CHRISTIAN ETHICS

Moral Theology
in the Light of Vatican II

Volume I: General Moral Theology
Newly revised edition

CHRISTIAN ETHICS

MORAL THEOLOGY
in the Light of Vatican II

Volume I

General Moral Theology

Newly Revised Edition

KARL H. PESCHKE, S.V.D.

WIPF & STOCK · Eugene, Oregon

Wipf and Stock Publishers
199 W 8th Ave, Suite 3
Eugene, OR 97401

Christian Ethics
Moral Theology in Light of Vatican II; Volume I
General Moral Theology, Third Edition
By Peschke, Karl-Heinz
Copyright © 1979 by Peschke, Karl-Heinz
ISBN 13: 978-1-62032-215-4
Publication date 5/1/2012
Previously published by C. Goodcliffe Neale, 1979

Reprint of the 2010 Theological Publications in India edition

Imprimatur
**The Most Rev. Dr. Ignatius Pinto
Archbishop of Bangalore
Archbishop's House
Bangalore
May 7, 2004**

CONTENTS

Abbreviations viii
Preface 1
Introduction 3

Chapter I: NATURE OF MORALITY AND
ITS ULTIMATE END 13
  A. Responsive character of Christian morality 14
    1. Holy Scripture 14
    2. Liturgy 17
    3. Christian theology 18
  B. The ultimate purpose of the moral demand 21
    I. Temporal happiness and welfare as ultimate purpose: eudaemonism, utilitarianism 23
    II. Ethics of self-perfection and temporal progress 29
    III. Morality for its own sake 32
      1. Kantian ethics 32
      2. Ethics of values 36
    IV. God's glory and kingdom as the ultimate purpose: theonomous ethics 39
      1. Teaching of Holy Scripture 40
      2. Theological reflection 44
    V. Salvation and the moral demand 48
      1. Role of salvation in Holy Scripture 48
      2. Role of salvation in theological thought 50
  C. The categorical character of the moral demand 53
  D. Openness to God's guidance and discernment of spirits 57

Chapter II: NATURE OF THE MORAL LAW 64
  A. Notion of moral law 65
    1. Concept of moral law 65
    2. Natural, revealed and human law 66
  B. Law of God in Holy Scripture 68
    I. Law of the Old Testament 68
    II. Moral law in the New Testament 75
    III. Distinctiveness of Christian ethics 84
    IV. Moral autonomy and theonomous ethics 92
  C. Natural moral law 95
    I. Concept of natural law 97
      1. The traditional concept 97
      2. The theological controversy over natural law 101

  3. Revised concept of natural law 105
 II. Properties of natural law 106
  1. Universality of natural law 106
   a) Extent of the universal knowledge
    of natural law 106
   b) Uncertainties in the teaching of the Church 109
  2. Immutability and dynamics 111
  3. Indispensability of natural law 113
  4. Personal and situational character 115
 III. Existence and ultimate basis of natural law 117
  1. Natural law as reflection of God's eternal decrees ... 118
  2. Natural law as based on the order of being 120
   a) General implication of the axiom
    "action follows being" 120
   b) Application to human activity 121
   c) Hume's critique and an answer to it 123
  3. Deontological and teleological foundation
   of moral norms 126
D. Human law 135
 I. Notion and necessity of human law 135
  1. Concept and properties of human law 135
  2. Attitude of the New Testament to human law 138
  3. Necessity of human law according to reason 140
 II. Object and substantive justice of the law 141
 III. Moral obligation of the law 146
 IV. Procedural justice and epikeia 149
  1. Procedural justice 149
  2. Epikeia 152
 V. Cessation of obligation and of the law itself 155

Chapter III: CONSCIENCE 158
A. Concept and nature of conscience 159
 I. Holy Scripture on conscience 159
 II. Conscience as moral faculty 163
  1. Views outside of Christian theology 163
  2. Concept of conscience in theology 166
  3. Conscience as subject to being 170
 III. Conscience as practical moral judgment 172
  1. Concept of the dictate of conscience 172
  2. Division of conscience 174
 IV. Stages in the development of conscience 175
B. The binding force of conscience 179
 I. The certain conscience 179

	II.	The vincibly erroneous and lax conscience 183
	III.	The perplexed conscience 185
	IV.	The doubtful conscience 186
C.	Formation of a certain conscience by means of reflex principles 188	
	I.	Nature and varieties of reflex principles 188
	II.	The systems of probability 190
D.	Freedom and commitment of conscience 195	
	1.	The right to freedom of conscience 195
	2.	Conscience and the civil law 197
	3.	Conscience and the teaching office of the Church 201
	4.	Duty to form one's conscience 205

Chapter IV: COMMUNAL ROOTS OF MORAL IDENTITY AND FUNDAMENTAL OPTION 208

A. Formative principles of moral identity 208
    I. The Bible as formative principle of the moral life 210
        1. The Bible as prime source of Christian identity 210
        2. Concrete shape of biblical moral identity 212
    II. The faith community as matrix of moral identity 216
B. Character formation 220
C. Basic intention and fundamental option 223

Chapter V: REALIZATION OF THE MORAL VALUE IN HUMAN ACTS 228

A. Concept and nature of the human act 228
    I. Concept of the human act 228
    II. Divisions of the voluntary act and effect 230
    III. The presupposition of freedom 232
        1. Freedom of will in Holy Scripture 233
        2. Theological reflection 236
B. Obstacles to human acts 238
    I. Impairments of required knowledge 238
        1. Ignorance 239
        2. Error 241
        3. Inattention 242
    II. Impairments of free consent 242
        1. Passion 242
        2. Fear and social pressure 244
        3. Violence 247
        4. Dispositions and habits 248
C. Sources defining the morality of human acts 250
    I. The object 251

	II.	The circumstances 254
	III.	The end intended by the agent 256
	IV.	Moral significance of the external act 260
D.	Preference rules and problems of the lesser evil 261
	I.	Preference rules 262
	II.	Imputability of indirectly willed effects 265
		1. Imputability of indirectly willed effects in general .. 265
		2. The principle of double effect 267
		3. Problems and controversies 269
	III.	Cooperation in the wrong deeds of others 277
	IV.	The ethical compromise 281

Chapter VI: THE MORALLY BAD ACTION: SIN 285
- A. Nature of sin 287
  - I. Biblical delineation of sin 288
  - II. Threefold dimension of sin 291
    1. The personal dimension of sin 292
    2. The social dimension of sin 293
    3. Sin as rejection of God 295
  - III. Mortal, grave and venial sin 296
    1. Different gradations of sins 296
    2. Mortal and venial sin defined 299
    3. Criteria for the objective gravity of sins 302
- B. Division of sins 305
  - I. Different kinds of internal sins 305
  - II. Sins of omission and commission 308
  - III. The capital sins 309
- C. Sources of sin 310
  - I. Temptation 310
  - II. Seduction and scandal 314
    1. Seduction 314
    2. Active and passive scandal 315
    3. Moral evaluation of scandal 318
  - III. Impact of a sinfully distorted world 320
    1. Solidarity in evil according to Holy Scripture 320
    2. Man's situation in a sinfully distorted world 322

Chapter VII: CONVERSION, VIRTUE AND PERFECTION IN HOLINESS 326
- A. Conversion 327
  - I. Man's need for conversion 327
    1. The call to conversion in Holy Scripture 327

		2. Universality of conversion and its continuous need 330
	II.	Nature of conversion 331
		1. Repentance of past evil deeds 331
		2. Return to God's salvific will 333
		3. Conversion as social event 334
	III.	Conditions of conversion 335
		1. Admission of sin and guilt 335
		2. Openness to the gift of grace 336
		3. Spirit and fruits of repentance 337
	IV.	Sacramental enactment of conversion 339
B.	Virtue 341
	I.	Nature of Virtue 343
	II.	The prime virtue and the many virtues 345
	III.	Fundamental requirements of virtue 347
		1. Moral knowledge and prudence 347
		2. Love of moral value 349
		3. Dominion over passions 350
C.	The universal call to perfection and holiness 351
	I.	Defective ideals 353
	II.	The call to perfection in Holy Scripture 355
	III.	Essence and universality of the call to perfection 360
		1. Nature of perfection 360
		2. Universality of the call to perfection 362
	IV.	Pathways to holiness 364
Bibliography 369
Index 373

ABBREVIATIONS

Holy Scripture
For the books of the Bible, the abbreviations of the Revised Standard Version (1966) are used.

Documents of Vatican II

DH	=	*Dignitatis Humanae*: Declaration on Religious Freedom.
GS	=	*Gaudium et Spes*: Pastoral Constitution on the Church in the Modern World.
LG	=	*Lumen Gentium*: Dogmatic Constitution on the Church.
NA	=	*Nostra Aetate*: Declaration on the Relationship of the Church to Non-Christian Religions.
OT	=	*Optatam Totius*: Decree on Priestly Formation.
SC	=	*Sacrosanctum Concilium*: Constitution on the Sacred Liturgy.
UR	=	*Unitatis Redintegratio*: Decree on Ecumenism.

The documents are quoted from *Vatican Council II. The Conciliar and Post Conciliar Documents*, ed. by Austin Flannery, 1988, revised edition.

Other abbreviations

AAS	=	*Acta Apostolicae Sedis.*
CIC	=	*Codex Iuris Canonici* of 1983.
DS	=	Denzinger-Schönmetzer, *Enchiridion Symbolorum*, 1967, 34th edition.
NT	=	New Testament.
OT	=	Old Testament (if accompanied by a number, *Optatam Totius*; see above).
S. Th.	=	*Summa Theologica* by Thomas Aquinas.

PREFACE

When this volume of "Christian Ethics" first appeared, in 1975, the Second Vatican Council had brought about many changes. Priests, lay-people and seminaries were looking for an overall orientation in moral theology on the basis of the teachings of Vatican II. This volume on general moral theology as well as the second one on special moral theology published three years later have tried to meet this need. The favourable reception the books received encouraged the author to continue with his work. He has sought to integrate the theological developments of the subsequent and recent years. In 1986 a revised edition of volume 1 appeared and in 1992 of volume II. 1996 volume I once again was being presented in a thoroughly revised edition and 2004 volume II as well.

Once again the author hopes that he has been able to meet the needs and expectations of the students of theology, the religious educators and the Christian faithful interested in the moral teaching of their faith, and that he will not disappoint any of his former friends.

The author wishes to thank sincerely Fr. Dermot Walsh, SVD, Fr. Peter Joseph, his former student at the University Urbaniana in Rome, now back in Australia, and Fr. George J. Woodall from the diocese of Nottingham for their reading and correction of the text under the aspect of English language.

INTRODUCTION

Christian ethics or moral theology is commonly defined as that part of theology which studies the guidelines a person must follow to attain his or her final goal in the light of Christian faith and of reason. Talk of *guidelines* causes most people to think directly of the moral norms which ought to be followed for this purpose. The elaboration of such norms is an essential task of moral theology. In this regard the definition describes what could be called an "ethics of doing". Aside from this however another task of moral theology needs attention, which could be called the "ethics of being". Besides the right and good actions it is primarily concerned with the type of person a human being and a Christian ought to be. "Moral goodness is a quality of the person, constituted not by rule-keeping behavior alone, but by cultivating certain virtues, attitudes, and outlooks."[1] The ethics of being focuses on the formation of character, patterns of actions, the right vision of life, the basic values and convictions which move a person to do what he or she believes to be right. For Christians the question to be asked is: "What sort of person should I become because I believe in Christ?" Looked at from this angle, the guidelines to be set up by ethics and moral theology also include the moral dispositions and virtues which a person ought to acquire and to possess. Of course, a person's being also bears on the human actions. The biblical metaphor of the good tree which bears good fruit expresses the truth that good actions have their origin in a good person. Vice versa however good actions will also have repercussions on a person's being.

Taking into considerations the above reflections, Christian ethics could be defined as that part of theology whose object is the foundations, attitudes and guidelines which enable a person to attain to his or her final goal. The theological character of the science involves that its study takes place in the light of reason as well as in the light of Christian faith.

---

[1] R.M. Gula, *Reason Informed by Faith* (New York: Paulist Press, 1989), 7.

Moral theology together with dogmatics makes up systematic theology. It treats in logical sequence the truths about God, his creation, the salvific work of Christ, the person as image of God and the creatures' way to God. Dogmatic theology is speculative in character, reflecting on the nature of God, of his creatures, and of the new creation in Christ. Moral theology on the other hand is more of a practical science. Availing itself of the theological and anthropological insights of dogmatic theology,[1] yet taking also into account the findings of the various anthropological and natural sciences, it draws consequences for the moulding of the human person as well as for the right actions and gives guidance to man in the realization of his final goal.

A presentation of *Christian* ethics implies that the ideals and norms presented are inspired by the sacred books of the Old and New Testament and related to what Christians believe about the world, God and each other. Above all it implies a permanent inspiration by the ideas, values and concerns of Jesus Christ. The disciple's faith in God and commitment to him has its roots in Jesus' faith in God and obedience to him.[2]

Closely related to moral theology is *philosophical ethics* or moral philosophy. It also endeavours to mould a person's character and to establish guiding principles for the moral life. But in contradistinction to moral theology, the latter excludes the positive revelation of the Old and New Testament as source of its moral knowledge and guidance. Moral philosophy draws its insights only from reason and from that general revelation which is granted to every person by the universal presence of the divine Spirit. To find another dis-

---

[1] At times the demand is made that moral theology start out with a theological anthropology (e.g. Domenico Capone, "Per un manuale di teologia morale," *Seminarium* 16, 1976, 482). However since dogmatic theology already includes a rather detailed Christian anthropology, this seems necessary only to a limited extent. It encumbers the subject matter of moral theology and tends to result in duplications. Nevertheless important elements of a theological anthropology are always inevitably contained in various parts of general moral theology, e.g. in the discussions about the destiny of man, the ontological presuppositions of natural law or the nature of perfection.

[2] Cf. Marcel Legaut, *Meine Erfahrung mit dem Glauben* (Freiburg: Herder, 10th printing 1979), 106.

tinction in the fact that moral theology would deal with the supernatural final goal of man and moral philosophy with a merely natural goal does not seem justified. In the concrete order of salvation there exists only one final goal common to all mankind which derives from the royalty of Christ over our present world. This is the unequivocal teaching of Vatican II. The council repeatedly and forcefully expresses its conviction that "all men are in fact called to one and the same destiny" (GS 22) and that "all, in fact, are destined to the very same end, namely God himself" (GS 24; cf. 29; NA 1). Of course the insight into man's final end will be of different character in moral philosophy and in moral theology. Since the latter is not only aided by reason and general revelation but also by the positive revelation of God in Scriptures and in Christ, it is to be expected that its insights into the final goal acquire a new dimension and are more complete.[1]

Moral theology is not without *presuppositions*. Every ethics, whether theological or philosophical, depends on two postulates in order to be possible, namely, freedom of will and accountability to an ultimate value. This does not mean that man has no experience of these realities. Quite the contrary, man's experience gives strong evidence for their existence. But this is an empirical awareness and not a rational proof.

---

[1] The elimination of the former dichotomy between theological and philosophical ethics and the essential convergence of the two is a most important advance in moral theology, greatly to be welcomed. Yet at the same time this newly acquired unity is threatened again by adverse trends from other sides. Armed with data gathered by cultural anthropology, theories of ethical pluralism are advanced. Yet neither from a theological or philosophical point of view nor in view of a convergent world in need of common standards can this be considered a progress. This is not to deny that legitimate differences in the preference and emphasis of certain moral values can and do exist. But if the ultimate calling and goal of mankind is indeed one and divine, then the ethical norms which give guidance to this goal must ultimately also converge and be substantially the same for all mankind. The practically universal agreement of the nations of today on the rights of man proves that such a convergence already exists in important regards. (Cf. Gerard J. Hughes, *Authority in Morals. An essay in Christian ethics*. London: Heythrop Monographs, 1978, 110-116; and Enrico Chiavacci, *Teologia morale* 2. Assisi: Cittadella Editrice, 1980, 221-226.)

Ethics must presuppose that man possesses freedom of will. If human activities were entirely predetermined by physical and psychological causalities, moral appeals to personal responsibility would be out of place. Man's actions could only be influenced by the pressure of physical or psychological forces. But this is not the way men experience themselves. Men experience themselves not merely as instruments in the hands of higher forces, but as creative agents, able to choose among alternatives and capable of self-determination. This is the constant and universal conviction of men in their dealings with each other.

The other presupposition is that man is accountable to an ultimate value or authority, which can claim his unconditional obedience. This ultimate accountability is what gives the moral demand its categorical character. Only on this condition is it possible to speak of moral duties in the strict sense which bind a person in conscience and which he or she cannot refuse to obey without becoming guilty. From the commitment to this supreme value human life at the same time also receives its ultimate meaning. It is not necessary that this supreme value or authority be thought of in terms of the Christian notion of God. It may be conceived in quite different images and even in only implicit forms. But it will always be a reality vested with absolute and therefore divine character. The affirmation and recognition of this reality ultimately takes place in an act of faith, even if only an implicit one.

Nevertheless Christian ethics presupposes that this reality is a personal God, one in nature, the creator of all that exists and a loving father of his creatures, particularly of men. The correct concept of God necessarily implies that the world as his creation is vested with a purpose and meaning. It equally implies that man as part of this creation has to respect this purpose and that this is his unconditional, categorical duty. In other words, the existence of God and man's accountability to an ultimate value are not two separate presuppositions. Rather the one is derived from the other; the categorical character of the moral demand is derived from the affirmation of the existence of God and of the world as his purposeful creation.

The fact that Christian ethics presupposes the existence of a personal God does not mean however that no proof for God's existence is possible. In fact Christian theologians, at least a great majority of them, are convinced that such a proof is possible (as long as the mystery of the Trinity is not involved). The question of the proofs for God's existence is dealt with in dogmatic theology, and moral theology can refer to it. However even if sufficiently known, the proofs are not convincing to all. This raises the question whether the arguments of moral theology can also be valid and convincing for those who do not share its concept of God, e.g. for an atheist. It must be admitted that moral demands which have their exclusive reason in the Christian understanding of God will not hold for those who do not accept this concept. However apart from the duties of worship, practically all other moral demands are at the same time also supported by more general insights of an anthropological and social nature. Nevertheless the unbeliever or atheist will earnestly have to ask himself whether his experience of an ultimate authority in the categorical imperative should not after all be interpreted in the Christian sense of a personal God.[1]

---

[1] The problem of the presuppositions of moral theology must be distinguished from the problem of *metaethics*. Metaethics together with normative ethics are two parts of the science of ethics. One calls the body of ethical statements and the actual normative argument normative ethics. Metaethics on the other hand is the discussion of the meanings or uses of moral terms and utterances about the nature of moral concepts. Metaethics "asks and tries to answer logical, epistemological, or semantical questions like the following: What is the meaning or use of the expressions '(morally) right' or 'good'? How can ethical and value judgments be established or justified? Can they be justified at all? What is the nature of morality? What is the distinction between the moral and the non-moral?" What is the meaning of related concepts like conscience, intention, responsibility, voluntary, etc.? (William K. Frankena, *Ethics*. Englewood Cliffs, N.J.: Prentice-Hall, 1973, 2nd edition, 5 and 96). In other words, metaethics is ethics without its normative body. This reduction seemed desirable to certain philosophers because no consensus could ever be reached concerning the normative parts of ethics. Many other philosophers however disagree and consider this reduction a regression. Strictly speaking, metaethics is a rather misleading term. It suggests a subject matter which goes beyond the scope of ethics and lies ahead of it. But this is not the case. The subject matter is eminently within the scope of ethics. To a large extent it is the subject matter of general moral theology, which, more recently, is often also called fundamental moral theology. Especially the latter term seems to be much more suited to indicate what is really meant. Metaethics has also been referred to as analytical ethics, critical ethics, the epistemology of ethics or simply ethics.

Finally, to the extent that moral theology uses Holy Scripture, Christian tradition and the teaching of the Church's magisterium as sources of its moral discourse, it also presupposes a number of related truths as established by dogmatic theology. Such truths are, e.g., the divine mission of Christ, the inspiration of Holy Scripture and the Church's role as custodian of the Gospel. However these dogmatic truths are in no way presuppositions for the rational arguments based on considerations of natural law or of philosophical nature.

In its *method*, moral theology has always adhered to a methodological pluralism. Contemporary scholars likewise conclude that a methodological monism, i.e. the use of one method only, is insufficient, and rather opt for a plurality of argumentations converging in one evidence. The actual procedure in contemporary theological investigation confirms that this is indeed the way in which the research proceeds and solutions are sought.

The methods employed are partly of a positive nature, as used in the biblical and historical sciences, and partly of a speculative nature, as used by philosophy and speculative theology. Positive theology employs literary and historical criticism as its instruments. Here especially hermeneutics has its place, i.e. the methods to be followed for a correct interpretation of traditions, biblical texts and historical documents, the intentions of their authors and of the moral statements they contain. Beyond this however hermeneutics is understood today also in a wider, more comprehensive sense. "Moral theology as an hermeneutic science endeavours to reconstruct the genesis of norms. Which is the context of their origin and which is the history they have gone through?"[1] Elements of traditions are studied against the background of the intellectual history of the respective epoch and critically examined for the possibility of their application to the present times. Also the totality of the intellectual presuppositions in a reflecting subject falls within the scope of hermeneutic inquiry.

In detail, research in moral theology avails itself of the following four forms of argumentation. First of all, the moral teachings of the biblical writings are consulted; they have

---

[1] Klaus Demmer, "Hermeneutik," *Neues Lexikon der christlichen Moral* (Innsbruck: Tyrolia, 1990), 333.

always been granted a prominent place in theological argumentation. Secondly, the historical development of a doctrine or moral norm is examined, with particular emphasis of course on its history within Christianity, though its non-Christian history is by no means ignored. Thirdly, the official teaching of the ecclesiastical magisterium and the concrete praxis adhered to by the Church is studied (which can be considered a particular instance of the historical development of a doctrine). Special authority in this regard is given to the teachings of the councils and popes. Also the recently created national bishops' conferences possess a doctrinal authority of particular weight, though not equal to that of the popes or councils. The present teaching of moral theologians, their agreements and disagreements likewise require attention. It is not the individual alone but the Church community as a whole which, in continuing responsiveness both to biblical tradition and contemporary situations, unfolds ever more the faith entrusted to her. The Christian has no enduring identity *as Christian* apart from the Church. On the other hand the representatives of the Church must also give ear to the community of believers and grant them the right to participation.

Fourthly, a most decisive weight is accorded to the arguments of reason. They are formulated on a double basis, which can briefly be characterized as the ontological and eschatological points of departure. The ontological point of departure consists in the study of man's concrete, existing nature and of the world around him. These are inquired into in the light of philosophical and theological analysis. Yet of great importance are likewise the insights of the anthropological and natural sciences, such as psychology, sociology, economics, medicine, ecology, etc. Above all they give information about the consequences which man's actions have for him, for others, society and the world at large. Consequences do play an important role in the moral evaluation of an action, though not an absolutely exclusive one. Many consequences can be foreseen, and as far as this is possible, responsible action must place them into account. Others though are only known by experience; they must be considered retrospectively. This point of departure is quite commonly associated with natural law doctrine. The knowledge of what man is, what his possibilities are and the limits he cannot transcend, is indispensable for a realistic moral discourse. The attention given to the empirical sciences brings about that moral theology, today more than in former times, supports a method that is empirical and inductive.

However in order to decide what man should choose among the many possibilities open to him, the ontological point of departure alone is not sufficient. It must be complemented by the teleological and eschatological point of departure, which informs man about the goal to be achieved, the kind of person he should be and the work he is to do.[1] This insight can hardly be gained without some experience of intuitive nature combined with responsible discernment, especially where the personal calling and the life task of a person is concerned, but also with regard to the tasks which challenge a community always anew in the course of its history. The two chapters on the nature of morality and the moral law, above all the natural moral law, will treat these questions in more detail.

It is to be noted that the different types of argumentation are not always used simultaneously for the verification of a moral doctrine. Many modern problems find no mention in Holy Scripture or in the theological writings of the past. At other times a doctrine enjoys such universal acceptance that a detailed study of its past history is not necessary. On the other hand, controversial doctrines call for a careful study of all the available arguments. The speculative arguments in particular are hardly ever to be dispensed with.

Moral theology is divided into general and special. General moral theology treats of the general presuppositions of the moral act and the qualities with which every action must be endowed in order that it may contribute to man's final goal.

---

[7] The urgent need of a two-pronged approach in the argumentation of theological ethics has been pointed out with particular clarity by Heinz Dietrich Wendland. Protology, i.e. the study of existing nature as it is the result of creation, "does not exist independently of eschatology, the first things not without the last things and the primeval time not without the final time" (*Botschaft an die soziale Welt*. Hamburg: Furche, 1959, 143). Ontological considerations must find their complement in the critical scales of the eschatological realities (*ib.* 148-152). See the study "Eschatologisches Naturrecht" in *Naturrecht in der Kontroverse. Kritik evangelischer Theologie an der katholischen Lehre von Naturrecht und natürlicher Sittlichkeit* by K. Peschke (Salzburg: Otto Müller, 1967), 127-141.

The subject matter in question may seem somewhat abstract and dry. Nevertheless their study is indispensable. "Modern man not only wants to hear what is to be done, but also wants to know *why* it has to be done."[1] The themes to be dealt with are the nature of morality and its ultimate end; the revealed, natural and human law as the objective norms of morality; conscience as the subjective norm; moral identity and fundamental option; the realization of the moral value in human acts; sin as the morally bad action; conversion, virtue and perfection in holiness.

Special moral theology treats of the human behaviour in the different spheres and situations of human life. It is subdivided in two main parts. Part one deals with man's responsibility in the religious realm, part two with his responsibility towards the created world. Part one, on the religious realm, discusses the divine virtues of faith, hope and charity, the nature of divine worship and the different forms of worship. Part two, on the created world, treats of the virtues of love of neighbour and justice. This is followed by those realms which can be defined as "personal ethics," i.e. bodily life and health; honour, fidelity and truth; and sexuality. The latter, sexuality, is the transition to the other great realm, "social ethics." Starting with the smaller communities, it progresses to the greater ones: marriage, family, state and Church. These are followed by work, property, economy and - as a widening to the entire world - responsible care for creation.

---

[1] Helmut Weber, *Allgemeine Moraltheologie* (Graz: Styria, 1991), 85.

Chapter I

NATURE OF MORALITY AND ITS ULTIMATE END

For Christian theology, the moral character of human actions is essentially determined by their relation to God's will. Man's actions are morally good if they agree with God's will, and they are morally bad if they disagree with it. But God's will is not primarily expressed in a set of codified rules and laws. It is first of all an inner calling and a summons to accomplish a task within the universal plan of God for man and this world. Hence man's response to this calling determines the morality of his actions and of his entire way of life. If a man's response is faithful to his calling, his actions and way of life are morally good. But if he is unfaithful to his calling, his actions are morally bad. The first section of this chapter will, therefore, be concerned with the responsive character of Christian morality.

The calling of each man and woman is personal and unique, but still not isolated and without relation to the common calling of mankind. God has not only a plan for each individual, but a universal design for all of mankind and for the entire world. Each man's personal vocation is related to that superior, universal design and ultimately stands in its service. The ultimate goal of man and the world is an ultimate criterion for the moral goodness of his actions. Whatever stands in contradiction to this ultimate goal cannot be morally good, because it would frustrate the meaning of a man's existence and contradict God's purpose for man and the world. In fact, the question of the ultimate end of man is fundamental for the nature of morality. The different systems of morality are distinguished from each other precisely by their different conceptions of man's ultimate purpose. The second section will therefore deal with man's ultimate end.

The third section treats of the categorical character of the moral demand, which necessarily follows from the fact that in man's moral decisions, his ultimate end and the very meaning of his existence are at stake. A final section on the need of man's openness to the guidance of the Holy Spirit is meant to underline the truth that man's obligations cannot be deduced by simple, logical conclusions from the ultimate goal. The ultimate goal is known to man only in its approximate features and not in its full clarity. Furthermore man's precise contribution to it can only be the matter of God's personal call through his Holy Spirit.

A. Responsive character of Christian morality

Responsibility and responsible freedom are household words in current ethical debate. Existentialist philosophy has contributed much to their popularity. But the precise meaning of the terms is all too often left vague. The literal sense of the word responsibility helps much to grasp its true meaning. It means to say: "liable to give an answer for what one has done." Yet if one has to give an answer, surely one has to give it to somebody. The scholar of ethics must not escape his obligation to clarify to whom or to which authority a person is responsible.

Man is not primarily responsible to himself. A word-response relationship presupposes two partners. Only in a derived sense can one speak of a person's responsibility towards himself. Man is above all responsible to his neighbours and to the various social groups to which he belongs. He is responsible to the future generations, e.g. when exploiting the natural resources. Man has also a cosmic responsibility for the world at large, as mankind of today comes to realize more and more. Yet ultimately - and this is an elementary conviction of Christian faith - a person is answerable to God. This is the immediate consequence of the theological doctrine that God is the creator of the universe who has arranged everything according to his purpose, and man is his creature who has received a task from him to be fulfilled. Responsible then is the person who gives the appropriate answer to his or her calling by God.

1. Holy Scripture

At the beginning of all religious thought of Holy Scripture is the theme of the covenant.[1] At Sinai, Israel, the people

---

[1] "In the covenant of God with his people there is resumed the essence of the religion of the Old and New Testament" (J. Schildenberger, "Covenant," *Encyclopedia of Biblical Theology*, ed. by J. Bauer, 1970, 140).

that God had delivered from the slavery of Egypt, entered into a covenant with Yahweh. In accordance with his plan of salvation, he decides to grant the chosen people his privileged love, protection and salvation, and at the same time states his conditions which man in turn is expected to fulfil. "If you will obey my voice and keep my covenant, you shall be my own possession among all peoples" (Ex 19:5). By virtue of the covenant, Israel finds itself placed in a word-response relation with God from the very beginning of its history. God's word is revelation of his name and of the meaning of events, promise of his grace and guidance, yet also law and rule of life. Man's answer is the ready acceptance of God's word, trust in his promise, and faithful fulfilment of his command. "All that the Lord has spoken we will do" (Ex 19:8; 24:7).

The message of the prophets constantly refers to the covenant. Whether they unanimously denounce the infidelity of Israel towards her God, whether they preach the catastrophes which threaten a sinful people, it is because of the pact of Sinai. They enrich by other analogies and new aspects the covenant relationship between Yahweh and his people, which originally appeared primarily under a juridical aspect. Israel is the son, and Yahweh the father (Hos 11:1-4; Jer 31:20). Israel is the flock, and Yahweh the shepherd (Ezek 34:11-23). Israel is the spouse or wife, and Yahweh the bridegroom or husband (Is 54:1-10; Jer 2:2f; 31:3f; Hos 1-3). These images, especially the last, make the Sinaitic covenant appear as an encounter of love (cf. Ezek 16:6-14). The attentive and gratuitous love of God calls in return for a love which will translate itself into obedience.[1]

Yet Israel did not remain faithful to the covenant. It turned to other gods, did not heed the Lord's word and disregarded his commandments. In consequence the ancient pact was found broken (Jer 22:8f; 31:32), just as a marriage which fails because of the adulteries of the wife (Hos 2:2-5; Ezek 16:15-43). Yet a new covenant is promised, which will be established at the end of time (Jer 31:31-34), which will renew that of Sinai (Ezek 16:60) and will bring about a change of heart and the gift of the divine Spirit (Ezek 36:26-28).

---

[1] See also Deut 6:5; 7:8-11; 10:12-15; 11:1.

This new covenant was entered into by God with mankind through his Son Jesus Christ. The word "covenant" figures in the four accounts of the institution of the Eucharist at the Last Supper (Mt 26:28; Mk 14:24; Lk 22:20; 1 Cor 11:25), but also in other passages of the New Testament (e.g. 2 Cor 3:6; Heb 8:6-13; 12:24). Jesus himself considers the promise of the new covenant, which was announced by Jeremiah and Ezekiel, fulfilled in his sacrifice. Placed thus "at the heart of Christian worship, the covenant theme is the background for the whole NT, even where it is not explicitly noted".[1] In contradistinction to the old covenant, which was a privilege of the people of Israel, the new covenant reaches out to all nations, for the blood of Christ has remade the unity of the human race (Eph 2:12-19). But no less than in the Old Testament, God expects from man an answer to his salvific action, the answer of faithful obedience and love.

In the OT God spoke his word through the mouths of Moses and the prophets. In the NT he speaks to mankind through his only begotten Son, who is the divine Word himself. Jesus proclaims the word (Mk 4:33; Jn 3:34), making known the mysteries of the kingdom of God (Mt 13:11 par). He conveys what the Father has taught him (Jn 8:28; 12:50). Men on their part are called to take position when confronted by this word. Those who accept it will bear fruit (Mt 13:18-23 par). Whoever hears God's word and keeps it, will have eternal life and God will make his home with him (Jn 5:24; 8:51; 14:23f; 15:7-10). But those who refuse it will be judged on the last day (Jn 12:48). Since Christ himself is the perfect answer to the love of the Father, his person and his actions become a model and example for the disciples. This is the reason for the repeated summons to the imitation of Jesus: "If any man would come after me, let him deny himself... and follow me" (Mt 16:24 par).[2]

The apostles and disciples of Christ continue to preach the word of God by proclaiming the message of the Gospel throughout the entire world. They offer to all men the "message of salvation" (Acts 13:26), the "word of life" (Phil 2:16), the

---

[1] "Covenant," *Dictionary of Biblical Theology*, ed. by X. Léon-Dufour (London: G. Chapman, 1988), 97.

[2] Also Mt 10:38 par; Lk 14:27; Jn 8:12; 12:26; 13:12-15; 14:6; 1 Pet 2:21; 1 Jn 2:6.

living word that discerns the hearts of men (Heb 4:12). Again, the word demands a decision and response from men. Some reject it (Acts 13:46; 1 Pet 2:8; 3:1), others accept it (1 Thess 1:6; 2:13), keep it in order to be saved (1 Cor 15:2; Rev 3:8), and put it into practice (Jas 1:21-25).

Thus a lasting drama is brought to pass around the word of God. God speaks to men in manifold ways: through Moses, through the prophets, through Jesus Christ, who is the Word made flesh. And man is called upon to respond to the word. "He who believes in the Word, who acknowledges and receives the Word, enters through Him into the life of the theological virtues of the child of God (Jn 1:12). He who rejects the word or scorns it remains in the darkness of the world and is judged thereby (cf. 3:17ff). Everyone must face this formidable prospect; openly, if he is brought into contact with the Gospel of Jesus Christ; secretly, if the divine Word is attained only under imperfect forms. To every man the Word speaks; He awaits an answer from every man, and man's eternal destiny depends upon his answer."[1]

2. Liturgy

The dialogical character of Christian faith and morality likewise finds expression in the liturgical and sacramental life of the Church. For, as Vatican II states in the Constitution of the Sacred Liturgy, "in the liturgy God speaks to his people, and Christ is still proclaiming his Gospel. And the people reply to God both by song and prayer" (SC 33). The songs and prayers contain as an essential element the praise and glorification of God, but they always equally express man's desire and readiness for a life in accordance with the will of God and the Christian faith. Thus by participation in the celebration of the liturgy, Christians constantly share in the covenant between Christ and the Church. "The structural pattern of the liturgy closely resembles that of salvation history, in that throughout we see a dialectic of revelation and response, the great God revealing himself as agape (1 John 4:8), seeking to evoke a response of faith from man. In Scripture we read of the *magnalia Dei*, the wonderful saving events of God, placing himself at the service of man for man's salvation. Through the liturgy this saving action continues to be present

---

[1] "Word of God," *Dictionary of Biblical Theology*, 1988, 670.

in history. And just as man was called to commitment by God through these saving events in the past, so too he is still being called to commitment by God through these same saving acts sacramentally present today. God's revelation of saving service calls man to a response of saving service on his part."[1] The liturgy and the sacraments voice and effect God's love, mercy, and saving grace. In turn, they demand of men the response of a corresponding life formation in harmony with God's will and in the fellowship of Christ.

The rituals and images of the Christian heritage are of no little relevance for the life of the faithful. "Explicit moral instructions are necessary but they are far less influential than the images or paradigmatic figures which influence our imaginations. The ways we see, judge, and act are all tied to the imagination, which is influenced by the communities to which we belong and to the images by which our communities live. More likely than not, then, only a small part of the moral life is influenced by the specific, conscious instruction which the church provides on moral issues. A considerably larger part is influenced by the church's effect on the imagination. With its heritage of ritual and religious images... the church is an indispensable point of reference for acquiring a Christian moral character and making moral decisions."[2] Even though this influence is exerted in different ways, the liturgy remains one of the privileged places where the faithful are put in touch with the Christian images. In it the Christian community acknowledges the sovereignty of God and so becomes a people according to the pattern of Jesus Christ.

3. Christian theology

Religion is essentially an encounter between God and man. God is concerned with man; he turns to him; he reveals himself to him. This makes religion possible. And man turns to God; he answers him. Christian religion too, and with special distinctness, understands itself as an encounter with the divine. God offers man his grace and addresses his word to him, and man is expected to answer in faith and love and in the fulfilment of God's will. This encounter takes place

---

[1] Donald P. Gray, "Liturgy and Morality," *Worship* 39 (1965), 29.

[2] R.M. Gula, *Reason Informed by Faith* (New York: Paulist Press, 1989), 200.

for the Christian in Jesus Christ. Christ is the message and revelation of the eternal love of God. In him God gave himself up for men on the cross, that man might give himself to God. But Christ is also, in virtue of his humanity, the answer to God's love for men. His life in loving dedication to the Father's will is the perfect response of mankind to God's gracious offer of communion with him. In fellowship and union with Christ, Christians are called upon to formulate their answer in the same manner as their master. "The response of the Christian should be that of a son, modelled on the filial response of the only-begotten Son and grounded in it."[1]

Man's response to God has two dimensions. There is a direct response to God, which is religion in the strict sense. Man responds to the revelation of God's glory, majesty and holiness, to his love and mercy in the divine virtues of faith, hope and love, and in the acts of worship. But there is also a second form of response. It is the response to the revelation of God's will with regard to this created world. The divine will is made known to men through the order of creation, the testimony of conscience, and to Christians also in the word of biblical revelation. Man's response consists in recognition and promotion of the created values, in the faithful fulfilment of the task assigned to him in the world as well as in the respect for the calling of his fellow-men and the rights resulting therefrom. This divine invitation in its twofold dimension is extended to men of all times. And all men are summoned to answer this call in willing obedience and responsibility.

The very core of moral decision is the spirit of obedience to God. It is saying yes to God's will. But this decision is essentially more than a simple saying yes or no to a fixed order. The understanding of God as a lawmaker, who presents men with a code of rules and laws which have literally to be followed, is not fully adequate. Today the conception of God has shifted to the designer of a task to be done. "God sets up a task to be done. Like any task it has a specific outline and a specific goal, but its details must be worked out by those who have responsibility. They must, out of their skill and alertness, expedite the task in terms of the continually

---

[1] Enda McDonagh, "Morality: Man's Response to God," in *Truth and Life*, ed. by D. Flanagan et alii (Dublin: Gill and Macmillan, 1969), 29.

changing situation and of the exigencies which emerge in the doing."[1] God gives responsibility to do the work and expects man to carry it out responsibly.

The moral decision requires humble and docile attention to the will of God. This includes that man seriously submits himself to the rule he has recognized as the will of God. Just as the self-communication of God to man has sought expression in human language, so has the response from man which that communication involves. The OT formulates God's will in divine commandments, and the NT provides a written account of the chief demands of Christian living. The written law is the attempt to express the internal reality of the call to divine sonship in some external, verbal formulas. "Such formulas are necessary and originate with Christ himself and the New Testament. They are, however, secondary to the internal reality and never in fact completely express it. They are always approximate and capable of fuller and better expression."[2] For this reason men and women are not only called to obey the law, but also to take care of it responsibly, so that it will express the will of God always more correctly and remain an authentic expression of the divine command in the varied conditions of time. Responsibility for the moral order entails the reasonable scrutiny and revision of principles.

Obedience to earthly authority does not dispense man of his personal involvement and direct responsibility before God. People must not be so submitted to the laws of earthly authorities that they lose sight of the all-embracing law of love of God and neighbour. In the judgment of the scribes, Jesus had repeatedly violated the law by disregarding certain Jewish precepts of ritual and ceremonial nature. But for him it was a matter of obeying the more important matters of the law: justice, mercy and love. No less dangerous is a legalistic minimalism which feels itself free from any responsibility where there is no written law or tradition. Narrow adherence to nothing but the codified rules is made an excuse for ignoring the total will of God.

Personal responsibility must therefore also move in where there are no rules. The complexity of modern life entails that

---

[1] Albert R. Jonsen, *Responsibility in Modern Religious Ethics* (Washington, Cleveland: Corpus Books, 1968), 183.

[2] E. McDonagh, *l. c.* 33.

whole areas of life have vastly outgrown the relatively simple plan of moral principles provided by handbooks and are not covered by detailed rules. "The principle of responsibility requires that the responsible man, salesman, general, politician or physician carry the spirit of the ethical principles which they adopt into those areas where no clear rules exist... Responsibility not only requires considered, conscientious commitment to principle, not only the careful critique of principle, but also a moral creativity."[1]

The word-response relation establishes a bond of a personal nature between God and man. But religion as community with God places man not only in right relation to God. To be in Christ necessarily means to be bound up with all those who have fellowship with Christ, who are called by Christ. Hence it belongs to the essence of religious living that it places man in the community with his neighbour. For although God calls man personally, each by his own name, he finds through the very acceptance of God's word the way opened to the love relation with his neighbour.

B. The ultimate purpose of the moral demand[2]

God calls men and women to communion with him and to the service of his will. And they are expected to answer this call in ready acceptance, in obedience and responsibility. This has been explained in the preceding section. The question arises whether there exists any further criterion by which a certain course of action can be determined as obedient or disobedient, as responsible or irresponsible. Accord or disaccord with God's call has been pointed out as the criterion of the moral goodness of an action. This criterion however is still of a very general and indeterminate nature. Can nothing more specific be said about the content of this call?

The common nature of men and the universal character of the word of God in Scripture point to a common goal and

---

[1] A. Jonsen, *l. c.* 195.

[2] A good exposition of the various currents and schools of philosophical ethics is contained in William K. Frankena, *Ethics* (Englewood Cliffs, N.J.: Prentice-Hall, 1973, 2nd edition). A pertinent, concise study of the question is given by Wolfhart Pannenberg, "The Kingdom of God and the Foundation of Ethics," in *Theology and the Kingdom of God* (Philadelphia: The Westminster Press, 1969), 102-126.

purpose of men. And this means to say, they point to a common calling. In fact according to the definition of moral theology, man's final goal is the ultimate criterion for the moral quality of an action. Those human actions are good which contribute to the realization of the final goal; and those actions are bad which lead man away from this goal and obstruct its realization. The more specific determination of man's ultimate goal and purpose is therefore of greatest importance for every system of moral theology and philosophy. Rightly ethics or moral theology can be designated as science of meaning.[1]

Recent ethical discussion pays increasing attention to the question of the meaning of existence. It is pointed out that insight into the meaning of existence supplies that comprehensive framework which makes moral judgments possible, provides the basis for their validity, and ensures unity to the ethical theory.[2] A definite view concerning the goal of a meaningful life enters in every ethical reflection as the condition of its contents.

More than any other doctrinal tenet, the conception of the meaning of human existence reveals the understanding a religion, philosophy or ideology has of man. It condenses their anthropology as if in a focal point and decisively influences their value judgments. Pope John Paul II therefore urges the fundamental importance of a correct grasp of the ultimate meaning of life. "The great task that has to be faced today for the renewal of society is that of recapturing the ultimate meaning of life and its fundamental values. Only an awareness of the primacy of these values enables man to use the immense possibilities given him by science in such a way as to bring about the true advancement of the human person."[3]

The different views with regard to the ultimate goal of man and of his activity can be categorized in four basic groups. The ultimate goal may be looked for in temporal happiness and welfare (eudaemonism, utilitarianism); in self-

---

[1] See Klaus Demmer, *Deuten und Handeln* (Freiburg: Herder, 1985), 14-16.

[2] In the multiplicity of empirical data any ethical theory can find its unity only in a definite meaning of life as the ultimate point of reference for human action (Wilhelm Korff in *Handbuch der christlichen Ethik*, vol. I, ed. by Anselm Hertz et alii. Freiburg: Herder, ²1993, 165).

[3] Apostolic exhortation *Familiaris Consortio* (1981), nr. 8.

perfection and temporal progress; in the realization of the moral value for its own sake (Kantian ethics, ethics of values); and in God's glory through the realization of his divine design (theonomous ethics). A further question in this line is the significance which accrues to man's salvation as a motive of his activity. The concept of salvation essentially belongs to the religious, theonomous forms of ethics. The questions which arise are how this motive is related to the motive of God's glory and kingdom, and whether it can be an ultimate goal of the moral act or only a secondary, subordinate one.

I. **Temporal happiness and welfare as ultimate purpose: eudaemonism, utilitarianism**

Eudaemonist ethics considers temporal happiness and welfare as the ultimate purpose of human life and activity. Pleasure and happiness is the only thing good in itself, while evil is what causes pain and sorrow. Good and right then is what is useful and profitable for achieving the goal of temporal well-being and success. Eudaemonism[1] accordingly is always utilitarian. But also vice versa, utilitarianism is always eudaemonist, at least the way it is most frequently understood. Furthermore, since the good or bad consequences decide whether an action is useful and therefore good or evil, eudaemonism and utilitarianism are likewise typical instances of consequentialism. Even where utilitarianism is not professed theoretically, it is very often the factual basis of conduct.

There are of course different temporal values in which happiness can be aspired to. Some attempt to find happiness in sensual pleasure (hedonism)[2]; others in riches, honour, social standing and power (such as a certain trend in OT ethics); others in the renunciation of sensual pleasure in favour of tranquillity and peace; and others in harmonic satisfaction

---

[1] The term "eudaemonism" is derived from the Greek word *eudaimonia* = happiness, prosperity.

[2] The term "hedonism" is derived from *hedonè* = pleasure. Advocates of the same were Aristippos (ca. 400 B.C.), Hegesius of Cyrene, Eudoxus and others. "It would be misleading to subsume under hedonism also the (esp. Anglo-Saxon) modern utilitarianism, since one is really dealing there... with an ethos" (K.H. Miskotte, "Hedonismus" in *Die Religion in Geschichte und Gegenwart*, vol. 3, ³1959, 112).

of all earthly needs, sensual, social, intellectual, cultural (Aristotle).¹ In our time a form of neo-eudaemonism has widely gained ground which appraises life (naturally man's life here on earth) as the highest good and value. But life is only a desirable good if it offers at least a moderate amount of enjoyment and happiness. The goal therefore is to maximize personal gratification and happiness, especially through the more immediate benefits of pleasure, comfort and material living standards.²

Eudaemonism may be private or social. Private eudaemonism is concerned with the happiness of the individual only. Social eudaemonism aims at the happiness and welfare of a social group. It may be predominantly concerned with the greatest possible welfare, influence and power of a selected group and its members (e.g. a family clan, a dominating aristocracy, a party)³ or of an entire nation (nationalism) or with the greatest happiness of the greatest number of people in general (as advocated by J. Bentham and J. Stuart Mill, the typical exponents of modern utilitarianism). Some authors consider as utilitarianism only this last form.⁴ Other authors distinguish between egoistic and particularistic forms of utilitarianism on the one hand and the universalist form on the other.

Eudaemonism has a great appeal because it is a simple, one-principle system with a concrete, tangible and persuasive goal. Man's desire for happiness is a universal reality, as

---

¹ See *Nicomachean Ethics*, book 1, c. VII-VIII. Aristotle also emphasizes the need of virtuous living, but ultimately as a means to happiness.

² Cf. B. Stoeckle, *Grenzen der autonomen Moral* (München: Kösel, 1974), 38-42. He critically asks, whether the presently advocated autonomous morality does not ultimately encourage a this-wordly neo-eudaemonism and ends up in it.

³ Marxist Leninism, Maoism and similar types of communist materialism belong to this category of utilitarianism. Good is, according to these ideologies, whatever serves the victory and sovereignty of the communist party, as the representative of the proletariat, and evil what is contrary to it.

⁴ Thus Rudolf Ginters, who himself advocates the theory of utilitarianism in the narrow sense; he calls the others forms ethical egoism (*Werte und Normen*. Düsseldorf: Patmos, 1982, 207-214).

Aristotle has correctly observed, something which a realistic anthropology has to take into account. Nevertheless eudaemonism as a system of human action suffers from grave shortcomings and, as Kant has shown with particular vigour, cannot serve as the basis for a morality worthy of its name.

The ultimate purpose of human activity and life is that value for which, in case of conflict, all the others are sacrificed. The spontaneous reaction against individuals or groups who concede the place of highest value to their temporal happiness and welfare is rejection and disgust, expressed in the word egotism. Why? The temporal happiness of an individual and even the welfare of a group is obviously a limited value, which cannot prove its right to preference in principle over the well-being of others. In more general terms, preference of limited values over more comprehensive values is always a distortion with disharmony and injustice in its train. Utilitarianism with its unconditional preference of temporal happiness and welfare over the higher, eternal values inverts the true order, disrupts and overthrows its.

Actually civil communities and states never admit, and cannot admit, the principle of unrestrained, private eudaemonism. And this is equally true of the relations of states to each other, which always resist the unlimited principle of social eudaemonism of their neighbour nations. Usually states succeed in preventing the worst excrescences of eudaemonist egotism of their subjects and of each other. But within the limits in which no vengeance of civil law or of other nations is to be feared, the principles of eudaemonist egotism have always flourished abundantly and not seldom brutally. Nevertheless eudaemonist ethics is most of the time not carried through with strict consequence. Men will often not succeed in opposing the voice of conscience, especially in cases of baser recklessness. The conviction of people and nations that such a voice exists is proven by the fact that they condemn and punish criminal recklessness perpetrated on utilitarian grounds even where it does not constitute an offence against positive law, e.g. in the Nuremberg trials (1946) against the crimes of the leaders of German National Socialism and in the subsequent prosecution of such crimes.[1]

Eudaemonism is also not able to give meaning to serious suffering, especially to long-lasting and incurable suffering. It remains nonsensical for this theory. Thus eudaemonism leaves unanswered one of the greatest problems of human life, and this again because it excludes the eternal values, which transcend this temporal order.

Evidently eudaemonist ethics is not in a condition to provide a solid foundation for the categorical character of the moral imperative, which characterizes every true morality. Eudaemonism is not able to give a satisfactory interpretation of the testimony of conscience which dictates that good is to be done and evil to be avoided, irregardless of consequences. The pleasurable and profitable are simply not identical with the obligatory, because they are not that ultimate end which nobody is allowed to neglect and disavow. They can be renounced without making a man guilty.

Finally a closer look reveals that feelings of happiness are not the one and all that people are after. People do not just want the feeling of doing good things; they actually want to do good things. They do not just want the sensation of being good persons, they want to be good persons. They do not just want the thrill of sensual and spiritual pleasure; rather they want the real world of a meaningful existence. It is wrong to assume "that what everyone is doing is just pursuing happiness. On the contrary, people have to be pursuing other

---

[1] The leaders of German National Socialism (1933-1945) did not offend against the laws of the German *Reich* of that time, since they themselves had enacted them in such a way as to legalize their criminal actions. Nevertheless they were called to account by an international court of the victorious allied powers. The basis for the trial was not a legal code of the international community of nations, which did not exist, but only a common sense of justice. The court condemned the national utilitarianism of the leaders of Nazi Germany as criminal on the strength of a natural law superior to all utilitarian interests. It must however be noted that the "international" court on its part put itself in the wrong by bringing to trial only the crimes of the defeated adversary and not - as its international character would have demanded - the criminal offences of all the participants of the war, as e.g. also the crimes of Stalin.

things."[1] What these other things are, one has to be prepared to find out.

At first sight the modern utilitarianism, which pleads for the greatest happiness of the greatest number, seems to avoid the pitfalls of the more particularistic forms of eudaemonism. The reproach of egotism cannot be raised against it, since its fundamental principle excludes it. Yet it too miscarries because of incurable defects. *First*, there are many different goods and values in which people find their happiness. Who establishes what worthwhile happiness is and has to be for everybody? The search readily ends with the tyranny of an intellectual elite or another power group which determines what happiness should be for a community.[2] Naturally the choice is also open to change of what should be valued as happiness. An open question likewise remains the order of precedence among the values of happiness. *Second*, eudaemonism provides no reason for preferring altruism to egoism or to exclusive concern for one's family or party. If happiness is the greatest good, how could a man be expected to sacrifice it (e.g. by loss of his limbs or life in a war) for the greater happiness of the rest? Eudaemonism offers no motive for this sacrifice. On the contrary, it makes it unintelligible. Where concern for one's fellow-man does not even on a long-term basis contribute to one's happiness, eudaemonism cannot establish the obligation of self-forgetful concern. *Third*, utilitarianism cannot hope to make sense, at any serious level, of integrity, fairness and

---

[1] B. Williams, "A critique of utilitarianism," in *Utilitarianism for and against* by J.J.C. Smart and B. Williams (Cambridge University Press, 1973), 113. R. Nozick illustrates the argument by the following, instructive thought-experiment (cited by J. Finnis, *Natural Law and Natural Rights*. Oxford: Clarendon Press, 1980, 95). Suppose you could be plugged into an 'experience machine' which, by stimulating your brain while you lay floating in a tank, would afford you all the experiences you choose, with all the variety you could want. But you must plug in for a lifetime or not at all. On reflection, is it not clear that you would not choose a lifetime of 'thrills' or 'pleasurable tingles' or other experiences of that type? For one wants to do certain things and not just have the experience of doing them; one wants to be a certain sort of person and not just have the pleasurable feeling of being it.

[2] The criterion to be chosen for the values of happiness is for Mill "the experience of intelligent people" (K.H. Miskotte, *l. c.* 113).

justice.[1] If a great amount of good for the members of a group can be achieved by inflicting some evil on one of them or on a minority, e.g. an unjust death sentence or removal of the minority, this should be allowed and even obligatory according to the utilitarian principle.

Certainly temporal happiness and welfare should also not be belittled. They are justified values. Human experience provides ample evidence that a certain degree of happiness and welfare is indispensable for a well integrated life and for efficient work. Therefore it cannot simply be wrong to strive after them. Indeed there is an intrinsic relation between value and happiness or joy. Every value is the cause of happiness or joy; the greater the value, the deeper the joy. Happiness and joy therefore are indications of values and help in their discovery. This is the positive function which they serve.

Just as it is not wrong to strive after health, a meaningful work, a stable home, the welfare of one's family, so it is not wrong to wish for the happiness and joy which they bring. But it is wrong to grant any of these values or even all of them together the place of a supreme and ultimate value. This does not agree with their temporal and transitory nature. But this precisely is the fundamental error of eudaemonism and utilitarianism. They raise these values to final ends.

As far as the literal meaning of terms goes, Christian ethics also could be called eudaemonist and utilitarian. For according to Christian ethics the reward for a good life is

---

[1] See David Lyons, *Forms and Limits of Utilitarianism* (Oxford: Clarendon Press, 1970), 161-197. B. Williams illustrates the point by the following example (*Utilitarianism for and against*, l.c. 105): Suppose that there is in a certain society a racial minority. It does no particular harm to the rest of the citizens, but also offers no particular benefits. Its presence is in those terms neutral. However the other citizens have such prejudices that they find the presence of this group very disagreeable. Proposals are made for removing in some way this minority. If we assume that programmes to change the majority sentiment are likely to be ineffective, then even if the removal would be unpleasant for the minority, a utilitarian calculation might well end up favouring this step, especially if the minority were a rather small one and the majority were very severely prejudiced, that is to say, were made very severely uncomfortable by the presence of the minority.

eternal happiness. And it considers as morally good whatever is useful for the realization of God's glory and man's eternal salvation. Likewise all systems which regard self-perfection or self-realization as the ultimate goal of the moral effort, e.g. humanism or existentialism, can in this literal sense be called utilitarian. The same can be said of ethics of values. They all deem morally good whatever is useful for the achievement of their goals, be it self-perfection or the realization of the moral values. Nevertheless this is not the meaning the terms have in actual philosophical and linguistic usage. Here they refer to ethical schools and ways of life which consider temporal happiness and welfare as the ultimate goal of human life. In order to avoid confusion and the risk of emptying the terms of any useful meaning at all, it is desirable to continue the adopted usage.[1]

II. Ethics of self-perfection[2] and temporal progress

Self-perfection, conceived in a naturalistic sense, is considered by humanistic personalism as the ultimate end of the moral effort. In psychological and psychotherapeutic literature it is frequently referred to as self-actualization and self-realization and promoted as the all-encompassing goal of human life.[3] Similarly existentialist thinkers often place the ultimate purpose of man in the realization of his true self and authentic personality. A religious type of the striving after perfection with the goal of self-sanctification is not seldom presented in Christian literature as the central task of moral life. It may

---

[1] It seems that the terms utilitarian and utilitarianism were first used by J. Bentham (1748-1832) and J. Stuart Mill (1806-1873). Kant was the first one to coin the term eudaemonist, and the principle of happiness adopted by the latter he called eudaemony. From there it was a small step only to the term eudaemonism.

[2] E. Coreth uses the term "Persönlichkeitsethik" to cover the various trends of the ethics of self-perfection ("Ethik," *Lexikon für Theologie und Kirche*, vol. 3, 1959, 1128f).

[3] "The concept of self-realization has gone through many variations from Nietzsche and Jung to Karen Horney, Erich Fromm, Kurt Goldstein, Frieda Fromm-Reichmann, Abraham Maslow, Carl Rogers, and others who seem to be searching for an all-encompassing theory of life's ultimate goal. With again another connotation, it appears in the context of existentialist thinking" (Charlotte Bühler, quoted by Viktor Frankl, *Psychotheraphy and Existentialism*. New York: Simon and Schuster, 1967, 45).

even constitute the moral ideal of entire religions. (The ideal of self-purification in Hinduism and kindred religions seems to amount ultimately to an anthropocentric ethics of self-perfection.)

What all these types of moral ideals have in common is that they centre ethics in man and more particularly in the individual person. They tend to be "individualistic", a word that again has a negative tinge, though less strong than the word egotism. The morality of self-perfection is man-centred and, if promoted within the context of religion, leads to an anthropocentric orientation of religion.

Vatican II thought it important enough to comment on the tendencies to individualism in ethics and to dissociate itself from them. It calls on the believer not to "content himself with a merely individualistic morality". The reason is that individualism does not sufficiently account for the social necessities, which are "among man's chief duties today" (GS 30, cf. 32).

The decisive deficiency of the morality of self-perfection lies in this that it centres in values of limited nature, leaving aside superior values which alone would merit to be the ultimate centre of attention and love. "To a degree these systems preserve the earnestness of morality, since they place man in a comprehensive framework of meaning, value, and law to which he must conform. But the ultimate in meaning and goal is always man and his own development and perfection."[1] Prayer, worship and religion are primarily viewed from the stand-point of the benefit they bring to man. With such an attitude man shuts himself off from the truest and deepest approach to God. The holiness of God can never serve as a means to man's self-perfection. Ultimately morality and religion must have the same centre: community and fellowship with God.

The humanistic ideal of self-perfection is even more limited than its religious counterpart. Very often it is conceived in the naturalistic sense of physical and intellectual vigour and beauty. For the physically or mentally sick and crippled it is not at all attainable, and the general decline of old age is nonsensical in this system. If the interests of self-actualization

---

[1] B. Häring, *The Law of Christ*, vol. I, 1966, 39.

happen to collide with the needs of the neighbour, this morality will easily lead to the neglect of his claims.

The main mistake of the ethics of self-realization, according to Victor Frankl, is the devaluation of the world and its objects to mere means for the person's self-actualizing ends.[1] Even the services rendered to other persons ultimately receive their meaning and moral goodness from the contribution they can make to the agent's self-realization. A love of the other person which is of no profit for man's self-actualization lacks meaning. Not only the material world but also other persons are ultimately placed in the category of means for the agent's personal good.

Furthermore men and women have many potentialities. Self-actualization conceives a person's life task to be the striving to realize as many potentialities as possible to the greatest possible degree. But experience shows that man has always more potentialities than he can realize. Which ones then will he realize? The ethics of self-perfection is not in a condition to offer a criterion for this choice. Man's only purpose becomes to grow exuberantly and rankly, without any further aim than to grow.

It must however be noted that a certain degree of intellectual and personal maturity is necessary before a man is able to serve his fellow-men and society efficiently. Therefore self-perfection certainly plays a justified role in human life, though it is not man's ultimate goal but rather an intermediate aim.

There are other ethical schools of thought which regard social and cultural progress and the creative development of the world as the ultimate end of the moral effort (Schleiermacher, Wundt, Teilhard de Chardin). They are faced with the difficulty of defining what real progress consists in, and they may define it too narrowly. A neglect of basic and central values will result in a deficient morality, e.g. if man is understood in a too narrowly materialistic way or if the transcendental openness of the world is rejected and accordingly any value to religion denied. But if justice is done also to the spiritual dimension of man and the values of religion, we

---

[1] V. E. Frankl, *Psychotherapy and Existentialism*, 1967, 37-58.

are faced with an ultimate end of human activity which is also the ultimate purpose of the moral effort in Christian religion, so far as the responsibility for this world is concerned.

III. Morality for its own sake

In the systems considered until now, actions are valued as good or evil according to their contribution to the realization of the values of happiness, self-perfection or temporal progress. The morally good is consequently not an independent, self-sufficient value. It is rather relative to another value, in whose service it stands and whose promotion or impairment is the measure of moral goodness. In contrast what the following moral systems, Kantian ethics and ethics of values, have in common is that they view the morally good as values in themselves, which receive their goodness not from their relation to another value, but should be realized only for the sake of their own worth and beauty.

1. *Kantian ethics*

Kant (†1804) gives the moral obligation a "formal" foundation in the categorical imperative, which is formulated thus: "So act that the maxim of your will could always hold at the same time as a principle establishing universal law." That is to say, the rule from which moral activity springs must be capable of becoming a universal law, and man ought to act as he would like all men to act. The categorical imperative is "formal" in the sense of containing no definite subject matter, but providing only a general principle and criterion of all moral commands and duties. This moral obligation must be fulfilled for its own sake; not for the hope of happiness, since this would be a mercenary ethics founded on pleasure or utility; nor for the sake of God as lawgiver and final goal, since - as Kant explains - an obligation imposed on men by God would result in turning men into slaves. Any heteronomous ethics, i.e. an ethics imposed upon men by an extraneous will, is unworthy of men, even if this be the will of God. Authentic morality must be autonomous, resulting from men's own insight, verified and approved by their reason. Kant's demand for moral autonomy has found a strong echo and is a much hailed tenet even today.[1]

This foundation of ethics has the merit of emphasizing the categorical character of the moral obligation against all utilitarian and eudaemonist ethics. Moral duty has absolute priority over profit and pleasure. Nevertheless it suffers from great shortcomings.

Kant pretends that man's dependence on a divine will and law would result in slavery. But how is it possible that man, who in the order of existence is evidently not independent, should be totally autonomous in the order of action? This is a contradiction. Kant is wrong in identifying dependence and slavery. Slavery is dependence on a person or thing that deprives man of his freedom to serve at his best the real purpose of his life. But in obeying God's will man is simply serving the true purpose of his life, and this is true freedom. On the other hand, if man had to obey only the authority of his own judgment on good and evil, as Kant's solution runs, this would speedily result in anarchy. It is an overestimation of himself if man is ready to submit only to his own authority

---

[1] In recent years attention has been drawn to another formulation of the categorical imperative by Kant: "So act that you treat humanity, in your own person as well as in the person of everyone else, always at the same time as an end and never as a mere means." The maxim coincides with the argument from the *dignity of the human person*, or at least is closely related to it, which is likewise often called upon today. The proposition enjoys widespread approval. Nevertheless its usefulness in the ethical discourse seems to be rather limited. If in a war the unjust aggressor is killed, is he still treated as an end in himself? In what possible sense? Certainly he is treated as a means, for his life is sacrificed as the means for the higher good of justice among nations. The problem is that the temporal existence of man is not an absolute value and therefore not the highest end. The lower value however may and even must at times be sacrificed if this should be necessary for the safeguard of the higher one. In a careful analysis of Kant's maxim, Bruno Schüller comes to the conclusion that the appeal to personal dignity yields very little normative content, and that there are actions which do indeed treat others as a means only, yet remain compatible with that person's dignity ("Die Personwürde des Menschen als Beweisgrund in der normativen Ethik," *Theologie und Philosophie* 53, 1978, 538-555; cf. the good summary in *Theological Studies* 41, 1980, 99-103). He agrees with D. Ross, who says of the Kantian axiom: "It has in fact great homiletic value; it is a means of edification rather than of enlightenment" (*Kant's Ethical Theory*. Oxford, 1969, 55; quoted in Schüller 548).

instead of inquiring after God's will for him. Kant himself, in his late years, felt the inadequacy of his tenet that the divine will must be excluded from ethics as a heteronomous principle. "The Opus Postumum shows that the elderly Kant is ready to grant a more immediate and real role to God as a moral legislator."[1]

Kant is equally too extreme when he rejects the hope of happiness not only as the ultimate goal of the moral effort, but also as any kind of motive at all. The desire for happiness is a helpful and justified incitement for man to pursue his true assignments. Certainly the usually vague inclinations must still be cleared up and further specified by reason and by confrontation with the moral demands. It is indicative and revealing that followers of Kant like Salomon Maimon (†1800), who feel indebted to the teaching of the great philosopher, nevertheless cannot agree that the desire for happiness should entirely be excluded from the motivation for good action.[2]

In the end Kantian ethics also provides an unsatisfactory basis for the categorical character, which it rightly attributes to the moral demand. What is at stake, according to Kant, if the moral obligation is not complied with? God's glory and man's happiness or eternal salvation are excluded as motives and goals of the moral effort. At stake is some kind of human dignity, which will suffer detriment in immoral actions. Offences against morality, then, must be omitted for the sake of avoiding such detriment. This is a rather idealistic and abstract sanction of the moral order, scarcely strong enough

---

[1] Vernon J. Bourke, *History of Ethics* (Garden City, N.Y.: Doubleday, 1968), 167.

[2] *Ib.* 171. Very firmly Albert Plé, OP, turns against Kant's mere ethics of duty and related tendencies in Christian quarters and argues for a more just place for the motif of happiness and pleasure in ethics (*Duty or Pleasure. A New Appraisal of Christian Ethics*. New York: Paragon House, 1987). Some assertions of the author however appear rather close to eudaemonism. Repeated formulations very strongly emphasize happiness and pleasure as the explicit end of human actions (e.g. 84, 91, 100). Compared with this, the deepest, most original longing of man for meaningful achievements and a meaningful life receives only scant attention. Nevertheless the author equally adverts that pleasure is not an end in itself and beckons to what is beyond it (107-9). In what this higher reality however consists is left vague by the author, and yet the answer to it is of decisive importance for any ethics.

to enforce obedience, especially under greater sacrifices. It does not confront man with the elemental choice between salvation and frustration, which alone gives sufficient grounds to a categorical imperative.

By excluding finally an ultimate end of morality in God and by basing morality on the individual's judgment of what he thinks could become a universal law, Kant's ethics ultimately leads to subjectivism. It is left to the individual's discretion to decide which actions would be acceptable as general laws. But there is no assurance that the choices will be morally reasonable and just. Whoever is in favour of nudism, abortion, free access to drugs, prohibition of certain foods (e.g. meat of cows), suppression of religion as superstition etc., will readily agree that these options should be adopted as principles establishing universal law. There is no criterion superior to man's private views and authority. If however by common agreement certain obligations were extracted as general norms binding for everybody, the decision whether a way of acting is acceptable as a common law would inevitably be based on the other criterion whether these laws are profitable for the community, serve the common interest, promote progress, etc. In other words, the last criterion for the moral obligation would be social utilitarianism or some kind of social and cultural progress. Kant's formal ethics in itself does not provide any definite guidance towards a definite moral ideal.

W. Pannenberg calls attention to the most divergent and even vicious usages to which Kant's formal imperative lends itself. Adolf Eichmann, who organized the extermination of the Jews in Nazi Germany, insisted at his trial in Jerusalem 1961, "that he had always acted according to Kant's imperative. He clearly envisioned the extermination of the Jewish people as a universal law to be universally followed. Fanatics of other strains can likewise wrap themselves in Kant's formal imperative. Kant's formal ethics does not in fact provide certain guidance toward the humanistic ideal he espoused."[1]

John Rawls wants to avoid such gross abuse of the categorical imperative by a further development of Kant's approach through his contractual theory of justice. His point of departure is that each one and all together should draw

---

[1] W. Pannenberg, *Theology and the Kingdom of God* (Philadelphia: Westminster Press, 1969), 104.

up the best possible rules of justice for an ideal society, yet under the "veil of ignorance". That is, nobody knows which place he will obtain in this society: whether he will be rich in it or poor, intelligent or dull, healthy or handicapped, white or black.[1] It is evident that in this society nobody would plead for the extinction of the Jews; he himself could be one of them. Nevertheless the theory does not resolve the other difficulties mentioned above affecting the imperative of Kant, such as the affirmation of nudism or of free access to drugs as a universal right.

Nonetheless this does not mean that Kant's categorical imperative or Rawls' version of it are without value for the discernment of moral norms. Every moral norm must indeed be suited for universalization, i.e. it must be of such a nature as to be valid for any person or group placed in a situation of a like kind. A norm which does not meet this criterion cannot be a valid moral principle. This however is only a negative criterion for the discernment of moral norms, not at the same time a sufficient criterion for what positively can count as a moral duty. True, the theories of Kant and Rawls are useful helps for producing moral norms, just as the golden rule is such a help;[2] only that by themselves they do not suffice.

2. Ethics of values

Ethics of values goes beyond the purely formal principle of the categorical imperative by maintaining the existence of moral values with concrete content. These values are thought of as some sort of ideal entities, somewhat like Plato's ideal forms. They are not merely subjective conceptions, but essences in the ontic realm, though not physically existing entities. In consequence, the moral values are not rationally deduced from any ultimate end of human life. They are rather perceived by

---

[1] *A Theory of Justice* (Oxford University Press, [7]1986), 12.

[2] In substance the categorical imperative is a philosophical formulation of the golden rule of love of neighbour. The latter, too, has its great merits, but also certain limitations, as is shown in the chapter on love of neighbour in volume II. Kant, it is true, objects against such an identification (*Grundlegung zur Metaphysik der Sitten*, BA 69), for A. Schopenhauer however the categorical imperative is just a "veiled expression" of the long-known golden rule (*Die beiden Grundprobleme der Ethik*. Leipzig, 1927, 220f).

a kind of intuition, i.e. by a certain feeling for value (Max Scheler, Nicolai Hartmann, Wilbur M. Urban). In a way similar to aesthetics and arts, where values are perceived by a spontaneous inner sentiment for the artistically beautiful, the moral value is perceived and esteemed by an immediate spiritual appreciation. And just as the aesthetic value is loved and realized for the sake of its own beauty, so also is the moral value to be loved and realized for its own sake. In this regard, insofar as the criterion for the morally good is not man's happiness nor a divine will nor a divinely willed ultimate goal (this latter relation is not completely excluded by Scheler), but simply the inner beauty of the good, the ethics of values coincides with Kantian ethics. However, as already said, the ethics of values admits of the existence of a variety of concrete moral values, such as justice, courage, self-control, brotherly love, truthfulness, faithfulness, humility. And the axiological ethicists also tend to think that the morally good fulfils or perfects a person in the direction of self-realization.

Ethics of values attempts to overcome any kind of utilitarian relativism inasmuch as the values are defined as ideal entities which are independent of any further purpose and goal. At the same time the empty formalism of Kant is replaced and filled by the concrete values of a material ethics. Ethics of values also accords a fairer place to happiness in man's moral life than Kant does. Although it is true that happiness does not establish the ethical value but follows from it, the experience of a value is by nature connected with a corresponding feeling of happiness, which is quite legitimate. Nicolai Hartmann says that the man who pursues happiness will not find it, but happiness "opens itself to him who sets his gaze... upon the primary values".[1]

In spite of this, ethics of values is not able to give the final answer to the moral question. Ethics of values ascribes the perception of moral values to an irrational feeling. Similarly, and even more so than in Kant's ethics, it is left to the individual's discretion to decide which are the moral values that are worthy to be accepted and to be realized. There is no criterion superior to a person's subjective feelings. Mere

---

[1] Nicolai Hartmann, *Ethics*, vol. I (London: George Allen and Unwin, 1967), 150.

feelings however are fallible. This lack of a superior, objective criterion for the morally good creates a void, which will easily be filled by the criteria of eudaemonism and utilitarianism. "Lacking a criterion that determines the nature of the good, ethics will continue to fall back upon the satisfaction to be derived as the best norm for action."[1]

Another difficulty not satisfactorily answered by axiological ethics is the priority among values in instances of conflict, where out of two values only one can be realized while the other has to be sacrificed. For example, it may be demanded of a father to deny his faith or else his child will be put to death. He finds himself in a conflict between faithfulness to his Church and fatherly love.[2] Which of the values is to be preferred? Since axiological ethics regards all moral values in principle as equal and does not admit of a supreme value to which the others are subordinated, no criterion is available to solve the conflict.

Again, just like Kantian ethics, so also ethics of values is not able to provide a satisfactory basis for the categorical character of the moral demand. What is at stake if the moral obligation is not complied with? At stake is the realization of certain moral values, which will not be brought into being. Everybody will agree that this is regrettable, just as everybody will find it more or less regrettable if aesthetic values are destroyed or not realized. But it does not appear too difficult to put up with such a loss. Precisely because the moral values are independent entities and not related to any superior purpose of God's glory or man's salvation, the system is unable to provide a peremptory sanction of the moral order. Axiological ethics misses the stern inexorability of a divine will uncompromisingly avenging offences against the moral law and demanding atonement for its infringements.

Finally the nature of the value entities remains mysterious and without satisfactory explanation. Their existence as independent essences in the ontic realm or in a similar mode of being lacks proof.

---

[1] W. Pannenberg, l. c. 108.

[2] Richard Wurmbrand reports the case of a Protestant pastor by the name of Florescu, whom communists in a prison in Rumania wanted to compel to betray his brethren. When he resisted all other tortures, they finally brought his fourteen year-old son and began to whip the boy in front of the father. The boy was beaten to death (*Tortured for Christ. The Voice of the Martyrs*. Glendale, Calif., 1969, 36).

It is however a lasting merit of the ethics of values that it has accorded a fairer role to man's emotions in the realm of morality. There is a need to overcome the emotional starvation of man resulting from unilateral concentration on rational principles and categorical imperatives. Ethics also has to give attention to the value responses which re-echo in the heart of man, make him sensitive to the beauty of moral goodness and call forth his love, devotion and enthusiasm for it. Likewise it is a correct observation that man grasps his moral task within the wider, universal horizon of meaning (which will be unfolded in the following) in an act of intuition and faith. In this, ethics of values is right. Yet the intuition has as its object not a multiplicity of a priori values, but ultimately the one comprehensive value of a personal calling. Complementary to the generic ethics derived from the common vocation of mankind, the personal calling then forms the basis of an individual existential ethics.[1]

IV. God's glory and kingdom as the ultimate purpose: theonomous ethics

Every ethics which affirms the existence of an unconditional "ought", and only that is an ethics worthy of the name, requires for the justification of this "ought" a purpose which is unconditional itself.[2] No temporal, transitory value can

---

[1] A more recent theory akin to the ethics of values is emotivism (C.L. Stevenson, A.J. Ayer). For emotivism the qualification of a behaviour as morally "good" is a matter of emotion or feeling, not of an insight based on rational criteria. As an emotional attitude, the value of the good cannot be communicated by rational conviction but only by emotional influence. Correspondingly, just as for the ethics of values, it holds for emotivism that the lack of a more universal criterion beyond emotion or feeling must lead to a moral subjectivism which does not offer a sufficient basis for general moral principles.

[2] W. Korff formulates the thesis: "Every ethics which establishes the claim of an unconditional ought requires for the justification of this ought a metaempiric, metalogical, theologic reference point of meaning" (*Theologische Ethik: Eine Einführumg*. Freiburg: Herder, 1979, 73). The thesis expresses a very valid truth, although the question must be asked whether the reference point of meaning is indeed totally metalogical. This point is ultimately God, his providence and wisdom. Yet according to a strong philosophical and theological tradition, God's existence and provident wisdom can be proven by arguments of reason.

establish an unconditional, ultimate claim. Such a claim can only emanate from an absolute, supreme value and purpose, i.e. from a purpose rooted in the divine being and will. Christian ethics therefore searches for the ultimate purpose and meaning of human life and of history in God's will and decrees. Nothing determines its particular character more comprehensively and decisively than the biblically founded Christian understanding of the ultimate end.

The option for a definite purpose of life is however not forced upon humans. They embrace it in a free decision of their will. Of course they ought to opt for the purpose which is in harmony with the divine will. But they can also prefer options of their own making and desire, though at a high cost: the loss of ultimate meaning. The choice of a purpose for one's life is therefore a most crucial decision. "The grasping of meaning is more than merely ethically relevant; it can already be defined as a moral option of elemental character."[1]

1. Teaching of Holy Scripture

As the moral command has, according to Holy Scripture and to Christian theology, its origin in God, so it has also in him, his glory and his kingdom, its ultimate purpose.

According to the *Old Testament*, God's praise and glory are the highest end and purpose of man and of all creation. In his external works God manifests his majesty, his holiness, his name to men. And he wants men and all creatures to glorify him through their word and existence. "Let them give glory to the Lord, and declare his praise" (Is 42:12; cf. 42:8-12; Jer 13:16; Mal 2:2). The glory of God is the content above all of the psalms, which summon sun, moon and stars, seas and mountains, plants and animals, men and all nations to join in the praise of the Lord (e.g. Ps 96; 145; 148; 150). Manifestation of and contribution to God's glory is the reason for their existence and therefore their assignment and duty. All God's sons and daughters will be brought from afar, "every one who is called by my name, whom I created for my glory, whom I formed and made" (Is 43:7).

---

[1] K. Demmer, *Sittlich handeln aus Verstehen. Strukturen hermeneutisch orientierter Fundamentalmoral* (Düsseldorf: Patmos, 1980), 165.

In the book of Genesis, Yahweh gives man authority over all the earth and charges him to "subdue it" and "have dominion" over it (Gen 1:28 and 2:15). Hence man has the task to develop and to shape the world after the example of God, its creator, and in cooperation with him. The world did not yet attain its final form with the six days of creation. It is still waiting for an ultimate completion and transformation, which God will bring about in a future time. "For behold, I create new heavens and a new earth; and the former things shall not be remembered or come into mind" (Is 65:17; cf. 66:22).[1]

In other OT texts, especially in Wisdom literature, fellowship with God is felt to be the supreme goal of moral action. More important than all individual goods is the friendship with the Lord. Guided by this knowledge, the psalmist prays: "A day in thy courts is better than a thousand elsewhere. I would rather be a doorkeeper in the house of my God than dwell in the tents of wickedness" (Ps 84:10).[2]

Nevertheless this understanding of man's destiny coexists with another motivation of moral conduct, which is at least equally strong and which is of eudaemonist nature. Earthly blessings are the promises given for a good life and for Israel's faithfulness as a nation, such as worldly possessions, abundance of children, long life, victory in war, a glorious Jerusalem, etc. Alongside these goods, the universal spiritual values of God's reign only maintain themselves with much difficulty.[3]

---

[1] Gradually, and especially during the Exile, the conviction developed "that in the final age of the world God would bring the variable course of history to a close and complete his creation. This view of history, which achieved greater consistency as time went on, is a phenomenon which gives Israel a unique place in the spiritual history of mankind... Israel brought up the question of the meaning of history in a deeper and more comprehensive way than any other people" (Rudolf Schnackenburg, *Christian Existence in the New Testament*, vol. 2. Univ. of Notre Dame Press, 1969, 189).

[2] Also Ps 27:4; 63:1-4; 84:1-4; Jer 9:23f.

[3] Walther Eichrodt concludes that "no proper comprehension of the dominant goal of all ethical action was ever attained" in the OT (*Theology of the Old Testament*, vol. 2. London: SCM Press, 1967, 365).

The *New Testament* vision of the meaning of human life and of history resumes the valid elements of the OT tradition, but also adds interpretations and images of its own.

Glorification of the Father in heaven was the concern of Jesus during his earthly life (Jn 8:49f; 15:8; 17:4; cf. Lk 2:14). St. Paul exhorts his Christians: "Whether you eat or drink, or whatever you do, do all to the glory of God" (1 Cor 10:31; cf. Eph 1:12; Col 3:17). In many doxologies the early Church proclaims the invitation: "To our God and Father be glory for ever and ever" (Phil 4:20; Eph 3:20f; 1 Tim 1:17; Jud 25). The reason is that "from him and through him and to him are all things" (Rom 11:36). In the Book of Revelation God reveals himself as "the Alpha and the Omega, the first and the last, the beginning and the end" (Rev 22:13; also 1:8; 21:6). Thus all creation has its centre in God and is called to contribute to his glory.

The idea of God's glory as the ultimate purpose of creation in general and of man in particular gains a new fullness and concreteness in Christ's preaching about the kingdom. Just as the kingdom of God is the principal motive in Christ's ethical teaching, so it is also the most characteristic description of man's ultimate end in the Gospels. The metaphor implies that the will of God is the highest authority for men, and that mankind as well as all of creation find their salvation in the fulfilment of this will. "Seek first the kingdom and his righteousness, and all these things shall be yours as well" (Mt 6:33 par). The kingdom of God is the greatest and most important treasure for which a man must be ready to sacrifice everything else (Mt 13:44-46). Nothing is more urgent than that a man be prepared and worthy to be admitted to it (cf. the parables of the king's banquet, Mt 22:1-14; 25:1-12). Participation in the kingdom and its blessings is Jesus' most important promise in the beatitudes (Mt 5:3-12) and to those who follow him (Lk 18:28-30). The unity of both concepts, of God's glory and of the establishment of his kingdom, is very aptly expressed in the first petition of the "Our Father", where Christ teaches his disciples to pray foremost of all: "Hallowed be thy name. Thy kingdom come" (Lk 11:2 par).

The theme of the kingdom of God, as Jesus had developed it, is not absent in the primitive Church either.[1] A still greater emphasis however is placed on the parousia hope, i.e. on the expectation of the second coming of the Lord for the final judgment and the completion of all things in his eternal kingdom. Christ's invitation to his kingdom is here replaced by the call to be prepared for the second advent of the Lord, which is considered the last event which will bring about the final establishment of the kingdom of the Lord.[2]

Another comparison speaks of the otherworldly dwelling with God as the true homestead of man. Christians have no abiding city in this world. They are strangers and pilgrims here on earth. Their homeland is in heaven (2 Cor 5:8f; Phil 3:20f; Heb 11:13-16). Sometimes the person of Christ acquires a cosmic character. Not his kingdom but he himself is described as the ultimate end of history. This thought is developed in the epistle to the Colossians (1:15-20) and in Ephesians 1:10: This is God's "plan for the fullness of time, to unite all things in him, things in heaven and things on earth." Christification of mankind, then, and of all things would be the goal of history.

In the Book of Revelation the concept of the kingdom of God is complemented by the metaphor of the new Jerusalem, whose appearance will reward and crown the struggle of the children of God against the forces of evil. The seer sees "the holy city, new Jerusalem, coming down out of heaven from God". And he hears "a great voice from the throne saying, 'Behold, the dwelling of God is with men. He will dwell with them, and they shall be his people, and God himself will be with them'" (Rev 21:2f; also 21:10). The new Jerusalem is again of cosmic character, comprising all creation, since it is also described as "a new heaven and a new earth" (Rev 21:1). The same thought occurs in the second letter of St. Peter. "Waiting for and hastening the coming of the day of God... we await for new heavens and a new earth in which righteousness dwells" (3:12f).

---

[1] Acts 14:22; 28:23; Rom 14:17; 1 Cor 15:24-28; 2 Thess 1:5; Rev 11:15.

[2] 1 Cor 1:7f; Phil 1:10f; 1 Thess 3:13; 5:23; Jas 5:7f; 1 Pet 1:13; 4:7.

2. Theological reflection

When Scripture describes the ultimate end of man as God's glory, his kingdom, the new Jerusalem, the unity of all things in Christ, the new heaven and the new earth, such assertions are still very descriptive and indeterminate. For the elaboration of the moral norm, a more precise and scientific definition of the ultimate goal of man and creation would be desirable. Nevertheless the statements of Holy Scripture contain some very basic insights.

First, creation is not the event of a blind fate or irrational demiurge, but the outcome of a wise and provident creator, who has structured it according to a discerning plan and comprehensive purpose. Second, this purpose is most intimately related to the divine realities and is therefore lastly of a religious and not profane character; it culminates in the fellowship and community with God. Third, the final goal is not primarily centred in the individual's perfection and bliss, not even in the welfare of social groups; rather it embraces mankind as a whole and beyond it the totality of creation; it is of universal and cosmic nature. And fourth, this goal brings about a condition far better than the present one. It relativizes all present achievements and denies to any human institution the status of the final answer. It ever anew challenges man to transcend the limitations of the present and affirms the possibility of reform and improvement. The final answer to man's longings will be given not in terms of earthly attainments, but in terms of a transformation that belongs to another world.

The following expositions concerning the ultimate goal of man and creation are above all inspired, though not exclusively, by the Pastoral Constitution on the Church in the Modern World of Vatican II (cf. especially GS 33-39). Its contributions to this question are of great value indeed.

Christians, on pilgrimage towards the heavenly city, should seek and savour the things which are above (GS 57). This includes their obligation to foster communion with God through the praise of his name, through prayer and contemplation, through liturgical worship in community, through the sacramental life. For the human is ultimately "directed toward and subordinated to the divine, the visible to the invisible, action to contemplation, and this present world to that city yet to come, the object of our quest" (SC 2; cf. 10).

Yet the vocation of Christians to community with God and to divine worship in no way decreases, but rather increases, the weight of their obligation to cooperate in the development of this world, to contribute to earthly progress, and to work for the perfection of creation (GS 57). In relation to this world, God's glory is achieved by the unfolding of the Creator's work and the realization of the divine plan in history. Men "can rightly look upon their work as a prolongation of the work of the creator, a service to their fellow men, and their personal contribution to the fulfilment in history of the divine plan" (GS 34; also 67). Hence men attain to community with God by the contemplative life of worship as well as by their active cooperation in the realization of the divine designs. This truth has been expressed from of old by the apposite motto of the Benedictine Order: *Ora et labora*, pray and work.

The unfolding of God's creation in particular is accomplished by the completion of several basic tasks. Man is called to subdue the earth and all that it contains, to cultivate and to keep it. He is ordered to this by God already in paradise (Gen 1:26-28; 2:15). This duty is again and with new emphasis pointed out by Vatican II: "By the work of his hands and with the aid of technical means man tills the earth to bring forth fruit and make it a dwelling place fit for all mankind;... in doing so he is realizing the design, which God revealed at the beginning of time, to subdue the earth and perfect the work of creation," and to devote himself to the service of his fellow-men (GS 57; also 34). Man is to harness the potentialities of the earth and to develop nature by his work, but at the same time also to guard and to keep it.

In a like manner man has the task to maintain and develop himself. "Human activity proceeds from man: it is also ordered to him. When he works, not only does he transform matter and society, but he fulfils himself. He learns, he develops his faculties, and he emerges from and transcends himself. Rightly understood, this kind of growth is more precious than any kind of wealth that can be amassed. It is what a man is, rather than what he has, that counts" (GS 35; cf. 57). Society is to help men in their task of developing their abilities and of maturing to full human dignity. The social order "must constantly yield to the good of the person" (GS 26; cf. 9). The welfare of the human person comprises the fulfilment of the basic needs of food, clothing, housing and a life in peace and liberty. It involves "that a person finds a certain measure of social recognition and does not constantly experience the rejection and contempt of others. And finally it pertains to the weal of the person that someone can trust, believe, hope and love... inclusive of the dimension of the religious sphere; it contradicts the welfare of the person to be compelled to live in such conditions that those ways of acting are impossible to him."[1]

The commitment to the progress of the earth furthermore involves participation in the life of social groups and promotion of the union of love among mankind. Indeed man cannot even find his full humanity except through a sincere gift of himself (GS 24; 57). It devolves on him to foster the process of wholesome socialization in the civic, economic and political realms, and this on the national level as well as on the level of mankind as a whole. For God did not create man for life in isolation, but for the formation of social unity. "This solidarity must be constantly increased until that day when it will be brought to fulfilment; on that day mankind, saved by grace, will offer perfect glory to God as the family beloved of God and of Christ their brother" (GS 32).

The contents of the ends and tasks set forth here are, in spite of all existing pluralisms, shared by men to a large extent. This is confirmed by the conventions on human rights. Nevertheless differences remain. The meaning of life, the calling of man and the nature of human welfare are decisively determined by the respective image of man and the fundamental anthropological and religious options. They are not the same everywhere. It is also to be granted that the ends and tasks of moral striving proposed here only offer a framework, within which, for Christian believers too, different moral options to some extent appear possible. Nonetheless the aforesaid ends offer an orientation indispensable for a basic discernment and are an essential help for a well-founded judgment.

---

[1] H. Weber, *Allgemeine Moraltheologie* (Graz: Styria, 1991), 159.

Through dedication to the said tasks in the service of creation and mankind, man is preparing the material for the celestial realm (GS 38). Therefore, concludes the council, "let there be no such pernicious opposition between professional and social activities on the one hand and religious life on the other. The Christian who shirks his temporal duties shirks his duties towards his neighbour, neglects God himself, and endangers his eternal salvation. Let Christians... carry out their earthly activities in such a way as to integrate human, domestic, professional, scientific and technical enterprises with religious values, under whose supreme direction all things are ordered to the glory of God" (GS 43). It is a mystery of human history, but nevertheless a reality, that the earthly and the heavenly city penetrate each other (GS 40).

Earthly progress is of vital concern to the kingdom of God, says Vatican II. Nonetheless it must be carefully distinguished from the growth of Christ's kingdom (GS 39). Although the Christian vision of the future is characterized by confident hope, its mark is not a naive optimism. "This must be said, because some theologians, especially of the secularizing sort, do seem to have come close to reducing Christian hope to a brash optimism based on the achievements of secular man and hardly to be distinguished from old-fashioned theories of progress."[1] The many individuals who have suffered for a lost cause, whose ideals have been defeated, who have been victims of injustice, misery, pain of body and agony of spirit defy any theory which considers merely worldly progress as the ultimate end. The eschatological understanding of the kingdom does not allow any particular social program to be mistaken for the kingdom. The kingdom is always more than secular progress. It is the realization of the thoughts of God which are not the thoughts of men. The kingdom ultimately culminates in the fellowship with God and the communion of saints.

The time for the consummation of the earth and of humanity is unknown to us. Neither do we know how all things will finally be transformed and how creation in its final perfection will look. Such knowledge is beyond human insight. As deformed by sin, the shape of this world will pass

---

[1] John Macquarrie, *Three Issues in Ethics* (New York: Harper and Row, 1970), 142.

away. And the new dwelling prepared by God will answer and surpass all the longings for peace which spring up in the human heart (GS 39).

Taking up at this point the language of Holy Scripture, the Council explains that the Lord himself "is the goal of human history, the focal point of the desires of history and of civilization, the centre of mankind, the joy of all hearts, and the fulfilment of all aspirations.... Animated and drawn together in his Spirit we press on towards the consummation of history which fully corresponds to the plan of his love: 'To unite all things in him, things in heaven and things on earth' (Eph 1:10)" (GS 45; cf. 10).

V. Salvation and the moral demand

Besides the glory of God and his kingdom, the books of Holy Scripture also indicate with great frequency man's salvation as the purpose of a good life and as the motive for obeying God's commandments. Salvation holds a very important place among the motives and goals of the moral effort in Holy Scripture and subsequently also in the piety of the Church. The question arises as to the role and rank of this goal. May a Christian aim at salvation as the principal goal of his moral action? Or must the motive of salvation always be subordinated to the glory of God as the centre of all values? How is the aim of man's personal salvation related to the goal of God's glory and kingdom? Finally, is there also a temporal aspect to salvation and is there a place in it for liberation from temporal evils? These are the questions to be studied in the following.

1. *Role of salvation in Holy Scripture*;

Salvation is as much a key biblical concept as the concepts of God's glory and kingdom. The notion of God who saves his people is a recurrent theme in the *Old Testament*. This salvation is often a liberation from temporal afflictions, but it also constitutes an eschatological promise. Whenever Israel found herself in a time of crisis from which God delivered her, she experienced God's salvation. Especially at the time of the exodus God saved Israel by ransoming her from the power of Egypt (Ex 14:13; Ps 106:7-10; Is 63:8f). But also on many other occasions the Patriarchs and the chosen people experienced the saving hand of God. In each time of impending disaster, therefore, Israel turned to Yahweh in order to be saved. She knew that besides her God there is no saviour (Is 43:11f; Hos 13:4; 1 Mac 4:30).

The title "saviour" for Yahweh becomes a major theme of prophetic eschatology. Prophecies concerned with "the last days" describe under various pictures the final salvation of Israel. Yahweh will save his people by leading them back to their land (Jer 23:6-8). He will save his sheep by bringing them to good pasture (Ezek 34:22f). He will deliver the house of Israel from all its impurities by giving it the gift of his Spirit (Ezek 36:26f). Salvation will be the essential act of Yahweh in that future time of grace when he will come to restore his people and all the earth in justice and holiness (Is 45:21-25; 52:7-10; 61:10f; Jer 31:7-9). To achieve it, he will send his servant, who will be made a light to the nations, that the Lord's salvation may reach to the ends of the earth (Is 49:6.8).

Salvation obtains an even more important place in the *New Testament*. The Gospels regard salvation as the purpose of Christ's life. He has come to earth to save that which was lost (Lk 19:9f; Jn 5:34; 6:39f), to save the world and not to condemn it (Jn 3:17; 12:47). The evangelists Matthew and Luke underline Jesus' role as saviour from his very infancy. The child conceived by Mary shall be called Jesus, because "he will save his people from their sins" (Mt 1:21). The angels announce to the shepherds the glad news that to them is born that night a saviour (Lk 2:11). Zechariah and Simeon hail in Mary's child the dawn of salvation promised by the prophets (Lk 1:69-71.77; 2:30). And the preaching of John the Baptist makes ready the ways of the Lord, so that "all flesh shall see the salvation of God" (Lk 3:6).

The message of the apostolic community has for its object the salvation of Jews and Gentiles (Acts 13:26.47; 28:28). The good news about Christ is defined as the "message of salvation" (Acts 13:26; cf. 11:14). Christ is the saviour (Acts 5:31; 13:23), and "there is no other name under heaven given among men by which we must be saved" (Acts 4:12). The apostles then offer men the only "way of salvation" (Acts 16:17).

The letters of the apostles preach salvation as the meaning of Christ's life. God desires the salvation of all men (1 Tim 2:4; 4:10). For this reason he has sent his Son as saviour of the world (Heb 5:8f; 1 Jn 4:14) and has made the Gospel an instrument for the salvation of every believer (Rom 1:16). In preaching it, an apostle has no other purpose but the salvation of men (1 Cor 9:22; 10:33). Salvation is also the meaning of the Christian life. The Gospel confronts men with a choice between salvation and doom, life and death (2 Cor 2:15f; 2 Thess 2:10-12). In the fear of the Lord they must work out their salvation (Phil 2:12), which is the object of the Christian hope (1 Thess 5:8f). Salvation is the final event at the end of time. God guards those who are chosen "for a salvation ready to be revealed in the last time" (1 Pet 1:5). The manifestation of the Lord and saviour will bring about "the salvation and the power and the kingdom of our God and the authority of his Christ" (Rev 12:10).

Man's salvation is likewise described under many other concepts and metaphors, such as consolation and reward, the peace and justice of God, liberation, divine sonship, vision of God, and above all as eternal life. For Christ came, "that whoever believes in him may have eternal life" (Jn 3:15).[1] Salvation appears as the human side of the glorification of God and of the presence of his kingdom among men. People who give God his glory, men who belong to his kingdom, are the ones who are saved. Those on the other hand who refuse to glorify God and reject the invitation into his kingdom call down perdition upon themselves.

2. *Role of salvation in theological thought*

Theologians regard the striving after salvation as lawful and even as obligatory, although they usually judge it to be subordinated to the glory of God as the centre of all values. For there is only one ultimate goal, and that is God's glory and kingdom. On the other hand, the biblical teaching does not give the impression that man's final salvation is to be only a secondary motive in the endeavour to live a life faithful to God's will, and that it would be a distortion of the right order to aim at salvation directly as a principal goal. It is

---

[1] Also Mk 10:30 par; Jn 5:24; 10:10.28; Rom 6:22, 1 Tim 6:12; etc.

hard to find in the holy books a definite subordination of man's salvation to any other purpose or goal.

There is doubtless a concern for a person's salvation which is legitimate. The innate desire of the human heart for happiness cannot simply be qualified as the expression of an imperfect personality. The unrest of the soul which longs for rest in God is implanted in the human heart by the creator himself. True, the striving of human beings after happiness always again stands under the suspicion of an egoistic self-interest. Indeed men often pursue the goal of happiness in selfish ways. But the striving after the salvation of the soul in the Christian sense is something altogether different from a merely self-centred type of happiness. Salvation is a condition which - unlike pleasure - does not comprise only the fulfilment of some particular inclinations in man; it concerns the good of the whole person and beyond it of the whole people of God. Salvation is community with Christ, who is himself both Saviour and Salvation; it is union with God. Since salvation signifies then a condition in which everything is right and whole, and a state which is by its nature centred in God, Holy Scripture does not find objection in placing salvation and eternal life before men as the ultimate reward for a faithful life and the final goal to be aimed at by them.

Furthermore man is able to strive after any kind of goal only if he experiences it in some way as good and valuable, i.e. he must find joy and fulfilment in its realization. This joy and inner fulfilment is willed by God as a spontaneous sense and criterion for man to discover the valuable and is an incentive to strive after its realization. Joyful appreciation, then, is so essentially connected with any kind of value in general, and also with the highest values of God's glory and kingdom in particular, that without this sense of appreciation a value could not be pursued, because it is not even understood and known as such. Happiness accordingly has a positive function and is not merely a human weakness, just to be tolerated. God himself is infinite happiness and beatitude. Taking this into consideration, man can hardly be blamed for being moved by inferior motivation when he pursues genuine values because he experiences them as the fulfilment of his longings or when he adheres to God's will because this is his salvation.

But if man is justified in striving after salvation as the final aim of his life, and if on the other hand God's glory and kingdom are to be the ultimate end of man and all creation, is man then not confronted with two ultimate goals? But only one goal can really be the ultimate one. In fact both, man's salvation on the one hand and God's glory and kingdom on the other, are two aspects of the same identical reality. Man's final salvation consists only and solely in the reign of God, and wherever the kingdom of God is, there is necessarily salvation. Both goals are always realized together. The ultimate purpose of God's demand is with regard to God, his glory, and with regard to man, salvation.

The close unity between the kingdom of God and the salvation of man should make it plain that salvation has also a temporal, terrestrial dimension, just as the kingdom of God also has a temporal dimension and includes a commitment to the development of the world. Salvation therefore may not be too narrowly understood as reward and happiness in the other world to the neglect of man's concern for the conditions of this world and of his calling to improve them. Such a tendency would indeed be liable to the criticism of Marx and others that religion betrays the cause of the poor in the world.[1]

Pope Paul VI does not hesitate to affirm that the Church "has the duty to proclaim the liberation of millions of human beings, many of whom are her own children - the duty of assisting the birth of this liberation, of giving witness to it, of ensuring that it is complete."[2] She joins in the effort and struggle of men to overcome everything which oppresses them, famine, chronic disease, illiteracy, poverty, injustices in international relations, neo-colonialism.

---

[1] It was the particular concern of liberation theology to overcome any other-worldly bias in Christian religion and to commit the Church to the cause of the poor and to the liberation from oppressive structures. Some basic writings to the theme are *A Theology of Liberation* by Gustavo Gutierrez (Maryknoll: Orbis, 1973); *Salvation and Liberation* by Leonardo & Clodovis Boff (Maryknoll: Orbis, 1984); and *Introducing Liberation Theology* by the same (Maryknoll: Orbis, 1987).

[2] Pope Paul VI, apostolic exhortation *Evangelii Nuntiandi*, 1975, nr. 30. Note the entire, careful discussion of liberation theology by the Pope, nrs. 30-39.

Yet Christian ethics could not agree that liberation be restricted to the mere dimension of economics, politics, social and cultural life. "The Church links human liberation and salvation in Jesus Christ, but she never identifies them, because she knows through revelation, historical experience and the reflection of faith... that in order that God's Kingdom should come it is not enough to establish liberation and to create well-being and development."[1] The earlier reflections on the ultimate goal of human life have shown that temporal welfare alone does not suffice to give meaning to human life, least of all to the lives of those many people who are never able to attain this goal of well-being.

It must also never be forgotten that liberation includes as one of its most urgent tasks the struggle against the bonds of selfishness and sinfulness in man's own heart. The best structures remain ineffective and soon become inhuman if those who live in them do not undergo a conversion of heart and free themselves from the serfdom of sin. "As the kernel and centre of his Good News, Christ proclaims salvation, this great gift of God which is liberation from everything that oppresses man but which is above all liberation from sin and the Evil One, in the joy of knowing God and being known by him, of seeing him, and of being given over to him."[2]

C. The categorical character of the moral demand

In every moral decision, and above all when his moral integrity is endangered, man senses that his response to God involves his very existence, his salvation. The moral obligation is expression of an imperious will, which commands unconditional obedience. In contradistinction to hypothetical rules, e.g. the rules of logic, aesthetics, grammar, which are stated for temporal ends and which bind only insofar as a man determines himself by his own choice to attain these ends, the moral laws are categorical. It is not left to a man's free choice whether he wants to follow them or not. They demand unreserved obedience and do not permit denial of submission, because they are concerned with the very purpose of man's existence and with the very goals of the Creator himself.

---

[1] *Ib.* nr. 35.
[2] *Ib.* nr. 9.

Holy Scripture is deeply conscious of the categorical character of God's command.[1] God will not permit his will to be disobeyed without avenging it. The *Old Testament* assures lasting blessings to those who obey God's commandments and laws, but it threatens severe chastisements to those who disobey them. The statutes of the Sinai covenant, which stand at the very beginning of Israel's history, are sanctioned by the promise of blessings and the menace of curses (Ex 23:20-28; Lev 26; Deut 28; 30:15-20). The prophetic books are full of references to divine judgments on the just and sinner. Yahweh will bring Israel and the nations which have sinned against him to trial (Is 3:13f; Amos 1f; Zeph 3:8). He appears as a shepherd, who sorts out the good and the bad in his flock (Ezek 34:17-22), as a labourer in the harvest who threshes out the grain (Is 27:12; Jer 15:7), as a gardener who selects the good figs from the bad ones (Jer 24:4-10). Also in the books of the wisdom literature the idea of retribution is well attested. "Every one will receive in accordance with his deeds" (Sir 16:14).[2]

The primitive teaching conceived of retribution as taking place in this world. "Victories and defeats, prosperity and trials, sickness and want, fruitfulness and abundance of offspring, happiness, health and wealth, friendship, love and honour were all counted as retribution coming from God."[3] However this doctrine had its difficulties, since the just man also was not rarely found to be afflicted by tribulations (cf. the Book of Job), while the evil-doers seemingly prospered. Nevertheless these incongruities did not destroy the firm conviction of a just retribution for good and evil. The concept of retribution simply went through a process of spiritualization. In the Book of Wisdom the idea of retribution is absolutely transcendent. Retribution here consists either in everlasting union with God and in a share in his eternal kingship and dominion, or alternatively in the loss of them (Wis 1-6). Death and life become the expression for transcendent recompense (Wis 5:15).

---

[1] Cf. the articles "Judgment" and "Retribution" by Wilhelm Pesch, *Encyclopedia of Biblical Theology*, ed. by J. Bauer, 1970, 442-449 and 764-770.

[2] Ps 1; 62:13; Prov 24:12; Eccl 12:14; Wis 1:7-12; Sir 16:11-13.

[3] "Retribution," *Encyclopedia of Biblical Theology*, 1970, 766. Cf. Deut 4:40; 28; Judg 2:11-15; Prov 3:1f; 10:27-30; 22:4f; etc.

Nature of Morality and its Ultimate End 55

The purpose of the divine judgments is first of all the vindication of God's honour. Yahweh is vitally concerned about his glory and the hallowing of his name, and he will not leave unavenged their contempt (Is 48:11; Ezek 39:21). But the divine chastisements also stand in the service of God's grace. They are means of correction which, if possible, make for salvation. God will once again look upon his people if they return to him (Is 1:25-27; Ezek 14:21-23; Hos 2:15-23). This is even true of the pagan nations: Yahweh will smite and heal Egypt (Is 19:22) and show mercy towards the nation which repents (Jer 18:7f).

In the *New Testament* the expectation of a final judgment, which will take place on a certain day, occupies an important and even central place. Christ himself announces a decisive judgment over all mankind (Mt 25:31-46, etc.). This day will bring salvation for those who believe and do good, but damnation for those who refuse to repent and to believe, who do not show mercy but instead do evil.[1] The doctrine of the approaching judgment gives the New Testament a sense of profound seriousness. It calls for decisive action, a state of readiness and an honourable way of life.[2]

The nature of the retribution is essentially transcendental and spiritual. The ultimate alternative behind all metaphorical expressions is only one: eternal life or eternal death. "The result of the judgment is described as, on the one hand, eternal joy, blessing, honour, good estate, peace, happiness, and the blessed company of God; on the other, as darkness, weeping, gnashing of teeth, punishment by fire, fear and terror, torture and ruin, eternal separation from God."[3] The qualification of the retribution as eternal signifies that there is no escape and that it is transcendent. People are set before the face of God, whose standards are entirely different from those of the world. Only occasionally is a reference made to divine retribution of a temporal nature (Mk 10:30 par; Lk 13:1-5; 1 Cor 11:29f).

The criterion for the judgment is not any national or collective standard, but is of a purely religious and moral

---

[1] Mt 11:20-24 par; 12:41f par; Rom 2:6-11; 2 Thess 1:6-10; 2 Pet 2:9.
[2] Mt 24:42-25:13; Lk 13:1-9; Phil 1:9-11; 1 Thess 3:13; 1 Pet 4:7f.
[3] "Judgment," *Encyclopedia of Biblical Theology*, 1970, 447f.

nature. Everyone will be judged according to his attitude to Christ (Mt 10:32f; Mk 8:38; Jn 3:18) and according to his works.[1] And since all the works of fraternal charity have a hidden relation to Christ, even those who are not conscious of such a relation of their deeds will be judged according to the law of Christ. "As you did it to one of the least of these my brethren, you did it to me." And reversely, "as you did it not to one of the least of these, you did it not to me" (Mt 25:40.45).

This teaching of Holy Scripture most forcibly confirms the universal testimony of conscience that the moral demand is categorical and does not tolerate disobedience and contumacy. This testimony is first of all the experience and perception of a reality, just as joy or sorrow are experiences of facts, and not in the first place logical conclusions.

Nevertheless there are also *intrinsic reasons* which explain the necessity of a categorical, moral order and prove its need. These reasons are found in the truth that in the moral decision the very purpose of God's work is at stake and with it the meaning of man's existence. Under the presupposition that the purpose of human life and creation at large is the realization of God's plan for the world, the unfolding of his divine designs and the glory of God, the categorical character of the moral demand is a logical conclusion. It is man's unconditional obligation to respect this purpose and to contribute to its realization. To obey or to disobey the moral order means to serve or to obstruct God's glory and the establishment of his kingdom; it means to realize or to defeat the ultimate end of man and creation. As a consequence, also man's salvation or perdition is at stake in the moral decision. For acceptance or rejection of the moral demand in the final analysis means ultimate fulfilment or frustration of human life.

The conviction that man and the world exist for a purpose which has been decreed for them by God is however not a mere act of faith without further rational foundation. The supremely wise order in the entire creation and its organic, determined, single-minded evolution give eloquent witness to this, that the universe has been created according to a coherent, purposeful plan. Likewise the correct concept of God as the wise and provident source of all beings leads to the compelling

---

[1] Mt 12:33-37; Rom 2:6-11; 2 Cor 5:10; Jas 2:14-26.

conclusion that God has set a purpose to the world and endowed it with a value worthy of its Creator. This argument will once more be taken up in the following chapter in the discussion of God's eternal decrees.

D. Openness to God's guidance and discernment of spirits

Since the concrete nature and design of the ultimate goal of human history and creation is not known to men but only to God alone, mankind needs to be open to the guidance of the Holy Spirit. Through his inspirations the Holy Spirit moves men and women again and again to choose the way which God wants them to go when the insights of reason come to an end. The Church has always been conscious of the need for such guidance, as is testified by her teaching on the seven gifts of the Holy Spirit.[1] In our present age the charismatic movement has been reminding Christians of all denominations with no little success of the need for openness to the promptings of the Holy Spirit and to his activity in the midst of God's people.

"If we are going to maintain that the basic structure of the Christian moral life is to respond to the initiative or call of God, then, with God as the center of value for us, we need to see all things in their relation to God and to integrate all things into our love of God. Discernment helps us to do that. It is an important part of our effort to make an authentically personal response to God."[2] Naturally the question immediately arises as to how a man can discern whether his ideas and desires come from God or from some other source of merely natural and less pure character. The discernment of spirits is not an easy task. It is a matter which requires great care and discretion. Theological and spiritual writers therefore have tried to define criteria and develop rules for the discernment of spirits.

Holy Scripture frequently speaks of God as the source of good insights and decisions. But it is also greatly concerned

---

[1] See Is 11:2f, the liturgy of Pentecost and of the sacrament of confirmation. The seven gifts of the Holy Spirit are wisdom and understanding, counsel (or right judgment) and fortitude, knowledge and piety (or reverence), and fear of the Lord.

[2] R.M. Gula, *Reason Informed by Faith* (New York: Paulist Press, 1989), 317.

that the spirits which move and influence a person be carefully tested. St. Paul lists among the charisms given in the Church "the ability to distinguish between spirits" (1 Cor 12:10). There are some who possess the gift of discernment in a greater degree than others. Nevertheless all Christians are expected and admonished to exercise discernment. "Test everything," St. Paul writes to the Thessalonians, "hold fast what is good, abstain from every form of evil" (1 Thess 5:21f). And St. John warns: "Beloved, do not believe every spirit, but test the spirits to see whether they are of God" (1 Jn 4:1). The discernment of spirits requires the readiness to change of mind and the effort for a life pleasing to God. "Do not be conformed to this world but be transformed by the renewal of your mind, that you may prove what is the will of God, what is good and acceptable and perfect" (Rom 12:2; cf. Eph 5:6-11; Phil 1:9f).

Every man and woman is challenged to take personal responsibility for the faith-decisions they make. Authority alone does not suffice to discover God's will. Even sincere leaders in the faith are not always right. Divinely constituted authority can help to gain greater clarity in the interpretation of God's will, but it cannot substitute for a person's own moral decision. Therefore every person must open the heart to God and be attentive to his word and call. This opening up to God demands prayer. "Prayer is truly relevant, both for the apostle *and* for the ordinary Christian, insofar as it is in prayer that we hear God and discover his will for us in the specific circumstances of our life."[1] The urgency of prayer for the discernment of spirits is a well-known doctrine in the tradition of Christian spirituality and of other religions as well. Yet a merely occasional prayer, said perhaps in the moment a decision has to be made, is not sufficient. The art of interpreting God's will requires an experience of God and a sensitivity for his intentions for us and the world. The tuning in to God's will presupposes perseverance and fidelity in prayer. In view of this it can justly be said that "the roots of moral knowledge are contemplative".[2]

Hand in hand with the spirit of prayer must go the striving after goodness and truth. Those who are led by God's

---

[1] Thomas H. Green, *Opening To God: A Guide to Prayer* (Notre Dame, Ind.: Ave Maria Press, 1977), 47.

[2] Daniel C. Maguire, "The Encyclopedia of Bioethics," *Theol. Studies* 41 (1980), 758.

Spirit keep the commandments, especially the commandment of brotherly love, while those moved by false spirits do not; rather they pursue selfish ambitions (1 Jn 3:10.24; Jas 3:13-18). Impartial listening to the Spirit is impossible for those who are under the influence of selfish desires, biased interests and preconceived ideas. Discernment of spirits demands detachment from bias and partiality. Docility to the Holy Spirit presupposes a heart which is humble and ready to listen. One does not presume that a proud person is listening to the Spirit. This is why knowledgeable directors have always discounted alleged divine phenomena in proud or disobedient people. Of course, the search for truth also demands the striving after accurate information. The gathering of relevant data, it is true, does not yet create the sufficient precondition for correct discernment of what is to be done; right discernment however is also not possible without the knowledge of the facts. Insufficient or false information abets false decisions.

Prayer and experience of God, striving after goodness and humility of heart are basic preconditions for the discernment of spirits. Nonetheless even the man of prayer and the saint are not automatically assured of a correct grasp of God's will in every individual case. The rules for the discernment of spirits are aids which try to assist a person in discerning the will of God. The more important ones are the following.

1. God always works in peace and usually slowly. At the end of a time of deliberation a choice is made, which is based not only on certain facts, but also on the harmony of the choice with the voice of the heart. God does not want to create turmoil. Rather, conflicts of the soul will cease, as is to be expected, once a person has attained to harmony with God. Decisions which conform to his will are accompanied by inner peace.[1] "The signs of peace, delight, and harmony are signs which tell us which course of action is most consistent

---

[1] T.H. Green illustrates this point by an example from a country where many families are poor. A seminarian feels confronted with a dilemma: He wants to continue for the priesthood and yet his family is in financial need. Should he leave or should he stay? What really is God's will for him? In this case it is very helpful to ask: "How do you feel about it when you are most at peace? - when you are at prayer and emotionally quiet and most open to whatever the Lord wants?" Very often the seminarian will reply: "At such times I always feel God is asking me to persevere and he will take care of my family. It is only when I am reflecting on it outside of prayer that doubts arise." In such a case one can confidently say that it is God's will for him to persevere (l. c.·51f).

with the sort of persons we are and want to become"[1] and with the task assigned to us by God.

2. Enlightened discernment usually needs the help of objective evaluation by others. It has been said that he who guides himself has a fool for a guide. This does not mean to say that a person should never make decisions entirely on his own responsibility. But it is undoubtedly true that he who listens only to himself is lacking in prudence. In matters of divine inspirations the possibility of illusion and self-deception is so great that an objective evaluation is indispensable.

3. The workings of the good spirit are discerned by the good results which ensue and the workings of the false spirits by the evil results. "For no good tree bears bad fruit, nor again does a bad tree bear good fruit; for each tree is known by its own fruit" (Lk 6:43f; cf. Mt 7:15-20; 12:33-35). At first sight this seems to be not much more than a platitude. Perhaps this is the reason why this criterion, which is so clearly expressed by Christ, is hardly mentioned by the spiritual writers. Moral theologians today emphasize the need of paying attention to the consequences of actions when judging them. Some teachings sound very ideal in theory, but are dismal in practice. They may speak of justice, equal rights, scientific progress, better life. But if their fruits are disregard for religion, commitment to violence as a normal means of strategy, light-minded destruction of human lives, creation of new outlaws and the like, then the fruits have judged the tree.

4. For Christians in particular a basic criterion for the discernment is a person's love for Christ. According to Holy Scripture nobody can confess the lordship of Jesus except under the influence of God's Spirit, and no one who curses the Lord can be speaking by the influence of this Spirit. "By this you know the Spirit of God: every spirit which confesses that Jesus Christ has come in the flesh is of God, and every spirit which does not confess Jesus is not of God" (1 Jn 4:2f; cf. 1 Cor 12:3). "Discernment of spirits is only possible for a person who looks on life from the perspective of one committed to God in Christ and through the Spirit."[2] Christians

---

[1] R.M. Gula, *l. c.* 325. This criterion is also found in K. Rahner. Peace, calm, quiet, joy as signs of the choice in harmony with God's will are opposed to pungency, bustle, noise as signs of the wrong one (*Das Dynamische in der Kirche*, Freiburg, ³1965, 138).

[2] R.M. Gula, *l. c.* 317.

find the pattern of their lives in the life of Christ. Better than anyone else he embodies the fundamental direction which human life has to take in response to the presence of God. "To know God's will is basically to test our inspirations against the scriptures in which God is revealed to us through his Son."[1] For this reason Holy Scripture should be the most important meditation book of every Christian.

5. A last criterion finally is the bond with the community of faith. The single most important community for Christians is the Church. Flat disregard of the teachings of the Church is a clear indicator of inauthenticity. "Whoever knows God listens to us," the first letter of John asserts, "and he who is not of God does not listen to us. By this we know the spirit of truth and the spirit of error" (1 Jn 4:6). This does not mean that justified disagreements with magisterial teachings are not possible. They are. But it means that the teachings of the magisterium of the Church must always seriously be taken into consideration and in cases of doubt enjoy presumption in their favour. The moral tradition is a major source for ethical insight. Therefore the Church is the necessary context for giving the Christian's moral life its identity.[2]

In this context the communal setting of moral decision-making deserves attention. The person becomes, decides and acts in community. This is true for Christians and non-Christians alike. The communal setting is always a critical component of ethics. The moral identity of a person is decisively determined by the community to which he belongs. The question has to be taken up later on again. Precisely here the justified concerns of the theories of the ethics of discourse and of communitarianism seem to be found. According to the ethics of discourse the validity of moral norms is based on the consensus of the members of a community gained by means of a common discourse.[3] In contradistinction to the approaches of Kant and

---

[1] T.H. Green, *l. c.* 51.

[2] For a detailed treatment of the norms for religious assent within the Church, see "The ecclesiality of faith," vol. II, 2004, ch. I, pp. 60-67.

[3] A prominent proponent of the theory is Jurgen Habermas, *Justification and Application. Remarks on Discourse Ethics* (Cambridge, Mass.: MIT Press, 1994). See also William Rehg, *Insight and Solidarity. A Study in the Discourse Ethics of Jurgen Habermas*, (Berkeley, Calif.: Univ. of California Press, 1994).

Rawls based on the individual, communitarianism underscores the necessary role of the community in the discovery of the moral norms.[1] It has been explained above that men have only an approximate knowledge of the ultimate end of mankind and creation, and that in comprehending this end they must let themselves be guided always anew by God's Spirit. At the same time the ultimate end is the most fundamental criterion for the moral norm, hence its correct comprehension is of such basic importance. Obviously the knowledge of this end by the individual will be more limited than the joint understanding of all the members of a community. True, a full discernment of God's plans is not possible for the community either, and its understanding will always be in need of completion and correction. Nevertheless the community's understanding of man's destiny will surpass that of the individual. By common discourse the members of the community must therefore arrive at an ever better understanding of their destiny as well as of the mediate goals and the moral demands resulting therefrom (which discourse may take place in conventions, synods, round-table conferences etc., but also by means of publications). And the mediator of the moral knowledge will fundamentally be the community with its traditions.

Vatican Council II is convinced of the fact that an immediate guidance by the Spirit exists among the people of God. It is aware of the need to be open to his inspirations and thus receive insights which reason alone cannot attain. "The People of God believes that it is led by the Spirit of the Lord who fills the whole world. Moved by that faith it tries to discern in the events, the needs, and the longings which it shares with other men of our time, what may be genuine signs of the presence or the purpose of God" (GS 11). Christ is "at work in the hearts of men by the power of his Spirit;... he quickens, purifies, and strengthens the generous aspirations of mankind to make life more humane and to conquer the earth for this purpose" (GS 38).

---

[1] For the theory, see Daniel Bell, *Communitarianism and Its Critics* (Oxford Univ. Press, 1993). C.F. Delaney, ed., *The Liberalism-Communitarianism Debate. Liberty and Community Values* (Lenham, Md.: Rowman & Littlefield, 1994).

Nature of Morality and its Ultimate End 63

This guidance is not given to Christians alone, although they receive "the first fruits of the Spirit" (Rom 8:23). Grace is at work in the hearts of all men of good will. For "since all men are in fact called to one and the same destiny, which is divine, we must hold that the Holy Spirit offers to all the possibility of being made partners, in a way known to God, in the paschal mystery" (GS 22). This statement of the council expresses the important realization that all men receive the guidance of the Holy Spirit in the pursuit of their vocation, even though with different immediacy and clarity.

Chapter II

NATURE OF THE MORAL LAW

If man has been given an objective final end by the Creator, he will be under the obligation to make this objective end his subjective end - in other words, to strive after it. And when he looks to that end, an order which has to be followed will become visible to him: the moral order. This moral order is shown to us through the moral law.

Norms and law are often experienced as burdensome and limitations of man's freedom. They evoke little enthusiasm. Men tend to contradict and resist them. Today this tendency is still further enhanced by the great emphasis placed on personal freedom. Nevertheless there is also general agreement that man needs moral norms and institutional protection. Written formulations of the law are not mere luxury items. They are indispensable aids for man in his endeavour to give a meaningful order to his life and to protect it from chaos. They represent the accumulated wisdom of the ages. Evaluated in this light, the written moral law is not primarily a burden, but rather a relief which frees a person from the arduous task of elaborating the moral norms for himself or herself ever anew.

From the outset it should also be rightly understood that the moral law is not to be identified with any code of written precepts. Although handbooks of moral theology and ethics strive to elaborate concrete moral norms, and are expected to do so, they are never in a condition to offer complete compilations of all of man's moral obligations. Likewise human verbalizations time and again do not express the moral obligation as perfectly as would be desirable. This is because the moral law is only secondarily a formulated, written law. Originally and primarily it is an unwritten law, inherent in the structure of man's being and of the world around him. Man must know the written moral law and respect it in order to lead a good life. But more is demanded of him than the merely literal observance of the written law in order to live up to his total vocation.

A. Notion of moral law

1. *Concept of moral law*

Law in the most general meaning is any constant way of acting or reacting, any directive rule of activity. Thus we speak of the laws of physics, chemistry and biology, which work by causative, physical necessity. We speak of the laws of grammar or of arts, which direct free human activity, yet with regard to closer, contingent goals. Moral theology deals with those laws which result from man's obligation to orient all his activity towards the ultimate goal. In the latter two cases the law does not effect physical necessity, but ideal, moral constraint.

a) Moral law in its most universal meaning is a directive ordering man's activity towards the ultimate end. This definition includes obligatory demands as well as counsels, recommendations, permissions. It comprises common laws, concerning all men or groups of men, and personal commands, resulting from an individual call addressed to an appointed person. It includes permanent rulings, e.g. the duty to honour contracts, and temporary, singular orders, e.g. a prohibition of public gatherings during a time of epidemic.

According to definition, every genuine moral law must be good and holy in the sense that it must guide human activity to contribute to the realization of the final goal of human history and of creation, and that it prevents men from obstructing the attainment of this end. Although at first sight it might seem an exaggeration that every moral directive must be a guideline towards the ultimate end, one must keep in mind that even "our daily work" and ordinary everyday activities are expected to contribute to "the fulfilment in history of the divine plan" (GS 34). Therefore the moral directives must be formulated in such a way that these ordinary activities also can really fulfil the task of contributing to the realization of the final goal.

A norm which does not contribute at all to the final end has no moral force binding the will. A command, if not intrinsically related to the final end, must at least through its circumstances be conducive to the end. Thus when God forbids our first parents to eat of the tree of knowledge and when he demands of Abraham the sacrifice of his son, the relation of these commands to the supreme goal consists in this that they prepare and educate man to acknowledge God's divine sovereignty and man's created dependence. A norm, finally, which results in frustration of the ultimate goal is morally evil and its observance unlawful.

b) Moral law, in its narrower meaning, is a directive of obligatory, general and stable character, ordering man's activity towards the ultimate end. Only in this sense can moral law be the object of special moral theology, since only rules of general and stable character can be formulated by a normative science. The unique, individual call resulting from unparalleled, individual conditions escapes the normative science, because the latter has no knowledge of the singular individuality, at least not beforehand.

With regard to the obligatory character of moral law, moral theology is not exclusively concerned with the obligatory but also with the advisable, expedient and permissible. Nevertheless the obligatory rules constitute a very weighty part of the moral directives, and they alone are usually called laws.

2. *Natural, revealed and human law*

Law as the moral norm of human activity is distinguished in natural moral law, the revealed law of the Old and New Testament, and human law.

The natural moral law or simply natural law is that moral order which arises from the nature of man and creation and which can be recognized by man's reason. It is also called divine natural law, because its origin is ultimately traced back to the will of God who created nature and who therewith also willed the laws resulting from it.

The norms contained in the word of the Holy Scriptures of the Old and New Testament are looked upon as *revealed divine law*. They may spell out obligations of natural law in order to clarify them, as for example the ten commandments (with exception of the third commandment on the Sabbath rest). Or they may enjoin additional obligations, of a positive nature, such as the ceremonial law in the Old Testament or the orders of the apostle Paul in the New Testament that women should veil their heads when they pray and should keep silence in the church. The language of natural or revealed *divine* law however needs clarification. It leaves the impression, "God has revealed his will to man in the form of concrete commandments by way of immediate allocution and still continues doing so. Such however was not the case with the «ten commandments», such also never was the case later on." What appears under the formula «divine laws» is always the more or less adequate insights of human beings as to what is morally right. Nonetheless their qualification as «divine laws» can be perfectly legitimate if they prove themselves, confirmed by experience, to be truthful ways for the realization of the divinely willed destiny of men. "Then the believing community can say, it has indeed now discovered the structures of order, implanted in the world by the creative «word», and has traced therewith the will of God."[1]

Distinguished from divine law, whether natural or revealed, is *human law*. Its immediate source of origin is human authority. Human law may also reaffirm obligations of natural law, e.g. the prohibitions of murder or stealing. Yet in many other cases it contains regulations which are not direct requirements of natural law, but which to a certain extent depend on the free, though reasonable will of the lawgiver, e.g. the voting age or the time needed for the prescription of a debt. Even where the object of human legislation is natural laws, the sanctions for transgressions of these laws, which are usually added by criminal law, are not pre-established by natural law. They can and do vary according to the judicious will of the legislator. Also the very choice of the natural laws which shall be included in a penal and civil code to a considerable extent depends on his will. All human laws therefore owe their existence to some extent to an act of will of the lawgiver, by which they are posed and put into force. They pertain to the category of positive laws.[2]

Human law is subdivided into the civil law of the state and the ecclesiastical law of the Church, which in the Catholic

---

[1] Alfons Auer, "Der Mensch als Subjekt verantwortlichen Handelns," in *Leben aus christlicher Verantwortung*, vol. 1, ed. by J. Gründel (Düsseldorf: Patmos, 1991), 31f. "Among the theologians a consensus is practically had today that the moral and juridical norms of the Bible do not directly originate from God as to their *express contents*, even where God is referred to as the one who speaks and gives the norms" (H. Altmeyer, "Gott als Gesetzgeber und Garant des Sittengesetzes," in *Schuld, Sühne und Erlösung*, ed. by K.J. Rivinius. Steyler Verlag, 1983, 72).

[2] 'Positive' is understood here not in the sense of affirmative, constructive or valuable and as a contrast to negative, but in the sense of posed (from the Latin *positum*) and decreed by an act of will of the lawgiver. The difference between moral and human law is well explained by Johannes Messner, *Social Ethics* (St. Louis/London: Herder Book Co., 1965), 164-169.

Church is called canon law. The canon law is contained in the Codex Iuris Canonici (= CIC).

Human law and moral law are related to each other, but still different, as the above expositions have shown. This has to be kept in mind, since the two orders are often confused. Object of human law is the common weal and the public order. Human law touches solely external acts. Accordingly it covers only a restricted part of our moral obligations. From the moral point of view, therefore, not everything is permitted which is not forbidden by the human law. Moreover human laws do not always fully agree with moral laws. Unjust laws however do not oblige in conscience, and often it is not even lawful to obey them. This means that from a moral point of view they are not valid laws at all. The question has to be dealt with in more detail below. Just human laws on the other hand bind in conscience. For this reason moral manuals have always included human law in the treatise on law as the objective norm of morality.

B. Law of God in Holy Scripture

I. Law of the Old Testament

1. *Historical reality of Israel's law.* When the Old Testament speaks of the laws, precepts and commandments of the Lord or when the New Testament refers to the law of the old covenant, they always have in mind the collection of laws which is called *the Torah*. It is contained in the first five books of the Old Testament, the Pentateuch, whose author according to ancient biblical tradition is Moses. Therefore it is also called the Mosaic law. According to the counting of the Talmud, the Torah contains 613 precepts and prohibitions. They are of religious, social and moral nature. Besides norms of natural law, they comprise numerous cultic prescriptions and regulations of civil law, which have the character of positive laws.[1]

---

[1] Norms of natural law are, e.g., the ten commandments with exception of the commandment of Sabbath rest (Ex. 20:3-17), the social norms of Lev 19:11-18.32-36, and the Shechemite Twelve Commandments (Deut 27:15-26). Positive laws of cultic nature are the commandment of Sabbath rest (Ex 20:8-11), the norms concerning peace and sin offerings (Lev 1-5), and the celebration of the appointed feasts (Ex 23:14-17; Lev 23). Positive laws of civil nature are the legislations in Ex 21:2-22:19 and the various laws concerning murder, sexual offences, court procedures, etc. in Deut 21-25.

These laws look back on a long tradition. In part they date back to the 12th and 11th century before Christ, although other parts of it have been added at later times. It is no longer maintained that the entire Torah has been compiled and written down by Moses himself, just as he is no longer considered the sole author of the Pentateuch. Nevertheless Moses must have been a lawgiver for Israel in more than a rudimentary sense. For only a firm foundation of Israel's identity as a nation could have enabled it to resist the influence of Canaan, when Israel settled in this land.[1]

Authors assume that the original ethos of Israel "was situated in the tribe, the clan and the family. The ethical formulations were subjected by a later editor to the covenant, as a protective and legitimizing arrangement instituted by Yahweh."[2] This procedure doubtless also holds true for the laws which Israel borrowed and adapted from the legislation of the neighbouring nations. They pre-existed in the legal practice of these nations and were given their divine authority in Israel only at a later stage.[3] A comparison of Israel's law with the Babylonian Codex Hammurabi of the 17th century B.C. or the Assyrian and Hittite law collections of the 14th-13th century B.C. shows many parallels as to content and even formulations.

Nevertheless there are also important differences between them, and Israel's law possesses its own distinctive marks. Israel did not merely copy the laws of the neighbouring nations; rather they were subjected to a process of selection and adaptation. Here in particular is room for the special

---

[1] "Only a Mosaic lawgiving can explain the remarkable force and persistence of the true personality of Israel, in spite of all the cases of adaptation and receptive borrowing in their new home" (Walther Eichrodt, *Theology of the Old Testament*, vol. I, Philadelphia, 1961), 84.

[2] Franz Böckle, *Fundamental Moral Theology* (New York: Pueblo Publishing Co., 1980), 131. According to A. Auer, recent research has convincingly proven that the decalogue, i.e. more precisely the "second table" or the fourth to tenth commandment, is of nomadic or semi-nomadic origin and older than the Sinaitic covenant and revelation (*Autonome Moral und christlicher Glaube*. Düsseldorf: Patmos, 1971, 56-61).

[3] Many will agree with F. Böckle's conclusion "that the essence of the moral order under the old covenant arose as the result of a historical process and therefore cannot be understood as the original divine law" (*ib.* 133).

guidance and inspiration of Yahweh in the formation of the law, of which Israel is so deeply convinced.

2. *The distinctive character.* If one seeks to define the distinctive character of Israel's morality and law, then attention must first be drawn to the consistency with which the entire law and all spheres of human life are placed under the absolute rule of Yahweh. Not only the ethical norms and cultic regulations, but also the secular laws derive their validity from being a direct command of Yahweh. Any breach of them is an outrage against Yahweh himself. "It is just this manifest concentration on the religious ordering of the national life as its indispensable foundation, which indicates a spiritual achievement without parallel in the ancient East."[1] Moral action is in Israel inseparably bound up with the worship of God. This means that God regards obedience to the law equally important as the worship of himself. Consequently every faithful performance of a duty acquires the nobility of an act of worship.

Moreover Israel's monotheism provides a principle of absolute unity for the moral and legal order: one Judge of all the earth with one law for all. Israel's law does not know of any class-distinction in the administration of justice, a practice which is quite common in other ancient codes of law. We hear nothing of any special law for the rulers, the priesthood, or the aristocracy. Every member of God's people is equally bound to the God of the covenant, the king as well as the simplest subject. This fact is particularly evident from the activity of the prophets, who proclaim their judgment irrespective of persons.

A further consequence of the concentration of the moral authority in a single divine will to the exclusion of any other authority is the absence of magic as a substitute for compliance with the moral obligation. Egyptian priestly teaching, for example, provided the deceased with magical means (e.g. a consecrated scarabaeus) which should enable the heart to hide its sins before the judges of the dead. In neo-Babylonian

---

[1] Walther Eichrodt, *Theology of the Old Testament*, vol. I (London: SCM Press, 1961), 75. The same conclusion is reached by R.E.O. White, who writes: "It is impossible to exaggerate the significance of this inherited conception of the God before whose eyes the moral life has to be lived, and before whose judgment the soul must eventually pass" (*Biblical Ethics*. Exeter: The Paternoster Press, 1979, 15).

Nature of the Moral Law 71

times magic of all sorts was the popular means of influencing the invisible powers. In ancient Yahwism there is neither another divine power which could neutralize Yahweh's verdict against the sinner, nor has his power limits so that a magical formula could compel the desired result against his will. Salvation can only be found in obedience to the holy will of God.

Another noteworthy feature of Israelite law finally is a high regard for the human person. This respect manifests itself in the absence of gross brutality in the punishment of the guilty. While in the Code of Hammurabi or in the Assyrian law bodily mutilations are not unusual at all, such as the cutting off of the hands, the cropping of the nose or ears, the plucking out of the tongue, branding, or cutting off of the breasts, they are not customary in Israel. "There is evidence here of a genuinely noble humanity and a deepened feeling for equity as traits of Israelite law. This can hardly be explained except in terms of the knowledge of God - that God who created man after his own image and therefore protects him, even when he is liable to punishment."[1]

3. Besides its merits, however, the Mosaic law doubtless also has its *limitations*. It is not a perfect law. It constitutes only the beginning of salvation history and still expects the fulfilment of its hope for integral redemption. Therefore it cannot cause surprise if it is still affected by limitations.

A historically conditioned shortcoming of OT morality is the limiting of fraternal love to the Jewish community, in it included also the aliens who had settled among the Israelites (Lev 19:33f; 24:22, Deut 10:18f). Fraternal love does not extend to the foreigners (e.g. the Samaritans). Much less does it extend to the national enemy, who is devoid of any right. Of course this was the universal attitude in ancient Eastern society. Nevertheless it remains a defect in moral insight. Other examples of historical limitations are polygamy, the right to divorce which was a right only for the man (cf. Deut 24:1-4), and the attitude towards the personal enemy. Although hatred and vengeance against a neighbour are banned by Lev

---

[1] W. Eichrodt, *l. c.* 79.

19:17f,[1] love of one's enemy remains rather restrained by the ideas of justice and expiation, as is illustrated by the *lex talionis*: "Eye for eye, tooth for tooth" (cf. Ex 21:23-25; Lev 24:17-20; Deut 19:21). Even the psalms often display a spirit of vengefulness, while prayers for the conversion of the enemy remain rare.

A limitation of farther reaching bearing concerns the understanding of the very nature of laws. The problem results from the close interweaving of moral precepts on the one side and positive laws of juridical and cultic nature on the other. It is a common occurrence that these two different kinds of laws are not sufficiently differentiated in the early and less developed states of cultures. This deficiency harbours the danger of wrong evaluations and of conflicts. Moral laws are of a more universal nature and less subject to change than positive laws. They are expressions of the order of creation and in that capacity possess an element of immutability. Positive laws on the other hand, whether civil or religious, are much more conditioned by historical circumstances and the concrete state of development of a society. Therefore they must be given sufficient room for the possibility of change in order to adapt ever anew to the varying needs of the different times and places. The lack of flexibility will otherwise lead to obsolete laws which are antiquated, without purpose and even counterproductive.[2]

This was the danger which confronted the ancient Jews in their uncompromising adherence to the Torah. This is to a large extent due to the particular understanding which the

---

[1] Restraints in man's attitude towards his personal enemy and occasionally even the spirit of forgiveness are likewise enjoined by Ex 23:4f; Prov 24:17f; 25:21f; Sir 28:1-7.

[2] Thus a number of laws in the Torah were merely sustained for the sake of tradition, though they had lost their meaning long since, e.g. the prohibitions to eat the meat of a great number of animals, among them not only the pig, but also the hare, the water hen, various lizards and anything in the waters which has no fins and scales (Lev 11; Deut 14:3-20). The same holds for the perpetual statute to eat neither fat nor blood (Lev 3:17). Out of proportion and in civilized nations universally abolished is also the OT imposition of death penalty for such offences as working on the Sabbath day (Ex 31:15; Num 15:32-36), adultery, incest, homosexuality and bestiality (Lev 20:10-16; Deut 22:23f). The numerous chapters in Leviticus and Deuteronomy devoted to norms concerning the sacrificial cult are likewise of very limited moral significance.

Jews had of the Mosaic law. They respected the Torah very highly as a gift of God. They regarded it as a law which was not only more perfect than that of other nations, but simply perfect altogether. And moral perfection consisted in the perfect fulfilment of the law.[1] The possibility that this law might have to be reformed and replaced by another, more perfect one was not seriously considered, even though the prophets repeatedly foretold the institution of a new covenant which would surpass the old.

With their great respect for the Torah the Jews inclined to seek righteousness in a most literal observance of all the different commandments, rulings and laws. The situation was still more aggravated by the fact that many supplementary laws and traditions of the elders were added, which likewise claimed unreserved obedience. This promoted the development of a legalism which upheld the letter of the law, even though it already came into conflict with the demands of justice, mercy and love. This was the situation at the time of Jesus. The great danger to man's faith, inherent in these misconceptions, was clearly perceived by Christ. Most of his controversies with the Pharisees and scribes revolved around their narrow, legalistic practice of the law. The ever increasing bitterness of the conflict contributed not a little to the rejection and final condemnation of Christ. But the truth of his message prevailed. The new covenant fulfilled what the old covenant contained in promise, but was not able to attain.

4. The realities of law and order in the Old Testament doubtless find their most characteristic expression in the Torah. Nevertheless besides the Torah with its precepts and commandments, the fact of *a moral order in the world* is still set forth in another, less juridical way, and that is in the Wisdom literature. Its authors are deeply impressed by the wise order they find everywhere in creation. They express this experience in the graphic description of wisdom as a master-workman who is beside God from the beginning, before the heavens were made, and who serves him in the creation of all that exists.[2] Wisdom is the ordering power behind

---

[1] "The obedience [towards the Torah] is one beyond dispute. Man has no right to ask for the justification of the precepts" (Wolfgang Schrage, *The Ethics of the New Testament*. Edinburgh: T. & T. Clark, 1988, 57).

[2] Job 28:20-27; Prov 3:19f; 8:22-31; Wis 9:9; Sir 24:3-9.

creation and the origin of all individual orders. The nature of wisdom could also be rendered by "primeval order", "world reason" or "meaning inherent in the world".

Wisdom does not exist and operate in isolation from men. Quite the contrary, she calls out to men to listen to her and to live in harmony with the order she has established. "Does not wisdom call, does not understanding raise her voice? ... To you, O men, I call, and my cry is to the sons of men" (Prov 8:1.4; cf. 1:20f). "It was obviously the opinion of the teachers that man is addressed from creation by a desire for order from which he cannot escape. This desire for order addresses, in the first instance, man's completely personal life. It is the basis and source of ethical behaviour."[1] Those who listen to the voice of wisdom "will understand righteousness and justice and equity, every good path" (Prov 2:9). In a second instance, the impulse for order also extends to the public, national life. "By me kings reign, and rulers decree what is just; by me princes rule, and nobles govern the earth" (Prov 8:15f).

Men are well advised to listen to the counsel of wisdom. For disregard of her voice has dangerous consequences. Calamity and panic, distress and anguish will strike those who believe they can ignore her (Prov 1:22-33). Harmony with wisdom is life, discord with her is death. This is an outright ultimatum.

The means for gaining insight into the right way of life is above all the good and evil consequences of an action. The blessings or misfortunes resulting from an action are frequent motives attached to the counsels of the wisdom teachers.[2] The motivations for doing good and avoiding evil are almost always of a temporal, profane nature. This gives the wisdom rules a naturalistic, utilitarian character.

The inductive method of judging actions from their consequences of course requires a thorough acquaintance with the facts of living. Great weight is therefore attributed to the experience of the fathers and elders. By listening to them, the young people will gain understanding and come to the

---

[1] Gerhard von Rad, *Wisdom in Israel* (Nashville and New York: Abingdon Press, 1972), 158.

[2] For example Prov 6:6-11; 14:29f; 17:13f; 22:22-25; Sir 3:17f.26f; 20:24-26; 37:29-31; 41:12f.

right knowledge of what is good and evil (cf. Prov 1:8f; 4:1-5; Sir 3:1).

Besides the word of the Torah, then, Yahweh has at his disposal still another means to teach man, namely the voice of the order of creation. "Yahweh obviously delegated to creation so much truth, indeed he was present in it in such a way that man reaches ethical terra firma when he learns to read these orders and adjusts his behaviour to the experience gained."[1] The entire tenor of the teachings of the wise men leaves no doubt that this voice can be readily understood by everybody who is prepared to listen (see also Job 12:7-9; Prov 1:20f).

The conviction that besides the Torah the demands of the moral order are made known to men in still another way is however not limited to Wisdom literature alone, although here it finds its most articulate expression. The Old Testament knows of a moral experience and of the awareness of concrete moral duties even prior to the Sinaitic covenant. Adam, Eve, Cain, Noah, Joseph and his brothers, all have a knowledge of good and evil. All feel bound by an unwritten law. This law reveals itself in the hearts of men as well as in the conscience of the group. But it is always conceived as the voice of God.

II. Moral law in the New Testament

1. *Old law and New Testament.* The New Testament evinces the firm conviction that the OT law derives from God as its author. Yet with equal determination it holds that the old covenant was only a preparation for Christ and therefore of transitory nature. The noblest function of the many ceremonial prescriptions was to symbolize in advance the Christian mystery, to awaken the yearning for the promised Messiah, and to excite a sense of sin and of need for the redemption which Christ was to bring.

For this reason, i.e. because the old law was essentially a preparation, it was destined to lose its binding force (Rom 7:1-6; Gal 2:16-19). "The law and the prophets were until John; since then the good news of the kingdom of God is preached" (Lk 16:16). The old law had only the task of an

---

[1] G. von Rad, *l. c.* 92.

educator for the new covenant in Christ (Gal 3:23-26). It lost its reason of existence with the coming of Christ and came to an end (Rom 10:4). The council of the Apostles of Jerusalem confirms this fact (Acts 15:7-11.28f). According to the letter to the Hebrews, the death of Christ was the point of time when the New Testament took its beginning and the new covenant was inaugurated and put into force (Heb 9:15-17). Accordingly in the sphere of NT morality the people of God is no longer bound by the old law. Yet this does not mean that everything in the Old Testament has ceased to bind. The theory that the ten commandments of the OT are of no concern to Christians was firmly rejected at the Council of Trent (DS 1569). The OT legislation gave the natural moral law binding force under an additional title, i.e. that of the Sinaitic covenant. This title ceases, but the other - human nature - remains. And moreover the New Testament imposes the natural obligations, or at least some of them, anew (cf. Mt 19:16-19; Rom 13:8f).

Not only for Christian tradition, but also for the New Testament itself the Old Testament remains an authority which is higher than that of customs and pagan philosophy, and which retains the dignity of "holy scriptures" (Rom 1:2). Paul repeatedly uses OT passages and examples to back up his teaching in general[1] and his moral exhortations in particular.[2] Of course it is understood that the Old Testament is no longer an independent authority for Christians; it is relativized and transcended by the authority of Christ.[3]

2. *Nature and character of the new law.*[4] The existence of a moral law in the New Testament was denied by some

---

[1] Rom 4:3-8; 9:6ff; Gal 3:15-18; 4:21-31.

[2] Rom 4:23f; 12:19f; 1 Cor 6:16; 9:3-10; 10:6-11; 2 Cor 8:13-15; Gal 3:6-9.

[3] Cf. the competent study on the authority of the OT in the parenesis of the NT by W. Schrage, *Die konkreten Einzelgebote in der paulinischen Paränese* (Gütersloh: Gerd Mohn, 1961), 228-238.

[4] See Josef Fuchs, "The Law of Christ" in *Human Values and Christian Morality* (Dublin and London: Gill and Macmillan, 1970), 76-91. Enda McDonagh, "The Natural Law and the Law of Christ" in *Invitation and Response* (New York: Sheed and Ward, 1972), 22-37.

of the Reformers, who misinterpreted the texts about the freedom of Christians (cf. Rom 10:4; Gal 3:23-26; 5:1). This gave rise to two definitions of the Council of Trent, which declared that other things besides faith are commanded in the Gospel (DS 1569) and that Christ our Redeemer is also a lawgiver (DS 1571).

Commenting on the impression Jesus' words made on the people, the evangelists note that "the crowds were astonished at his teaching, for he taught them as one who had authority, and not as their scribes" (Mt 7:28f; cf. Mk 1:22; Lk 4:32). "All the people hung upon his words" (Lk 19:48; cf. Mk 11:18). Jesus was not preoccupied with legalistic pedantries concerning rituals, religious laws and traditions of the elders. His concern was a most radical obedience to God's unconditional claim upon man's life and a total availability to the innermost stirrings of the Spirit. Jesus' instructions and parables bring this message home in ever new forms and ways.

This emphasis prevails throughout the New Testament. The new law is primarily an internal law. The main stress is on man's internal responsibility before God and the law of the Spirit. Paul finds a particularly striking difference and even opposition between the old and the new law in this that the Mosaic law is an external, written code, whilst the law of Christ is a law of the Spirit. "For the written code kills, but the Spirit gives life" (2 Cor 3:6). Therefore Christians are to "serve not under the old written code but in the new life of the Spirit" (Rom 7:6). The New Testament is a covenant in the Holy Spirit, who has been poured forth into the hearts of men (Rom 5:5), who leads and teaches them from within (Rom 8:14). From the living communion with Christ flows the "law of Christ" as an inward law. So it says in the Scriptures: "I will put my laws into their minds" (Heb 8:10). Through "the law of the Spirit of life in Christ Jesus" (Rom 8:2) Christians know "the just requirement of the law" and also fulfil them (Rom 8:4).

Nevertheless to man under original sin even the law which corresponds to his own inward being appears as something contrary and to that extent an outward law. For this reason the New Testament repeatedly and most earnestly warns Christians to flee sin and "the works of the flesh" and instead to "walk by the Spirit" and bear the fruits of virtue, goodness and holiness.[1] The dangers which come from man's old, sinful nature made it necessary to set up lists of vices, which those who want to enter God's kingdom must absolutely avoid (1 Cor 6:9f; Gal 5:19-21; Col 3:5-10). Moral norms were formulated as a protection against the "carnal man" from within. But they have also a positive purpose besides. They serve as aids for a peaceful life and provide an orientation on the way to perfection.[2] Hence, although the new law is fundamentally an internal law, in a secondary sense it is also a formulated, written law.[3] In the thought of Paul, the Christian community is called to formulate the exigencies of the law of the Spirit and the believers are expected to obey this authority.

Ethical directives are given in the Bible by way of commandments and precepts, but also in images, examples and parables. "The Bible says what it has to say about the moral life in the forms and genres of laws and imperatives, to be sure, but also in narratives, parables, sayings, and other literary forms... Its ethical material both illumines the moral life with images to help us interpret what is going on and, in some instances, it prescribes behavior, such as in the ten commandments, the great commandment [of love], and the instructions of St. Paul. The proper use of the Bible in either instance involves an ongoing dialogue between the faith experiences of the biblical community and those of today."[4]

3. *Concrete precepts and commandments.* The concrete precepts and commandments of the new covenant pertain to the greatest extent to the category of natural moral laws. There are only a few injunctions which have the nature of positive laws, and they are of a religious nature.

a) In the case of the *moral precepts* one has to distinguish between those of Christ in the synoptics and those of the letters of the NT. In interpreting the precepts of Christ,

---

[1] Rom 6:12-18; 8:12f; Gal 5:16-25; Eph 4:22-24; 1 Pet 2:11f.

[2] For example Mt 5:21-24.27f.44; 19:16-19; 25:31-46; Rom 13:1-9; 1 Cor 7:10f; Eph 5:21-6:9; 1 Thess 4:1-8.

[3] According to Thomas Aquinas, the fundamental element of the new law is the grace of the Holy Spirit, whilst the external laws are only a secondary element (S. Th. I-II 106,1; 106,2; 108,1).

[4] R.M. Gula, *Reason Informed by Faith* (New York: Paulist Press, 1989), 181f.

attention has to be given to the particular style and literary character of Jesus' teaching. Jesus most of the time uses a figurative, metaphoric style in his moral instructions, which makes his demands more often than not appear radical and exaggerated. "Give to everyone who asks." "Leave father and mother, wife and children, and hate your own soul." "If your hand or your eye is leading you astray, cut it off and cast it away." "Never worry about food or drink. The morrow will look after itself." "Do not invite your friends or your brothers. Invite the poor, the maimed, the lame, the blind."[1] These precepts cannot be taken literally as they stand and put into practice. Their purpose is a different one. They are meant to challenge men to a most radical obedience towards God and to an ever greater perfection. "The one thing that all such sayings clearly enforce is the unlimited scope of God's commands. They leave no room for complacency. It is impossible to be satisfied with ourselves when we try our conduct by these standards."[2] The challenges of Christ become guideposts on the way we must travel in seeking the true ends of our being under the kingdom of God.

The moral precepts of the apostles, on the other hand, are rules of conduct which are moral laws in the strict sense of the definition. They are intended to be taken literally. "Contribute to the needs of the saints, practise hospitality." "Repay not evil for evil." "Children, obey your parents in everything." "Fathers, do not provoke your children, lest they become discouraged." "Let every person be subject to the governing authorities." "You elders, tend the flock, not as domineering over those in your charge but being examples to the flock." "You that are younger be subject to the elders. Clothe yourselves, all of you, with humility toward one another."[3] Christian tradition has always considered these precepts as norms which ought to be put into practice as they stand, not only by Christians but by all men on the earth. In

---

[1] Examples for the didactic style of Christ: Mt 5:21-24.39-42; 6:25-34; 18:7-9; 23:8-10; Lk 14:12-14.

[2] C.H. Dodd, *Gospel and Law* (Cambridge: University Press, 1965), 61; see the entire, very helpful chapter 3: "The Ethical Teaching of the Gospels", 46-63.

[3] Examples for the moral teaching of the apostles: Rom 12:9-21; 13:1-7; Eph 5,21-6,9; Col 3:12-4:1; 1 Thess 5:14-22; Heb 13:1-5; 1 Pet 2:13-17; 5:1-5.

two cases however questions have been raised in recent times, that is concerning the moral judgment of Paul in matters of the social status of women and of slavery.

As to the social status of women, Paul teaches that wives should be subject to their husbands, although in the same breath he also exhorts husbands to love their wives (Eph 5:21-29; Col 3:18f). He certainly does not intend to say that wives should obey their husbands unconditionally, even if they demand something which is sinful. Besides, the rather general form of the exhortation allows for a great latitude in interpretation. True, it must be admitted that Paul asserts a subordination of wives under their husbands. His frame of mind is more hierarchic than democratic. Nevertheless Paul recalls in his letters with praise a number of women who have worked hard with him for the Gospel and laboured with him side by side (Mary, Tryphaena, Tryphosa, Persis, Euodia and Syntyche) and calls them co-worker (Prisca), sister (Apphia), diakonos (Phoebe), and apostle (Junias).

With regard to slavery, Paul nowhere urges or even recommends this institution, and therefore its abolition in no way contradicts his teaching. Rather its abolition agrees with his principle that we are all one in Christ and that "there is neither slave nor free, there is neither male nor female" (Gal 3:28; also Col 3:11). Paul put up with an institution which the tiny, young Church was unable to change anyway.[1]

b) As for the *positive precepts*, the teaching of Christ in the Gospels contains only two. They concern the two most fundamental sacraments of the Church. They are the mandates of the Lord himself to baptize all nations in the name of the Blessed Trinity (Mt 28:19) and to celebrate the Lord's Supper in his memory (Lk 22:19; cf. 1 Cor 11:24f).[2]

---

[1] It strikes as though that Paul did not disapprove of slavery even in his letter to the Christian brother Philemon, to whom he sent back the runaway slave Onesimus with the plea for clemency. If the encyclical *Veritatis Splendor* lists slavery among the actions evil in themselves (nr. 80), then this judgment does not find an equally clear expression in the writings of the New Testament.

[2] There are still other sacraments which take their origin from the NT Scriptures. But they are not enjoined by express precepts. Either they are derived from concrete practices of the early Church, such as the laying on of hands on those to be ordained priests (1 Tim 4:14; 2 Tim 1:6) or the anointing of the sick with oil (Jas 5:14f), or from a particular authority given by Christ, such as the power to forgive sins (Mt 16:18f; 18:18; Jn 20:23).

The positive precepts in the other writings of the New Testament above all concern Church discipline. In 1 Cor 11:5-16 Paul orders that women have to cover their heads with a veil when they pray. Although such a custom still exists in some regions today, it has long since ceased to be a binding precept. 1 Cor 14:26-40 gives instructions on how to use the gifts of tongues and prophesy in the assemblies, and orders that women should keep silence in the churches. This ruling is also no longer enforced. Another positive law is the regulation in 1 Tim 3:2 and 3:12 that those who are elected bishops and deacons should have been married only once.

Some other positive precepts result from the decision of the council of the Apostles in Jerusalem, which decreed that in principle Christians are no longer bound by the Mosaic law, yet in a sort of compromise still imposed upon the Gentiles to "abstain from what has been sacrificed to idols and from blood and from what is strangled and from unchastity" (Acts 15:29). These are essentially precepts of the OT ritual law, whose end Christ is (Rom 10:4). Already in the first letter to the Corinthians Paul held that objectively there is nothing wrong with eating food offered to idols (1 Cor 8). And also the prohibitions to abstain from blood and from what is strangled soon fell into oblivion. Only the obligation to refrain from unchastity always remained in force, but this is an obligation of natural law.

Apart from the two mandates of Christ, which are most venerable to Christians because he doubtless wished them to be kept as long as his Church existed, the great measure of freedom of the spirit with which the Christian community has handled the positive laws of the New Testament, even though they are part of the inspired books, is surprising.

4. *Natural moral law in the New Testament.* In distinguishing metaphoric forms of precepts in Jesus' teaching from others which have to be taken literally and in examining the moral teachings of the apostles as to their continued validity, a criterion has been used which is of a more comprehensive nature than Scripture alone. This criterion is the conformity of the biblical precepts with the rights and needs inherent in man's nature and the duties resulting therefrom. It is the criterion of natural law. Does the New Testament know of a

natural moral law and accept it as an authority of universal character?[1]

a) *The teaching of Christ.* Christ himself, in setting forth his teaching, appeals to the established order of creation as a pointer to the law of God. One remarkable instance is his view of divorce. The law of Moses, he says, permitted divorce. However it was only "for your hardness of heart he wrote you this commandment. But from the beginning of creation, 'God made them male and female'..., and the two shall become one. What therefore God has joined together, let not man put asunder" (Mk 10:5-9). That means, the very nature of man, as created by God, points, if properly understood, to the norm of permanent monogamy. Although Moses found it necessary to permit divorce because of the shortcomings of the people, it is not in full accord with the mind of God when he made mankind. Now that the kingdom of God has come, the original form of the natural order must be restored.

Also the commandment of love of enemies is supported by an argument taken from the order of creation. Men must love their enemies because the heavenly Father "makes his sun rise on the evil and on the good, and sends rain on the just and on the unjust" (Mt 5:45). Since men are expected to love their creator, this implies that they cannot exclude from their love anything loved by the creator, also not the "the ungrateful and the selfish" (Lk 6:35). Otherwise their love would not be sincere and undivided. This is in substance a natural law argument for the duty to love enemies.

On several occasions Christ presupposes the knowledge of good and evil as self-evident and known, e.g. where he says in the dispute on the clean and unclean, "what comes out of a man is what defiles a man," and then numbers a list of evil deeds considered as sinful by his hearers independent of his teaching (Mk 7:20-23). Christ's sermon on the last judgment equally presupposes a knowledge of good and evil in all men, since all will be judged according to the works of mercy which they did do or did not do to their neighbour (Mt 25:31-46; see also Lk 12:57). As a general measure for

---

[1] For the teaching of the New Testament on natural law in general, cf. J. Fuchs, *Natural Law* (Dublin: Gill and Son, 1965), 14-37; B. Schüller in *Readings in Moral Theology No. 7: Natural Law and Theology*, ed. by C.E. Curran and R.A. McCormick (New York: Paulist Press, 1991), 72-98; for the testimony of Paul in particular, see W. Schrage, *l. c.* 187-228.

the morally good, he points out the "golden rule", which is a norm naturally known: "Whatever you wish that men would do to you, do so to them" (Mt 7:12).

b) *The teaching of the apostle Paul.* For Paul the natural law is a self-evident domain, which raises no problems as such. If he deals with it, it is only in subordination to the themes of law, sin and grace, which are his direct concern. In the first three chapters of the letter to the Romans, Paul is preoccupied with the moral condition of the heathen world and the need of redemption of all mankind. Such a need exists only if there is guilt and sin, and this presupposes that the heathens have a true knowledge of God and their moral obligations. And in fact, Paul argues, they have such knowledge. Man's reason derives it clearly from the reality of creation (Rom 1:19f.32). This is why Paul can write of the guilt of the heathens, although they are without the Law and without Christ. Their wrong deeds are vices because they are repugnant to man's nature and to the moral order demanded by it.

The classic Pauline text on natural knowledge of the moral law is found in the second chapter of Romans. "When Gentiles who have not the law do by nature what the law requires, they are a law to themselves, even though they do not have the law. They show that what the law requires is written on their hearts" (Rom 2:14f). The wider context of the whole chapter shows that there is a general subjection of all, of heathen, Jews and Christians, to the same moral order and to the same judgment according to this norm (vv. 1.12). It is therefore clear that in the thought of Paul the distinction between good and evil is founded in the nature of things, not only for heathens but also for Jews and Christians. The Mosaic Law does not establish the difference between good and evil, but rather teaches men about what is already good and evil before it has been declared as such by the Law. For this reason Paul can say that the good works of the heathen constitute a fulfilment of the demands of the Law. They "do by nature what the law requires" (Rom 2:14). It appears then that the law of God was written on the heart of man by the very fact of his creation by God. Now such a law, which is derived from nature as its source and which is made known to man by reason and conscience, is nothing else than the natural law as defined by moral theology and ethics.

Natural law continues to exist and to be valid also within the law of Christ. Although the OT Law has lost its validity, those precepts which are part of the natural law remain a binding norm independently of the Law. In this sense Paul can say that the Christians also fulfil the just requirements of the Law, even though they are set free from it (Rom 8:2-4). The catalogue of pagan vices (Rom 1:29-31) is consequently repeated for the Christians and is presented as a list of sins which exclude men from the kingdom of God (1 Cor 8:9f; Gal 5:19-21; 1 Tim 1:9-11). Paul's exhortations that Christians should "give no offence" to anybody and through their good conduct "command the respect of outsiders" (1 Cor 10:32; Col 4:5; 1 Thess 4:12) presupposes moral norms and criteria which are common to both, Christians and outsiders alike.

Much of the moral teaching of Paul is based on judgments of reason as to what is good and evil, without reference to the OT Law or commandments of Jesus.[1] It proves therefore that the natural law has become part of the "law of Christ". Fulfilment of its obligations by the power of Christ is the way of life of those who belong to his kingdom.

III. Distinctiveness of Christian ethics

In the preceding reflections it has been pointed out that many laws of the Old Testament have parallels in the legislations of the neighbouring nations and that most of the laws of the New Testament pertain to the category of the moral norms which man can know by nature, i.e. pertain to the natural law. This raises the question of the distinctive character of Christian morality. Is Christian morality different from the morality of people who are not Christians? If so, in what does this difference consist? The question has been livelily discussed in recent years and has found different answers.[2]

1. *The traditional view* commonly affirms a distinctive content of Christian morality. Although by far the largest part

---

[1] For example Rom 1:29-32; 13:1-7; 1 Cor 7:1-5; 8:4-6; Col 3:18-4:1.

[2] A helpful collection of representative contributions to the question is found in *Readings in Moral Theology No. 2: The Distinctiveness of Christian Ethics*, ed. by C.E. Curran and R.A. McCormick (New York/Ramsey: Paulist Press, 1980).

of the moral laws can be discovered by reason and therefore is accessible to all men, there are some ethical values and norms which are specifically Christian.

The reason why two sets of moral norms are asserted is the doctrine of the condition of man before and after the redemption of Christ. Prior to the redemption by Christ, man is held to be in a state of "pure nature" (*natura pura*), i.e. in a state without the divine life of grace.[1] To this state natural moral norms correspond, which are arrived at by the insights of reason and which are obligatory for all men. After redemption man receives, in addition to his natural life, the divine life of grace. To this new state additional norms correspond, which are only accessible to those who possess this life of grace and of course which are obligatory only for them. Their principal source is the positive, divine revelation of the Old and New Testament. Catholic moral theology generally holds that these additional norms surpass the values and norms of a merely human morality, although they do not contradict it. Protestant tradition tends to see a greater discontinuity between the human and the Christian; Christian ethics challenges human morality and at times contradicts it.

What do revelation and faith concretely add to ethics? Scripture teaches that Christians have received the gift of a new life from Christ, the life of grace, mediated in baptism. The new life calls for a new, different way of conduct. The new attitudes include the divine virtues of faith, hope and charity, love of enemies, humility, spirit of sacrifice and acceptance of sufferings in the fellowship of the cross. In the realm of worship, the sacraments in particular impose duties which are exclusive to Christians.

2. *A more recent view* on the other hand maintains that Christian ethics has no distinct content of its own. Among contemporary authors this seems to be the more common view. Nevertheless this second opinion cannot simply be called the modern one. Already Francis Suarez (†1617) held this

---

[1] Originally mankind possessed this state of grace, but it was lost through the sin of the first parents, Adam and Eve, in paradise (cf. Gen 3).

view.[1] It is likewise found in the manuals of Genicot-Salsmans, Göpfert, Vermeersch, Hürth-Abellan, and Regatillo-Zalba.[2] The theologians Hürth and Abellan summarize the position as follows: "All moral precepts of the new law are also precepts of the natural moral law. Christ did not add any further moral precept of a purely positive kind to the natural moral law.... That holds also for the precept of love.... The obligation to love God and one's neighbour for God's sake is an obligation of the natural law."

It is important to note that the authors just mentioned distinguish between ceremonial and moral precepts in the new law. If Christ did not add any moral precepts to the natural law, he evidently added new ceremonial precepts (though not purely ceremonial), namely the sacraments. They are indeed divine laws of a positive nature, but they do not pertain to the category of moral laws in the strict sense.

Recent authors who subscribe to this view are A. Auer,[3] J.-M. Aubert, E. Chiavacci, C. Curran, J. Fuchs, R. McCormick, B. Schüller, D. Tettamanzi, J. Walter, the Anglican theologian J. Macquarrie,[4] F. Böckle,[5] and others.

3. *The arguments* for the second opinion are the following. A weighty argument is based on the study of the facts. The data of both experience and history produce no clear evidence

---

[1] F. Suarez, *Commentaria ac Disputationes in Primam Secundae D. Thomae: De Legibus*, lib. X, c. 2, nrs. 5-15. Suarez also makes reference to Thomas Aquinas I-II, q. 118, art. 2. Here Thomas distinguishes between sacraments and moral precepts. As to the latter, the new law adds nothing beyond that which is already contained in the old law, because it is by natural reason that we are directed towards the works of virtues.

[2] E. Genicot/I. Salsmans, *Institutiones Theologiae Moralis*. vol. I. (Brussels, 1951), nr. 90. E.A. Göpfert, *Moraltheologie*, vol. I (Paderborn, 1923), nr. 33. A. Vermeersch, *Theologiae Moralis Principia, Responsa, Consilia*, vol. I (Rome, 1947), nr. 153. F. Hürth and P.M. Abellan, *De Principiis, de Virtutibus et Praeceptis*, vol. I (Rome, 1948), nr. 66. E.F. Regatillo and M. Zalba, *Theologiae Moralis Summa*, vol. I (Madrid, 1952), nr. 359.

[3] A. Auer, *Autonome Moral und christlicher Glaube* (Düsseldorf: Patmos, 1971), 160f. A great part of the book is dedicated to the study of the universality and distinctiveness of biblical ethics.

[4] *Readings in Moral Theology No. 2*, l. c. 35f (Aubert), 299f (Chiavacci), 77 (Curran), 8 and 11 (Fuchs), 168 (McCormick), 217f and 229f, (Schüller), 55f (Tettamanzi), 96 and 107 (Walter), 126f (Macquarrie).

[5] F. Böckle, *Fundamental Moral Theology*, l. c. 224f.

of a distinctive content of Christian ethics. For all moral precepts of the Old and New Testament parallels can be shown in other cultures and religions. This is true of love of enemies, the virtue of humility, the spirit of sacrifice or endurance in suffering. This also holds for the virtues of faith, hope and charity, even though outside of Christianity the content of faith is different and much less detailed.

The teaching of the magisterium is guided by the conviction that the answers it gives to moral questions are intelligible and valid for all men of good will. This is particularly evident in the socio-economic doctrines of the social encyclicals since Leo XIII. The Pastoral Constitution on the Church in the Modern World of Vatican II, which covers the whole realm of moral life, "resolutely addresses not only the sons of the Church and all who call upon the name of Christ, but the whole of humanity as well" (GS 2). The justification for this appeal is the persuasion of the Church "that her message is in harmony with the most secret desires of the human heart, since it champions the dignity of man's calling" (GS 21). All men have the same ultimate vocation and "enjoy the same divine calling and destiny" (GS 29; also 22, 24, NA 1). And if Christ reveals the commandment of love as the basic law of human perfection, he likewise assures "that the way of love is open to all men" (GS 38).

As to the intrinsic reasons, two arguments are put forward. First, in order to have insight into the meaning, justification and weight of the moral precepts formulated by Holy Scripture, man needs a rational criterion which enables him to understand their intrinsic goodness. This criterion is the consonance of the precepts with the needs and aspirations of human nature. But this is a criterion shared by all men and not exclusively by Christians. If the existence of such a criterion were denied, the alternative would be a purely voluntaristic positivism. God dictates his precepts and man has to submit to them in blind obedience without an understanding of their reasons. This would not be worthy of man nor of his creator, who has endowed man with reason precisely in order to understand.[1]

---

[1] For a careful discussion and refutation of the voluntarist position see Gerard J. Hughes, *Authority in Morals* (London: Heythrop Monographs, 1978), 4-10. Additional problems for the voluntarist position are, first, the verification of the claim that certain precepts have indeed been revealed by God and are not after all of human origin and, second, the difficulty of interpreting precepts whose meaning man does not understand.

Considerations of the same kind apply to the imitation of Christ as moral guide for Christian life. A genuine understanding of Christ as the standard of authentic humanity is not possible without a previous awareness of the essence of such humanity. Without this awareness Christ could not be perceived as an example. The ideal of authentic humanity is prior to its incarnation in an example. "There is a hermeneutic circle here: Christ interprets for the Christian the meaning of authentic humanity or mature manhood, but he is acknowledged as the Christ or the paradigm of humanity because men have interpreted him as such in the light of an idea of authentic humanity that they already bring to him and that they have derived from their own participation in human existence."[1]

Second, since the concrete final destiny is ultimately one and the same for all mankind, there is existentially also only one essential morality common to all men, Christians and non-Christians alike. This is a new argument, based on theological insights not available to the older theologians. In order to understand this argument, it has to be noted that the traditional distinction between a state of "pure nature" and a state of grace is paralleled by a corresponding distinction between a natural and supernatural ultimate end. The problems surrounding these distinctions and the new answers given to them will be dealt with in detail below (cf. "The theological controversy over natural law"). The distinctions always laboured under difficulties and their artificial character has been more and more felt. Vatican II has at last overcome the impasse: In the concrete order of human existence, all men share in the fruits of Christ's redemption. In the hearts of all men grace is at work, and all men have one and the same ultimate end, which is divine (cf. GS 22; 24; 29; NA 1). Now, since the moral order is decisively determined by the ultimate end of man, the moral order must essentially be the same for all men as well. Besides, since man's very nature is modified by the presence of grace everywhere, all men are confronted

---

[1] J. Macquarrie in *Readings in Moral Theology No. 2*, l. c. 123.

with the same, concrete order of being, which likewise must result in the same moral order for all.[1]

4. *The specific contribution of faith* to ethical perception. If the recent theories are correct and if Christian morality cannot claim a distinct content of its own, does this not mean that in the last analysis Christian morality is without a particular identity? Is not the assertion of certain secularised forms of Christianity, that to be a Christian is simply to be a human being, after all correct? Are not all the rest dispensable paraphernalia?

This is a conclusion drawn too fast. The previous chapter has shown that there are a variety of ethical schools, but not all are of equal value. The claim of the recent theologians is not that Christian ethics may coincide with just any of these schools. The assertion rather is that Christian ethics coincides with that kind of human morality which is authentic and genuine. This is the virtue of only one of the schools, theonomous ethics. This is the form of ethics espoused by Holy Scripture.

The great merit of Holy Scripture is that it has helped men and women of all times to grasp correctly the meaning of life and their calling by God. In the labyrinth of the many ethical opinions it has always given them safe guidance and direction. "Christianity does not establish a new or different morality, but it makes concrete, clarifies and, above all, focuses

---

[1] Within the second opinion, *two variants* can still be distinguished. Some theologians deny the existence of a specifically different material content in Christian morality, but admit of a specific Christian intentionality and motivation. This is the view of J. Fuchs (*Readings in Moral Theology No. 2*, l. c. 6-8; 14-18), J.-M. Aubert (*ib.* 36) and J. Walter (*ib.* 102). Others however object that one cannot conceive of a new intentionality and motivation which does not also result in a newness of activity. They therefore hold that there is neither a distinct content nor a distinct intentionality of Christian morality. Since all men have the same destiny, they are also able to share in the same intentionality. This is the view of C. Curran (*ib.* 77) and D. Tettamanzi (*ib.* 55f). - Perhaps it might be helpful to distinguish between intentionality and motivation. Intentionality is determined by man's moral goals, and these Christians share with all men of good will. Motivation on the other hand is a wider concept. Also ideals and examples which incarnate moral values in exemplary form are motives. The example of Christ is of this nature, and this motive can rightly be called distinctively Christian.

on a particular person, Jesus Christ, the deepest moral convictions of men."[1] Through the aid of revelation men have access to the moral truths with greater facility and sureness (cf. DV 6).

Of particular importance is the proper foundation of ethics and the correct vision of man's ultimate goal. Already the Old Testament clearly recognizes that the moral imperative has its foundation in the authority of God. Not the individual, not the tribe nor the nation is the measure of all things, but God's sovereign will. His rule extends to all spheres of life. He does not merely expect acts of worship. He claims the consecration of man's entire life to his service. As the goal of this service Holy Scripture perceives God's glory, his kingdom and man's salvation.

Also distinctive in the ethics of the New Testament is obviously the normative place which is assigned to Jesus Christ and his teaching. His word and concrete way of life reveal the truth about man and his destiny. Christians are called upon to make Jesus' form of existence their own and to realize it in their lives. Nevertheless this form of existence is not something which otherwise lies outside the scope of human nature or even contradicts it. Rather Christ fulfils man's nature. "Or, better expressed, he both contradicts it and fulfils it - he contradicts our actual condition but fulfils what we have already recognized deep within us as true human personhood."[2] Vatican II can therefore say that "whoever follows Christ the perfect man becomes himself more a man" (GS 41; cf. 11).

In the light of the anthropological and theological foundations and the vision of the final goal adopted by Holy Scripture, biblical ethics gathers, develops and ranks its moral norms. This results in a process of selection, modification, accentuation and stimulation, which is at work in all of Holy Scripture, beginning with the Old Testament and continued in the Gospels of the New Testament and the apostolic writings. The early Church was confronted with a confusing and contradictory plurality of ethical doctrines and principles in the Greek and Roman world. It was necessary for it "to make a decisive and critical separation, in which the Christian

---

[1] J. Macquarrie in *Readings in Moral Theology No. 2*, l. c. 142.
[2] J. Macquarrie, *l. c.* 124.

faith formed its new options in accordance with the Old Testament standards and with the 'way of thinking of Jesus Christ.'"[1]

In this process of critical separation, NT ethics for example rules out any forbidden foods, magic forms of piety, polygamy, discrimination against the state of unmarried life, while it opts for fraternal love, especially towards the most needy, love of enemies, self-control in sexual life and humility. Other norms undergo a modification, such as the norms concerning divorce, sanctification of the Sabbath or cultic laws in general. Other changes concern the rank attributed to certain moral attitudes and values, as illustrated by the emphasis given to openness for the inner law of the Spirit or to the virtues of love, faith, chastity and spirit of sacrifice.

What holds for the early Church, also holds for the moral teaching of the Church today. "The originality of Christianity in the moral field does not lie in the sum of principles which have no parallels elsewhere.... Christian originality consists rather in the overall conception into which man's quest and aspiration was directed by faith in the God of Abraham, in the God of Jesus Christ" and by the place which the various moral principles do or do not occupy in the spiritual structure of Christianity.[2] The biblical materials set the boundaries for all proposed norms from whatever source they come. Some will be considered in bounds for Christian ethics, others out of bounds.

The message of Christ has also a stimulating effect for the moral deportment. Who enters into the horizon of meaning disclosed by Christ can no longer content himself with a mere external fulfilment of the law; he must look after a good heart. He can likewise not be satisfied with a moral minimum, but is challenged to conducts of devoted love and generous service, which reach into the realm of the evangelical counsels. By the fact, finally, that the moral instructions are not proposed merely in abstract norms, but frequently presented in stories, parables and images, the moral striving receives concrete, vivid impulses.

---

[1] Joseph Ratzinger in *Readings in Moral Theology No. 2*, l. c. 182. See also Hans Halter, *Taufe und Ethos: Paulinische Kriterien für das Proprium christlicher Moral* (Freiburg: Herder, 1977), 488-491.

[2] J. Ratzinger, *l. c.* 177.

IV. Moral autonomy and theonomous ethics

The moral norms of Christian ethics can also be arrived at by reason, so it has been explained. They must be legitimized before the tribunal of reason in order to have obligatory force. It must also be possible to establish their validity independently of Christian revelation or any other positive revelation for that matter. From this the conclusion has been drawn that every valid form of ethics, Christian ethics included, must be autonomous. Christian ethics too must aim at autonomy.[1]

The tenet that all moral norms need a rational justification is indeed a valid proposition. The terminology chosen however is easily misleading. As it is commonly understood, moral autonomy means man's independence from moral injunctions external to him, including any divine law and will. The autonomous man creates the moral law on his own authority, with responsibility only to his own person and values. This however is not the teaching of Christian theology;[2] it is, to be sure, also not that of the advocates of the autonomous morality in the Christian context.

The idea of a totally independent, autonomous morality was first formulated by Kant. For him it means an ethics which is not only free from any considerations of happiness and profit, but also free from any demands imposed upon man by God. Moral goodness is a value in itself, and it merits to be realized for the sake of its own dignity, not for the sake of any external authority who wills it, be it even the authority of God. There are other conceptions of autonomous morality, which are of utilitarian, humanist or existentialist

---

[1] This thesis has been formulated above all by A. Auer, *Autonome Moral und christlicher Glaube* (Düsseldorf: Patmos, 1971). It is critically reviewed by B. Stoeckle, *Grenzen der autonomen Moral* (München: Kösel, 1974). F. Böckle adopts the thesis and terminology of Auer and attempts a "theological justification of moral autonomy" in *Fundamental Moral Theology* (New York, 1980), 46-63. This thesis is a characteristic thrust of Böckle's book. Trutz Rendtorff in *Handbuch der christlichen Ethik*, vol. I, edited by A. Hertz and others (Freiburg: Herder, ⁴1993), 210-215, once again shows reservations. He refers to Karl Barth's criticism of autonomous morality in the name of God's sovereignty and warns against an inhuman overestimation of ethical rationality.

[2] In the encyclical *Veritatis Splendor* John Paul II sees in such an understanding of the autonomy a serious danger for the faith and warns against it (nr. 35-41).

provenance and the like. They all have in common the categorical rejection of a foundation of ethics in God or an absolute ground of being and in ideas of Christian faith or of religious nature in general.[1]

These ethical theories have been discussed earlier and their insufficiency been shown. Man is evidently not an independent being in the order of existence. He has not created himself. The structures of his being have been laid down for him by someone else. How then could he be independent in the order of action? How could he create the moral norms for his activity in absolute autonomy and independence from the source of his being? This is a contradiction and an unrealistic illusion.

Man is as little the autonomous creator of his moral norms as he is the creator of his own being. He has to submit to the structures according to which he has been created and to the purpose for which he has been made. Moral principles are to be accepted rather than to be created, because they are demands of reality and of man's destiny. Not man is the origin of the moral order, but the supreme intelligence and wisdom which has made everything and also assigned to man his task and purpose. This supreme reality may be given many names. Yet if Christians and many other religions call it God, it is no other reality than that.

"For a Christian or for a believer in a transcendent God an autonomous morality independent from God, or also for a non-believer a morality independent from an ultimate value or a basic meaning of existence, such an autonomous morality is a nonsense.... Without ultimate meaning neither a normative ethics makes sense, nor a system of values, nor a single precept, nor finally the discernment of the norm intrinsic to conscience."[2] In this precise sense Christian ethics is theonomous.

On the other hand it is true that man's conduct cannot be controlled, today less than ever before, by a mere reference to ecclesiastical authorities or holy books. Man wants to know

---

[1] Cf. "Die neuen Prospekte: Szczesny, Schulz, Habermas", in B. Stoeckle, *l. c.*, 23-32.

[2] Enrico Chiavacci, *Teologia morale*, vol. II: *Complementi de morale generale* (Assisi: Cittadella, 1980), 229f. See the entire, worthwhile chapter "Il dibattito sull'autonomia della morale," 227-246.

the intrinsic reasons for his moral obligations and their rational justification. This implies independence from a purely authoritarian imposition of the moral norm. It does however not imply that moral norms are superfluous, neither those of Holy Scripture nor those of the religious and civil communities. "Norms are not only *socially* necessary, they are also *morally* necessary. What is good and meaningful is not a matter which depends on the arbitrariness of the subjects. True, the experience of meaningfulness is indispensable for human activity, but in what meaningful activity consists is a question of reality.... It is a matter of long experience, communitarian experience of humans who scrutinize reality in the quest for the meaningful and strive to form and transform it correspondingly. Norms are, so to say, long-standing experiences in regard to good and evil, cast in rules."[1]

According to a theological opinion, reason alone is not in a condition to fathom out the origin and the goal of man and consequently not his responsibility either. This being the case, "the exposition of the moral demand necessarily stands in need of the aid of faith".[2] One has in mind the faith of Christian revelation. However the previous deliberations of the distinctiveness of Christian ethics have shown that such dependence of reason on biblical faith is not certain and is contested by many theologians. Even though for reason the origin and goal of man always remain somewhat shrouded in mystery, this is also true for faith. "For our knowledge is imperfect", and as long as we are in this world we only see as "in a mirror dimly" (1 Cor 13:9 and 12).

Yet it is a correct insight that reason is not man's only access to reality. There are also the powers of intuition and the guidance of the Holy Spirit. There are inspirations which do not come from reason but from the heart. The method to gain them is not logic but contemplation. If faith is understood in this sense of intuitive contemplation and openness to the Spirit, it can indeed be said that the knowledge of the moral demand is in need of faith. Without doubt this faith is realized to the highest degree in biblical revelation, but it is not limited to it. It is a potentiality of every God-fearing heart.

---

[1] K.-W. Merks, "Autonome Moral," in *Moraltheologie im Abseits? Antwort auf die Enzyklika «Veritatis Splendor»*, ed. by D. Mieth (Freiburg: Herder, 1994), 65f.

[2] B. Stoeckle, *l. c.* 89; cf. 86f.

It remains certainly true that this faith cannot assert itself arbitrarily. It must be able to legitimize and prove its moral insights and principles before the tribunal of reason. But in the process of the shaping of the ethical principles, faith is the more creative power and maintains the leadership. "Faith needs continuous confrontation in order to call forth its possibly hidden implications; reason on the other hand requires the creative-emancipatory impulse which emanates from the operation of faith in history."[1]

C. Natural moral law

"The natural law, as an idea, is almost as old as philosophy itself. Since the Greeks first began to philosophize it has appeared in every age and can be described as a sort of recurring decimal in the history of thought."[2] It has had its great moments of eclipse. It has been presented and defined in many different ways.[3] It has been criticized and at times been assailed scornfully. But it has never been vanquished. No alternative has ever been found which could substitute for it.

Since the time when Catholic moral theology developed as a separate discipline, natural law has been one of its steady components. Especially great was the influence of Thomas Aquinas in this regard.[4] Also in Anglican ethics the natural

---

[1] Klaus Demmer, *Sittlich handeln aus Verstehen. Strukturen hermeneutisch orientierter Fundamentalmoral* (Düsseldorf: Patmos, 1980), 156.

[2] Michael B. Crowe, "Natural Law Theory Today," in *The Future of Ethics and Moral Theology*, ed. by R.A. McCormick and others (Chicago: Argus Communications, 1968), 78.

[3] At times the plurality of definitions and interpretations is alleged as an argument against natural law. However this is the fate of many basic concepts. Love and justice have found many different definitions and interpretations, and yet nobody doubts their existence and need.

[4] The natural law doctrine of Thomas Aquinas is a good illustration of the dangers of anachronisms. Time and again mention is made of his definition of natural law (*lex naturalis*) as a rule of action common to man and all animals (I-II, q. 94, a. 2), which he adopted from the Roman lawyer Ulpian. He is then criticized for his narrow-minded, physiological understanding of natural law. However the terminology of Thomas differs from our present one. The rule of action which corresponds to the specific, rational nature of man is called by him law of nations (*ius gentium*). Only from the 16th century on does the term *ius gentium* refer to international law and *lex naturae* assume the meaning which is attributed to it today.

law doctrine has found a firm place. The attitude of the Protestant Churches, on the other hand, is more divided. In the first three centuries after the reformation, natural law still served as the foundation of Protestant jurisprudence. Only after the secularization of natural law by representatives of this jurisprudence, such as Pufendorf (†1694) and Thomasius (†1728), did Protestant theology of the 19th century turn in disappointment against it. And only then did the opposition between Catholic and Protestant attitudes towards natural law emerge.[1] Yet more recently Protestant ethics also gives new attention to the question of natural law.[2]

The term natural law refers to those moral insights which man is able to know by means of his reason, independently of the verbal revelation of God. The word "natural" in the term has the meaning of (1) not supernatural, i.e. not communicated in a supernatural way; (2) not positive, i.e. not the result of a command of a legislative authority, as in positive human or divine law; (3) found in and derived from the nature of man. These explanations show that the doctrine of natural law deals with the question of natural ethics as a whole. Natural law, the moral law of nature, natural ethics and natural morality are synonyms.

Natural law doctrine is of fundamental relevance above all on two accounts. First, it is the basis of a moral order of universal character and constitutes a source of ethical wisdom which Christians share with all mankind, for it rests upon that reality which is shared by all men: their common humanity and existential conditions. Secondly, natural law is the only adequate safeguard against arbitrary exercise of political and legislative power. It is the final court of appeal against unjust, prejudiced laws of human authorities.

---

[1] See the very informative article by Hans Liermann, "Zur Geschichte des Naturrechts in der evangelischen Kirche," in *Festschrift Alfred Bertholet gewidmet* (Tübingen: J.C.B. Mohr, 1950), 294-324.

[2] See K. Peschke, *Naturrecht in der Kontroverse. Kritik evangelischer Theologie an der katholischen Lehre von Naturrecht and natürlicher Sittlichkeit* (Salzburg: Otto Müller, 1967). Heinz-Horst Schrey, "Diskussion um das Naturrecht 1950-1975," *Theologische Rundschau*, Neue Folge 41 (1976), 59-93.

I. Concept of natural law

1. *The traditional concept*

According to traditional moral theology, natural moral law is that law of human conduct which arises from human nature as ordered to its ultimate natural end and which is recognized by the natural light of reason.[1] That is to say, the subjective medium of cognition is reason alone. The objective ground, in which the moral law is recognized and from which it is derived, is, on the one hand, man's natural (not supernatural) ultimate end and, on the other, human nature not elevated by grace. In distinction from this, the Christian moral law (the "law of Christ") has as its medium of cognition reason aided and supplemented by faith, is ordered towards the supernatural ultimate end, and is based on human nature as elevated by grace. It must however be noted that there is no contradiction between nature and grace or between the natural and supernatural ultimate end. The supernatural end lies in the same direction as the natural, although it necessarily leads beyond it.

A particular difficulty is posed by the question of the precise *concept of nature* in the natural law doctrine. Which exactly is the human nature that serves as the source of the moral order? Some regard the essential, metaphysical nature of man as this source. One has in mind that nature which in all the varying conditions of time and space always and everywhere remains the same. Naturally the laws derived from this nature would also always and everywhere be the same; they are immutable. But it is rightly objected that such a nature is an abstraction which never exists as such and which also cannot be marked out with certainty. Besides, and this seems a still weightier objection, it is not comprehensible why the changeable conditions of human nature are not equally sources of the moral obligation. Indeed moral handbooks formulate many such obligations, as for example the obligation to adequate schooling in the developed societies of today.

---

[1] Cf. M. Zalba, *Theologiae Moralis Compendium* I, 1958, nr. 316: "Lex naturalis est divina creaturae rationalis in finem ultimum naturalem ordinatio, necessaria, in ipsa natura expressa, naturali lumine rationis percepta."

Others distinguish between the empirical, factual nature of man and his ideal essence. Man's factual nature comprises all the physiological, biological, psychological and sociological structures and mechanisms in which human life exists and unfolds. Yet it often shows distortions, as for example a sluggish temperament or sadistic constitution. If the concrete human nature were to serve as the basis of the moral order, these traits would entitle a person to an indolent life or to sadistic gratification. Evidently no serious philosopher or theologian could agree to such conclusions. Accordingly only the ideal essence or nature of man can serve as the source of this moral law. This solution avoids the pitfalls of a possible biologism, psychologism and sociologism. The problem however is how the ideal nature can be distinguished from the factual one with its possibly deformed traits. The answers to this remain vague, divided and vary according to cultures and times. A precise knowledge of this nature is wanting.

Others again consider reason as the essential, primary element of natural law. The moral law is an order of reason. Morally good is what is according to reason. This view is correct insofar as reason definitely plays an essential role in the knowledge of natural law. Yet it is only one of the constituent principles of natural law, namely the subjective medium of cognition. Reason is not able to create the concrete moral order out of its own depths without a confrontation with outside reality. In this process reason has to judge whether certain modes of conduct are morally good or evil. According to which objective criterion is this done? This question is not answered, and it is the crucial one. "Reason as such guarantees neither humanity nor love."[1]

Still others regard the full actuality of man's nature as the objective source of the moral order. It comprises his empirical, factual being together with "the ends designed in the physical and psychical instincts of his nature".[2] The physical, biological and social structures in which human life exists as well as the generic and individual traits of the human person have indeed an influence on the moral order and

---

[1] W. Schrage, *The Ethics of the New Testament* (Edinburgh: T. & T. Clark, 1988), 15.

[2] J. Messner, *Social Ethics* (St. Louis/London: B. Herder Book Co., 1965), 18.

therefore are sources for it. But this factual nature of man includes as one of its very important components also the ends designed in the physiological, psychical and spiritual inclinations and aspirations of the human person. These ends answer the question of how the potentialities of man and of the world around him should be used. Since these ends result from human existence and determine it, they are called by Messner "existential ends". And since they set before man aims which have to be realized, they impart to ethics a teleological character.

In harmony with universal and established human experience, the following survey of the existential ends can be given (based on Messner): self-preservation, including bodily integrity and social respect; self-perfection, including the enlargement of experience and knowledge and the improvement of the conditions of life; procreation and education of children; concern and care for the spiritual and material welfare of one's fellow-men; social fellowship for the promotion of common utility; commitment to goodness and value in its absolute, transcendental form, especially union with God through worship of him.[1]

The knowledge of these impulses and aspirations and the comprehension of their proper functioning is gained in the

---

[1] Cf. J. Messner, *l. c.* 19. The scope of the last end has somewhat been broadened here compared with the wording of Messner. In a similar way, John Finnis presents a list of seven basic values, which however seem less organic than the existential ends of Messner. They are the following: life, knowledge, play, aesthetic experience, friendship (sociability), practical reasonableness, and religion. Procreation is subsumed under the value of life (*Natural Law and Natural Rights*. Oxford: Clarendon Press, 1980, 86-90). An almost identical list is compiled by Germain Grisez (*The Way of the Lord Jesus*, vol. I: *Christian Moral Principles*. Chicago: Franciscan Herald, 1983, 124). Aesthetic experience is, in his list, substituted by self-integration; and friendship is enlarged to justice and friendship. The basic values are not *moral* values in themselves, but rather the object of the moral actions. No hierarchical order exists among them, just as there is no such order among the existential ends of Messner. The same difficulties therefore arise for the basic values as for the existential ends - as discussed above in the following - in establishing a priority in cases of conflict among them. For a discussion of the positions of Finnis and Grisez see R. McInerny, "The Principles of Natural Law," in *Readings in Moral Theology No. 7: Natural Law and Theology*, ed. by C.E. Curran and R.A. McCormick (New York: Paulist Press, 1991), 139-156, and the answer of the two authors, *ib.* 157-170.

same way in which insight into the nature and proper functioning of other realities and living things is gained: by means of outward and inward experience. An example may help to clarify the interplay between the existential ends and the other factors of empirical nature. The study of human nature shows that the energies of the human body are limited; if overtaxed, exhaustion will lead to breakdowns and even death. These are empirical facts. Which are the conclusions to be drawn from this? The existential ends give the answer. One of these ends is self-preservation. It demands that an over-exertion of a person's energies be avoided in order to preserve his health and life. This is the moral demand.

However this may not be the only conclusion possible. Among the existential ends is also that of social fellowship for the promotion of common utility. One could imagine situations of national emergency which might justify and perhaps even demand the risk of an exhaustion of one's energies for the sake of the common good. This means that the demands of two existential ends are in conflict. How is this conflict to be solved? This question is not answered with sufficient clarity by Messner.

The solution is provided by the criterion of man's ultimate end. According to the definition of natural law, human nature is not the only objective source for the cognition of the moral law. Combined with it is the ultimate end. It is this end which determines the order of priority among the various existential ends. In instances of conflict between two existential ends, that end prevails which is more urgent for the realization of the ultimate end. Moreover whenever the sacrifice of one of the existential ends (e.g. procreation) serves the ultimate end better, this sacrifice is allowed; at times it may even be demanded. The criterion of the ultimate end also solves problems resulting from disordered traits in human nature, e.g. a sadistic constitution (if the problem cannot already be solved by the existential ends). In view of God's creative and salvific purpose for man and this world, a sadist has the obligation to renounce his devious desires and to avoid situations which could trigger his destructive tendencies.

In summary, then, the result of the discussion about the concept of nature in natural law doctrine is this. The concept of nature in the definition of natural law refers to the full reality of man's nature with all its empirical features and existential ends as well as to the nature of all those beings to which man's activity is related. Yet this nature is never the source of the moral order alone by itself, but only in combination with the requirements of the ultimate end.

Hence it is not correct to say that nature alone provides the basis for the moral norm. This would be correct only if nature were understood in so wide a sense that the ultimate end of creation were considered part of this nature. One might justify this on the grounds that existing reality is already a partial realization of God's plan and is intrinsically ordered to the ultimate end. However it must be noted that the ultimate end is contained and predesigned in existing nature only in an incomplete blueprint, just as the architectural masterplan for a building is only imperfectly revealed in a construction which is not yet finished. Besides man has also a transcendental destiny, which is his most important one. Preferably therefore the traditional distinction between nature and ultimate end as two complementary sources of the moral norm is to be retained.

2. The theological controversy over natural law

Traditional natural law theory encounters various criticisms and objections. It is argued that its claim to universal validity is defeated by the widely divergent moral codes of different peoples and times. Natural law does not do justice to the historical character of the moral norm. It is too legalistic and unable to respond to the personal claims of God's grace and of love. It lacks eschatological orientation. It succumbs to the naturalistic fallacy by drawing conclusions from the existing facts of reality to what man should do; yet from what actually is one cannot conclude to what morally ought to be. The objections will find their answers partly in the expositions on the properties of natural law, partly in the discussion of its existence. There is however still a further objection, and this shall be answered here. It is of theological nature and therefore only raised in theological quarters.

Protestant theologians often turn energetically and sometimes sharply against Catholic natural law. One of the basic reasons for their dissatisfaction with Catholic natural law is the way Catholic theology relates it to the law of Christ or the law of the supernatural order of grace. According to

Catholic moral theology there is the ethic of natural law, derived from a nature not exalted by grace, which obliges all mankind, non-Christians and Christians alike, in an equal way. To these general moral laws other obligations are added on a second level, binding for Christians only, which result from their supernatural life. Behind this concept is the Catholic doctrine on nature and grace, in which nature appears as the fundamental condition of man, to which grace is added in a second instance and more or less as an accident.

The nearly unanimous criticism of Protestant theologians against this "two-storey-theory" is that the life of grace, which is superior in value compared to the life of nature, is placed in the subordinate condition of a quasi-accident. Moreover the Catholic supposition that there exists a nature deprived of the state of grace which would be nevertheless basically good is attacked as wrong. Also wrong therefore is the assumption that a law deduced from this nature is basically good and without any reservations acceptable as a norm for a Christian life. Exponents of this criticism are K. Barth, E. Brunner, J. Ellul, H. Thielicke and others.

Yet Protestants themselves find the greatest difficulties in offering satisfying solutions. From a corrupt nature only a corrupt law can be deduced. But how can a corrupt law be prescribed as a norm binding in conscience? Brunner and even more so, Thielicke are in serious difficulties to prove the binding force of ethical norms not taken from Scripture. In the system of these authors such norms are always accompanied by the doubt as to whether they are not in reality perverted because derived from a perverted nature.

K. Barth, in his early years, seemed to offer a solution not much more satisfying: an ethical biblicism.[1] It would be only through the word of God in revelation that man could know what is good. But if this were true, non-Christians would have no means to arrive at valid moral norms, since they do not have the Bible. And no common ground would exist for the moral order of a society where non-Christians and Christians live together. However it turned out later on

---

[1] Deeply dissatisfied with Barth's method to deduce moral laws by means of analogies from Holy Scripture, the Protestant theologian H. Thielicke asserts that he would prefer Catholic natural law rather than adopt Barth's kind of supernatural law (cf. *Theological Ethics*, vol. II. Philadelphia: Fortress Press, 1969, 580 and 583).

that in Barth's mind the word of God comes to man not only in the historical revelation of Holy Scripture, but also in the revelation given to every man by the working of the Holy Spirit.[1] This is possible because the redemption of Christ is not limited in its effects to the baptized. The grace of Christ is active everywhere, though not everywhere known as such and less efficacious and powerful among non-Christians than among Christians. Thus the opposites of nature and grace, of a pagan world in the state of pure or corrupt nature and of a Christian world in the state of grace, find their unity in a christological universalism. The truth is that after the redemption of Christ there is no longer a nature completely deprived of grace. The grace of Christ is working at all times and everywhere, even among non-Christians. And as a consequence, there is basically not a double morality of the state of nature and of the state of grace, but only the one morality of a mankind under the influence and dominion of Christ and his Holy Spirit and his grace.

The Catholic side came to similar insights and conclusions in the efforts of Teilhard de Chardin, K. Rahner, Ph. Delhaye, H. de Lubac, H. U. von Balthasar and others. The Constitution of Vatican II on the Church in the Modern World explains that Christ restored to the sons of Adam the divine likeness which had been disfigured from the first sin onward. "In Him God reconciled us to himself and to one another, freeing us from the bondage to the devil and of sin, so that each one of us can say with the apostle: The Son of God 'loved me and gave himself for me'" (GS 22). And the Council continues in the same article: "All this holds true not for Christians only but also for all men of good will in whose hearts grace is active invisibly. For since Christ died for all, and since all men are in fact called to one and the same destiny, which is divine, we must hold that the Holy Spirit offers to all the possibility of being made partners, in a way known to God, in the paschal mystery" (GS 22; cf. 29; NA 1). It is on the basis of this solidarity and this common destiny of mankind,

---

[1] Expressions like gospel, revelation, word of God, faith, Christ often gain in Barth's language a significance which transcends their historical meaning. They then denote the hidden word of God which addresses itself at all times to all men, the hidden gospel which reveals itself continually and everywhere to people, the universal Christ who influences and unites people always.

that the Council addresses itself in the above-mentioned Constitution "not only to the sons of the Church and all who call upon the name of Christ, but to the whole humanity as well" (GS 2).

Conclusion: The distinction between a purely natural ethics on the one hand and a morality only for Christians on the other therewith underwent a revision of great moment. There is no longer any fundamental difference between natural and Christian ethics. Neither can such a difference be asserted by reason of human nature from which the moral law is derived, because in Christ not only Christians but all men of good will are reconciled to God, receive the Holy Spirit, and are under the influence of grace. Nor can it be asserted by reason of the character of the ultimate end, "since all men are in fact called to one and the same destiny". There is only a difference in the knowledge and understanding of human nature, of the ultimate end and by that of the moral law; a difference, certainly, which is still important and which is not to be slighted. Christian faith imparts to man an insight into human nature, the final goal and the moral order which is deeper, fuller and more to the point than the insight gained by reason alone.[1] If God found it necessary to reveal this knowledge to men, particularly in his Son Jesus Christ, they doubtless have reason to value this revelation highly. The importance of the message of Jesus is most forcibly underscored by the voice from the cloud on the mountain of transfiguration, which bids men: "This is my beloved Son, with whom I am well pleased; listen to him" (Mt 17:5 par).

Positive Christian revelation[2] furthermore specifies the moral obligations resulting from the divine life of grace by positive divine precepts above all in the realm of the virtue of religion, such as the sacraments. These specifications are, like charisms, free gifts of God's grace.

---

[1] K. Barth formulates that the insights given by Christian revelation into the nature and destiny of man and the world are "toto coelo" superior to anything philosophical knowledge has been able to offer (*Church Dogmatics* IV/2. Edinburgh: T. & T. Clark, 1958, 724f).

[2] Positive Christian revelation is that revelation which expressly and in a "positive" way has been put down in the writings of the Old and New Testament. It must be distinguished from the general revelation, which is granted to all men and women through the action of the Holy Spirit in their hearts.

3. Revised concept of natural law

When we bear in mind the criticisms against the former Catholic concept of natural law and take into consideration the new understanding of non-Christian mankind and its ultimate end as developed by Vatican II, we find that the traditional definition of natural law needs adjustment. Although the changes in the wording of the definition may appear as only minor ones, they give expression to a significant revision in the theological understanding of the concept.

Natural law is that law of human conduct which arises from the full reality of human nature as ordered to its ultimate end and which is recognized by means of reason, independent of positive Christian revelation.

The concept of human nature is to be taken in a rather wide sense. It refers - as already explained earlier - to the full reality of human nature with all its generic and individual traits as well as to the nature of all those beings to which man's activity is related. It likewise comprises - in contradistinction to the traditional doctrine of natural law - those modifications of nature which are effected by Christ's redemptive work, not only in the baptized but in all mankind, and includes that share in grace which all men possess.

The ultimate end is no longer merely the natural one. It is the concrete, final destiny of man, which is, as the Council asserts, one and the same for all men, and divine.

Finally, with regard to the subjective medium of cognition, this medium is reason not aided by positive Christian revelation. However this must not lead to the false conclusion that reason in the definition is understood as completely withdrawn from the influence of grace. All cognition of reason in concrete mankind is everywhere influenced and guided by grace and the Holy Spirit, although in the case of non-Christians in a completely hidden way. Hence the medium of cognition is reason not aided by Christian revelation though under the influence of grace.

Natural moral law as described in the definition embraces the whole natural moral order. From the natural moral law must be distinguished natural right, which only covers that segment of natural moral law which is concerned with the realm of justice and the juridical order between men. Often however the two terms, natural law and natural right, are interchanged. The precise meaning of the terms in the mind of an author must therefore be learned from the context in which they are used.

II. Properties of natural law

1. *Universality of natural law*

The natural moral law binds every man at all times and in all places, for its basis is the very nature of men. In its essential characteristics it is common to all. All are called to attain the same final goal and to respect the same existential ends in essentially the same way, even if this way presents a varied picture in the details of its realization.

No one is free from the obligation of fulfilling this duty; no one is superior to the guidelines which show him the way to it; no one is beyond good and evil. Even those who are temporarily or permanently without the use of reason are not excepted from this obligation. Although they do not sin subjectively in offending against natural law, they break it materially and therefore can and often must be hindered from doing so (e.g. mentally sick persons who endanger the lives of others).

Of course no law can be binding in conscience as long as it is not known. But whoever has the use of reason, cannot remain ignorant of the natural law for long, at least not of its basic principles. By the very fact that man has a nature existentially oriented towards certain ends and that he has been given the power to recognize his essential obligation to contribute to the realization of these ends and not to obstruct them, the natural law becomes known to him.

a) Extent of the universal knowledge of natural law

A careful distinction has to be made between the objective reality of natural law and the knowledge men have of this reality. The objective reality of natural law is universal in a similar way as the physical or biological laws of nature are. They are truths which exist and are operative even if not known by men. The concrete knowledge of natural law on the other hand is not universal in the same way. Man does not possess this knowledge in a fully developed form from the beginning. He must evolve it, just as he evolves other

Nature of the Moral Law 107

forms of knowledge, as for example that of the physical or biological laws.

Scholastic theology distinguishes between primary and secondary principles of natural law. Primary principles are those norms which can be known with certainty by every normal man in possession of his reason. They are self-evident from his nature. All men are aware of their existence, just as all men are aware of the most fundamental laws of nature, e.g. the law of gravity. Secondary principles on the other hand are those further conclusions of natural law which are less universally known and more readily subject to error.[1]

The primary principles of natural law are self-evident, but not moral judgments a priori. They are conditioned by experience. Yet once experienced, they are immediately evident to the practical reason. As soon as the development of reason enables a person to grasp the notions the primary principles convey, they are recognized as evident. Messner qualifies them as "synthetic judgments a priori".[2] Indeed one has every reason to expect that nature will assure in man the knowledge of these principles which are indispensable for a meaningful life.

The most universal principle of natural law runs: "The known good must be done and evil must be avoided." Reason takes this way of acting for granted. Yet this principle is of merely formal nature, since nothing is said about what is in its contents (materially) good or evil. What is good and worthy of man's desire? The most general and basic answer to this

---

[1] At other times the criterion for the distinction is sought in the absolute or relative validity of a norm. Primary principles are those norms which enjoy absolute validity, while secondary norms are those which permit exceptions. This however seems to be the less common understanding of the distinction. Besides, the present tendency to question the existence of moral "absolutes" and to reduce the norms possessing absolute validity to only one or two renders this type of distinction unavailing and of very little practical use.

[2] J. Messner, *Social Ethics*, l. c. 61. "In order to obviate misunderstandings it may be observed that to emphasize the dependence of moral insight upon experience does not mean that general moral principles are founded upon experience; rather it means that experience is a prerequisite for the apprehension of their evident truth as well as of their general validity" (*ib.* 32).

is given by the following principles, which are equally evident to all people.[1]

Maintain and promote your bodily life.

Maintain and promote social coexistence.

Duties of state of life (and parental duties in particular) are to be answered.

Lawful authority (and parents in particular) must be obeyed.

What you do not wish others to do to you, do not do to them ("the golden rule").

Leave to every one and give to every one what is his.

Contracts must be honoured.

Also the principle that due honour is to be accorded to the supreme being is often included in the list. Doubtless as soon as the notion of God is grasped rightly, this duty is an immediate conclusion. But the phenomenon of pantheism and still more so of atheism today shows that de facto not all men possess this notion nor are aware of this obligation.

All the other moral norms are considered secondary principles. Ignorance and error may obscure and distort them, even in entire nations and cultures. They are subdistinguished into proximate and remote conclusions of natural law. The proximate conclusions enjoy a wider range of acceptance and are more readily agreed upon. The commandments of the second table of the decalogue and the precept to honour God pertain to them. Also many of the human rights belong here, although others pertain rather to the category of remote conclusions, as for example the principle of the equal dignity of all men or the right to freedom of religion.

The remote conclusions require a more advanced understanding of the nature of man and are often discerned only under great difficulty. Anyone who grasps the situation properly and can think rightly must necessarily agree to them. But the difficulty of surveying all the concrete data makes it possible for the uneducated to be invincibly ignorant of some of them even for a long time. And sometimes this is true even for the educated, as in the case of slavery or of the judgment that women are human beings of lesser rights. It is also

---

[1] See *ib.* 59. Likewise Karl Hörmann, "Die Unveränderlichkeit sittlicher Normen im Anschluss an Thomas von Aquin," in *Sittliche Normen*, ed. by W. Kerber (Düsseldorf: Patmos, 1982), 37.

possible that a community chooses a rule of conduct for the realization of an existential end which is not a completely wrong but a less perfect one, as for example polygamy. Some remote principles may even remain controversial among the very experts for a longer period of time (e.g. direct killing of a tyrant or suicide by hunger strike).

An insufficient understanding of human nature, e.g. of the equal dignity of women or the nature of the family, naturally leads to deficient moral norms. This also holds for inadequate anthropological ideals. Yet apart from this, allowance must be made for cultural and social patterns which can condition moral norms, particularly those of a more complex nature. "Human nature used as a first-hand criterion of moral action is the result of a complex process of comprehension, which includes both interpretation and evaluation."[1] Different cultures can lead to different norms, which possess their justification side by side. Also within the same culture complex situations at times admit of different evaluations and answers. An attitude of tolerance is called for here.

b) Uncertainties in the teaching of the Church

The official Catholic Church, especially in the last hundred years, has often motivated her statements and decisions on moral issues by arguments taken from natural law. And since natural law is of universal character, these decisions have been understood as the objective norm of moral conduct for all men. Yet repeatedly non-Catholics have been of a different opinion on these moral issues. Thus they have rejected the claim of the Catholic teaching authority to give universal norms in her moral decisions, and with this claim they frequently reject her teaching on natural law and even the doctrine on natural law altogether. In recent times such controversies have above all developed with regard to questions of medical and conjugal ethics.[2]

It is particularly in this regard that Protestants voice their criticism that Catholic natural law and ethics are not distrustful enough of themselves; a defect that is said to result in the claim of a correctness which overestimates itself. Also Christian

---

[1] K. Demmer, *Deuten und Handeln* (Freiburg: Herder, 1985), 148.

[2] Cf. the questions of therapeutic abortion, artificial birth control, artificial insemination or sterilization for eugenic reasons.

ethics is in need of a constant critical checking, to determine whether its norms represent correctly enough the true demands of the natural and biblical law.

In fact the remote principles of natural law do not always lie perfectly open even for Catholic moral teaching. It often needs a long time of study and evolution until the most correct conclusion is found. Thus the doctrine of religious toleration attained its full maturity in Catholicism only with Vatican II, and the teaching on conjugal love shows a process of growth, in which the most recent modification is the new evaluation of the ends of marriage by the Council Vatican II.[1] Such limitations in insight and in the ability to grasp moral realities in their full range call for humility in theological discussions and for openness to revising possibly incomplete formulations.

Considering this fact that even Catholic ethics does not always present the most perfect solutions in its moral teaching, the question may arise whether this must not shake the confidence of her believers and of men in general in the Church and her moral theology. However an attitude of overall scepticism would certainly be a wrong and unjust reaction. Shortcomings occur in all sciences. Although we know, e.g., that experts in physics have repeatedly been in error about the exact laws of nature and physicians have often applied wrong treatments,[2] we still entrust ourselves to them in our

---

[1] In the bull *Dum diversas* of 1452 Nicholas V declared the enslavement of heathen and the enemies of Christ as permitted (later by Paul III in the bull *Veritas ipse* of 1537 disapproved). Gregory XVI (encyclical *Mirari vos* of 1832, DS 2730f) and Pius IX (encyclicals *Nostis et nobiscum* of 1848 and *Quanta cura* of 1864; cf. DS 2977-9) rejected freedom of religion and conscience, freedom of expression and press. Pius XII declared, in various statements, the sacrifice of an organ as lawful only on the basis of the principle of totality, i.e. in favour of one's own health, not in favour of organ transplants inter vivos (*AAS* 44 [1952], 782, 786f; 45 [1953], 747; 48 [1956], 461f; 50 [1958], 693).

[2] Instructive in this regard is the case of the physician Ignaz Semmelweis (1818-1865). In his time many women died of childbed fever and, unexplainably, more died of it in the hospitals and university clinics than at home. Simply by experience Semmelweis discovered that the infection rate in the hospitals was drastically reduced if the physician washed his hands when going from sick to healthy women in the maternity wards. He reported his findings in a congress and urged his colleagues to wash their hands before going from sick to healthy women. But being rather young and without a name, he was contradicted, ridiculed and rejected by the very professors of medicine. He was vindicated only twenty years later, when the need of asepsis was confirmed by the discovery of the bacteria.

corresponding problems. The reason for this is the very rightful conviction that these scientists, in spite of their errors, are still able to contribute more efficiently to the best possible solution of a problem in given circumstances than those who are not experts. The same is true in the realm of morality and justice. Moral theology and ethics may not always present the best solutions. But in a doctrine of theirs, commonly accepted by the experts, the presumption favours the correctness of the teaching. "In the matter of morals, as in other professional matters, the non-specialist acts responsibly by following a trusted expert."[1] To accept the decisions of a competent authority still involves the least risk and is the most prudent way of acting.

2. *Immutability and dynamics*

A prominent trait of the modern man's understanding of himself and of nature is his perception that all things are in the process of evolution, subject to change and historically conditioned. Vatican II also is aware of this fact. "Mankind substitutes a dynamic and more evolutionary concept of nature for a static one" (GS 5). This calls for new efforts of analysis and synthesis. But the Council likewise asserts "that beneath all that changes there is much which is unchanging" (GS 10). Permanence and historicity alike characterize the nature of man and his world.

Immutability of natural moral law means that as soon as human beings endowed with reason had appeared, certain fundamental norms concerning good and evil emerged from their nature, and these will exist as long as human nature exists. There is a constant in human nature which remains throughout all historical and cultural change.

Yet in the moral sphere, as in every other, men have to learn by trial and error and by patient scientific effort. The laws of physics have always existed, immutably; but their discovery by men was a slow process, accompanied by many mistakes. It is not different in the realm of morality. There has been a long evolution in moral consciousness from the days of primeval man up to the present day. This evolution is marked by many blunders and by ignorance of laws which

---
[1] R.M. Gula, *Reason Informed by Faith* (New York: Paulist Press, 1989), 209.

we regard as fundamental nowadays, e.g. freedom of religious beliefs, equality of rights of all men, humane treatment of prisoners of war. Ignorance of these rights and laws does not say that they did not exist before. Objectively they have always had validity. But here as well as in all other sciences, man's insight into these laws had to proceed from imperfect to perfect knowledge. This kind of evolutionary process does not signify a mutability of natural law itself, but only an alteration of human insight into it.

There is however also the fact that man himself and his conditions of existence change. This can be seen from a glance at the course of development from Neanderthal man to the present day. Such changes indeed bring about alterations in the norms of natural law which are objective and real. As man and his living conditions change, the application of the same, basic principles leads to different conclusions. This signifies a historicity and mutability of natural law in the proper sense.

The changes may result from alterations of human nature itself. One cannot a priori exclude that such mutations still take place. However scholars like Teilhard de Chardin consider the biological evolution of man practically to be closed. "In fact the question of such an evolution and its effects on moral theology hardly plays a role in contemporary discussion."[1] If some moralists speak of changes of man's nature, a closer look usually reveals that they only refer to changes caused by civilization and culture.

The changes in man's conditions of existence however are many, and they accelerate at an ever faster pace. "There seem to be two ways in which the changes in man take place one of them primarily inward, intellectual, and spiritual, whereby formative images and ideals are created and projected, and the other primarily physical, consisting in the techniques and apparatus whereby man carries out his operations. Clearly, however, the two ways are very closely related."[2] Changes of this type often result in modified or new demands of natural law. Examples are the trend, brought about especially

---

[1] Andreas Laun, *Die naturrechtliche Begründung der Ethik in der neueren katholischen Moraltheologie* (Wiener Dom-Verlag, 1973), 152.

[2] J. Macquarrie, *Three Issues in Ethics* (New York: Harper and Row, 1970), 46.

by better schooling and education, to increase the citizens right to political codetermination, above all by means of democratic vote; or the greater need of birth control on account of the drastic reduction of infant mortality; or the duty, graver today, to undergo a therapeutic amputation in view of the new possibility of anaesthesia and antisepsis.

Thus natural law is by no means a static reality, but a reality of dynamic character. The evolution from taboo ethics to the principles of the Atlantic Charter and of human rights demonstrates how dynamic a power natural law is. Yet this dynamics is immutably related to the order of being from which natural law derives, with the result that wherever nature is the same, the demands of natural law are also the same.

3. Indispensability of natural law

In the true sense of the word no dispensation from natural moral law is possible, at least not from the side of human authority. Since human nature and the ultimate end, from which natural law derives, are not created and set up by man but by a power superior to him, natural law likewise exists independent of man's assent. It is withdrawn from his power of free disposal. For Christians, as for many other religions as well, the power which created man and claims him unconditionally is God. The origin of the order of natural law is accordingly likewise God. Natural law is identical with God's will. Evidently man has no authority over a law of this status. Exceptions or dispensations from natural law based on purely human authority are usurpations of a right man does not possess. They are violations of the divinely willed order.

The possibility however that God himself may allow an exception from natural law in some extraordinary case cannot simply be excluded, as long as this exception does not contradict God's own nature. Suspension of a natural moral law by a special divine intervention seems just as possible as suspension of natural physical laws in miracles. God's command to Abraham to sacrifice his son Isaac can be considered such an exception. Instances of this kind of course always demand an express positive divine revelation. More recent instances of such exceptions can at times be found in the lives of saints. For example, the Swiss farmer Nicholas of Flüe (†1487), father of 10 children, was ordered by the voice of God to leave his wife and children (the youngest was only a few months old) and to lead the life of an eremite. What would have been irresponsible for another father to do, was proven genuine in his case by the signs surrounding his vocation; e.g. he abstained from all food for almost 20 years.[1]

If dispensation from natural law in the true sense is not possible, exceptions from it in an improper sense are nevertheless conceivable and indeed do occur. This is the question of epikeia in natural law.

The doctrine of epikeia was developed particularly by Aristotle. It gained influence in Christian ethics when this doctrine was adopted by Albert the Great and Thomas Aquinas. Yet in the writings of these authors epikeia only refers to certain exceptions from human laws, made by private authority in some particularly difficult case. The need for such exceptions arises from the fact that human laws are often imperfectly formulated, either because the legislator did not find the right words, or because certain instances which should or should not have been covered by the law (usually borderline cases) escaped his attention. In such instances the subject of the law is at times entitled to exempt himself from the law and to disregard it. The justification is ultimately the greater justice of the natural law. This doctrine will be discussed more in detail below in the section on human law.

If natural law is the justification for the use of epikeia with human laws, what could serve as justification for the use of epikeia with natural laws? In order to answer the question, a distinction must be made between the objective order of natural law on the one hand and the formulation of these laws in human words on the other. The objective order of natural law is the structure according to which man has been created. It is the work of God and does not permit of dispensations, as has been explained earlier. The formulations

---

[1] As another example can serve Jeanne D'Arc (†1431), who was ordered by heavenly voices to take charge of the French army at the age of 17 and to free the country from a long, disastrous occupation by the British. The same voices also ordered her to dress as a soldier and wear man's clothing. For any other woman of her time this would have been unthinkable and gravely scandalous. But unmistakable proofs confirmed the authentic character of her mission, e.g. she revealed secrets to the Dauphin Charles which he alone knew.

of natural law however are the work of man. They are subject to the imperfections of human language and insight in a similar way as the wordings of human laws are. In order to compensate for these imperfections, epikeia may at times be called for.[1]

Thus for example the majority of the traditional manuals of moral theology consider the prohibition of lying as a precept of natural law which permits of no exceptions. But if in a concrete case somebody is confronted with the alternative to save an innocent life by a lie or to give the would-be murderers the fatal information which they demand, many an upright person might feel justified in making an exception and telling a lie. He or she may come to the conclusion that the wording of the prohibition is too narrow and that the real demand of natural law, or the real will of God, in this particular case is different. The decision to resort to an exception in this situation is an instance of epikeia from natural law in the asserted, improper sense. It can be defined as an exception from the human wording of a natural law in a case of conflict where a person's conscience has gained the moral certainty that the wording is deficient and should not be applied. Of course the use of epikeia in such cases demands an upright sense of responsibility before God, the ultimate source of every moral obligation.

It ought to be noted that in contradistinction to human law, which of necessity is drawn up in human words and created for the greater part of the cases, the natural moral law is essentially an unwritten law and possesses all-inclusive validity. Epikeia in the latter case automatically leads to the alteration of the norm concerned. The natural moral law "is not after all drafted for the greater part of the cases, it claims a universal validity without exceptions".[2]

4. *Personal and situational character*

Traditionally the natural law doctrine only knows the three qualities dealt with so far. The fourth quality added here can be considered a fruit of the debate about situation

---

[1] This is also the opinion of J. Fuchs, "Epikeia Applied to Natural Law?", in *Personal Responsibility and Christian Morality* (Dublin: Gill and Macmillan, 1983), 185-199.

[2] K. Demmer, *l. c.* 70.

ethics in the years 1950-1970.[1] Situation ethics strongly emphasized, although in a one-tracked way, the uniqueness of any situation and of the person acting in it for the ascertainment of the moral demand. In studying the pertinent literature, it is surprising how widely scholars of ethics and moral theology are agreed in their conviction that situation ethics does not provide a sufficient basis for the moral life. But it is equally surprising how great a popularity situation ethics enjoyed at that time. Situation ethics could have hardly had such an appeal if it had been without any valid concerns at all. Indeed it contains some criticisms of traditional moral teaching which deserve to be taken seriously.

Natural moral law derives from the nature of man and his ultimate end. Inasmuch as this nature as well as the ultimate end are common to all men, one justly concludes to the universality of natural law. But beyond their common nature, humans also possess individual properties and talents, which make up their personal, unique nature. Likewise their contribution to the realization of the ultimate end is a unique calling. These features are equally the basis for moral obligations, yet obligations of a personal, unique kind. The awareness of these realities has led, in post-conciliar moral theology, to a noticeable shift of accent from "human nature" to the "human person". In the past one was easily inclined to the opinion that moral handbooks present the sum total of moral obligations and that persons who just fulfil these rules already have done their full duty. Handbooks however can only provide a framework of obligations derived from the common nature of men, insofar as this nature is more or less the same in all human beings. But they are not in a position to define those moral obligations which derive from the concrete uniqueness of each person. That means that the moral claims

---

[1] Existentialism by its nature inclines towards situation ethics; its most extreme exponent is J.P. Sartre. Situationist positions are also found in some Protestant authors, such as K. Barth, D. Bonhoeffer, P. Lehmann and R. Bultmann, and that with the argument that God's sovereign freedom cannot be bound by any moral code. The most popular champions of this ethics were J.A.T. Robinson, *Christian Morals Today* (London: SCM Press, 1966) and J. Fletcher, *Situation Ethics. The New Morality* (Philadelphia: Westminster Press, 1966); idem, *Moral Responsibility. Situation Ethics at Work* (Philadelphia: Westminster Press, 1967). They emphasize the unrepeatable, ever unique nature of the concrete answer of love.

addressed to the individual person are not just limited to what is written in the books. Karl Rahner calls this to mind in his treatment of an existential ethics.[1]

Beyond this, all morality also has situational elements of historical, cultural, social and other nature. Moral principles may not be applied mechanically to situations which are similar and yet not entirely equal. Situations have to be studied carefully before moral conclusions are drawn. It is necessary to gather relevant data, recognize facts and do empirical research before making a moral decision. Different circumstances may require different answers. Any parent who has brought up two children knows that the accomplishment of the same goal often requires some modification in approach because of differences in personality. "A sensitivity is therefore demanded for each particular situation, which makes the finding of the moral norm more laborious than one is generally ready to admit."[2]

On account of the reasons indicated, moral behaviour cannot be limited to a legalism, faithful to the mere letter of the law, but rather must be directed towards the realization of the comprehensive human values as well as to one's personal destination and calling. Here reference is also to be made to what has been said about the dialogical character of ethics in chapter one.

III. Existence and ultimate bases of natural law

The existence of a moral law is a universal experience of men. "Deep within his conscience man discovers a law which he has not laid upon himself but which he must obey.... For man has in his heart a law inscribed by God." According to it he will be judged (GS 16; cf. DH 3). This law is a natural endowment of man. It tells him of certain moral principles which he is bound to obey, independently of his individual will.

---

[1] K. Rahner, "On the Question of a Formal Existential Ethics," in *Theological Investigations*, vol. II (Baltimore: Helicon Press, 1963), 217-234.

[2] Johannes B. Lotz, "Philosophische Bemerkungen zum Finden und Gelten sittlicher Normen," in *Christlich glauben und handeln*, ed. by Klaus Demmer and Bruno Schüller (Düsseldorf: Patmos, 1977), 161.

Referring to the universal witness of conscience, Vatican II expresses its firm conviction of the existence and binding force of natural law, whose principles "spring from human nature itself" (DH 14; cf. GS 36). The Council "reminds men that the natural law of peoples and its universal principles still retain their binding force. The conscience of mankind firmly and ever more emphatically proclaims these principles" (GS 79). Everybody has to respect "the limits of the natural law", whether they are public authorities or individual citizens (GS 74). Holy Scripture itself expects and demands respect for this order from all men, Christians and non-Christians alike, as has been shown earlier.

The intrinsic reasons which confirm the existence of a natural moral law are two. The one is taken from the existence of a divine plan for this world, based upon God's eternal decrees; the other is inferred from the axiom "action follows being". Both require a detailed presentation. A discussion of the controversy about the deontological and teleological foundation of ethics shall follow.

1. *Natural law as reflection of God's eternal decrees*

Natural law, as moral law in general, has been defined as the law of human conduct ordering man's activity towards the ultimate end. This means to say that the moral law presupposes the existence of an ultimate end and of a purpose for the world. On the other hand it will also be true that, if there is an ultimate end and if the world has a purpose, this must necessarily result in a purposeful world order and a moral law for man. Moral theology of the past has developed this argument with the aid of the doctrine of the divine decrees. This is to be explained and unfolded in the following.

a) *Christian notion of divine decrees*. It is an essential part of Christian doctrine that God is the creator of the world. From eternity he sees all possible worlds in which his infinite perfection can be reflected. Yet he has freely chosen to create in time a particular world to share in his divine goodness and to manifest his glory. In his eternal vision God knows the all-embracing end of the whole world and the partial ends to be appointed for individual creatures. By his decrees, then, he settles that all things shall be created in such a way and with such abilities that through their appropriate activity they are able to contribute to the divine plan.

Thus the eternal plan and decrees of God - also called the eternal law - embrace absolutely all created operations and laws of operation: the activities which do not come within the scope of free will and those by which rational creatures move freely to their end; the necessary laws which govern the activities of irrational creatures and the moral laws which are to be observed freely. In the eternal plans and decrees of God, all the laws of nature and also the moral laws ultimately have their origin and consistency.

b) *Existence of divine plans and decrees*. Holy Scriptures are of the firm persuasion that God has a very well-defined plan for this world and above all for mankind. This plan has its aim in God's glory and universal reign and in the salvation of mankind, as has been shown above (cf. chapter I, pp. 39-53). Furthermore God's universal wisdom is regarded as the ultimate fount of the marvellous cosmic order in the world (Job 28:20-27; Wis 8:1; Sir 42:15-25) as well as of the moral order (Prov 8:14-36; Bar 4:1). Divine wisdom has judiciously "arranged all things by measure and number and weight" (Wis 11:20).

In regard to the proof from reason, the conviction that God rules the evolution of creation and no less the course of human history according to divine plans and decrees essentially springs from the thought that God as supremely wise cannot act without a plan. To do so would result in a desultoriness, impairing divine glory in a way unbecoming of God. Vatican II takes for granted the existence of a divine plan for the world and of corresponding laws. Individuals as well as communities have to conform their actions to them. Hence, the norm of human activity is this: "to harmonize with the authentic interests of the human race, in accordance with God's will and design, and to enable men as individuals and as members of society to pursue and fulfil their total vocation" (GS 35; also DH 3).

Another strong evidence for the existence of a purposeful world order and a plan underlying creation is taken from experience. This evidence is available and plain even to those who do not believe in God, if they look at reality without prejudice and keep their minds open to the truth. We observe in the cosmos and in human nature the working out of stable laws, creating and warranting meaningful interrelations between beings, and a wise ordering of the whole world. We likewise notice the process and aspiration of a surprisingly purposeful evolution in the history of creation and mankind. The deeper the human mind penetrates the mysteries of nature, the more wonders he discovers of an astoundingly wise order and marvellous interaction in the world.

c) *Moral law as consequence of God's plan and decrees.*
By the simple fact that a certain goal has to be reached, all those actions which are not conducive to the goal and which obstruct it are immediately and generally excluded as rejectable. Likewise the goal to be realized dictates, at least in a general way, the positive steps which have to be taken in order to achieve the task.[1] If therefore the world has been created according to a certain plan for a purpose to be realized, this will necessarily include a law of action and operation for all that exists, obviously also for men. From the existential destination of men and women to the service of God's purpose, a law of action necessarily results for them which they must follow if they are to fulfil the tasks assigned to them. The existence of a divine plan for this world involves the existence of a law or order in nature that makes the realization of this plan feasible and that guarantees it. In the case of men, and in harmony with their nature, this order has to be investigated and obeyed in free and responsible decision. This is the moral order or moral law. It is a natural moral law because it does not owe its existence to a supernatural revelation, but to a finality inherent in the nature of creation.

2. *Natural law as based on the order of being*

a) General implication of the axiom
"action follows being"

The axiom "action follows being" (*agere sequitur esse*) is one of the ultimate ontological principles, which admit of no further proof in the strict sense, but which can only be explained in order to show their evidence. The meaning of

---

[1] See the party-politics of communism, which decides what is lawful or rejectable by the criterion whether a certain conduct serves the aims of the party or not.

the axiom can be that action is later in temporal and logical sequence than being. But of interest in this context is the other meaning, that the quality of an action is determined by the quality of the being which is its cause, or that a thing acts according to its nature.

The origin of an action is the nature of a thing, while the action is that which is caused. In other words, the nature of a thing is the cause, and the action is the effect. Yet according to the principle that nothing is without sufficient reason (*nihil sine causa sufficiente*), every effect must find its sufficient reason in its cause. Hence action must find its sufficient reason in that being which is its cause. This means, negatively formulated, that action cannot be of another nature than its cause. It cannot be of a different or more comprehensive quality than its source. Positively formulated, action must be of the same nature as its cause. Rightly it has been said that no philosophy could deny this scholastic axiom, at least not practically.[1]

In all beings the activity is conditioned and determined by being, that is, by the proper nature of a thing and its relation to the world about it. In non-rational beings this determination is of compulsive character. Nature is for them a necessitating norm. Not so with man. He is not totally bound by necessity to the norm of his own being. With regard to the actions subject to his free will, he can freely comply with the norm he recognizes or deliberately ignore it. However he cannot ignore the laws of his being without suffering the negative consequences of such discord. A man can choose to take heroin. But if he does so, he will ruin his health and life. He can disregard the laws of static calculation, but the building will collapse.

b) Application to human activity

In this context we are only concerned with man's free, moral activity. According to the axiom "action follows being", man's moral obligation must be derived from and measured by the nature of his being. Man's nature is taken here in its broadest meaning, with all its natural and supernatural constituents and endowments. Applied to actions of the moral

---

[1] B. Häring, *The Law of Christ* I, 1966, 228.

order, then, the axiom could be formulated: The order of action must correspond to the order of being; or: The ought rests on what is.

Accordingly men must act in harmony with their nature. A contrary attitude is condemned to frustration, failure and defeat, since it attempts actions for which the means do not exist or which do not find the necessary preconditions in nature to be efficient and sensible and therefore turn out to be preposterous. Hence the law of human action is determined by human nature, and this is universally true for all human actions, the free actions included. Consequently there is a natural moral law.

The task of ethics and moral theology is to recognize the human beings as they really are in their true nature with all their essential relations, and to derive therefrom the moral laws which are to direct their activity. There cannot be any doubt that men have many qualities and conditions in common. This must result in corresponding common obligations, which can be formulated in general laws. The individuality of a person of course, by which he or she differs from other humans, will be the source of individual obligations not comprehensible by general laws. Yet these peculiar, personal calls will certainly not contradict those general obligations which result from the nature a person has in common with others.

It is also a matter of fact that nature at the same time shows constancy and mutability. This means that moral law is immutable and mutable insofar as nature in general and human nature in particular are immutable and mutable. Therefore philosophers and theologians justifiably point to the historicity of moral law and demand that its historical relativity must be taken into consideration.

The order of being also comprises the inclinations and aspirations of nature which strive to effectuate their corresponding goals. The knowledge of just these inclinations and aspirations is of greatest importance for the formulation of the moral imperative.[1] And here again we meet with man's relation to God and with his existential orientation towards the ultimate goal. Man does not bear the ultimate meaning within himself, but can only be understood in his relation to God and to the

---
[1] Cf. the existential ends, p. 99.

divinely established plan, to the realization of which he is called to contribute. From this existential reference it follows that man may not merely look at the given, concretely existing nature of himself and the surrounding world for the deduction of the moral law. This is only one of the constituent principles of the moral order, the ontological determinant. He must never fail to look, at the same time, to the goal he is assigned to promote and to realize and for which he is ultimately destined. This is the other constituent principle, the teleological and eschatological determinant.

c) Hume's critique and an answer to it

The basic thrust of the argument just developed is, that the moral law is inherent in the structures of nature, just as physical or biological laws are inherent in it. The careful study of nature, and in particular of men's nature, reveals these structures and enables them to know the moral laws which must govern their actions. From the existing facts of reality conclusions are drawn as to what men ought to do.

Against this form of argumentation Hume raised an objection in his "Treatise" of 1739-40, which objection has become known as the principle "no ought from an is".[1] His argument is that one cannot conclude from what actually is to what morally ought to be. While this objection has enjoyed much discussion in philosophical quarters of the English speaking world, it has found surprisingly little attention among philosophers outside it. Catholic moral theology did not attend to it either until very recently. Nevertheless it is an objection which merits to be taken seriously and to be discussed.

The problem is this. The study of nature reveals the laws according to which beings function, the purposes for which they are made, and the good or bad consequences a certain way of conduct will have. Thus for example the study of nature reveals that a house built on sand without foundations will not last; or that teeth are made for chewing food and not stones. These observations present facts. They state what is or what will come to be if certain actions are done and certain conditions fulfilled.

---

[1] David Hume, *A Treatise of Human Nature*, book III, part I, section I, at the end.

Now Hume objects that from these facts no definite conclusions can be drawn as to what men morally ought to do. From the existence of certain laws of nature, from the purposes of certain beings, and from the bad consequences of a certain action one cannot conclude to the moral obligation to respect these laws and purposes and to avoid the bad consequences. Why could we not at times build houses without foundation? Why should we not use our teeth for biting through wires? The answer shall be given in three steps.

(1) The use of things according to their intrinsic laws and purposes guarantees their serviceable and efficient use. Contrary use frustrates and destroys them. If teeth are used for cutting wires, they will be destroyed. Everybody must agree that it is not reasonable to act like this. The duty of reasonable, purposeful, efficient use of beings is an immediate awareness of all normal men. Therefore men readily conclude from the knowledge of the purpose of a thing to the moral obligation of a corresponding, good use. This conclusion is generally correct. Nevertheless one can also conceive of exceptions. If one can save one's life by cutting with one's teeth a wire which is meant to explode a bomb, one may do so, even at the risk of breaking them. And quite in general the question arises why it is unreasonable to frustrate or destroy things. What is the deeper reason?

(2) The realization of man's existential ends is the reason why a purposeful use of beings and things is demanded. A contrary use will impair these ends. The existential ends have been outlined earlier. Briefly they are: self-preservation; self-perfection; procreation and education of children; concern and care for one's fellow-men; social fellowship for the common good; communion with God. The useless and dangerous construction of a building without foundation on sand, especially if it is a bigger one, contradicts the purposes of self-preservation and care for one's fellow-men. The arbitrary destruction of one's teeth contradicts the existential end of self-preservation.

Occasionally however the existential ends can also justify the use of a thing against its nature, namely if this were to serve these ends better. The mentioned instance of cutting a wire with one's teeth in order to save one's life, even though it will destroy them, is justified by the purpose of self-preser-

Nature of the Moral Law 125

vation as well. Self-preservation is served by many goods, and in a conflict, the more urgent good prevails over the lesser one.

But a further question is still to be answered. Why must the existential ends be respected and promoted? Why are they valued?

(3) The final answer is found in man's ultimate end. The existential ends must be respected and are values because through their furtherance the ultimate end is promoted, i.e. God's glory, his kingdom and the unfolding of his creation. Particular tasks implied in this end are, as explained above in detail (pp. 45-46), the subjection of the earth, the development of the human person, the promotion of social values and the union of love among all mankind. Ultimately then that use of beings and functions is good which best serves and promotes the purpose of God's plans. (The ultimate end is also the arbiter in cases of conflict between two existential ends, as already mentioned earlier.)

The ultimate end is the ultimate norm for the appropriate use of beings and things. As a rule the ultimate end is best served by the use of things according to their inherent purposes; therefore this use is obligatory. This obligation is favoured by presumption; it does not demand a special proof in each case. Occasionally however the ultimate end may be served better by the use of a thing against its nature, as in using one's teeth for cutting a fatal wire. Such a practice is likewise justified and often even demanded. But since this is the exception, it has the burden of proof.

Conclusion. Natural law doctrine formulates the principle: the order of action must correspond to the order of being. Or, the norm for human activity is determined by the nature of man himself and the nature of those beings to which his activity is related.

Negatively formulated, this means to say: In his actions men may never ignore the nature and laws of beings, i.e. they must always take them into account. A man may construct a house on sand, risking its collapse (e.g. for the production of a movie); but he must know what this implies. Positively stated: Men must act in harmony with the laws of beings, as long as the still higher law of the ultimate end does not demand something else. In following the laws of nature, men usually act well.

But it does not mean that nature provides the exclusive basis for the moral norms, or even only for some of them. This presupposed, Hume's principle "no ought from an is" indeed contains a valid insight. From the existing reality of nature alone no final conclusions can be drawn with regard to the moral obligations. The additional criterion of the ultimate end is required to gain these conclusions.

If however Hume's principle were to mean that the study of existing reality is of no avail for the elaboration of the moral norms, this would be a graver error still than the one criticized by him. Maybe the obvious falseness of such an assumption explains why many philosophers and theologians did not take Hume's objection seriously. Definitely the study of nature provides much data and many patterns and finalities which are truly relevant for the moral norm and constitutive for it. The norms for man's actions are indeed derived from the nature of beings, although not from it alone.

3. *Deontological and teleological foundation of moral norms*

The discussion about the deontological and teleological foundation of moral norms began in the years around 1970. It is a debate about the foundation and justification of moral norms. Even if the discussion in the meantime has abated, the issue is important enough to be presented and discussed in some detail.[1]

a) *Clarification of terms*. The terms "deontological" and "teleological" were first combined and contrasted in 1930 by C.D. Broad.[2] Deontological theories (from the Greek *deon* = duty) maintain that there are certain acts which are always

---

[1] A helpful collection of some basic articles and studies on the issue is found in C.E. Curran and R.A. McCormick, eds., *Readings in Moral Theology No. 1: Moral Norms and Catholic Tradition* (New York: Paulist Press, 1979).

[2] C.D. Broad, *Five Types of Ethical Theory* (New York: Harcourt Brace, ³1944), esp. 206-216.

ethically right or wrong, no matter what their consequences, e.g. suicide, abortion, adultery, rape, denial of faith, breach of the confessional secret, etc. Such absolute prohibitions are today often called "moral absolutes". Teleological theories (from the Greek *telos* = goal) on the other hand hold that the rightness or wrongness of an action is exclusively or at least decisively determined by the good or evil consequences which an action produces. All other considerations remain subordinate to this criterion. As long as the good consequences prevail over the bad ones, the action is ethically right. Thus, e.g., the suicide of a spy is morally right if this is the only safe means to safeguard vital, national secrets. Purely deontological and purely teleological theories are however ideal types. Most ethical theories are mixed theories, sometimes predominantly deontological and sometimes predominantly teleological.

The teleological theory, often also called proportionalism or consequentialism, is sometimes equated with utilitarianism.[1] If the equation is correct, all the arguments which militate against utilitarianism will also militate against the teleological theory. In fact the same objections have been repeatedly raised against both.[2]

However there are authors who maintain, and it seems correctly so, that utilitarianism is only one form of teleology. It is that form which seeks the good in temporal types of pleasure and happiness. It must be distinguished from other forms, particularly from Thomistic teleology, which seeks the good in quite a different end of man, namely in God's glory and reign. This distinction merits greater attention than it has

---

[1] B. Schüller takes this equation for granted and himself advocates a consequently teleological approach in the ethical argumentation (*Die Begründung sittlicher Urteile*. 1980, 286f). Definitely teleological are also the approaches of Franz Scholz ("Sittliche Normen in teleologischer Sicht," in *Stimmen der Zeit* 201, 1983, 707f) and Rudolf Ginters (*Werte und Normen*. Düsseldorf: Patmos, 1982, 193-195; 214).

[2] See John R. Connery, "Morality of Consequences: A Critical Appraisal," in *Readings in Moral Theology No. 1*, l. c. 244-266, and Harald Oberhem, "Teleologische Normenbegründung? Kritische Anmerkungen zu einem moraltheologischen Programm," *Theologie und Glaube* 71 (1981), 280-316.

received until now.[1] Differences in the definition of the ultimate goal quite naturally must result in differences between the teleological theories. The reason is that the ultimate goal at the same time serves as the ultimate criterion for the evaluation of the consequences of an act. If the criterion differs, the evaluation will also differ. Accordingly there are as many different forms of teleology as there are substantially different definitions of the ultimate end.

In the following, the arguments for the deontological and teleological theories shall be presented. It is interesting to note that each of the theories principally bases itself on one of the two arguments used above to prove the existence of natural law. The deontological theory bases itself chiefly on the argument from the order of being (at least in Catholic moral theology), the teleological theory on the argument from the final goal of man and creation.

b) *Argument in favour of deontology.* The principal argument for deontological norms is taken from the existence of an order of nature. All beings are equipped with their own qualities and faculties, which enable them to perform the tasks proper to them and - in the case of living beings - to provide for their existence. An analysis of these qualities and faculties and of the laws according to which they function permits conclusions as to the correct and rightful treatment and use of beings, including the treatment and use of man's own being, organs and functions. From there corresponding moral obligations result, because the correct, appropriate use of beings and respect for their nature are not left to the free discretion of men, but are moral duties.

The study of the nature of beings and especially of men, moreover, gives insights into the rights they can claim (and naturally also into the correlative duties they have). Thus women have the same rights as men, not primarily because this will produce good consequences, but because both possess the same nature and dignity. Cretins have the right to life as much as other human beings, because they share the same

---

[1] Cf. Lisa Sowle Cahill, "Teleology, Utilitarianism and Christian Ethics," *Theological Studies* 41 (1981), 605; 627-9. Idem, "Contemporary Challenges to Exceptionless Moral Norms," *Moral Theology Today. Certitudes and Doubts*, essays by various authors, Saint Louis, Mo.: The Pope John Center, 1984, 128f. See also the discussion in the same book, p. 201.

nature. Commutative justice demands equivalence between service and remuneration, as required by the natural law principle "to each one his own". God is to be worshipped, because man is his creature and subject and therefore must revere and obey him.

An analysis of the finalities and purposes of things permits conclusions as to their inherent needs and purposes. If these inherent needs and purposes are disregarded, the consequences will indeed be damaging and fateful. But one has not to wait for the bad consequences, in order to come to this conclusion. A watch is made to indicate the time. A simple study of its nature will reveal that one cannot use it as a hammer without destroying it. A knife is not made for eating soup; one can know it beforehand. The nose is not made for the intake of solid food; one does not need an experiment to know that an attempt to do so will clog it.

There is a common sense awareness which says: If things are treated and used according to their nature, they will serve men best. If however they are used in contradiction to their nature, they prove inefficient and often will be damaged or destroyed.

Does this mean that one may never use a thing contrary to its nature and thereby perhaps risk its destruction? This conclusion is often drawn, but it is not entirely correct, as has become clear in the discussion of Hume's objection. This is the limitation of the argument. From the laws and working mechanisms of nature alone no immediate conclusions can be drawn as to what is morally correct and right. That means to say, in order to safeguard a good of greater value than the one endangered by the "unnatural" use of a thing, one may resort to such a use. However such an onerous use is the exception and not the rule; therefore it needs a special justification. As long as the justification of an exception remains doubtful and is not morally certain, the duty to abide by the nature-ordained purposes and rights prevails. The moral certainty to the contrary must be the greater the higher the value is which is at stake.

In the realm of non-human goods such a proceeding has indeed always been admitted. Even though a watch will be destroyed if it is used as a hammer, one may use it like this if one can thus fix a hole in a lifeboat and save the passengers.

Objections have been raised and are raised if a human faculty or organ are used against their nature. Yet in principle one will have to admit exceptions also here. Even if a lie should contradict the faculty of language, many nevertheless consider it permitted if by means of it an innocent human life can be saved. Even if the function of the kidneys is the preservation of one's own life, it is allowed to sacrifice one in order to save another person's life.

The reservation that a higher value may justify the use of a thing contrary to its nature introduces, it has to be realized, a deliberation of teleological and consequentialist character. Deontological considerations alone are accordingly not sufficient for the foundation of the moral norm. This however is not something novel for Catholic moral theology, whether old or new. The only question is to what extent teleological considerations have to be taken into account. This has to be examined in the following.

c) *Argument in favour of teleology.* The argument in support of the teleological theory is rarely expressly formulated. It seems so simple and evident that it does not need much formulation and underpinning. Its thrust is that, confronted with two evils, one most choose the lesser one, or confronted with two good options, one must choose the better one. Faced with the loss of one innocent life or two, one must choose the loss of one life only. Confronted with the choice of building one school for 200 or another for 500 students, one must build the one for 500. Of course not only the immediate consequences have to be weighed, but also the indirect and remote ones. If the school for 200 students at the same time pacifies a disgruntled minority, it may after all constitute the greater value which has to be preferred.

The question of the consequences of a norm or of an action is a fundamental question of moral responsibility. Whoever loves his neighbour, must also be accountable for the consequences of his or her actions. "Seen in this way, the teleological idea definitely pertains to the inner circle of ethics.... Where the consequences of an action are taken into account, a person remains linked to concrete reality. There is a constant feedback from the actual conditions. One is more readily in a condition to verify the correctness of norms and decisions."[1] Consequently by the nature of its approach the teleological theory feels obliged to accord experience the place due to it in the drawing up of moral norms, be it one's own experience or that of others, or that of past generations (in the tradition).

The most decisive problem in the teleological argument is the criterion according to which the various values are weighed. If a member of a totalitarian party is commanded to shoot one of its ideological enemies, may he do so? If the criterion is the continued strength and victory of the party, the answer will be yes.[2] But if the criterion is the full reality of truth and the comprehensive good of all mankind, the answer will be no.

It is evident that the ultimate criterion for judging the good and evil consequences of alternative actions is that value which is considered the highest of all by a person or system. This however implies "that the discussion of the consequences already takes place under the supposition and influence of speculative evaluations and assumptions".[3] The question of the ultimate value of the moral demand has been discussed and answered in the previous chapter. For Christian theology it is the realization of God's glory and salvific reign and the unfolding of his creative plan for this world. What this more concretely implies, has also been explained earlier (cf. pp. 45f).

But it has also become clear, in the study of the ultimate end, that men only have an approximate knowledge of God's designs and eternal purpose. Therefore the use of this criterion is not just as simple and plain as the application of a metric measure. Although this criterion gives a definite orientation, it also often leaves men searching for the most appropriate answer.

A frequent objection against a purely consequentialist approach to the moral norm is the difficulty, first, of knowing all the proximate and remote consequences of an individual action and, second, of weighing them appropriately. The knowledge of the consequences to a high degree depends on

---

[1] H. Weber, *Allgemeine Moraltheologie* (Graz: Styria, 1991), 141.

[2] The attempted assassination of Pope John Paul II during an audience in St. Peter's Square on May 13, 1981, may well have been the conspiracy of a totalitarian system.

[3] H. Weber, *l. c.* 169.

contingent, empirical insights and information. In principle this makes the norms thus gained less certain. Arguments from the nature of beings on the other hand are less subject to such contingencies. True, they also require a certain amount of empirical knowledge; that amount which is necessary for a sufficient understanding of the nature of those beings with which moral laws are dealing. But the knowledge needed is not as vast as that required for a purely consequentialist evaluation.

In the search for the moral norm men accordingly stand in need of all the aids available to them. One of the aids remains the study of the nature of things and their inherent laws and purposes. These laws and purposes however are by no means alien to the ultimate end. Rather men and all beings have been equipped with them precisely in view of that end which they are called to serve and to realize. Since these laws and purposes are endowments for the realization of the ultimate end, their observance will benefit humans and creation by an inner necessity and logic. Experience confirms it: in respecting these laws and purposes, men usually fare well.

d) *Complementary character of the two forms of argumentation.* Also traditional moral theology admits that there is only one supreme and highest norm of morality, just as there is only one ultimate goal of men. This supreme norm is the whole-hearted love of God and neighbour. The ultimate criterion for the moral value of an action is whether it contributes to God's creative and salvific plan or not; whether it promotes the human community in accordance with God's calling or not.

As the supreme norm, this criterion has absolute character. It does not admit of exceptions. Are there, besides it, still other norms of absolute character? This is possible, but on condition that they derive their validity from the supreme, ultimate norm of morality. Prohibitions of actions which always contradict the love of God and neighbour possess, in a derived and secondary way, absolute character themselves. This is true, for example, of the absolute prohibition of the seduction of others to sin.

On the other hand it is not possible to establish norms with absolute character which do not derive their existence from the above mentioned absolute norm, but from other

Nature of the Moral Law 133

sources. They are not in a condition to legitimate their claim of *absolute* authority; unsolvable tensions and collisions must be the consequence. On account of their different origin, a complete harmony and accord of the norms is not guaranteed. Men find themselves exposed to diverse norms of absolute character, which in instances of conflict cannot all be satisfied at the same time. Since all claim absolute authority, none can be sacrificed, which however is required because of the conflict.

For example, those who regard the prohibition of lying as an absolute, exceptionless obligation (as Kant and many, especially older, Catholic theologians do), cannot permit a lie even in defence of the lives of innocents, persecuted by a hostile government, be they Jews, deformed children destined for euthanasia or involved Christians. But would fraternal love not demand the defence of the innocent? The person who subscribes to the absolute prohibition of lying is confronted by the unsolvable dilemma between a moral principle of deontological nature and the precept of fraternal love. Absolutes of this kind are the ones which leave the "fatal impression that the faithful observance of this claim of an absoluteness without exception in certain cases increases suffering and evil in the world, while the moral norms as God's commandments after all ought to help people to realize life·in a fuller way".[1]

The result of the preceding deliberations is that norms with absolute character are possible, and in this there is agreement with tradition. But they are possible only on teleological grounds, and in this there is agreement with the recent theologians. Absolutes of this kind accordingly may never only describe the object of an act (as the deontologically grounded absolutes of traditional morality did), but must always also include the purpose of the act and therewith a teleological element. Such absolutes are, e.g., "It is wrong to lie in order to enrich oneself with alien goods." "It is wrong to beat a child for reasons of sadistic pleasure." "It is wrong to abort a foetus to avoid social embarrassment."

All these considerations argue in favour of a teleological position. However there are also important factors of deon-

---

[1] H. Altmeyer, "Gott als Gesetzgeber und Garant des Sittengesetzes," in *Schuld, Sühne und Erlösung*, ed. by K.J. Rivinius (Steyler Verlag, 1983), 79.

tological nature, and entirely indispensable ones, which have to be taken into account. A very important element of deontological nature is the supreme criterion of morality, the ultimate end, which is itself not established teleologically but by deontological affirmation and reasoning. Furthermore, as has been shown earlier, the study of the nature of beings provides essential information as to their most efficient use and as to the inherent needs and rights of humans, while a treatment of things contrary to their nature is condemned to inefficiency and often enough has injuries in its train. Such drawbacks and detriments have to be avoided as far as possible. This establishes a presumption in favour of the duty to treat and use things according to their nature and to respect the rights of others. The basis of this presumption is of a deontological nature.

Affirmation of these deontological factors as essential for moral deliberation on the one hand and endorsement of man's ultimate end as the supreme criterion of morality on the other would make it meaningful to speak of a position of moderate teleology. But the position outlined is also well characterised by the term Thomistic-Christian teleology.[1] In order to justify this terminology, however, a slight modification or at least a further specification of the usual definition of teleological theories is required. These theories should not be understood as systems which determine the morality of an action so exclusively by consequences that no room at all is left for deontological considerations. Such considerations remain essential and indispensable. But the last decision whether deontologically established rules are to be followed, as favoured by presumption, or whether in exceptional cases they should be overridden, is made solely by the criterion of the ultimate end. No doubt, only in this sense a Thomistic-Christian teleology is conceivable. This presupposed, the term describes the proposition here under discussion best.

In summary, then, the judgment on the morality of an action is not possible without a careful study of the nature of beings, i.e. without due consideration of the deontological factors involved. Much less is it possible without proper regard for the demands of the ultimate end, i.e. without due con-

---

[1] The terms Thomistic and Christian teleology are used by Lisa S. Cahill, *Theological Studies* 42 (1981), 605 and 629.

sideration of the teleological criterion of the moral law. Accordingly the deontological and teleological argumentation stand in need of each other. They are not mutually exclusive but of a complementary character.

D. Human law

The treatise on human law deals with the juridical order of society, be it the state or be it the Church (or similar religious bodies), insofar as this order is determined by laws which are enacted for the common good. It is not necessary that this law be a written code. It may consist of unwritten legal traditions and customs, especially in primitive societies. Nevertheless the laws of practically all civil communities of today are written codes, as is the law of the Church.

I. Notion and necessity of human law

1. *Concept and properties of human law*

a) The time-honoured *definition* of law by Thomas Aquinas is: law is an ordinance of reason for the common good, promulgated by him who has the care of the community.[1]

Law is an ordinance, i.e. it induces an obligation and is not merely a counsel. - It is an ordinance of reason, because it must be based on the insights of reason into what is good for the community. The mere will of a lawgiver is not sufficient reason for a valid law, nor are emotion and sentiments. - Laws can only be enacted for the common good and not for the private good of a few citizens. Even if a law concerns solely a smaller group of citizens, e.g. lawyers or teachers, the purpose of the law must in the last analysis be for the good of the whole community. - Promulgation is the official publication of a law so that it can come to the knowledge of the subjects. Promulgation is necessary in order that a law becomes obligatory. - Laws can only be enacted by those who have the care of the community, i.e. by those who are in charge of it as the legitimate authority.

The above definition defines law in a wide sense, insofar as ordinances also include temporary injunctions and individual orders, while law in the strict sense is a directive of obligatory,

---
[1] *S. Th.* I-II, q. 90, a. 4.

general and stable character. The definition also includes statutes and precepts of lesser communities, such as religious communities or even the family, since it refers to ordinances of anybody who is in charge of a community. However laws in the strict sense are those enacted by sovereign societies. Scholastic theology calls them "perfect" societies, because they are not in need of still other, higher societies to secure their goals, and in this sense are self-sufficient. Such societies are the state and the Church, the one in charge of men's temporal welfare, the other of their spiritual good. Finally it may not be necessary to define law as an ordinance of reason in order to preclude emotion or human caprice as sources of human laws, since this is sufficiently done by the determination that laws must be enacted for the common good.

Keeping these considerations in mind as well as the wording chosen for the definition of moral law at the beginning of this chapter, an alternative definition of human law might be: a directive of obligatory, general and stable character for the common good promulgated by him who is in charge of a sovereign society.

Precepts, statutes, orders differ from laws insofar as they are limited to smaller groups, often to individuals only, or, if imposed upon a public community, are merely temporary injunctions. Furthermore private authorities (parents, religious superiors, etc.) can also enjoin them. Under the moral aspect however there is hardly any difference between this group of ordinances and human laws.

b) *The properties of human law* serve to clarify its concept still further. A first essential property of human law is that it can be enforced. Second, human law is limited to external conduct only. Three further properties are formulated parallel and in contradistinction to the three traditional properties of natural law.

(1) Human law is *enforceable*. The reason is that coercion is necessary to compel also those members of society to obedience who tend to be lawless.[1] Without the coercive power of the law, the law-abiding subjects would be placed at a serious disadvantage, exposed to exploitation by those

---
[1] Thomas Aquinas, *S. Th.* I-II, l. 95, a. 1; q. 96, a. 5.

who are lawless, and ultimately impelled to abandon the law themselves. This must result in the collapse of the legal order. Obviously this would contradict its necessity. Yet for the sake of an equitable administration of justice, the exercise of coercive power is not a matter for the individual, but for the public authority alone, exceptions apart.

(2) Human law is *concerned with external conduct only*. The inner disposition, which is essential for moral conduct, is outside the scope of human laws. "Social order, which is the purpose of law, is guaranteed when the external conduct of the members of society is in harmony with the legal rules. Social order does not depend upon whether the motive of this conduct is consideration for others or fear of punishment."[1] Doubtless the proper motivation of subjects in their compliance with the law remains of great interest for the legislator as well. "The common good is certainly more perfectly realized when society is ruled more by love of justice than by fear of the police."[2] Legislators therefore can only welcome the efforts of those who strengthen the moral will of the subjects. But apart from the fact that human authorities are not able to judge internal dispositions, external compliance with the law suffices to secure the social order and the common good.

(3) Human law is *limited to particular groups* of people, in contradistinction to natural law, which is universal. Human laws oblige only those who are members of the community for which the laws are enacted. They are binding only upon the subjects of a particular state or union of states, such as the EU, or of a religious body like the Church.

(4) Human law is *historically conditioned*, much more so than natural law. As societies and their civilizations change, human laws inevitably change with them. Beside evolution, also social factors are a weighty reason for the contingent character of human laws. "In most cases the positive law enacted after the period of customary law, was effected by politically dominant groups to a greater or lesser extent in

---

[1] J. Messner, *Social Ethics*, 1965, 165.
[2] *Ib.* 165.

their own interest."[1] The actual legal order is seldom, if ever, the outcome of purely legal reasoning. It is likewise the expression of class relationships and compromises between contrary interests. Therefore it never embodies perfect justice. Nevertheless it has binding force for the sake of the common good, as long as it realizes a minimum of justice and order. However those in charge of the community have the obligation to adapt the law ever anew and ever more perfectly to the needs of the changing conditions and the demands of greater justice.

(5) Human law has *presumptive obligatory force*, but is open to exceptions and dispensations, in contradistinction to natural law. If the common good is to be secured and realized, subjects cannot be entitled to disobedience whenever they merely doubt the utility or justice of a law. Rather presumption favours the duty to obey the law. On the other hand, if a law is recognized as certainly unjust or detrimental, it does not oblige, at least as a rule. Furthermore in many instances authorities are entitled to grant exceptions or dispensations from the laws, e.g. by pardoning a delinquent. And if epikeia is a right of individuals in cases of imperfect formulations of natural law, it is such a right even more so with regard to human laws. Because of the importance of the question of epikeia, it shall be dealt with separately below.

2. Attitude of the New Testament to human law

When St. James says: "There is one lawgiver" (Jas 4:12), he does not thereby reject human law as superfluous, but indicates its supreme source. (This idea is most clearly expressed in Prov 8:15: "By me kings reign, and rulers decree what is just.") Moreover, although human laws are directly enacted to guarantee and to promote the common weal, their ultimate purpose is no less the final goal as established in Christ than it is the ultimate purpose of all responsible human activity. Since therefore God is the supreme source and ultimate goal of human law, the dialogical character of morality is also preserved in the obedience towards human laws.

---

[1] *Ib.* 187.

Nature of the Moral Law 139

Christ himself in his life and teaching gives us an example of obedience to civil law as well as to the cultic precepts of his people. When he was asked about the poll tax (Mk 12:13-17), i.e. whether it was lawful to pay taxes to Caesar, or not, Christ's answer was: "Render to Caesar the things that are Caesar's, and to God the things that are God's." Jesus' judgment was that the tax should be paid, although such obedience must not conflict with the rights of God. In other words, Jesus recognized the emperor's right to expect compliance with the laws from his subjects. The state, even the pagan state, has its importance in its own sphere, which is the common good. But Jesus makes it also clear that the state must lastly remain subordinate to God's will and depends on God's authority. He recognizes the jurisdiction of Pilate, even if he contests the justice of his judgment, and submits to the iniquitous verdict of death to the extreme of unresisting submission to it. In the same way Jesus pays the temple tax (Mt 17:24-27). He makes the pilgrimage to the temple at the prescribed liturgical times. He observes the Sabbath, though not in the barren formalism of the scribes.

The early Church adopted the same attitude to the public authorities as Christ did. Although reserved towards the Jewish authorities, and becoming increasingly independent of them, the early Church shows a striking loyalty to the Roman state and its institutions. Despite Paul's not always satisfactory experiences with the Roman authorities, there is not a word in his writings against the empire. On the contrary, there is the well known passage in Romans 13:1-7, which binds Christians in conscience to obey the government of the state. "Let every person be subject to the governing authorities. For there is no authority except from God, and those that exist have been instituted by God. Therefore he who resists the authorities resists what God has appointed." The public authority is God's servant for the common good. "Therefore one must be subject, not only to avoid God's wrath but also for the sake of conscience." Hence the Christian is to give what he owes the state authorities, and that is obedience, payment of taxes and respect. The same exhortations to reverence and obedience to public authorities are found in 1 Peter 2:13-17, where honouring the king is put next to fearing God. "Fear God. Honour the emperor." Similar exhortations are found in Titus 3:1-2, while in 1 Timothy 2:1-3 particular prayers for the authorities are recommended. We are probably dealing with a common topic in early Christian homilies.[1]

The religious Jewish authorities were soon replaced by the religious authority of the new Christian Church. Christ himself had conferred upon the apostles and their successors the task of governance over his Church. "He who hears you hears me" (Lk 10:16). "As the Father has sent me, even so I send you" (Jn 20:21, cf. Mt. 16:19; 18:18; 28:20). When the Jewish authorities tried to silence the apostles by a strict prohibition to continue their preaching of Christ and his Gospel, the apostles answer with a statement that is the moral basis for all resistance against unjust authority and immoral laws: "We must obey God rather than men" (Acts 5:29; also 4:19f).

3. Necessity of human law according to reason

Stable social norms are indispensable for peaceable communal life. They co-ordinate the activities of the many. They "provide the individual with the opportunity to acquire modes of behaviour that as a rule have every chance of success and set him free from his search for the best possible solution. They also make it possible for human relationships to be lasting and set man free from uncertainty with regard to the other's behaviour. In other words, norms and institutions are fundamental legal goods and man is dependent on them."[2] Although natural moral law also lays down man's social obligations, it alone is not sufficient to ensure the order of social life, especially not of the corporate life of bigger societies. This order can only be secured by human laws, and this for the following reasons.

(1) Natural law is frequently not so evident and clear in its particular requirements for everybody. What for example are the demands with regard to the equal rights of all members of a civil community, men and women, white and black alike? Or what are the rights of authors concerning their inventions, writings and compositions? Human laws clarify such uncer-

---
[1] Cf. R. Schnackenburg, *The Moral Teaching of the New Testament* (London: Burns and Oates, 1967), 235-244.

[2] F. Böckle, *Fundamental Moral Theology*, (New York: Pueblo Publishing Co., 1980), 205.

tainties. They make clear the requirements of natural law, also in its remote conclusions, for everybody.

(2) Human laws are needed to determine the concrete norms of conduct where the natural moral law can be complied with in different ways. Often several possible ways are open to comply with a social need, e.g. in matters of traffic laws, prescription of property rights, rulings for public worship, etc. It is not that natural law is totally indefinite concerning these issues. As to the regulation of traffic, e.g., it definitely demands that the safety of the road user be guaranteed. This can be done by right or by left side traffic. The legislator is free to choose one of the two alternatives; but his options are limited to one of the two. At other times of course also more options are available, but they are always limited. Within the frame demarcated by natural law, the choices of the social ordering power are very much a question of expediency, governed by the preferences of a society for certain values. But a decision is necessary to make a final choice, and this provision is made by means of human laws. At the same time the relative variability of human laws cautions that culturally conditioned variations of the same must not be absolutized. Equally the changing conditions of life demand always again revisions and adaptations of the laws to the new circumstances.

(3) Human law is finally necessary to secure the protection of those values which are of greater moment for the common weal. The sanctions attached to human laws are an indispensable means of education for men in their frailty and a shield against human malice. Were there no legal restraints checking the abuse of freedom and the violence on the part of evil men, the uprightly minded would be robbed of their liberty to act by law and public order would cease to exist.

II. Object and substantive justice of the law

a) *The object of human legislation in general* is, in harmony with the definition of human law, the common welfare. Human legislation has to safeguard and promote the common weal (1) by defining the rights and duties which the members of a society possess and by securing the realm of freedom needed to comply with the responsibilities founded upon man's existential ends; (2) by protecting the interior peace and order of the society and establishing external security; (3) by creating favourable conditions for social and economic progress and for the cultural, moral and religious life.

This implies that the will of the lawgiver is not the exclusive nor even the primary basis of the legal order. The criterion for the common good consists in the realization of objective, individual and social ends, which are binding for the lawgiver in the enactment of legal norms. "Enacted law is true law insofar as it conforms with the pattern of ends indicated in the essential reality of human nature and with the responsibilities based on this pattern."[1] This reality also includes man's existential destiny to strive after his ultimate end. Since all earthly goals are subordinated to God's glory and plan of creation, human legislation must never obstruct the attainment of this end, but on the contrary contribute to its realization. It must be kept in mind that outside God's kingdom and its justice there is no salvation for men and therefore also no common welfare in a true sense.

Every right implies a legal object over which a person is empowered to exercise control. Legal objects can be material things like machines or immaterial things like an invention. Also a person's services can become a legal object. A human person however can never justly become a legal object after the fashion of a thing, like a slave in ancient law.

b) Several *conditions to be fulfilled by a law* are singled out in order that a law be binding upon its subjects. Tradition usually lists four conditions: The object of the law must be morally permitted, and it must be just, possible and useful.

However the conditions are not adequately distinct. The second condition is more comprehensive than the others and includes all of them. If a law is just, nothing more is to be desired of it. A law whose object is impossible or morally not permitted is also unjust. Furthermore traditional manuals usually combine several heteronomous demands in the second condition, e.g. that laws must keep within the bounds of jurisdiction, distribute burdens in proportionate equality, and not be retroactive.

The matter gains greater clarity by a distinction introduced by legal scholars in this regard. Substantive justice or morality

---
[1] J. Messner, l. c. 191f.

of the law is distinguished from procedural justice.[1] The question about the object of human legislation concerns substantive justice of the law. Here pertain the demands that laws must keep within the bounds of jurisdiction and distribute burdens in proportionate equality. The demand that laws must not be retroactive pertains to procedural justice of the law. The latter shall be dealt with separately at a later occasion.

Keeping this distinction in mind, the following conditions can be listed which must be fulfilled by a just law.

(1) The law can only command what is *morally permitted*, and it can never command what is sinful. For all legitimate authority is in the last resort derived from God and is not allowed therefore to contradict his will by sinful legislation.

Accordingly a law can only command acts that are good or at least indifferent. It cannot order acts which are in principle evil, e.g. euthanasia of the incurably sick and disabled. Rather it is expected to forbid them. But for sufficient reasons a law may *tolerate* certain evils in society, e.g. false religious beliefs, superstitions, parties with totalitarian ideology, prostitution, and the like.

(2) The law must keep *within the bounds of jurisdiction* of the legislator; it may not exceed his competence. The legislator's competence is delimited by the nature of the society entrusted to his care and its particular common good. Thus state authority has no right to enact liturgical laws or to appoint bishops.

(3) The law must *respect the demands of distributive justice*. It must distribute burdens and privileges equally and according to the capacities of the subjects. A standard of proportionate equality must be observed. This is particularly true for the laws of taxation.

(4) The law must *not restrict rights without a real need* on the part of the common welfare. For example the state is not permitted to curtail exceedingly the right to private property,

---

[1] Cf. Lon L. Fuller, *The Morality of Law* (New York: Fawcett Publ., 1964), 110; and J. Finnis, *Natural Law and Natural Rights* (Oxford: Clarendon Press, 1980), 261.

to prohibit the erection of private schools, or to restrain unduly the freedom of movement. Exceptionally however it can forbid indifferent or even good acts if in the circumstances they prove dangerous for the common welfare, e.g. public gatherings, even in churches, in a time of a contagious plague.

(5) The law must be *physically and morally possible*. A law is physically impossible if it commands actions that are completely beyond the forces and means of a person. A lunatic man cannot be required to vote, and a dumb person cannot be obliged to sing the national anthem. The law is morally impossible if it commands what can only be done with great difficulty. Thus laws could not forbid all excursions by private car or order people summoned to court to report within half a day. (The latter instance illustrates that no hard line can be drawn between extreme difficulty and plain impossibility.) Such laws could not be kept by the greater part of the community. They would therefore create unrest and agitation and thus be to the detriment of the common welfare instead of to its furtherance.

If however only a part of the law is impossible, then the possible part must be fulfilled, in case the purpose of the law can be achieved by this compliance. For example a law demanding too high rates must nevertheless be fulfilled to the extent in which taxes are reasonable.

It follows from the above condition that a law cannot normally order heroic acts, since this would mean to demand what is morally impossible under ordinary circumstances. It could not command 14 hours work a day and only 6 hours sleep. Yet in exceptional circumstances human law would be allowed to demand heroic acts, namely if this is necessary for the defence of the common weal, especially military service in a just war, or for the witness of faith in times of persecution. Human law can also expect heroic acts from those who freely enter a state of life in which such acts are imposed, e.g. in religious orders.

(6) The law must be *useful and of benefit* for the common good. A law loses its force as soon as it becomes useless or even injurious to the community. Such would be the case if a law were to forbid all alcoholic drinks or animal experiments. Even laws which enforce moral duties, but minor ones, such

as the obligation not to lie, pertain to this category. Although the observance of the whole moral law contributes in some way to the public welfare, such laws would overburden public justice and be detrimental to the common weal. Hence human law should only order what is of more decisive concern for public order and social life. The fact however that a law does not prescribe the best means for the achievement of some task in the community, although it fulfils its purpose nevertheless, does not invalidate the law.

c) A special question concerns *internal acts as objects of human legislation*. Can human authority command internal acts? Purely internal acts, i.e. acts which are performed within the intellect and will, are not subject to the jurisdiction of social authority, since its only concern is the safeguard and promotion of the social order, which is external. This is certainly true of the civil authority, yet, according to the more common opinion of theologians today, also of the authority of the Church to govern the ecclesiastical society. As a matter of fact, the Church as lawmaker does not command purely internal acts. She is concerned with moral obligations regarding such acts only insofar as she interprets and clarifies the divine law, e.g. when she declares that in certain conditions God's law demands acts of faith, hope, contrition, etc.

Mixed acts however, i.e. external acts which require for their completeness and validity an internal act, can be commanded by the Church as well as by the state, e.g. the internal consent in the conclusion of contracts; the intention to swear in an oath; the application of certain Masses by priests according to the intentions prescribed by the Church. The obvious reason for this right is that otherwise public order and the common welfare could not sufficiently be cared for.

d) *Unjust laws* in principle do not oblige, i.e. laws which do not fulfil the six conditions listed above. However subjects are allowed, if need be, to renounce their rights and to obey the unjust law nevertheless, as long as it does not demand something which is morally evil. Sometimes this can even be necessary for the sake of the common weal. Thus, although a law which forbids all public religious processions is unjust, it may be lawful and even necessary to obey it in order to avoid still greater harm to the Church and the faithful.

If the rights of a third person are infringed by compliance with an unjust law, then fulfilment is only permitted under the condition that the third person could not reasonably object against such a procedure. Thus Pius XII does not blame a judge who fined an innocent priest or lay person according to an unjust law, but did so only that he might be able to continue his service as a judge for the greater benefit of the population.[1]

In case a doubt arises whether all the conditions necessary for a just and valid law are fulfilled, the law has legal force and obliges. The reason is that human laws have presumptive obligatory force, as has been explained earlier. On the one hand legislators usually have better insight into the reasons necessitating a law. On the other hand the stability of the social order would suffer too much if it were lawful to disobey the law whenever subjects have doubts about its justice and usefulness.

III. Moral obligation of the law

a) *Nature and basis of the moral obligation.* Just laws bind in conscience by reason of their intrinsic necessity for the common good. The helps of the common good are necessary for humans, because by nature they are social beings. They depend on the aid and cooperation of others for their own personal growth as well as for the realization of their calling to serve God's glory and his plan for the world. Human law therefore is rooted in the very nature of men and their final end. This is the reason why it has a moral character. Therefore Scripture says: "One must be subject, not only to avoid God's wrath but also for the sake of conscience" (Rom 13:5).

Man's conscience is spontaneously aware of the supreme jural principles such as: render to each one his own; lawful authority must be obeyed; contracts must be honoured; social evil-doers must be punished. Connected with these is the realization that it is morally bad to violate the definite rights of others. And if a person does so, i.e. if he deliberately and culpably violates a just law, he is in conscience bound to submit to just punishment. A punishment is just if it measures

---

[1] *AAS* 41 (1949), 603.

up to the importance of the law for the common welfare; as far as possible it ought to take into account the degree of personal guilt.

From the fact that human law receives its obligatory force from natural law and ultimately from God's will, it follows that "real law cannot exist in conflict with natural moral law. If an enacted law is incompatible with man's existential ends, it conflicts with the moral nature of law."[1] It has no real juridical foundation and confers no moral duty of obedience.

b) *Gravity of the moral obligation and penal law theory.* There is a widely held theory that many laws rightful in themselves do not oblige in conscience to comply with the demand of the law but merely to submit to the penalty imposed for violations. This is the theory of the so-called "penal laws".[2] The basic reason for this theory is the argumentation that the legislator, who can enact laws with stiffer sanctions, can also take care of the common weal by means which enjoin a less strict moral obligation upon the subjects. And where legislators do not bother or do not pronounce themselves in detail about the obligation in conscience of their laws, theologians are to define the moral obligation according to certain external and internal criteria and to declare which positive human laws are mere penal laws. These criteria are above all the manner in which the law is commonly received by the people and the object of the law.

The advocates of the penal law theory agree that it cannot be applied to ecclesiastical laws. Nor can it be applied to civil laws involving substantial rights of others and areas essentially affecting the common good, e.g. laws concerning just wages or bribery of court officials. Generally regarded as penal laws are local police regulations, hunting and fishing laws, traffic laws, mendicancy, military conscription, certain sanitary regulations, import laws and duties, and above all various forms of taxes. They all have in common that they are not direct conclusions from natural law principles, but

---

[1] J. Messner, *l. c.* 162.

[2] A monograph on the question of the existence of mere penal laws has been written by D. C. Bayne, *Conscience, Obligation, and the Law* (Chicago: University Press, 1966).

further determinations of those general demands which leave the legislator free to choose among various possible implementations.

Today however the theory of penal law is largely abandoned. The general objection to this theory is that the gravity of a law does not depend on the will of the lawgiver, and this for the following reasons.

(1) The legislator has not received his legislative power to be used arbitrarily but in order to secure the common good, which every member of the community is bound in conscience to safeguard and to promote. When the legislator therefore prescribes something as necessary for the common good, all his subjects are bound in conscience, even if he attaches no importance to this aspect. But if he misuses his power and issues arbitrary laws, then he cannot impose in conscience even the obligation of accepting the penalty for infringements.

(2) The legislator's task is to determine by enactment of positive laws more precisely the demands of natural law in the concrete conditions of time and history. The natural law itself requires and justifies the further determination of its general demands by positive human laws. Therefore human laws oblige in the same manner as the natural law which they determine.

(3) The source of moral sanctions is God alone and not the will of men. To what degree a positive human law shall oblige in conscience is to be derived from the nature of the law, or to put it differently, is to be derived from its importance for the realization of God's intentions. Men can only make out, clarify and explain the moral obligation which inheres in every just law independently of the human will. - One may also wonder which lawgiver wants his laws not to oblige in conscience but to be mere penal laws.

As a conclusion it must be held that every just law directly binds in conscience. The objection that this doctrine must in many instances result in an overstrain of the subjects is not valid, since the cases of overstrain and moral impossibility can be solved by epikeia. Therefore, when on country roads the driver chooses the wrong side because it is in better condition and feels no burden on his conscience as long as he endangers no one, it is not the theory of penal law which justifies his attitude but rather epikeia. Citizens are allowed to disregard a law whose observance here and now is not necessary for the common good. But if they are caught by the authorities, they would have to pay the fine. This could be considered the lasting truth of the penal law theory, although it is asserted for other reasons.

The degree of the moral obligation of human laws depends on the greater or lesser importance they have for the common welfare. From what has been said on the legislator's function concerning the creation of laws and the determination of their moral obligation, it must be concluded that he cannot impose a matter of certainly light importance under grave sin, nor a matter of certainly great importance for the common weal under venial sin only.[1] Spitting in a bus cannot be forbidden under grave sin, nor is plain disregard of the traffic lights ever a light matter. If many theologians have felt that the legislator is permitted to impose serious matters under venial sin only, they must be contested. The reason is that - as has been explained before - the assessment of the moral obligation of a law is not the legislator's task and does not depend upon his will.

IV. Procedural justice and epikeia

1. *Procedural justice*[2]

Procedural justice or procedural morality of the law is concerned with fair procedures in the handling of the law, as the term implies; i.e. it is concerned with the proper divulgation and administration of the law. It is not concerned with criteria for the appropriate content of the law, but rather with the conditions which rule its just and fair implementation. The conditions are the following.

(1) Laws must be *duly promulgated*. They must be made public in such a way that they are generally accessible and that those who are concerned can readily know them. Laws can be obeyed only on condition that they are known. In

---

[1] So also J. Fuchs, *Theologia Moralis Generalis*, Pars I (Roma: Università Gregoriana, 1960), 134.

[2] The issue of procedural justice is given particular attention by Lon L. Fuller, *The Morality of Law* (New York: Fawcett Publ., 1964), 46-108.

addition adequate publication is also necessary so that the public can evaluate them and subject them to criticism, if need be.

A law may enter into force with the moment of its promulgation or at some date fixed by the legislator. Laws which demand that citizens omit certain actions which so far had been allowed, e.g. the hunting of certain animals, or do certain actions, e.g. the insertion of anti-pollution devices in motor vehicles, must allow for a sufficient period of time between the promulgation of the law and its enforcement, so that people can adjust to the new law and not be caught unawares.[1] On principle it is not allowed to follow a new law during the time of suspension after promulgation (vacation of the law), and this because of the necessary uniformity of public life. However if the new law does not controvert a former law or if it is merely permissive and not contrary to the rights of a third person, it may be followed earlier.

(2) The effects of the law may *not be retroactive*, exceptions apart. Above all new penal laws may not be extended to past actions. This would violate the principle, respected by all civilized nations, that there be no penalty without law (*nulla poena sine lege*). If for example a new law guarantees copyrights for computer programs today, it would be unjust to penalize those who have copied programs yesterday. By their very nature, laws are prospective. Since they are supposed to rule human conduct, and since only actions which are not yet accomplished are subject to guidance, laws must in principle limit themselves to govern present and future conduct. Nevertheless at times situations can arise which recommend retroactive statutes or even make them imperative. Usually they are curative measures for the undesirable effects of outdated or defective laws of the past. Thus the former code of canon law contained a number of excommunications which no longer appear in the new code of 1983. Retroactively they cease to have effect also for those persons who incurred them at a time when they were still in force (cf. CIC 1313). Thus those who according to the old legislation incurred

---

[1] Laws of the Holy See are usually promulgated in the *Acta Apostolicae Sedis*. Their obligation begins three months after the publishing date of the issue of AAS in which they appear (i.e. not three months after the date on which the documents are signed), unless something to the contrary is stated (cf. CIC 8).

excommunications because they contracted marriage before a non-Catholic minister or had their children baptized by him are no longer subject to these censures.[1]

(3) Laws must be coherent, *not contradictory*; or, as another terminology prefers, they must not be incompatible or repugnant. Evidently contradictory laws place the subjects in the unfair condition of not being able to satisfy both laws at the same time. They end up being exposed to legal sanctions, whatever action they take.

(4) A just legal order must *heed legal continuity*. This implies that laws should not change too frequently. Otherwise many of the citizens will be left disoriented. The maintenance of continuity may even mean for the lawgiver that at times he must forego changes which in themselves may be improvements from the point of view of natural law. This applies if the change, owing to deeply rooted custom, proves to be detrimental to legal stability and the common utility. "Legal reforms, therefore, must be decided not simply according to natural law postulates but also according to factors of a positive law character."[2]

(5) Procedural justice finally demands *congruence between official action and declared rule*. There is a kind of reciprocity between the government and the citizens with respect to the observance of the law. Citizens are expected to abide by the rules of the law, and governments are expected to apply them without distortion to the conduct of the citizens. When this bond of reciprocity is violated or ruptured by a government, a general deterioration of the legal order will inevitably ensue. The congruence may be impaired in a great variety of ways: mistaken interpretation, ignorance, indifference, bribery, prejudice, discrimination, harassment. A frequent discrepancy between law and official action is the theoretical assurance of religious liberty by constitutions and the actual prosecution of religious activities by official action.

"The most subtle element in the task of maintaining congruence between law and official action lies, of course, in the problem of interpretation. Legality requires that judges

---

[1] These penalties have in fact already been abrogated, with retroactive effect, by the Motu Proprio *Matrimonia Mixta* of 1970; *AAS* 62 (1970), 262 (nr. 15).

[2] J. Messner, *Social Ethics*, 1965, 297.

and other officials apply statutory law, not according to their fancy or with crabbed literalness, but in accordance with principles of interpretation that are appropriate to their position in the whole legal order."[1] The experts of the law are expected to be fully acquainted with these principles (cf. CIC 16-19).

There are however times when the genuine good of the community and its members is best served by departing from the letter of the law. Such decisions call for a high degree of personal responsibility, especially if made by governments in matters of national concern. This is the question of epikeia, which will be dealt with in the following.

2. Epikeia

Epikeia (or epikia, epiky) is an interpretation of the human law not according to its letter but according to its spirit in those border cases which have not sufficiently been taken into consideration by positive law.[2] St. Thomas regards epikeia as a virtue, the daughter of prudence and equity. "Epiky as readily inclines one to accept burden and strain beyond the letter of the law if its intent and purpose and the common good demand it, as to hold oneself free from the onus, when one must assume in all fairness that the lawgiver does not will to impose such a burden in altogether singular circumstances - or at least not in the specific manner prescribed by the letter of law."[3] Therefore if a law provides for a minimum wage which is too low, or has become too low because of inflation, the true spirit of epikeia will move the employer to pay more than the letter of the law requires, if not by raising the wage, then at least in the form of other benefits.

From this it is apparent that epikeia is not evasion of the law, but the spirit of that freedom from the mere letter of the law which St. Paul had so much at heart and which aims at a nobler fulfilment than the mere letter prescribes. Epikeia maintains the superiority of the unwritten, intrinsic law inherent in human nature over the codified norms of positive law.

---

[1] Lon L. Fuller, l. c. 96.

[2] Other ethical schools speak of moral emergency, of supralegal law, of "unavoidable sin". Ascetic theology speaks of presumed permission.

[3] B. Häring, *The Law of Christ* I, 1966, 281.

In the narrow sense, epikeia is a restrictive interpretation of the law by private authority excusing one from the observance of the law in some particularly difficult case in accordance with the genuine meaning of legislation. Moral handbooks usually confine epikeia to this second narrow sense. Frequently manuals hold that epikeia is an interpretation of the law in accordance with the true mind of the legislator and not, as formulated here, with the genuine meaning of legislation. Yet it is rightly advanced that the legislator himself may at times be too narrow in the understanding of his laws, and that one can imagine legitimate exceptions which the legislator himself might not be willing to approve.[1] Besides in today's democratic societies legislators are usually not individual persons but legislative bodies. Laws are often the result of a compromise. It is therefore difficult, if not impossible, to identify the precise mind of the legislators behind the law.

Christ himself practised and taught the virtue of epikeia. Thus he states that the Sabbath was made for men (Mk 2:27) and ignores the Sabbath law in order to heal the illnesses of people (Mk 3:1-5; Lk 13:10-17; 14:1-6; Jn 5:1-16; 7:21-24; 9). He permits his disciples to pluck ears of grain on the Sabbath day to appease their hunger and quotes, against his critics, the example of David who ate together with his men the bread of the Presence in the temple in an emergency, although he and his men were not allowed to eat this bread, but only the priests (Mt 12:1-8). He likewise mingles and dines with publicans and sinners, disregarding the law of pious Jews which forbade them to do so, yet obeying the higher law of his salvific mission (Mk 2:15-17; Lk 15:1f).

The inner justification of epikeia is the following. First, the legislator often is not in a condition to foresee all the circumstances which may arise in any given situation and cover them all in the wording of a general law. Second, laws can often not follow fast enough the developments of life and the changes in society. Being tailored for past conditions,

---

[1] The case of a parish priest of poor health is reported, who 20 years before the reform of the eucharistic fast 1957 (which until then required total abstinence from midnight on until the celebration of the last Mass) would take a broth between his Sunday Masses at 7 a.m. and 9 a.m. He argued, with some good reason, that the Church must permit him to get the strength for his work if she wants him to do it.

they are not always able to do full justice to the needs of the present. Thus positive laws necessarily remain imperfect and deficient. Human legislation itself has therefore the legal duty to admit of the right of its subjects to resort to the law of epikeia, so that the unavoidable deficiencies of the law can be compensated.

Evidently epikeia is an exceptional thing. It may only be employed with prudent discretion. When making use of it, the following conditions and cautions should be observed.

(1) Epikeia, as discussed in this context, only applies to positive laws. To the extent that legislations render natural laws, it cannot be applied. Thus it is not permissible to use fraud and lies in order to secure a piece of public land for a charitable purpose or a Church building. The use of epikeia in matters of natural law has been discussed earlier and is subject to much greater restrictions.

(2) The hardships and disadvantages resulting from fulfilment of the law must be unproportionately great and outweigh the benefits to be hoped for from compliance with it. This only unfolds the demand, contained in the very definition of epikeia, that it must remain in harmony with the genuine meaning of legislation. Epikeia must be justified by the superior needs of the common good and ultimately by the demands of the ultimate end of mankind. One has to weigh against each other, on the one side, the importance of a law for the common weal as well as the negative consequences resulting from its disregard and, on the other side, the hardships and detriments accruing from its fulfilment.

(3) Consultation with others is very much urged, especially in instances of more important exceptions. Individuals can easily deceive themselves as to the validity of their reasons. Therefore they do well to avail themselves of the more detached advice of others. This is probably also the reason for the following condition, commonly found in handbooks.

(4) In doubtful cases recourse to the superior is required, unless it is unproportionately difficult to approach him. In instances however where the use of epikeia is certainly justified, recourse to the superior is in principle not necessary. If the law does not bind because of inner reasons, an additional

dispensation from the superior is not required.[1] At times an obligation might exist to inform the superior about what one is going to do.

(5) Epikeia cannot be applied to laws that void acts (invalidating laws) or to laws that render persons incapable of undertaking certain legal actions (incapacitating laws). The common welfare requires that certainty be had about the validity of such acts. Thus for example civil law usually declares a last will invalid if it is written without a date. Or youths under the age of 18 are declared incapable of obtaining a driver's license. J. Fuchs admits a rare possibility of epikeia with regard to incapacitating laws in very extreme cases and gives the example of matrimonial impediments.[2]

Epikeia is usually thought of as a right applying only to the individual and private sphere. Yet the right of epikeia exists no less in the realm of public law. In a state of emergency the government of a democratic community is entitled to measures exceeding the powers provided in the constitution, if this is necessitated for the safeguarding of essential ends of the community. Nevertheless the government remains bound to give an account of its actions to the legislative authority as soon as possible.

V. Cessation of obligation and of the law itself

1. *Cessation of obligation.* The obligation of the law ceases by causes which exempt or excuse from the law, by dispensation, and by privilege.

a) That person is exempted from the law who ceases to be its subject. This may come about through a change of age, profession or rank, but also through a change of domicile. If e.g. a person leaves the country of his residence in which there is for Catholics an obligatory holy day and enters another country where no such obligation exists, he is not bound to observe the holy day in the other country, for whatever reason he leaves his country.

b) That person is excused from the law who is invincibly ignorant of it. According to canon law ignorance also excuses

---

[1] This is also the opinion of J. Fuchs, *Theologia Moralis Generalis*, Pars I, l. c. 140.

[2] J. Fuchs, *l. c.* 139.

from the penalty, but not from the effect of invalidating or incapacitating laws (CIC 15; 1323, nr. 2). A person who has committed an abortion but is ignorant of the fact that it is censured by an excommunication does not incur the penalty (although she or he nevertheless sins gravely). On the other hand, a merely civil marriage of Catholic partners contracted without dispensation from the bishop remains invalid, even if the partners were unaware of this requirement.

Physical impossibility equally excuses a person from the observance of the law. A paralysed person cannot appear in court and a prisoner cannot go to Sunday Mass. Moral impossibility, i.e. if the observance of the law results in great hardship for the subject, also generally excuses from positive human laws. It does not however excuse from those human laws which only render a prohibiting natural law, e.g. laws prohibiting murder, perjury, rape, denial of faith, unless the natural law itself permits of exceptions, e.g. purloining of another person's property in order to save one's life. The exceptional cases in which human laws can require heroic acts have already been mentioned earlier. For the other laws the maxim holds that the more important the law is, the greater an inconvenience is required to excuse a person from it.

Partial impossibility excuses totally from the observance of the law if the obligation is indivisible. Thus, if one vows to make a pilgrimage but finds one cannot reach the shrine, one need not even begin the pilgrimage. If the obligation is divisible, the possible part of it must be observed. An obligation is divisible if that part of it which can be observed is sufficient to attain the end of the law. Thus who cannot absolve the entire elementary school, must at least absolve that part which is possible for him or her.

c) A dispensation is a release from the law in a special case by the legitimate authority. Apart from this, the person remains bound by the law, For example a student may be dispensed from classes in order to attend the wedding of her brother. A dispensation, to be lawful, can only be given for a sufficient reason, which must be in proportion to the gravity of the law. It need not be so great, however, as would be required to excuse one from the observance of the law. The interpretation of a dispensation must be made in the strict sense (cf. CIC 92), except if the dispensation is given in the interest of the common good or, in the realm of ecclesiastical law, "motu proprio", or if the dispensation is already contained in the legal enactments.[1]

d) A privilege is a right granting a favour not due by law. While a dispensation usually releases from the law only temporarily, a privilege is a permanent special ruling. Thus members of the armed forces often have the privilege to use the public means of transportation free of charge if they are on duty. Privileges may be granted by the legislator or by those who have received the respective power from him. Their responsibility for the common good requires them to grant privileges only when the common good is safeguarded. Odious privileges, which curtail the rights of others or place a burden upon them, must be interpreted strictly; e.g. the exemption of private schools from taxes does not automatically include property of theirs used for commercial purposes. Favourable privileges, which are a burden to no one, can be broadly interpreted; e.g. the privilege granted to a confessor to absolve from reserved sins.

2. *Cessation of the law itself.* a) Extrinsically a law may cease through the act of the legislator or through contrary customs. A new law abrogates a former law if it expressly states this, or if it is directly contrary to the old law, or if it regulates anew the entire subject matter of the old law. In case of doubt the revocation of an earlier law may not be presumed, but as far as possible the later law must be harmonized with it. If the new law is only partially contrary to the old, then the old law is repealed only in part (cf. CIC 20f).

b) Intrinsically a law can lose its force because its purpose ceases to exist. If the purpose of the law ceases in its whole extent and for all, the law ceases entirely. The prohibition of public gatherings during an epidemic, for instance, ceases when the epidemic ceases, even if it is not expressly repealed. If the law creates great difficulty for certain persons only, these may use epikeia. If the law brings to some no advantages, but also no loss, it must be observed for the sake of the others. Thus the banns of marriage must be published even when the parties know that there is no impediment.

---

[1] Cf. H. Jone, *Moral Theology*, 1963, nr. 74.

Chapter III

CONSCIENCE

The moral precepts as objective norms of morality can be compared to signposts and markers on the road, which indicate the direction the traveller must take in order to reach his goal. The mere existence of the signposts however is not enough to help people on their way. They need a sense to perceive the signs, to select from among them the relevant ones, and also to help them where there are none. They also need a knowledge of the goal to be reached. This sense is a person's conscience. It is that moral faculty which tells people subjectively what is good and evil and which manifests their moral obligation to them.

While the doctrine on conscience in the years immediately after the Council Vatican II attracted only moderate interest, it is receiving increased attention today. Personal responsibility in decisions of conscience is accorded a high rank. And indeed conscience is an irreplaceable barrier against human arbitrariness. Its destruction is the precondition for totalitarian rule. In this perspective the Council speaks of the dignity of conscience and of the great importance of freedom (GS 16f). "Contemporary man is becoming increasingly conscious of the dignity of the human person; more and more people are demanding that men should exercise fully their own judgment and a responsible freedom in their actions and should not be subject to the pressure of coercion but be inspired by a sense of duty" (DH 1).

The frequent appeal to conscience however also raises questions. In the name of conscience the state and its law are opposed. In the name of conscience one dissociates oneself from the value standards of society. In the name of conscience one abandons traditions and refuses to take directions from the Church. A tendency emerges towards a "'privatization' of conscience, which withdraws into its 'own responsibility' with the claim that conscience is not accountable to others, or even could be subjected to scrutiny by them".[1] The opinion gains ground that moral judgments are a matter of the individual only. Conscience becomes an alternative to norms and moral law. Thereby the impression can be created that norms are only for those under age. With this "the tendency goes hand in hand to withdraw 'personal decisions', by appealing to conscience, from rational discussion and objective scrutiny. The 'retreat to conscience' thus can become a cheap alibi for the rejection of self-examination and self-correction and a means to cover one's refusal to take advice, as is characteristic above all of ideological justification."[2] The permanent task of the formation of conscience is not seen. But where men and women assume responsibility *before* their conscience, they also have responsibility *for* their conscience.

A. Concept and nature of conscience

I. Holy Scripture on conscience

The Old Testament. The word conscience, in Greek *syneidesis*, is of Hellenistic origin. It should therefore not come as a surprise that the word conscience does not occur in the Old Testament, except for Wisdom 17:11. But the reality itself of conscience is not unknown to the Old Testament writers. Expressions used for this reality are "mind" (at other times translated "loins") and "heart". The words are frequently coupled together (Ps 26:2; Jer 11:20; 17:10; 20:12). At other times the term "heart" alone is employed (Gen 20:5; Ps 7:10; 24:4; Jer 17:1; 31:33). From the beginning of salvation history the phenomenon of the conscience which condemns man after sin is known; e.g. Adam and Eve after they had eaten from the forbidden tree, Gen 3:7-10; Cain after he had killed his brother Abel, Gen 4:9-14; David whose heart smote him because he had numbered the people against the will of the Lord, 2 Sam 24:10. Equally known is the conscience which praises man for his justice: "My heart does not reproach me for any of my days" (Job 27:6; also Ps 17:3; 26:2f; 139:23f). The judgment of conscience is for the Old Testament ultimately

---

[1] Robert Schlund, *Schöpferisches Gewissen* (Freiburg: Herder, 1990), 15.
[2] *Ib.* 16f.

the voice of God, a fact that is especially evident in the example of Cain's remorse for his crime.

In general interest in conscience in the OT is rather limited. The main reason is the conviction that God and man directly confront one another. "This immediacy in the experience of God leaves Old Testament man relatively uninterested in an authority in his own inner self. It is God himself who instructs him and who says what is to be done and to be omitted. His word gives the knowledge of good and evil."[1] Therefore the OT is primarily concerned with the constant listening to the word of God. And when occasionally something after all is mentioned about the reality of conscience, it is seen in relation to Yahweh. "He it is who gives knowledge to the heart and from whom alone the pure and upright heart (= the good conscience) can come. The thought that the heart (conscience) is an independent reality in man is alien to the Old Testament. It always appears as a limited and relative reality, related to God and defined by him."[2]

The New Testament. Christ himself and the Gospels do not use the term conscience either, although Christ most earnestly warns against the obscuring of a person's spiritual "eye" in the soul when he says: "If the light in you is darkness, how great is the darkness" (Mt 6:23). And on the other hand he commends: "If your whole body is full of light, having no part dark, it will be wholly bright, as when a lamp with its rays gives you light" (Lk 11:36). John resumes the Old Testament manner of expression and speaks of the heart which condemns or reassures a person (1 Jn 3:19-21). But in the other writings of the New Testament the term conscience occurs repeatedly, and especially Paul develops the doctrine concerning it.[3]

Paul, in using the word conscience (*syneidesis*), was taking up a term which was frequently used from the first century before Christ onwards in popular philosophy and

---

[1] Helmut Weber, *Allgemeine Moraltheologie* (Graz: Styria, 1991), 189.

[2] *Ib.*

[3] Cf. R. Schnackenburg, *The Moral Teaching of the New Testament, 1967,* 287-296; Wolfgang Schrage, *The Ethics of the New Testament.* Edinburgh: T. & T. Clark, 1988, 195ff.

ethics. The characteristic mark of this spiritual function is the personal and spontaneous reaction before or after some moral decision; but awareness of moral values is of course necessarily presupposed as its foundation.

This latter meaning, awareness, is more closely adhered to than is usual with us when Paul says that, by proclaiming truthfully the word of God, "we would commend ourselves to every man's conscience in the sight of God" (2 Cor 4:2) or when he hopes that what he is, is "known" to the "conscience" of the Corinthians, that is, that his uprightness may be discernible to them (2 Cor 5:11). The use of "for the sake of conscience" in Rom 13:5 is a request to act not merely out of fear of God's wrath, but also out of appreciation for the inner goodness of the moral command.

Often conscience is characterized as a "witness" (Rom 2:15; 9:1; 2 Cor 1:12). It accompanies our actions as an incorruptible witness within us and can also be called upon to attest the truth of our assertions. When dealing with the "weak conscience" of those who consider it illicit to eat meat offered to idols (1 Cor 8:7-13; cf. 10:23-30), the apostle speaks partly of the antecedent judgment of conscience, which is erroneous in this case, and partly of the reaction of the subsequent conscience, because the conscience of the weak finds itself "defiled" if they eat sacrificial meat. Subsequent conscience is also described in Romans 2:15 under the image of mutually accusing and defending thoughts, and in 2 Cor 1:12 under the metaphor of a witness who testifies for Paul that he behaved in the world with holiness and sincerity. The expressions, found in the other writings of the NT, "a pure conscience" (Acts 24:16; 1 Tim 3:9; 2 Tim 1:3) and "a good conscience"(Acts 23:1)[1] and the opposite "a corrupted conscience" (Tit 1:15) equally include the approving or disapproving judgment of subsequent conscience.

The judgments of conscience are not merely natural insights, but judgments enlightened by faith. According to the first letter to Timothy, moral judgments proceed as much from conscience as they do from faith. "The aim of our charge is love that issues from a pure heart and a good conscience and sincere faith" (1 Tim 1:5; cf. 1:18f; 3:9). And while in 1 Cor 8:10 the judgment on the morality of the good is passed

---

[1] Likewise Acts 24:16; 1 Tim 1:5 and 19; Heb 13:18; 1 Pet 3:16.21.

by conscience, it is passed in Rom 14:23 by faith. "Whatever does not proceed from faith is sin." It is difficult to attribute a special sense to the word faith in this context. But it is also not necessary. "For to St. Paul, faith is the whole attitude of the Christian, assimilating his judgements of moral worth too. The Christian is not divided within himself, with a natural economy and a supernatural one, there is only one judgement of conscience, and it is determined by his belief."[1]

Convictions of conscience, it is to be noted, do not automatically entitle a person to carry them out without any further considerations. The right to follow them is limited by the criterion of love. The conviction that Christians may eat all foods and even meat offered to idols is correct according to Paul. But not all share this conviction. Having a "weak conscience", some believe that they must abstain from certain foods and from meat offered to idols. This being so, those who have a strong conscience must show consideration for the weaker brethren. They may not eat from the disputed foods in the presence of the weaker brethren if this could seduce them to act against their conscience and therewith to commit sin (Rom 14 and 1 Cor 8). From the fact of the "weak", i.e. the erroneous, conscience it follows that for Paul conscience is not ipso facto the voice of God. It has more the function of examination than that of creating norms. Conscience is "not so much a guiding authority, establishing in its own right the substance of what is required, as a critical authority, using certain criteria to judge what people do or fail to do. What is to be done is prescribed not by conscience but by the commandments, or else the community is to determine it."[2]

Conscience finally is a universal endowment of all men. In Romans 2:14f Paul shows he is convinced that the "Gentiles who have not the law do by nature what the law requires" and hence are a law to themselves. The next verse then determines more precisely by what means they have the possibility to fulfil the moral law without knowledge of the written law: "They show that what the law requires is written on their hearts, while their conscience also bears witness and their conflicting thoughts accuse or perhaps excuse them."

---

[1] R. Schnackenburg, *l. c.* 294.
[2] W. Schrage, *l. c.* 195.

"This passage bears witness to Paul's view, a view perhaps not uninfluenced by Stoic thinking, but wholly translated into Christian terms, that everyone possesses a faculty of making moral judgements, and a conscience."[1]

In summary, it can be said that conscience receives a growing attention in the Bible. While the Old Testament and the Gospels rather know God who is speaking and man who is listening, the other writings of the New Testament increasingly also reflect on an endowment in man which judges his deeds and omissions. This endowment however is completely imbedded in the world of faith and orientated by it. At the same time conscience is also soberly seen as a reality with limitations, which results from its creaturely condition. It appears as a reality which is in need of divine grace for its cleansing and purification. Apart from that it is to be noted that conscience is not a key notion in Holy Scripture, and in the New Testament as well it remains a theme of subordinate importance. For the Bible "the key word in ethics is not the word 'conscience', an expression for something subjective and individual; for the Bible the distinctive words rather are 'obedience' and 'love' or 'service', which always give expression to a relation beyond one's person or subjectivity."[2]

II. Conscience as moral faculty

A distinction must be made between conscience as moral faculty, which manifests to men their moral obligations and impels them to fulfil them, and conscience as practical moral judgment, which tells men in the concrete situation what their moral obligations are.

1. *Views outside of Christian theology*

The experience and knowledge of Holy Scripture that there is a voice in man which demands of him to do the known good and which accuses him if he refuses to obey this call, is actually a universal phenomenon. No culture has yet been found in which conscience is not recognized as a fact. Generally among primitive peoples, expressions such as

---

[1] R. Schnackenburg, *l. c.* 293.
[2] H. Weber, *l. c.* 193.

"heart" and "loins" replace the word conscience. An ancient Egyptian text reads: "The heart is an excellent witness" and one must not transgress against its words; "he must stand in fear of departing from its guidance". Seneca expresses the same thought when he speaks of a holy spirit dwelling in man, "an observer and watcher of good and evil in us" (Epist. 41,1). Although in the process of secularization in modern times the religious aspect of conscience was given up, Kant still thought of conscience as the "consciousness of an interior court of justice in man".[1]

But empiricism gave conscience a psychological interpretation and derived it from sociological conditions and needs (H. Spencer, E. Durkheim) or even from oppression by civilization (F. Nietzsche, S. Freud). Thus, although the existence of conscience was not denied, its authority as a competent judge of good and evil was challenged and rejected.

Particular influence was gained by Freud's theory about conscience as a "superego". The superego is a set of demands and habits learned from parents and from society which require the individual to live and act according to prescribed rules and standards. These habits and rules however are repugnant to the individual's true nature and deepest inclinations rooted in the unconscious. To resolve this conflict, Freud demands that the oppression by the superego be more and more reduced, so that men's actions are only determined by the claims of their deeper, true nature and by the needs of a sensible coexistence with the outside world.

These views about conscience however were not adopted by the philosophy of the 20th century. On the contrary, it has been concerned with doing justice to the phenomenon of conscience in such representatives as M. Scheler, N. Hartmann, M. Heidegger, K. Jaspers. Heidegger sees in conscience the "call of care", which keeps existence from the impersonal "man" and which is open for the "voice of being". Jaspers understands by conscience that voice speaking to man "which is man himself".

Also in depth psychology conscience has been given, already early, a more just place especially by C. G. Jung.

---
[1] See the historical survey in W. Dupré, "Conscience," *New Catholic Encyclopedia* IV, 1967, 196f.

Also he knows (the same as Freud) a kind of superstructure of the ego, the "persona". It is an outer cover of man's personality, whose purpose is to hide the individual's true nature and at the same time to make a particular impression on the surrounding world. On the road to an authentic personality, one must part from the persona and be to the outside world what one is within. The confrontation with the deepest core of the person in the unconscious brings more and more a new centre of the human personality to the foreground: the "self". The self appears on the scene like a secret counsellor and is the place where ethical decisions are made. It conveys "a feeling of what one ought to be and might be. To deviate from this presentiment means taking the wrong path, it is the way of error and disease."[1] Jung thinks that if the word conscience did not have such powerful religious connotations, he would use this term. It would "describe this court of appeal excellently".[2] In other words, if abstraction be made from certain religious associations, the self can be defined as conscience.

Psychologists today regard it as a settled question that conscience is a genuine sense of self-esteem and appropriate striving. "Indeed, we may safely say that, except for a few 'psychopathic personalities,' conscience is a normal development within every human being. It is an indicator - something like a fever thermometer - that tells us some activity on our part is disrupting or has disrupted, an important aspect of our self image."[3]

The moral behaviour of humans is doubtless and to a considerable extent also subject to the influence of the social environment. Yet if empiricism sees in conscience nothing else but the result of social and cultural sways, a satisfactory answer must also be given to the question regarding the principles according to which the rules of moral and social conduct develop, which communities impose upon their mem-

---
[1] Quoted by J. Goldbrunner, *Individuation. A Study of the Depth Psychology of Carl Gustav Jung* (University of Notre Dame Press, 1964), 130.
[2] *Ib.* 130.
[3] Gordon W. Allport, *Pattern and Growth in Personality* (New York: Holt, Rinehart and Winston, 1963), 134.

bers from childhood on. Are these rules simply arbitrary, tyrannical inventions, or are they not rather the outcome of secular experience based upon the needs of the community, whose orderly existence must be safeguarded and whose development must be fostered? And if these rules are in the service of the preservation and growth of the community, it is further to be clarified, whence the members of the community know the kind of growth and progress they should aim at. The ultimate answer is that they know it by their conscience, which alone gives everybody the necessary, usually intuitive insight into the goals of nature and into the plan of God with the world.

True, this much must be conceded to Nietzsche and Freud that norms of moral and social conduct can also be at times the result of the pressure of those in power and of erroneous conclusions by the community. But the generally most meaningful order in the world and in society proves that the outrages upon conscience and its errors are deplorable deviations, but by no means constitute the essence of conscience. The inner experience man has of himself and the great judiciousness of so many civil and moral laws speak another language. If there is nonetheless so much failure and evil in the world, then men know quite well that this is all too often because the insights and judgments of conscience have been disregarded.

2. *Concept of conscience in theology*

Scholastic theology and the traditional manuals of moral theology commonly consider conscience not as a separate moral faculty, but as a particular instance of the operation of reason. Conscience is the process in which the general norms of the moral law are applied to a concrete action which a person is about to perform or has performed, telling the person what his obligation is here and now or judging his past acts. In this view conscience is a herald which voices the objective law and a deputy which applies it to the concrete, individual situation. Conscience accordingly is considered a judgment of the practical reason. This is also the understanding of Thomas Aquinas. Accordingly the synderesis as the core of conscience is a habitus of reason for him.[1] His understanding of conscience is in substance intellectualistic.[2]

A different understanding of conscience is advanced by Augustine and the Franciscan school. For Augustine conscience is the place of the innermost encounter between God and man, and therefore the voice of God. Conscience is the divine centre of the person, where he is addressed by God. In it he is aware of God and the soul. In line with this thought Bonaventure and the great mystics of the Middle Ages place the innermost ground of conscience in the "scintilla animae", the spark of the soul. At other times they describe it as the peak of the soul. It is that centre of the soul where man encounters God and is least accessible to the contamination of sin. In later scholastic and moral theology, however, this view found less attention.[3]

Conscience is not mere reason, because it is more than a mere executive agent of pre-existent moral laws, whose only task it is to apply the laws to concrete situations here and now. Otherwise persons with the sharpest intellect ought to possess the best consciences, which is not the case. Conscience first and foremost informs a person about his personal calling in the context of God's plan of creation. This calling reason cannot deduce by purely intellectual operations from merely rational premises. Reason alone is also not sufficient to explain the strong elements of an emotional nature connected with the judgments of conscience, especially with consequent conscience.

Besides the perceptive function conscience also has a volitive quality, and this even primarily, which inclines and urges a person to accept the known good and to realize it. This impulse flows from the vital awareness of man's innermost

---

[1] *S. Th.* I, q. 79, a. 12.

[2] For a good, brief presentation of the teaching of Thomas Aquinas on conscience, cf. Wilhelm Ernst, "Gewissen in katholischer Sicht," *Internationale Katholische Zeitschrift "Communio"* 11 (1982), 155-159. The subject of conscience does not find great attention in Thomas. Of the more than 600 "quaestiones" of the *Summa Theologica* not a single one is dedicated to this theme; only a few scattered articles deal with the question. A longer reflection on conscience is found in *De Veritate* (q. 1 and 17).

[3] For a concise presentation of the Augustinian tradition, cf. Anselm Hertz, "Glaube und Gewissen," in *Handbuch der christlichen Ethik*, vol. 3, ed. by the same et alii (Freiburg: Herder, ²1993), 52-58.

self that in the attitude assumed towards the moral values his true being and his salvation are at stake. Nevertheless conscience evidently is also not identical with the power of the will, since man may will and do what is against his conscience. In fact both functions, the perceptive and the volitive, must be attributed to conscience.

Recent theologians generally resume the tradition of the Franciscan school and place the conscience in the ground of the soul. They consider it a reality deeper than reason and will and distinct from both, the centre of the human person. This is the view of F. X. Linsenmann, A. Koch, T. Müncker, K. Golser, F. Furger, R. Spaemann,[1] A. Auer, F. Fuchs and J. Gründel.[2] "Conscience is more than mere reason, more than mere will, more than mere feeling, it is the depth of human existence, the innermost core of the person in his directedness towards God and in his ultimate sustenance by him."[3]

Accordingly conscience is a faculty in its own right, distinct from reason, will and feeling. It is that faculty, situated in the very depth and centre of the human person, which accords to man an understanding of his meaning and destiny, an awareness of the divine purpose behind the world, a perception of his personal calling within God's plan, and an experience of the imperative character of this calling. Implied in this is the spiritual and emotional urge to comply with the demands resulting from the call. All this makes it plain that conscience by its very nature has a religious dimension. It is the place where a person is called to responsibility before God. This is the reason why disobedience to its voice entails the guilt of sin.

With these explanations in mind, conscience can be defined as that faculty which makes known to man his moral obligations and urges him to fulfil them. It is not primarily

---

[1] Franz Xaver Linsenmann, *Lehrbuch der Moraltheologie* (Freiburg, 1878), 86-89. Anton Koch, *Lehrbuch der Moraltheologie* (Freiburg, 1907), 84-86. Theodor Müncker *Die psychologischen Grundlagen der katholischen Sittenlehre* (Düsseldorf, 1934), 26, 130-169. Karl Golser, *Gewissen und objektive Sittenordnung* (Wiener Domverlag, 1975), 161. Franz Furger, *Einführung in die Moraltheologie* (Darmstadt: Wissenschaftl. Buchgesellschaft, 1988), 52f; 59. Robert Spaemann, *Moraltheologische Grundbegriffe* (München: C.H. Beck, ^{4}1991), 79-81.

[2] For the last three theologians, see W. Ernst, *l. c.* 162f.

[3] A. Auer, quoted by W. Ernst, *l. c.* 163.

a theoretical or scientific knowledge of moral values and of good and evil; rather it shows man what his ultimate calling and the divine Spirit require of him individually as his personal obligation and leads him to perceive the binding force of these requirements. Not only the requirements of human nature, but also of grace and the divine Spirit are manifested by conscience, since in our concrete world man is everywhere under the influence of Christ's grace and of the Holy Spirit. By means of this influence all men are enabled to strive after their common, ultimate vocation, which according to Vatican II is one and divine for all mankind (GS 22). This does not mean that the operation of divine grace is also experienced by men as such. People who do not believe in God will reject any religious explanation of conscience. But also in their case the experience of the absoluteness of the claims of conscience is implicitly a religious experience. Therefore Vatican II can consider obedience towards conscience as an implicit faith in God, which works salvation for them (see LG 16).

Because of its religious dimension, conscience is also called the voice of God, as has already been mentioned before. The demand of absolute obligation, which is inherent in the dictate of a certain conscience, can ultimately only come from God. On the other hand conscience can evidently err, and that nobody would like to attribute to God. How then is the assertion to be understood, that conscience is the voice of God? "Conscience is the voice of God in this way: beyond errors themselves it manifests to me the will of God; not in the sense that God wills its errors, but in the sense that God wills the good faith and the love of the good, of which it remains an expression."[1]

Throughout it has been noticed that the conscience of individual men and even more so conscience in various societies does not speak everywhere with the same voice. Nevertheless there is also, in spite of all differences, a basic core of common perceptions. Scholastic theology therefore has distinguished the elementary ground and nucleus of conscience, which has been called synderesis (or synteresis) since the 12th

---

[1] Guido Gatti, *Temi di morale fondamentale* (Leumann, Torino: Elle Di Ci, 1988), 135.

century,[1] from the developed habitus of conscience. The synderesis is the habitus of the ultimate moral principles which are immediately perceived by the practical understanding. The most universal principle of synderesis is, that the good must be done and evil must be avoided. Man's knowledge of his existential ends and of the basic moral principles flowing therefrom must equally be attributed to the innate faculty of synderesis.[2]

On the basis and under the orientation and impulse of synderesis the further growth and acquisition of practical moral knowledge takes place. For the development and further unfolding of its elementary contents experience, education, instruction and study are of fundamental importance. The moral judgments are to a great extent determined by these (of course historically conditioned) factors and dependent upon them. In this process the objective moral law, although also with its limitations by place and time, becomes more and more a personal possession. Not in the last instance is a deeper practical knowledge of the authentic moral values acquired by the very practice of the good. The habitus of conscience, which develops in this way, is the presupposition and source of the practical judgments and dictates, which tell a person his moral obligation in the concrete situation.

3. Conscience as subject to being

The observation that the moral norms of society are open to imperfections and the postulate of man's responsible freedom lead to a tendency to want the moral norms to be set up by personal conscience alone. "The individual conscience is accorded the status of a supreme tribunal of moral judgment which hands down categorical and infallible decisions about good and evil. To the affirmation that one has a duty to follow one's conscience is unduly added the affirmation that

---

[1] The term synteresis is probably due to a slip of a copyist in writing the word *syneidesis* in St. Jerome's Commentary on Ezechiel in the middle of the 12th century. The term synteresis itself however is also found in earlier writings with the meaning of *conservatio*, preservation.

[2] To these basic principles pertain the already mentioned primary principles of natural law, e.g. maintain and promote your bodily life; maintain and promote social coexistence, duties of state of life (such as parental duties) are to be answered; the golden rule; leave and give to everyone what is his own (see p. 108).

one's moral judgment is true merely by the fact that it has its origin in the conscience."[1] The decision about good and evil becomes a matter of the autonomous and "creative" conscience.

Obviously such a view does not do justice to human nature. Just as the common physical and biological nature of man is the source of corresponding common, definite laws for all, likewise the common nature and destiny of man is also the source of common tasks and moral obligations for all. "Deep within his conscience - Vatican II writes - man discovers a law which he has not laid upon himself but which he must obey" (GS 16).

As appealing as the thought of a creative fashioning of moral norms may appear, it is subject to reservations. It pertains to the essence of morality to be independent of the will of man. Although the moral law is inscribed in the heart of man (and in this sense autonomous), it is not created by him or in any other way dependent upon his mere will. "Conscience is an organ of 'seeing' or 'hearing'. Both metaphors express the same: it falls upon conscience to perceive a reality outside of itself, i.e. insofar as it is morally significant."[2] Doubtless the impulse of conscience also ought to engage the creativity of a person. But the norms and models which a person finds in this process are determined by the reality they are concerned with. Conscience is not creative in the sense that it is drawing up the moral claim, rather it is creative in the further discovery and unfolding of that claim and its application to concrete situations.

Also relevant for the question of the basic orientation of conscience is the understanding of the meaning of life and therewith of the ultimate end of man. If the meaning of life is self-realization, then conscience will have to be primarily subject-oriented.[3] Yet if the ultimate end of man is the glory of God, the building of his kingdom of justice and peace and the further unfolding of the work of creation, as this is the

---

[1] John Paul II, encyclical *Veritatis Splendor*, 1993, nr. 32

[2] Andreas Laun, *Das Gewissen: oberste Norm sittlichen Handelns* (Innsbruck: Tyrolia, 1984), 94.

[3] J. Fuchs comes to this conclusion, *Für eine menschliche Moral*, vol. II. Freiburg: Herder, 1989), 147. For him "morality essentially means this: to accept oneself as a personal subject and to realize oneself as this particular self" (148); it means: "true self-realization" (162).

view of the Bible and of Vatican II (GS 34, 57, 67), then conscience appears object-oriented. Certainly the particular task which falls to each one within this great work is only known to him alone in his heart. But the contribution to be made in the realization of the common work must ultimately stand in the service of "the fulfilment in history of the divine plan" and the unfolding of the creator's design (GS 34). This directs man to a task outside of himself and signifies for conscience an orientation toward the object and the actual world of being.

The moral law is inscribed in the hearts of men. This inner law is not simply identical with the moral laws and precepts in the handbooks of ethics and moral theology. No doubt, the formulated norms are an essential help in the formation of conscience. Yet the norms of the manuals only stake out a framework of moral obligations, as already explained earlier. The moral good in its variety and richness is much more than what general laws can express. "Not everything that is morally good for the individual is already concretely set forth in the general moral norm of an ethics derived from being and essence, even if it also cannot contradict this norm and depart from the moral order in which God's will in principle is made known."[1] Precisely under this aspect men and women are called to self-reliant definition of the moral demand, which can be called creative in a good sense. Moreover one has soberly to reckon with the possibility that moral norms formulated by men can be subject to imperfections, which perhaps personal conscience has to set off and to correct. Not every judgment of conscience which departs from an external moral norm is an erroneous conscience, albeit an invincibly erroneous one. Certainly dissent from a moral norm commonly upheld requires a high degree of responsibility. The question will be given more attention below.

III. Conscience as practical moral judgment

1. *Concept of the dictate of conscience*

The faculty of conscience goes into action when the morality of a concrete line of conduct, which a person wants to follow or has followed, and the moral obligation in the

---
[1] R. Schlund, *Schöpferisches Gewissen* (Freiburg: Herder, 1990), 77.

concrete situation are to be judged. The moral faculty then formulates a judgment, which is called the dictate of conscience or also simply conscience (as in the expression "antecedent conscience").

Conscience in this sense is defined as an ultimate, practical judgment on the morality of a concrete action, commanding to do what is good and to avoid what is evil. It is called a *practical* judgment, because it is related to the "praxis" of the moral activity. In most cases this judgment is not reflexive but spontaneous. The judgment of conscience is expressly reflected upon especially in instances of doubt or of resistance and disobedience to the dictates of conscience.

Conscience is called an *ultimate*, practical judgment in contradistinction to a practical judgment of speculative nature. The first concerns a person's concrete action in a concrete situation; the second formulates general moral principles concerning the morality of human actions in the abstract without relation to the concrete activity of a person here and now. The principles and norms collected in moral handbooks or catechisms are practical judgments of speculative nature.

The dictate of conscience contains a double element. The first element is the judgment on the morality of a concrete action which a person intends to perform or has performed, or which he intends to omit or has omitted. This judgment can be erroneous, because conscience may judge a line of conduct to be right which is objectively wrong and vice versa. The second element is the command and obligation that what has been recognized as good must be done or should have been done, and what has been recognized as evil must be omitted or should have been omitted. This obligation is categorical. It is not only always right to follow it, it is obligatory to do so.

Just as the faculty of conscience is not merely a collection of pre-existent moral norms, so the concrete judgment of conscience is not merely an act in which general moral norms are applied to a concrete action here and now. True, such an application also takes place, but it is always accompanied and completed by a person's fundamental awareness of his or her personal destiny and individual calling in the service of the intentions of God and the plan of creation. Even the general moral laws are formulated under the influence of this awareness which men have of the purpose and meaning of their lives and the world at large. It is for that reason that the general laws can appeal to the consciences of men, because ultimately the laws have been formulated under their inspiration and control.

2. Division of conscience

Conscience can be *antecedent or consequent*. It is called antecedent if the judgment on the morality of an action and the obligation to perform or omit it is passed before the action is translated into reality. The antecedent conscience commands, exhorts, permits, or forbids. Conscience is called consequent if it evaluates a deed already done or omitted. The consequent conscience approves, excuses, reproves, or accuses.

Conscience can be *certain or doubtful*. A certain conscience passes judgment without fear of error. For moral certainty it suffices that all reasonable fear be excluded. Thus a person who is convinced that he has paid back the 200 dollars he owed to his friend has a certain conscience. An absolutely certain conscience however can still be erroneous. For example, if the debt is paid in instalments, it may still be true that the person is mistaken and that only 150 dollars have been paid. The doubtful conscience on the other hand is uncertain concerning the morality of an action. Therefore it suspends its judgments; or it passes judgment but with reasonable fear of erring. Thus a youth who doubts whether it is right for him to see a controversial movie has a doubtful conscience.

Conscience can be *right or erroneous* according as the practical moral judgment agrees or disagrees with the objective norms of morality. The person who judges that it is not right to get a divorce simply because his wife is no longer beautiful has a right conscience. An erroneous conscience is either invincibly or vincibly so. The invincibly erroneous conscience is inculpable, since the person has no awareness of the possibility of error. If Hindus believe they may not eat the meat of cows, their conscience is erroneous from a Christian point of view. But for the Hindus this error is invincible, since their religion teaches them that cows are sacred. The vincibly erroneous conscience on the other hand is culpable, because with some good will its error could be corrected, e.g. if a white judge is aware that he too uncritically accepted the testimony of a doubtful witness against a black defendant.

The perplexed conscience and the judgments of the lax and scrupulous conscience are species of the erroneous conscience. The perplex and lax conscience will be dealt with separately below. The scrupulous conscience is less an erroneous than a sick conscience. Scrupulosity is the persistent, gnawing, unreasonable fear that one has offended God or is about to do so. The scrupulous person is in constant dread of sin where there is none, or of grave sin where there is only venial sin. The roots of this state of doubt and fear are not primarily of rational character; they are above all to be sought in disturbed emotions. Vaguely the afflicted person himself feels that his doubts are futile and should be despised; but he is unable to escape them. If need be, it may be advisable to refer the afflicted person to a psychiatrist. Frequently however psychiatric help is not available or feasible. In such cases the priest can try the supportive kind of help which the more traditional methods have advocated. He then will endeavour to inform himself about them.[1] Fortunately the problem has lost much of its urgency today. Together with the elimination of legalism in moral and ascetic theology in recent decades, the instances of scrupulosity have become much rarer.

In ethical discussions today a strong stress is often laid on the distinction between moral goodness or badness and moral rightness or wrongness. This distinction corresponds with the traditional distinction between a certain conscience (which judges something in firm conviction as morally good or evil, whereby it can err) and a right conscience (which correctly judges something as morally right or wrong). What is morally good must not necessarily be morally right, and vice versa. If a person because of his religion believes, that he cannot admit a life-saving blood transfusion for his child, then he does something which on account of his inner belief is morally good, but objectively not morally right.

IV. Stages in the development of conscience

A distinction must be made between the evolving conscience in childhood, which is predominantly an authoritarian

---

[1] See the very good and helpful treatment of scrupulosity in G. Hagmaier/R Gleason, *Counselling the Catholic* (New York: Sheed and Ward, 1964), 145-173. For some basic moral principles in guidance see H. Jone, *Moral Theology*, 1963, nr. 91.

conscience or a "must-conscience", and the mature, adult form of conscience, which can be qualified as an "ought-conscience". It is of greatest importance that on the way to adulthood the authoritarian must-conscience of the child develops into the personal ought-conscience of the grown-up, mature person.

Some authors speak of superego instead of must-conscience. However this terminology is more readily exposed to misunderstanding, since for Freud, who introduced the term superego, this is essentially an oppressive, unauthentic superstructure of the human psyche, whereas the must-conscience is a necessary and therefore genuine stage in the development of the person. Those who adopt the term superego accordingly expressly caution that the superego, although basically a principle of censorship and control, "still has a positive and meaningful function in our personalities. In children, the superego is a primitive but necessary stage on the way to genuine conscience. In adults, the superego functions positively when integrated into a mature conscience to relieve us from having to decide freshly in every instance those matters which are already legitimately determined by convention or custom."[1]

In the view of many psychologists, the must-conscience of the child evolves out of parental commands, restrictions and prohibitions. Some form of punishment often accompanies these commands. The child of course does not know why he must or must not do certain things. He complies with the orders because they are prescribed by his parents. He spontaneously submits to their competence and knowledge, and he must also fear their punishment if he disobeys. Although initially submission is rendered only as far as the parents' control reaches, the child gradually "interiorizes" the external voice of authority and follows their orders and norms even when he is alone.

More recently however greater attention is also given to the rule of imitation and identification in the formation of

---

[1] R.M. Gula, *Reason Informed by Faith* (New York: Paulist Press, 1989), 128. In the same way Louis Monden writes: It would "be a fatal mistake to try, as it were, to skip the superego stage in the formation of the young conscience. The superego is necessary; the child cannot do without it. However, it depends to a great extent on the parents whether, in relation to the later development of conscience, that superego will be a permanent prison or the protecting shell which opens at the right moment" (*Sin, Liberty and Law*. London: G. Chapman, 1966, 121).

the child's value patterns and ideals. Imitation and identification play a role in the development of conscience which is at least equal to that of commands and prohibitions, and probably superior to them.

Thus the early stage of conscience is formed, which is due to the internalization of parental and social rules and ideals.[1] Inasmuch as these rules are in harmony with the child's true nature, they contribute substantially to the formation of an authentic conscience. But if they disregard the child's real constitution, they give rise to kinds of "superegos" and "personas" which do violence to and suppress the true personality. Furthermore the must-conscience is inclined to limit the moral obligations to certain areas, i.e. to those areas which are covered by the parental and social norms. The other areas appear to be morally indifferent and left to a person's free discretion, which is a legalistic contraction of the moral obligation. The imitation of examples, though, can transcend this framework, but can after all not fully compensate for this inadequacy.

As the child grows older and progresses towards adulthood, the must-conscience is to give way to the mature ought-conscience.[2] The ought-conscience is no longer primarily sustained by fear of punishment and external imitation. Rather it originates from the conviction of the inner value of the moral obligation, from the inner law of a person's nature and the divine calling as spelled out in that centre of the human person which is a person's true self. Emphasis has shifted from imitation and parental and social control to personal responsibility. There remain many "musts" in adulthood, but they spring now from a sense of duty to build and not to tear down one's personality

---

[1] At times the "superego" stage of conscience, which is primarily formed in early childhood through the child's relation to the parents, is distinguished from a more developed stage of conscience based on conventional morality, which is formed in interaction with the social group. This then is followed by the third stage of the ought-conscience. This threefold division is based on the theories of J. Piaget and L. Kohlberg (see G. Grisez, *The Way of the Lord Jesus*, vol. I. Chicago: Franciscan Herald, 1983, 89f). The superego stage of conscience and the conscience guided by convention are however both forms of the authoritarian conscience, and their limits seem to be substantially of the same nature.

[2] According to Jean Piaget the transition from the "heteronomous" to the "autonomous" conscience occurs at about seven years of age in normal children.

and from a sense of responsibility for the common good and for the kingdom of the Lord.

Fundamentally there can be no opposition between an adult conscience and the "musts" of moral law. (The must-conscience to the greater extent reflects the moral law of the community.) For the aim of the law is to express and clarify what one ought to be by one's human abilities and the divine calling. "Hence in principle the adult person will acknowledge and welcome in the law the imperative of his own striving towards human and Christian adulthood, even though he may be clearly aware of the imperfections in its formulation and thus of the corrections he must introduce into it. To be in principle hostile and opposed to every law may safely be considered an infallible sign of immaturity."[1] At times however there will be instances where the deeper ought-conscience recognizes the norms of the must-conscience as inadequate, and that all the more, the more deficient views and alienating interests have influenced the formation of the must-conscience. The modified norm may simply be grounded in a clearer insight and the transition to it may ensue without greater conflicts. But the detachment from the old bonds can at times also be coupled with considerable pain and guilt feelings, e.g. if one is dealing with a deeply rooted, unauthentic ego-ideal.

Not always the transition from the must-conscience to the adult ought-conscience is successfully effected. Physical, intellectual and moral adulthood do not necessarily go together. One person succeeds in forming a personal conscience. The precepts and values he has learned from others he is able to incorporate as part of his own inner attitude and conviction. To the outsider, a person whose conscience is thus self-reliant will create the impression that his moral and religious life comes straight from the heart and has its roots in a harmonized personality. His relationships with his fellow-men are not blocked by a mechanical application of principles and regulations.

But it is different with people whose consciences remain authoritarian and do not reach maturity. Their moral behaviour easily appears forced, a matter of principle with little warmth of feeling. For them the demands of conscience remain a foreign body, external or even in opposition to the true, inner

---

[1] Louis Monden, *Sin, Liberty and Law*, l. c, 102.

self. It is by no means necessary that they should experience conscience as a foreign body, because from childhood on the moral demands of the social environment have been absorbed and interiorized. Yet ultimately these people do not live from the depth of their soul, but do what others expect of them.[1]

There are many stages possible in the transition from authoritarian to mature conscience. Perfect maturity of conscience, such as realized by those saints who were only ruled by St. Augustine's principle "Love and do as you will", is certainly rare. It makes part of authentic adulthood self-critically to acknowledge what has remained infantile in oneself and how far short one's spiritual stature falls of the full adult stature of Christ. This will make a person all the more ready to listen to what the law can provide as a help and correction of one's own views and unreliable leanings.[2] Such acceptance of the law is not immature submission proceeding from fear and external constraint, but is approval resulting from the insight into one's limitations and from the knowledge that the moral laws are fruits of the experience and common work of many generations. However once a person has sufficiently formed his conscience by attending to the law of nature and of grace, by purifying his intentions and gathering solid information, there comes a moment when he must be able to rely on his own conscience, because no mere legality can sufficiently answer God's personal call and invitation.

B. The binding force of conscience

I. The certain conscience

1. A certain conscience must always be obeyed when it commands or forbids. It may always be followed when it permits something. Paul states that "whatever does not proceed from faith is sin" (Rom 14:23). According to the context, he

---

[1] For the characterization of the developed and undeveloped adult conscience, cf. R. Egenter and P. Matussek, *Faith, Freedom and Conscience* (Dublin: Gill and Son, 1967, 118f; compare pp. 91 and 115).

[2] The prohibition, existing in many states, of the sale of fire weapons without special license is based on the experience that private persons often do not know how to handle them prudently. The same is true of the prohibition of the sale of narcotics.

means to say that every action which is not performed with the certain conviction of its rightfulness is sin.

The reason for the principle is that conscience is that appropriate faculty of man which tells him what his moral duties are. Conscience as the sense of right and wrong in man is the necessary consequence of a divine plan for the world and of a purposeful world order. For neither the order of nature nor the divine plan can be realized without a sense in man informing him about the place falling to his lot in the world and the role he has to fulfil in it. Through the mediation of conscience everybody gains the necessary insight into the laws he is to respect in the order of creation and the tasks he is to fulfil in the service of God's plan for the world. It is the competent and indispensable guide given to man to discern his vocation and moral obligation. Therefore to disobey this faculty is to disobey the moral order, is to disobey the will of God, and this is sin.

2. The certainty required for the judgments of conscience generally need not be a strict moral certainty, but a wide moral certainty is sufficient.

Strict moral certainty excludes any reasonable fear of error. Strict moral certainties are the assumptions that people will not kill arbitrarily, that Catholic priests or Anglican ministers baptize validly, that the apostles Peter and Paul met death in Rome; the opposites would contradict the normal behaviour of rational beings and the assured rules of historical verification. Wide moral certainty is accompanied by a slight yet negligible fear of error, because the possibility of error is of little probability. The assumptions that physicians will act responsibly and with competence or that drivers will respect the basic traffic rules are wide moral certainties. Wide moral certainty is equally the supposition that an action cannot be pernicious and can therefore lawfully be performed if several competent moral theologians regard it as licit, although others are of a different opinion. The wide moral certainty could also be characterized as a very high probability. It has also been termed "prudential certainty".

Wide moral certainty is sufficient for licit operation in the general conditions of life, because frequently only this certainty can be obtained. Always to require strict moral certainty for lawful action would burden life with many anxieties and render it intolerable. God does not command the impossible.

Only in a few cases is wide moral certainty insufficient, namely, where a value is so important that not even a slight risk can be taken to damage it; e.g. when the recovery of a leading personality is of great importance for the common good (in which case one will call in not only one, but three physicians), or if at the visit of a foreign head of state multiple precautions are taken to guard against any unpleasant incident.

3. The invincibly erroneous conscience must be followed just the same as a certain conscience which is right.[1] Therefore he who lies to help a neighbour out of a difficulty, convinced that to do so is an act of charity, actually does perform a laudable act of fraternal charity; and should he act contrary to his erroneous conscience he would sin. On the other hand, whoever thinks that it is a sin to say "oh hell" and nevertheless says it sins, although, as a matter of fact, the expression is not sinful in itself.

Paul's statement that "whatever does not proceed from faith is sin" actually refers to an erroneous conscience. In the Roman community there were some Christians who believed that the use of meat and wine generally was forbidden (Rom 14:2-21). Paul asserts that those who judge that for Christians no food is "unclean" were right. But the food "is unclean for any one who thinks it unclean" (Rom 14:14), and such a man "is condemned, if he eats, because he does not act from faith" (Rom 14:23), In 1 Corinthians 8, Paul examines a similar problem. It concerns the meat from pagan sacrifices which was offered for sale in the public markets. Although the right knowledge is that there are no "gods" and hence that there is nothing against eating meat from such fallacious sacrifices, nevertheless those who think such meat forbidden would sin if they ate it. "Their conscience, being weak, is defiled" (1 Cor 8:7). The ultimate and decisive measure of morality is therefore, according to Paul's clear teaching, one's subjective conscience, even if it judges wrongly. A confirmation

---

[1] Catholic moral theology has not always held this principle with the same clarity and firmness of conviction as now. Very informative insights into the history of this doctrine in Catholic tradition are offered by Karl Golser, *Gewissen und objektive Sittenordnung* (Wiener Domverlag, 1975), 37-77.

of this doctrine can be found in the words of Christ which he addressed to the Pharisees: "If you were blind, you would have no guilt" (Jn 9:41). That is, if the Pharisees were unable to detect their errors concerning the person of Jesus, they would be excused from sin; but as a matter of fact their consciences were not invincibly but vincibly erroneous, and therefore they were responsible for their wrong-doing.

The inner reason for the axiom is that a certain conscience, even if it erroneously proposes something as good or bad, proposes it as one's moral obligation and as the will of God. To disobey this certain, though erroneous judgment of conscience would mean to disobey what is subjectively believed as one's moral duty and God's will; therefore it would signify sin.

Were man not entitled and bound to follow the certain judgments of his conscience on the ground that it can sometimes err, he would be handed over to complete lawlessness without the possibility of any trustworthy decision. On the other hand, by submitting to his certain conscience he acts in a way which enables him, in spite of occasional errors, to best realize what is good and to avoid what is evil. Although there is a risk of objectively wrong decisions, it is remote; while it is proximate if the judgments of conscience were simply disregarded under the pretext of the wrong generalization that conscience is unreliable.

The possibility of erroneous judgments of conscience should however make man cautious in his decisions and open to the advice of others. Especially in case of fanatic convictions the immediate danger of blind prepossession exists. Whoever becomes aware that he is in such a state of mind, has the urgent duty to examine his "judgments of conscience" with great care. Yet after having done what is in one's power to come to the correct decision, one has the right and duty to follow one's conscience also in instances of invincible ignorance.

As far as the erroneous conscience of others is concerned, one has in principle to respect their honest convictions. It can be advisable to tolerate an erroneous opinion and to be silent about it, if the error is not particularly damaging and if the attempt to correct it would cause greater detriment, e.g. if serious quarrel and aversion would result. Yet if the error is in some regard detrimental, as is mostly the case, it will certainly be a work of charity to find a way of removing it. And where the erroneous conscience even threatens fundamental goods and rights of others, one is obliged to oppose it firmly and to prevent the injustice within the scope of the possible. Thus if a religious fanatic believes that he ought to kill a representative of his religion pleading for tolerance, then the police can and must hinder the potential murderer, if they come to know about his intentions, and take him into custody.[1]

Note that the unavoidable cannot be sinful, even though one falsely believes it to be a sin. Thus a gravely ill daughter does not sin if she cannot travel to the funeral of her father, even if she thinks she has by this gravely offended against the duty of filial love.

II. The vincibly erroneous and lax conscience

(1) The *vincibly erroneous conscience* cannot be followed as a legitimate rule of action. Conscience is vincibly erroneous if it dawns on man that his moral outlook might not be entirely sound or if he is aware of being careless and irresponsible in his decisions. Thus a physician may have examined a patient only hastily with the result that he is not able to make a responsible diagnosis. With such a state of mind a person is not allowed to act or to appease himself, since he would voluntarily expose himself to the danger of committing error and sin.

Before a person with a vincibly erroneous conscience can act, he must first remove his doubtful state by searching after the truth. If he is not able to do so for the moment, he must postpone the action, or he must follow the safer line of action. If a motorist doubts, whether he may still drink another glass of wine, the safer alternative is not to drink another one.

(2) Akin to the vincibly erroneous conscience is the dulled or *lax conscience*. The lax conscience is inclined, on insufficient grounds, to judge a thing to be lawful which is sinful, or something to be a light sin which is actually a grave one. In a light-minded and sometimes frivolous way

---

[1] Nov. 1995 Premier Rabin was shot in Tel Aviv, "by order of God", through the student Yigal Amir, who regarded Rabin's consent to Palestinian autonomy as treason. Had the police known about the intentions of the student, they would have had the right and the duty to place him under detention.

the lax conscience does not face up to the gravity of the moral obligation. A businessman, for example, may regard the defrauding of huge tax amounts as a light matter only and some cheating in the quality of his goods as normal, lawful business practice.

A person who is of lax conscience has the general and grave obligation to reform this state of mind, since it exposes him to the danger of sin and since it must, as a rule, be considered as vincibly erroneous. He must pay much more attention to doubts that occur to him than others need do, and he may not readily disregard them as mere scruples. But if such a person is unaware of his state of conscience and does not recognize, even in a general way, the malice of an action or his duty to make further investigation, his conscience must be regarded as invincibly erroneous and he would be excused from sin in this particular case. Nevertheless the causation of this state of mind may well have been accompanied by guilt. It can result from the refusal to search for and recognize the truth. This free refusal which prevents the proper knowledge is culpable. "The goodness or evil of the person do therefore not begin with the moment in which conscience has spoken and do not depend only on obedience or disobedience to its judgment; they extend to the very elaboration of its judgment and depend on its obedience or disobedience to the truth."[1]

A lax conscience is usually the result of lukewarmness in the service of God, as depicted in the book of Revelation 3:15-20. Christ counsels the lax members of his Church to buy from him the remedies for their lukewarmness. These remedies are a re-vitalization of religious life and faith in God, the probing of conscience and repentance, and zeal in doing good works. God himself announces his visitations as a remedy. The antithesis to a lax conscience is the tender conscience or the delicate conscience, which is characterized by a clear and vigilant discernment of the good.

(3) A particular variety is the *compensatory conscience*. Through a bothersome preoccupation with small and quite innocent details of morality it attempts to conceal a fundamental

---

[1] G. Gatti, *l. c.* 136.

lack of generosity in the spiritual life.[1] This compensatory supersession is intended to divert attention from the unwillingness to live up to one's true vocation. A client with these "tepidity scruples" tries to obtain from the spiritual guide the assurance that he has not really offended against his moral duties, which is true with regard to the defects confessed, but not with regard to the deeper lack of faithfulness. Therefore, in spite of possible approval by the priest or counsellor, the counselee's deeper self will not be at peace. The treatment of this type of scrupulous unrest must bring to consciousness the secret lack of generosity by an understanding, patient, sincere conversation. The troubled person must realize that his unrest is an invitation to a real change of heart and to a more faithful answer to the call of divine grace. Akin to the compensatory conscience is the pharisaic conscience, which attaches great importance to small things and makes light of serious matters (cf. Is 5:20).

III. The perplexed conscience

The perplexed conscience is a type of erroneous conscience which, in a conflict of duties, fears sin in whatever choice it makes. A widowed mother, who has received many benefits from a friendly family whose father has caused a car crash of which she was a witness, will easily find herself in the conflict between the obligation of gratitude to her benefactor and the obligation to tell the truth in court, where she is cited as a witness.

In such instances, if the decision can be delayed, one must first postpone the action in order to obtain information and deliberate on it. But if the decision cannot be postponed, one must choose what appears to be the lesser evil or - if this is impossible to settle - either of the alternatives. The observance of these norms presupposed, there is no question of formal sin, since it is impossible for the person to escape

---

[1] Adrian van Kaam speaks of "life-guilt". This guilt does not refer to one or other incidental transgression. It results from a basic refusal to respond to one's personal call. Accordingly it is vague and undefined (*The Vowed Life*. Denville, N.J.: Dimension Books, 1968, 124f). It may manifest itself in tepidity scruples, but it can also seek escape in other forms of distraction, e.g. in restless, dissipating activities, even of charitable nature.

both alternatives of the perplexing situation together. Impossibility and lack of freedom however preclude sin.

A further guide for such instances is the rule that precepts of natural law ordinarily precede precepts of positive ecclesiastical and civil law, supposing that the moral gravity of the conflicting precepts is approximately the same. Hence if a nurse feels obliged by precept of the Church to go to Sunday Mass and bound by charity to stay with a critically sick patient, the obligation of charity should be preferred to the obligation of the ecclesiastical precept. Furthermore precepts which are certain prevail over those which are merely probable or doubtful.

The perplexed conscience is classified as a type of erroneous conscience, because objectively only one of the two conflicting obligations can be binding. It would contradict justice and the wisdom of God if man were confronted with two equally binding obligations, of which after all he can fulfil only one.

Such conflicts more readily occur in individuals who are less acquainted with the moral norms. However this does not preclude the possibility that even the experts and an entire community may for some time be in a state of perplexity as to the prevailing obligation in a particular conflict of duties or rights. The commentaries of the Catholic bishops' conferences on the encyclical "Humanae Vitae" concerning the artificial means of birth control can serve as an illustration.

IV. The doubtful conscience

Conscience is doubtful if it is in a state of uncertainty as to the lawfulness or obligation of an action, whether conscience suspends its judgments or whether it inclines to one side, but with the fear that the contrary might equally be true.

The doubt may either concern the existence of a law and moral principle (*dubium iuris*) or the existence of a fact (*dubium facti*). The question whether therapeutic abortion is lawful is a doubt concerning a principle, whilst the question whether the growth in the uterus of a sick woman is a tumour or a child is a doubt concerning the existence of a fact.

Another distinction is that between speculative and practical doubt. The former is concerned with the theoretical truth of an ethical doctrine (e.g. whether the killing of a tyrant may sometimes be lawful); the latter deals with the lawfulness of an action to be performed here and now (e.g. whether it is lawful to kill this particular tyrant here and now).

Norms for action with doubtful conscience

The basic principle reads: In a practical doubt about the lawfulness of an action one may not act. The reason is that by acting with a doubtful conscience, a person would expose himself to the danger of injustice and sin, and that itself is injustice and sin. Therefore a hunter who doubts whether what he is aiming at is an animal or a man, is guilty of homicide if he kills, even if it turns out that he slew an animal.

Action in instances of a doubtful conscience is regulated by the following rules: The action must be postponed until certainty can be reached. Practical certainty can be gained *directly* by solving the doubt through reflection on the case in the light of general principles, through consultation of experts and pertinent books, through clarification of the facts, etc. The effort one is obliged to make in order to acquire certainty is to be measured by the importance of the values which are to be safeguarded. "Prudence forbids us to devote excessive attention and research to trivial matters because this would rob us of the spirit of joy in doing good and, most of all, because it would greatly hamper the fulfilment of more urgent and more important duties."[1]

If the doubt cannot be solved directly - but only then - one may attempt to gain practical certainty *indirectly* by the application of the so-called reflex principles. These do not solve the theoretical doubt about the existence of a law, right, or fact (e.g. whether an accused person is guilty); but certainty is obtained as to what one may or must do here and now (e.g. in doubt presumption favours the accused). The reflex principles will be dealt with in detail in the next section.

If there is no time or possibility to solve the doubt, one must opt for the safer alternative, that is, one must favour the alternative which excludes the danger of sin and injustice most certainly. Hence if somebody doubts whether the drug LSD is allowed, he may not take it. If no safer side can be

---

[1] B. Häring, *The Law of Christ*, vol. I, 1966, 172.

discerned, the situation amounts to a perplexed conscience, and the person may choose whatever alternative seems best to him.

C. Formation of a certain conscience by means of reflex principles

I. Nature and varieties of reflex principles

Reflex principles are rules of prudence which do not solve a doubt concerning the existence of a law, moral principle, or fact by intrinsic or extrinsic evidence, but only indicate as to where, in cases of insoluble doubt, the greater right is usually to be found and the lesser evil to be feared, and which side therefore is to be favoured as long as the doubt persists. The principles are gained by inference from the common circumstances of such cases and the ordinary happenings of life, from general experience and observation. In default of actual evidence, the reflex principles give subsidiary solutions, which will not in all instances do justice to the parties concerned, but which at least guarantee that in the majority of cases injustice is avoided and the rights of those concerned are safeguarded best. If, e.g., in a court case two parties claim the same estate, the safest solution would be had if one side were able to procure intrinsic evidence of his ownership by submitting unequivocal documents. But if no party is able to do so, the lawsuit will often be settled by application of the rule of prudence: in doubt, the condition of the possessor is the better, i.e. of that possessor who at present lives on the land, cultivates it or actually uses it in another way. This principle will not always do justice to the party which is not in possession; and the arbitration therefore remains subsidiary. But according to common experience, the solution of the doubt thus gained is the right one more often than not.

The most comprehensive of the reflex principles, to which all the others can be reduced, is the rule: In doubt, we must stand on that side where presumption stands, Presumption is understood as a conjecture as to where in cases of doubt the greater right commonly lies and the lesser injustice is to be feared. This side is supposed to be within his rights until the truth of the contrary is proved.

The other reflex principles specify more in detail where in doubt presumption stands. They are the following:
1. In doubt, the condition of the possessor is the better. (*In dubio melior est conditio possidentis.*)
2. In doubt, favour the accused; or: crime is not to be presumed, but to be proved.
3. In doubt, presumption stands on the side of the superior.
4. In doubt, stand for the validity of the act (e.g. the validity of the matrimonial bond, cf. CIC 1060, or the validity of an examination or an appointment to an office; however doubtful contracts are usually not upheld by civil law.)
5. In doubt, amplify the favourable, restrict the unfavourable. (*Favorabilia sunt amplianda, odiosa restringenda.*)
6. In doubt, presumption stands for the usual and the ordinary; or: follow daily and ordinary experience. (E.g. in doubt whether an apparition is miraculous or a mere imagination, the latter is to be assumed.)
7. In doubt, favour the customary and hitherto approved.[1]
8. A doubtful law does not oblige (*lex dubia non obligat*), i.e. presumption stands for liberty.

With regard to the last principle, "a doubtful law does not oblige", it must be noted that this principle can be applied only in instances of common doubt, i.e. when the law is doubtful among the very experts. If an undisputed law is solely doubtful to a particular person in a particular case, then such a doubt must be dealt with like a doubtful fact; e.g. if a man doubts whether it is lawful to help his friend in stealing some articles from a car repair shop. To instances of doubtful facts the following rules apply:

(I) *If there is a risk of serious spiritual or temporal harm (be it to oneself, to another person or to a community), which one is obliged to avoid by an indubitable law, the*

---

[1] J. Gründel arrives at this rule: "To depart from customary and hitherto moral action, without the support of weighty reasons, is irresponsible" (J. Gründel, *Normen in Wandel*. München: Don Bosco Verlag, 1980, 122); likewise B. Schüller in *Christlich glauben und handeln*, ed. by K. Demmer and B. Schüller (Düsseldorf: Patmos, 1977), 282.

safer alternative must be chosen. Therefore one may not enjoy even the rare pleasure of the narcotic heroin because of the great and immediate peril of addiction with all its ruinous effects. A hunter may not shoot in doubt whether the object is an animal or a human being. In administering the sacraments, one must decide in favour of the opinion that safeguards the validity of the sacrament with certainty.

(II) *If there is only question of the honesty of an action, where no risk of serious spiritual or temporal harm is involved, one is not bound to opt for the safer alternative.* Therefore if one doubts whether one may cross a property, whether there is a sacred holy day with the obligation to go to Mass, whether a watch offered for sale is smuggled, one is not obliged to follow the safer way and to make a detour round the property, to attend a Mass or to decline the possibly smuggled watch. The reason is that no serious damage is to be feared, even if the contrary should turn out to be true.

II. The systems of probability

The side where presumption stands is usually to be favoured, as long as the contrary is not proved. A man is presumed to be innocent as long as it is not certainly proved that he has committed a crime. The condition of the possessor is the better, as long as there is no certain proof for the right of the contesting other side.

Yet especially concerning the principle "a doubtful law does not oblige" a controversy exists whether liberty can always be favoured as long as the law is not morally certain, or whether reservations are called for and liberty can only be favoured when its side is more probable or at least equally probable compared with the case for the obligation of the law. This controversy led to the systems of probability, in tradition less felicitously called "moral systems", i.e. the systems of rigorism, probabiliorism, aequiprobabilism, probabilism and laxism, which caused many passionate altercations among moral theologians in the past, especially during the 17th and 18th centuries. It has cost the moral theologians much effort and thinking. The dispute does indeed concern not a merely peripheral problem, but the significant question after the greater right of the law or of liberty. In the course of the dispute the weight shifted ever more in favour of liberty.

An example will help to characterize the five systems briefly. In 1917 the Holy Office gave the response that Catholics may not attend spiritistic seances even as mere spectators (DS 3642). However since then new insights into the nature of spiritistic phenomena have been gained, which incline some theologians to a more generous attitude in this matter. Could therefore today a Catholic possibly attend a spiritistic seance as a mere spectator? The various moral systems would judge the matter in the following ways. Rigorism would contend that even if 80-90% of the theologians favour permission to attend a spiritistic seance, the old law still prevails and attendance remains forbidden. Probabiliorism would demand that the majority of the theologians must favour a permission, otherwise the prohibition remains in force. Aequiprobabilism would grant permission if at least 50% of the theologians were in its favour. For probabilism 30% would do. And for laxism even one or two contemporary theologians in favour of a permission would suffice to allow attendance. More in detail, the tenets and principles of the various systems are the following.

Rigorism or tutiorism maintains that, in doubt, one must always opt for the law, even if liberty from the law is most probable, since the part of the law in principle is the safer side.[1] It has been rejected by Pope Alexander VIII (DS 2303). Equally rejected has been *laxism*, to which even a tenuous probability suffices for exemption from the obligation of the law.[2] Laxism has never been taught as a theoretical system, but has been followed only practically by certain moral theologians in their solutions of doubts. It has been rejected by Pope Innocent XI (DS 2103). Both systems contradict the

---

[1] Rigorist would be the tenet that a Catholic organist may never, not even occasionally, play the organ at the religious service of a Protestant church, on the grounds that this would conflict with his Catholic faith.

[2] A laxist attitude is had if a priest celebrates the Holy Eucharist with rice cake on the grounds that one or the other theologian considers it possible that Christ's intention, when instituting this sacrament, was just to use the ordinary food of the people and not necessarily wheat bread.

principle, though from opposite sides, that moral certainty is the basis for lawful action. - Excluding these two extremes, the following three systems are propounded in moral theology:

1. *Probabiliorism*, which will depart from a safe view in favour of the law only for a more probable view in favour of liberty. The basic argument for it is the following. In doubt one must opt, as far as this is humanly possible, for the safer side, i.e. for the side which is most likely to exclude sin; and that is the side of the law in cases where the opinion in favour of the law is more probable or equally probable. However if the opinion in favour of freedom is more probable, one may opt for this side, since the danger of sin is only slight and therefore negligible.

Against this the following objection is made. To follow a law which is only probably just does not exclude the danger of injustice and material sin. Thus the observance of the decree of the Holy Office, issued Dec. 14, 1898, which forbade Catholic sisters in the service of the sick to call a non-Catholic minister to a non-Catholic patient, even if the latter should ask for him, had become obsolete and in many instances unjust long before it was abolished by the "Directory for Ecumenical Matters" of May 14, 1967.[1] In this case the rigorous observance of the old law certainly did not most exclude the danger of sin. The present directory not only obliges the Catholic staff in hospitals to call the non-Catholic minister if the patient should ask for him, but the personnel is obliged to advise ministers of other religious groups spontaneously and to afford them every facility.

2. *Aequiprobabilism*, which allows abandoning the view in favour of the law when the view in favour of liberty is equally probable. It bases itself on the argument that in doubt one must follow the opinion which most excludes the danger of error. Therefore one must follow the more probable opinion, if there is one. If however the opinions in favour of the law and in favour of liberty are equally probable, one may choose whichever alternative one likes. The reason is that in such instances the danger of error is always equally great, whichever

---

[1] D. Prümmer regards the decree of the Holy Office still valid in his *Manuale Theologiae Moralis* of 1958, vol. I, no. 526.

side one prefers. Aequiprobabilism is the system associated with Alphonsus of Liguori, who adopted it and gave it repute.[1]

These considerations appear reasonable and convincing. On the other hand it seems unreasonable to demand that an opinion must first find approval of at least 50% of the competent theologians before it can be followed. The answer to the difficulty appears to be this. If a person is able to form his opinion only on the basis of the number of authors for and against it, and is not in a condition to gain a personal understanding of the supporting reasons behind the opinion, then indeed it seems that he could only opt for a view which enjoys the support of the majority of the authors or at least of 50% of them. But if in addition to the support of some, maybe five or six, competent authors a person is able to form for himself the judgment that the arguments advanced by these authors are indeed well founded, then this is a sufficient basis to follow the view held by them.

3. *Probabilism*, which holds that one may follow the opinion in favour of liberty as long as it is well-founded, even though the contrary opinion be more probable. Probabilism bases itself on the following arguments. First, liberty is entirely "in possession" as opposed to legal obligation, because man's liberty precedes any formulated law. Therefore man has an indubitable, certain right to liberty, which can only be restricted by the obligation of an indubitable law. Second, the right to liberty is so high a good that it can only be limited by an even higher good. Yet the good effect of a doubtful law is of doubtful nature itself, which cannot be considered a higher

---

[1] There is however still another distinction found in the writings of St. Alphonsus, which says that only in doubt concerning the *existence* of a law one can follow the opinion equally probable in favour of liberty; but in doubt concerning the *cessation* of law one is to follow the opinion equally probable in favour of the law. But recent historical research seems to show that the original intention of Alphonsus was rather a pure aequiprobabilism. It was more for external reasons that he had to modify his theory and draw closer to probabiliorism, because of a prevailing attitude of anti-probabilism in his time in Italy, not only among theologians but also among civil rulers. (1768 the Jesuits, who favoured probabilism, were expelled from the kingdom of Naples.) Cf. Louis Vereecke, *Storia della teologia morale moderna* IV: *Storia della teologia morale nel XVIII secolo* (Roma: Accademia Alfonsiana, 1975, mimeographed notes), 115-122.

good than the certain right to liberty. In consequence, man's rights are better safeguarded if in instances of doubtful laws he retains the liberty to make his choice in full independence. This does not mean that he excludes from his choice the means indicated by the law. He can still opt for them, but he is not exclusively bound to what the law proposes.

Against this argumentation it is objected that man is subject to the demands of natural law from the first moment of his existence. Accordingly man's subjection to the law is as early as his right to freedom. And the observance of this basic order is not less a value than that of freedom. In answer to this, probabilism points out that only the unwritten moral law is implanted in man's nature. Yet human formulations of the moral law and most particularly positive laws are posterior to man's freedom, and they may indeed unduly restrict freedom because of the imperfections which accompany human formulations time and again.

Against the argument that in doubt one must always opt for the side which excludes error most, probabilism advances the following consideration. Although the opinion in favour of the law may be more probable, it is not in the best interest of the moral order to oblige man to the sole alternative of the law. Rather the possibility to make one's choice in a way which agrees best with the will of God is still greater if man is allowed to choose freely between the different alternatives. For once man has been fixed on the sole, though more probable alternative in favour of the law, he is without the possibility of opting for the other opinion, which is also still probable. But he is able to choose among all alternatives, if he is allowed to apply the principle: in doubtful matters freedom (*in dubio libertas*). For the rest, the difference between probabilism and aequiprobabilism does not seem too great if - as explained above - the more probable opinion does not only depend on the number of authors, but also on one's personal conviction concerning the arguments advanced by them.

A doctrine is considered probable if it is supported by various scholars who are (1) known for their seriousness, (2) considered authorities in the field of research concerned, and (3) "probati", i.e. are accepted as approved teachers within the Church. Commonly five or six authors of this nature are regarded as sufficient to establish a probable opinion.

In the Declaration on Religious Freedom, Vatican II itself defends a very broad-minded concept of human freedom in a significant statement. There we read: "The principle of the integrity of freedom in society should continue to be upheld. According to this principle man's freedom should be given the fullest possible recognition and should not be curtailed except when and in so far as is necessary" (DH 7).

D. Freedom and commitment of conscience

1. The right to freedom of conscience

The certain judgments of conscience are, as has been shown above, the proximate subjective norm of human activity. These judgments a person is bound to follow faithfully and he cannot disobey them without incurring guilt. To the strict obligation to follow one's certain conscience corresponds the right to act according to one's conscience; in other words, a man has the right to freedom of conscience. This is one of the basic freedom rights of men. It has also been included into the Universal Declaration of Human Rights by the United Nations (art. 18). From the right follows, as Vatican II declares, that a person "must not be forced to act contrary to his conscience. Nor must he be prevented from acting according to his conscience" (DH 3).[1]

The right to freedom of conscience accordingly comprises two claims. The first one is the right not to be forced to act contrary to one's conscience; this right is unconfined. The second claim is the right not to be restrained from acting according to one's conscience; this right meets with restrictions where it happens to collide with the demands of the common welfare. Are sectarians entitled to blare their propaganda hostile to the Church from loud-speakers of their belfries in the towns of South America? Should the burning of widows in India be considered the legitimate right of a free conscience, since it gives expression to a lofty concept of marriage? Can conscience entitle religious fanatics to hijack planes and shoot hostages in order to compel compliance with their demands?

---

[1] The right to freedom of conscience has also been asserted by Leo XIII in his encyclical "Libertas praestantissimum" of June 20, 1888, cf. DS 3250.

Conflicts and incompatibilities of this kind have their reasons in the faulty judgments of an erroneous conscience. It has been explained earlier that, even though a person has the obligation to follow an invincibly erroneous conscience, society has the right to defend itself against dangerous outgrowths of these errors, the simple reason being that error cannot claim the same right as the truth.

Vatican II states: "In availing of any freedom men must respect the moral principle of personal and social responsibility: in exercising their rights individual men and social groups are bound by the moral law to have regard for the rights of others, their own duties to others and for the common good of all" (DH 7). If an individual or a group is not able to meet these demands, society has the right to defend itself against such misguided threats. "The responsibility of providing such protection rests especially with the civil authority" (DH 7). Governments must however limit their defensive measures to that minimum which suffices to guarantee the just claims of the citizens and of the common welfare.

The above reflections show that freedom of conscience is not a right without problems and difficulties. The difficulties are still more aggravated by the undeniable fact that men have the tendency to twist and "cook up" the voice of conscience or to be negligent in its formation. Not without good reason a distinction has here been made between authentic convictions of conscience on the one hand and purely intellectual convictions on the other, which in an isolated way pursue their goals, but subconsciously are aware of not doing justice to reality in its entire complexity. It cannot be overlooked that in today's society the often invoked right to one's conscience against a majority or a positive law does not only meet with respect, but also with distrust.

Evidently freedom of conscience does not mean freedom *from* conscience. The person who disregards the voice of his conscience does not only sin, he is also guilty before the community. Crime consists precisely in this, that a person disregards the voice of his conscience in a serious matter. Likewise a twisted or negligently formed conscience is not the basis for immune and legitimate action. The citizen who causes encumbrances for the environment out of culpable ignorance of the law is not free from guilt. If society has the right to defend itself against the threats of an invincibly erroneous conscience, how much more does it have this right against a conscience which is vincibly and culpably erroneous. This raises questions concerning the relation of freedom of conscience to civil laws, to the teaching office of the Church, and to the duty of the responsible formation of conscience.

2. Conscience and the civil law

If in the question of the relation between conscience and the civil law attention spontaneously directs itself to possible conflicts between the two, their fundamental relation is nevertheless one of correspondence. In principle no contradiction exists between the fundamental right of freedom of conscience and the obligation to civil obedience, since conscience itself perceives this obedience as necessary and therefore as a moral duty. A refusal of civil obedience can only be an exception, about whose justification the objector - because the exception carries the burden of proof - must have moral certainty. In doubt presumption favours the legal order, which after all enjoys the approval of society (and therewith of the majority, and in many cases of the vast majority) and is supported by its will and conviction.

The Second Vatican Council therefore turns against "those who, while professing grand and rather noble sentiments, nevertheless in reality live always as if they cared nothing for the needs of society. Many in various places even make light of social laws and precepts" (GS 30). In contrast to this mind-set the Council exhorts that "everyone consider it his sacred obligation to count social necessities among the primary duties of modern man, and to pay heed to them" (ib.).

This of course does not preclude that the conscience of citizens at times can come into conflict with the law. Conflicts between conscience and authority are a problem as old as mankind. The Greek poet Sophocles (496-406 B.C.) provides a dramatic account for such a conflict in his tragedy "Antigone". King Creon had forbidden the burial of his enemy Polyneikes. His sister Antigone (daughter of Oedipus), buried him nevertheless, because it was her conviction that this act of piety was a demand of the gods. For this she was sentenced to death by the king.

Conflicts between the decisions of civil authorities and the individual conscience can readily arise, caused by shortcomings on either side. Authority will not always arrive at the most just and prudent decision. (Only laws enacted in honest conviction are here considered. Evidently criminal orders can never claim obedience.) At the same time the subject is far from being infallible in the judgments of his conscience.

The right to freedom of conscience is - as explained above - a fundamental human right and as such is also guaranteed by the modern democratic constitutional states. It implies that citizens may not be obliged by the public authorities to act against commands and prohibitions of their conscience. The injunctions of conscience accordingly have priority vis-à-vis the orders of the law. But this entails problems. Isn't the validity of the general order of law in principle subject thereby to the personal judgment of the individual citizen, whose judgment can evidently also be erroneous? Must this not curtail the necessary protective function of the law? Can the appeal to conscience, for example in case of the terrorist murder of a politician, free the terrorists from guilt and justify a claim of impunity? Where are the limits of the claim to freedom of conscience?

One conflict of conscience is expressly regulated in many states by the law: Nobody may be forced to do military service against his conscience. Military service however is at the same time a burdensome duty, and the objection against it can also stem from dread of the sacrifices and the efforts connected with it. How can it be discerned whether the objection stems from a dictate of conscience or whether it is a strategy to escape a disagreeable duty? The principal criterion for this is the readiness of the objector to accept an "unpleasant alternative". In question here as well as in other cases of the refusal of a civic duty is also the equality of burdens among citizens. In the case of an objection against military service, it is restored by the alternative of civic service. Unfortunately the state cannot attach an "unpleasant alternative" to every civic duty in order to counter possible conflicts with the freedom of conscience. There are limits to this possibility. The alternative in other cases then is possibly the imposition and acceptance of a penalty.

Two typical instances of the refusal of duties for reasons of conscience can be distinguished. (1) A duty, whose fulfilment is declined, directly contradicts the conscience of the objector, e.g. the professional duty to participate in an abortion; or the duty to take an oath as a witness in court; or the duty to undergo a protective inoculation. (2) A duty is declined which would indirectly promote actions of which conscience disapproves, e.g. the partial or general refusal to pay taxes or premiums to the sick-fund because they could be used for the financing of armaments or for abortions on sick-certificate.

Going beyond the mere refusal of a duty are actions of active resistance. Such actions can concern the reality itself judged to create a condition of injustice, e.g. the destruction of war material[1] or the terrorist murder of a politician;[2] or the action as such does not have a relation to the (real or supposed) injustice against which the protest of conscience is directed, but only has the meaning of giving force to the demands raised, e.g. the blockade of roads or bridges as a form of protest against a damage to the environment (e.g. through the construction of a roller dam).

With regard to the different instances of a refusal of duty and of resistance, it is to be accepted that the freedom of conscience accords a right to ward off actions which contradict a person's conscience. It does however not warrant a refusal of contributions which have been duly enacted according to the principle of equality of burdens. Thus a member of a legally established sick-fund, who considers the utilization of that fund for the financing of abortions on sick-certificate or of blood transfusions as contrary to his conscience, cannot derive from his conviction a right to retain his contributions. He cannot demand that *his* convictions be made the criterion for the validity of general legal norms. The same holds for the refusal of taxes as a protest against expenditure for armaments. The general payment of contributions does not violate the conscience of the one who pays; their payment in itself is not unethical or sinful. Very many of the allocations made from those contributions are indisputably legitimate. Moreover the individual allocations are not decreed by the

---

[1] Thus the group around the Berrigan brothers in the USA in 1968 burnt records of conscripts and in 1980 damaged rockets in an arms production plant (cf. K. Remele, *Ziviler Ungehorsam*. Münster: Aschendorff, 1992, 179; 183; 193).

[2] In 1968 Robert (Bob) Kennedy was shot by the Palestinian immigrant Sirhan B. Sirhan, because he considered him dangerous for the cause of the Arabs. In 1978 Aldo Moro, a Christian Democratic politician, was murdered in Rome by the Red Brigades.

person who pays, but by the legislator. The conscience of the latter is called upon indeed, when deciding upon the particular allocations. The only way to obviate the allocations rejected by a citizen is the appeal to the conscience of the fellow citizens to adjudge those allocations as immoral, and by this means to create a new majority which will repeal the legal norm in question. After all the citizen continues to demand all expenditures favourable to himself from the contributions.

Freedom of conscience furthermore grants the right, at least to a large extent, of acting in conformity with one's conscience, e.g. to witness to one's faith or to help the needy (e.g. refugees possibly unjustly treated by the state). Yet it does not grant a right to encroach upon the rights of others. If somebody violates the protected interests of others, such as life, health, freedom, property, he brings into action the protective function of the state. "Nobody can appeal to freedom of conscience to encroach upon the sphere of rights of his fellow-men, for homicide or physical injury, for constraint and damage to property."[1] To this also pertains the traffic blockade as act of "civil disobedience", although in this case exceptions could be thought of, since the encroachment is less trenchant.[2] In principle the blockade constitutes an interference with the constitutionally protected freedom of movement of the road users and their negative freedom of opinion. Methods of active resistance are illegal in a legitimately and democratically ruled state. The right to resistance only comes to life if an illegally acting government disregards the basic rights of its citizens in fundamental ways.

In a pluralistic society the state will inevitably be confronted with various convictions of conscience. It will therefore have to limit itself to an ethical minimum. And wherever a way can be found to do justice to the law and to the conscience of the individual, it has to be chosen. But unqualified indulgence towards abusive appeals to freedom of conscience must undermine the stability of the legal order and the trust of the

---

[1] J. Isensee, "Gewissen in Recht," in G. Höver/L. Honnefelder, eds., *Der Streit um das Gewissen* (Paderborn: Schöningh, 1993), 55.

[2] For J. Isensee however the traffic blockade is incompatible with the prohibition of violence, the duty to uphold the peace and the obedience due to the law (*ib.* 55f). It should be noted that a strike of public busses is not a traffic blockade. Only certain means of public transportation are cancelled, while the traffic itself remains unimpeded.

citizens. Therefore the state cannot simply exempt delinquents of conscience from punishment.

The common weal is secured only if the consciences of the citizens are in substance formed correctly. The correct formation of conscience therefore necessarily also becomes a concern of the state. This cannot be achieved by decree of law. The means to this rather are education of the youth in schools, the educational work of the mass media under public law, the example of the office holders, and the cooperation with those forces in society which can impart a coherent ethos. There are special expectations here in regard to the Churches as well as to religions in general. While for the state neutrality in matters of belief is a fundamental necessity, the Churches are bound to the Christian faith and to the moral claims resulting from it. On the basis of their faith a formation of conscience is possible which goes beyond the possibilities of the state. It falls upon the Churches to form and sharpen consciences for the enactment of just laws as well as for the loyal fulfilment of those laws.

3. *Conscience and the teaching office of the Church*

It is oldest Catholic tradition that the teaching office belongs to the essence of the Church, which office also includes orientations for the Christian moral life. Representatives of the teaching office are the bishops, individually and above all in common, and in a special way the bishop of Rome, who are called to this service, appointed and qualified for it. "The solution of Luther, born out of a personal plight, according to which above all the individual is guided by the Spirit, has been considered as too inadequate from the Catholic point of view. It has been felt that the perseverance in the truth, which Christ has promised to his Church, is secured by something further, namely by a special office or also service of its own."[1] The Second Vatican Council has expressly confirmed this tradition (LG 25) and has not left any doubt that the teaching office makes demands upon conscience, from which a person cannot prescind in his judgments and decisions (DH 14). - Although the following considerations have directly

---

[1] H. Weber, "Konkurrenten oder Weggenossen? Das Verhältnis von Gewissen und kirchlichem Lehramt," in *Das Gewissen*, ed. by J. Gründel (Düsseldorf: Patmos, 1990), 92.

in view the teaching office of the Catholic Church, they hold to a large extent also for other religious and social authorities who set down moral norms and give moral orientations.

The teaching office of the Church helps the believers to know what corresponds to a life guided by the Christian faith. All ethicists and theologians agree that conscience needs education and formation. Among the forces in society which are in a position to accomplish this educational work and, on account of their qualification, are also obliged to undertake it, is the community of the Church, and there again the teaching office holds a special place. "If I believe that the Church comes from the Lord, then the office of the Church has a right to be accepted as a primary factor in the formation of conscience, in the true formation of conscience itself."[1] In the midst of so many conflicting voices telling people what to do, and so many diverse communities projecting images of what makes life worthwhile, the Church is for her believers a basic help to hear the call of the Gospel more clearly. On the basis of the common faith in Jesus Christ and his Gospel, common convictions of a religious and a moral nature ensue for the members of the Church on a much larger scale than in a state community, whose world-view must remain neutral.

This does not exclude a certain pluralism of moral judgments also within the Christian Churches, even though within narrower bounds. Christian revelation does not offer express answers to all questions about correct conduct in the world. Human inquiry and deliberation are needed, naturally in the light of the Gospel and with the help of grace, which does not entirely exclude differences of moral opinions (e.g. concerning the lawfulness of capital punishment or the construction of nuclear power plants).[2] This does however not mean that in such instances all alternatives are of equal value. "Not every opinion which emerges is immediately acceptable simply for the reason that it emerges. Believers must be guided to see whether or not, in view of the conscientiousness and competence they discern in those who advocate alternatives,

---

[1] J. Card. Ratzinger, "Der Auftrag des Bischofs und des Theologen....," in *Internationale katholische Zeitschrift* 13 (1984), 532.

[2] Cf. GS 43: "Yet it happens rather frequently, and legitimately so, that some of the faithful, with no less sincerity, will see the problem quite differently."

a particular alternative can be situated within the realm of Christian morality."[1]

Moral obligations must in principle be intelligible and comprehensible. This however is not contradicted by the fact that men are not always in a position to form a sufficient judgment for themselves on particular moral questions. If in such a case they entrust themselves to the judgment of a competent, trustworthy authority, and especially to the teaching office of the Church, they act in a responsible way. The goodness of the moral command is in this case not grasped directly via intrinsic reasons, but indirectly via the competence of a trustworthy authority. In many other spheres of life men too must content themselves with indirect certainties of this nature. But where it is possible to gain a direct insight into the justification of an obligation, this is to be preferred. An inner insight usually makes a more judicious fulfilment of the command possible. The teaching office itself must strive to make its moral demands comprehensible to those who are looking for such an understanding.

The teaching office of the Church has an authority of its own, which comes from Christ. Yet this authority is not simply identical with the authority of Christ. The teaching office does not receive a new revelation, but only interprets the revelation given by Christ. In doing so, mistakes and errors can happen. This problem has attracted much attention especially in recent times. Very forcibly the question is being raised, how far a man has to submit his judgments of conscience to the judgments of religious authorities.[2]

Because limits of certitude are present on both sides, on the part of the believers as well as on the part of the teaching office, both sides ought to be cautious in their affirmations and rejections. Yet the presumption is in favour of the teaching office.[3] Its representatives are appointed for this office on

---

[1] J. Fuchs, "Gewissen und pluralistische Gesellschaft," in *Für eine christliche Moral*, vol. II (Freiburg: Herder, 1989), 176.

[2] For the question of religiously founded assent to the teaching office and of a possible dissent, see "The ecclesiality of faith," *Christian Ethics*, vol. II, ch. 1.

[3] The National Catechetical Directory of the U.S., *Sharing the Light of Faith*, of 1978 writes: "When faced with questions which pertain to dissent from non-infallible teaching of the Church, it is important for catechists to keep in mind that the presumption is always in favor of the magisterium" (nr. 190). See the pertinent expositions on this matter by R.M. Gula, *l.c.* 155-161.

account of their special competence and of their sense of faith. Furthermore the doctrinal assertions are formulated - the more important they are, the more carefully - with the aid and counsel of many experts and theologians. In comparison to such conclusions, the insights of the individual believer must be considered as far more limited and more exposed to error. Spontaneously individuals are aware of this, and therefore they do not feel at ease with moral judgments of their own which conflict with the decisions of the ecclesiastical authorities. And justly so! If an individual conscience stands against the opinion of the teaching office and of the experts, this ought to make the individual extremely careful, lest he become guilty of acting irresponsibly and with obstinate pride. Only well-founded certainty to the contrary can overthrow the presumption of right in favour of such an opinion and justify a decision deviating from it.

A subject must be so much the more careful, the more competent the superior is and the more advice from experts he received before formulating his decision. Naturally, if there is a difference of opinion among the experts and theologians themselves, whether a decision given by a superior authority in a moral controversy was the correct one, then a subject's dissenting conscience can no longer be classified as an individual's questionable opinion. The fact that even experts and theologians have similar doubts adds to the probability that the subject's dissent has some good reasons in its favour. One cannot deny that conscientious dissent under such circumstances possesses a great likelihood of being justified. Should an individual reach the sure conclusion that his contrary conviction is after all correct, he may follow this conviction if it permits something, and he must follow his conscience if it commands or forbids something to the contrary.

Authorities are not free from error. Even with the best of intentions they may at times be mistaken. The opposite danger however is no less real, namely that freedom of conscience is abused to justify unlawful disobedience to authority. Concerned about this, Vatican II expresses its apprehension. "There are many who, under the pretext of freedom, seem inclined to reject all submission to authority and make light of the duty of obedience. For this reason this Vatican Council urges everyone, especially those responsible for educating others, to try to form men with a respect for the moral order who will obey lawful authority." This task is of no less importance than the other one: to form men who will be lovers of true freedom and of an upright sense of responsibility (DH 8).

4. Duty to form one's conscience

Conscience is the ultimate subjective norm of moral conduct. This is uncontroverted. But it is in a like manner uncontroverted that it must seriously strive to conform to the demands of the objective world of truth. "Although each individual has a right to be respected in his own journey in search of the truth, there exists a prior moral obligation, and a grave one at that, to seek the truth and to adhere to it once it is known."[1] The sincere intention to do what is good does not suffice. A man simply must have good information in order to make good mature moral judgments. Truth and moral rightness are not autonomous creations of man's mind and conscience. Rather man is subject to the authority of the truth and must conform to it. This dependence includes the obligation to search for the truth. "The ultimate authority of moral principles is the authority of the truth; and truth in ethics is known only through the painstaking study of the facts."[2]

Since conscience stands in need of illumination and guidance, a man is responsible for its formation. To call upon the judgments of one's conscience without having striven to inform it properly is an insulting abuse. Unwillingness to inform one's conscience, "to use the best available resources to understand the truth of the moral situation facing one, is already an unwillingness to respond to the one true God".[3] The sources of information are the word of God, man's personal communion with Christ, the living faith of the Christian community, the moral norms handed down in society, and the findings of the ethical sciences. Finally also openness to

---

[1] John Paul II, encyclical *Veritatis Splendor*, 1993, nr. 34.

[2] Gerard J. Hughes, *Authority in Morals* (London: Heythrop Monographs, 1978), 89.

[3] Enda McDonagh, "Conscience: The Guidance of the Spirit," in *Truth and Life*, ed. by Donal Flanagan et alii (Dublin: Gill and Son, 1968), 129.

correction, readiness to dialogue, sensibility for a feedback and the acceptance of criticisms are important elements of the formation of conscience.

Formation of conscience however does not merely consist in the rational appropriation of a set of moral norms and principles and the acquisition of the necessary factual knowledge for a concrete judgment of conscience. "We make our decisions more out of the beliefs we live by and the habits we have formed than out of the principles we have learned."[1] The world of moral values to a large extent consists in a collection of traditions and religious observances, exemplary figures and ways of acting, stories and images, which are mediated by the communities to which a person belongs. "If one is deeply involved in the Christian community, its beliefs and stories will highly influence one's moral conscience."[2] The community's perspective and vision of the world will form and determine those of its members. Besides the Christian community, of course, there are also other social forces. Their images and stories can offer additional orientations, but they can also stand in conflict with the ones of the Gospel and rob them of their power. Via the mass media they can exert a considerable influence on people. It is therefore of fundamental importance which forces one will grant the decisive influence in one's life. This leads on to the question of Christian identity, which shall be dealt with in the following chapter.

A person who did his best to form his conscience and to reach an informed decision of conscience is by no means degraded in his dignity if he should nevertheless err in his decision. But the same "cannot be said of the man who takes little trouble to find out what is true and good, or when conscience is by degrees almost blinded through the habit of committing sin" (GS 16). If a person were careless in acquiring the knowledge necessary to form a prudent and responsible judgment of conscience or even disregarded his duty to do so, he would be guilty of a vincibly erroneous conscience, which is not a basis for lawful action.

---

[1] R.M. Gula, *Reason Informed by Faith* (New York: Paulist Press, 1989), 141.
[2] *Ib.* 143.

It is correct that on the one hand the knowledge of one's personal calling and of the moral responsibility derived from it is most directly experienced in the depth of one's own soul. But on the other hand the knowledge of the moral obligations is also decisively enriched, enlightened and deepened by the insights and experiences of the community, and there again particularly of the religious community. Only self-delusion and haughty pride will in superficial preference rely on their own insights without openness to the values of the community and docility to the teaching of those who have special competence and who are the God-willed authorities in questions of faith and morals. The formation of conscience must go hand in hand with the realism of humility, which is aware of the inevitable limitations of every individual.

Chapter IV

COMMUNAL ROOTS OF MORAL IDENTITY AND FUNDAMENTAL OPTION

The clear perception of the morally right in the moral law as well as the right formation of conscience are essential conditions for the moral action and determine it. However a further factor still merits to be taken into consideration, which influences the moral judgment and action, namely the community or the communities to which a person belongs and in which he or she lives. They form the moral identity of their members. This factor must receive attention in the following. Understandably special attention will be given, in this moral theology, to the community of the Christian faith. Appeals to isolated individuals are without effect, if they are not supported by a community which approves the values aspired to und promotes them. To a large extent moral attitudes have their roots here. Also civil laws and codes of ethics presuppose a corresponding support in the community. "A society is simply not viable if everything that should or should not be done needs to be spelled out in laws, rules, and regulations. Moral formation must undergird and supplement these."[1] Naturally it is equally a task of the members of a society themselves. At least to some extent it always also remains *their* responsibility to which communities they will grant an influence on their lives and which they will join more closely.

A. Formative principles of moral identity

The encounter with other cultures, especially those of Asia and Africa, shows that good and evil are evidently *also* concepts shaped by the community. This means, that moral evaluations and concepts "are relative to the respective society where they occur; that they are related to the values which

---

[1] Bruce C. Birch and Larry L. Rasmussen, *Bible and Ethics in the Christian Life* (Minneapolis: Augsburg, 1989), 122.

are upheld by this society, and that they are dependent on the historically and culturally conditioned understanding of this society".[1] This factor has until now received little express attention in the systematic presentations of moral theology. One realm where the normative force of the community is brought to bear in the teaching of the Church is the doctrine of the consensus of the faithful (*consensus fidelium*[2]) or also of the theologians. Of course, it is to be understood that such a consensus cannot be found out just by public opinion polls. It must be pursued in communion with the hierarchy of the Church established for the service of the Gospel and the people of God.[3]

Another realm is the tradition. In recent decades it has, wrongly, been rated in rather a disparaging way. Fundamentalists believe that it should be set aside for the sake of the "pure teaching" of the Bible or of natural law. But such an underrating does clearly not correspond to its real importance. The tradition offers that synthesis between the good news of the Gospel and the requirements of human existence in concrete society, which the human person living here and now needs.[4]

A "moral vision" is required to sustain "a common culture and a common commitment to moral values".[5] The moral

---

[1] Hermann Altmeyer, "Gott als Gesetzgeber und Garant des Sittengesetzes," in *Schuld, Sühne und Erlösung*, ed. by K.J. Rivinius (Steyler Verlag, 1983), 81.

[2] To be distinguished from the consensus fidelium is the sensus fidei. Under the latter "one understands the spiritual instinct of the believer for the truth of faith and of the Christian life. The Holy Spirit effects this spiritual sensitivity in those who sincerely believe in Christ." The consensus fidelium on the other hand is a particularly intensive form of the sense of faith; in it "the sense of faith of the majority of the believers flows together and thereby is marked by a special firmness of conviction" (A. Günthör, Anruf uttd Antwort, vol. 1. Vallendar-Schönstatt: Patris, 1993.34; see there the further treatment of the question, pp. 34-36).

[3] *Instruction on the Ecclesial Vocation of the Theologian*, 1990, nr. 39.

[4] In African culture the significance of tradition finds expression in the conviction of the vital bond which is seen to exist between the living and their deceased ancestors. "The existence of the living detached from the vital influence of the ancestors is inconceivable, just as the existence of the child cannot be considered in separation from the influence of its parents" (Mulago gwa Cikala, "Fin ultime de l'homme africain dans sa religion traditionelle et son accomplissement dans le Christ," in *Schuld, Sühne und Erlösung*, l. c. 227). The living must maintain this bond under pain of atrophy of their lives.

[5] Pastoral Letter of the Catholic Bishops of the USA, *Economic Justice for All* (Washington: NCCB, 1986), nr. 22f.

vision, the common culture and common commitment to moral values form a person's moral identity and need to be given attention. They have their roots in the community and only in a second step in the individual. "They must have a source in our communities and be nurtured over time. They must be learned and passed along from one generation to the next since they are social rather than genetic. Mature conscience and moral vision express *formed moral identity*, and formed moral identity relies upon living communities of character that have longevity. For Christians that community is the church. What such communities do is internalize moral vision and qualities as a kind of 'moral guidance system'."[1]

I. The Bible as formative principle of the moral life

1. *The Bible as prime source of Christian identity*

The Bible is the prime source for the basic values, virtues and vision which give Christians and the community of faith their particular identity. Scriptures are considered by the early Church a reliable guide in matters of faith and life. But not all that is necessary for moral life is found in the sacred pages. Direct moral exhortation *is* present in the sacred books, such as the Ten Commandments, the Sermon on the Mount, Pauline instructions. Yet it functions more as exemplary guidance than as comprehensive instruction. Instructions in 'the Way' are more akin to moral orientations than legislation, even when the language is the law-like language of moral obligation. A truncated use of Scripture is inclined to reduce the moral use of the Bible to an ethics of precepts only. Wise use of Scripture is sensitive to the varied dimensions of the moral life embedded in the biblical texts.

"In both the Old and the New Testaments *doing is intimately tied to being*. Those with ethical concerns most often approach the Bible asking, 'What shall we do?' The Bible resolutely tells us that what we do is dependent on who we are called to be."[2] According to the Bible, we cannot separate doing and being. We must ask, "What are we to do?" as well as "Who are we to be?" Scripture acts as a shaper of character as well as of conduct. This formation

---

[1] B.C. Birch and L.L. Rasmussen, *l. c.* 121.
[2] *Ib.* 165.

requires the long-term nurturing of faith and of the moral orientation flowing from it. If the distinctive contents of faith, the values and visions of the Church have not been internalized from study and meditation of the biblical resources, then it will not be possible to draw upon them meaningfully in the midst of moral challenges. The Bible is to be known for its basic values, ideals and orientations as well as for its practical applications to concrete moral issues. Basic attitudes such as the Hebrew affirmation of creation as good, Jesus' preferential option for the outcasts and sinners, or the conviction of the universality of God's saving will become determining factors for Christian action.

Apart from any explicit instruction, these attitudes shape the character of the disciple, but also of the community as a whole which the Church is called to be. For besides the question of right conduct and of the right sort of person which the believer should be, the Bible also asks about the right sort of community of believers, i.e. of the people of God, its growth and sanctification. The faithful are living stones of the spiritual house which is built upon Christ, the cornerstone, and upon the foundation of the apostles. "You are a chosen race, a royal priesthood, a holy nation, God's own people, that you may declare the wonderful deeds of him who called you out of darkness into his marvellous light" (1 Pet 2:9).

Direct moral exhortation *is* contained in the biblical writings. This cannot be ignored. Scripture is a source of moral imperatives. But much more pervasively moral formation is achieved by Scripture in indirect ways. "Psalms sung again and again in worship or read in quiet devotion foster certain 'senses' which take the form of virtues: a sense of gratitude, dependence, responsibility, humility, and awe, for example. These aren't 'exhorted,' they are nurtured in the course of prayer. Likewise, the recital of the great narrative accounts in Scripture, the telling of parables, and the hearing anew of the oracles and dreams of the prophets, create moral identity. It is not claiming too much to say that Scripture in the life of the Christian community has this moral vocation, to shape the personal moral identity of community members in keeping with the ways of God."[1]

---
[1] *Ib.* 45.

2. Concrete shape of biblical moral identity

In every religion there are certain basic meanings and reasons, which have a decisive formative influence on the lives of its adherents. They assume the role of motives for concrete moral choices and modes of actions. Among the biblical themes of this nature, characteristic for Christian moral identity, are the following.

a) A basic biblical theme of moral relevance is that of the covenant between God and his people. According to the Old Testament, Yahweh chose Israel by liberating it from Egypt with mighty hand and by concluding his covenant with it at mount Sinai (Ex 19-24; Deut 4:37-40). In the Sinaitic covenant Yahweh promises the people his protection and love and pledges the holy land. Israel in return is expected to obey the commandments of Yahweh and to walk in his ways. So the covenant teaches men that the moral law is not a free creation of men's autonomous will. They receive it from the hand of God and they are expected to obey it. All realms of human life are subject to the divine will. The New Testament continues the theme and understands itself as the "new covenant".[1] As the old covenant rested upon the act of God in delivering Israel from Egypt, so the new covenant rests in God's saving act, by which he has redeemed mankind through the death and resurrection of his Son Jesus Christ and has promised his kingdom to those who believe. And as the old covenant laid upon Israel consequential obligations, which were defined in the decalogue and in the law of Moses, so the new covenant commits to the Church the mandates of the Gospel and calls her to fulfil the will of the heavenly Father in the fellowship of Christ. This expresses the truth that God is the decisive source and motive of the moral obligation.

Closely connected with the theme of the covenant is the motive of reward and punishment. The reward of God's blessings and of eternal life is promised by Scriptures to those who are faithful to God's command and to his covenant, the punishment of divine visitations and eternal damnation on the other hand is threatened to those who disregard them. This theme has been dealt with more fully in the section on the categorical character of the moral demand (chap. I) and reference may be made to it here.

---
[1] Mk 14:24 par; 1 Cor 11:25; 2 Cor 3:6; Heb 8:6-13; 9:15; 12:24.

b) The truth that all life is placed under the dominion of God finds likewise expression in the theme of the kingdom of God. God reigns as a righteous and compassionate king, and men are accountable to him for the things they do. In the Old Testament God is described as a king who rules over the world (Ps 47; 93; 95-99; Is 52,7; Zeph 3,15 etc.). In Jesus' teaching the reality of the kingdom of God obtains a dominant role. It pertains to the nature of a kingdom that it claims authority and obedience. One cannot have a kingdom of God among men unless the rule of God has been accepted by them. The proclamation of the kingdom implies that the will of God must be done in all the spheres of life, everywhere. "Thy Kingdom come", this is the primary object of the Lord's prayer (Mt 6:10 par). In many parables Jesus points out the need to become worthy of the kingdom.[1] The kingdom constitutes the principal reward promised by him to those who accept his message.[2] It is a reward of a comprehensive nature. Its blessings are justice and love, joy and peace. These are not mere individual rewards, but always and necessarily turn into graces and benefits for the whole body of Christ. The kingdom of God together with God's glory has already been broached as a fundamental biblical description of the ultimate end of men; the expositions there may likewise be recalled.

Closely related to the theme of the kingdom is the theme, unfolded above all by the NT letters, of the expectation of the second coming of the Lord to bring about the consummation of all things in his eternal reign. It is a strong motive influencing the admonitions for the present world with its troubles. Christians must be "without blame" on the day of the Lord. With joyful readiness and free from moral offence they are to receive the Lord when he comes.[3] The early Christians rightly understood that the eschatological situation is an essential condition of human existence. Man is a pilgrim in this world. All of mankind is on pilgrimage towards the consummation of time. The goal is the full realization of the kingdom of God. But, insofar as the kingdom has already

---

[1] Mt 13:44-50; 22:1-14 par; 24:45-51; 25:1-12.31-46; Lk 19:11-27 par.

[2] Mt 5:3-10; 6:33; 19:12; 25:34; Lk 13:29.

[3] Rom 13:11-14; 1 Cor 1:7f; Phil 1:10; 1 Thess 3:13; 5:1-11.23; Tit 2:11-13; Jas 5:8; 1 Pet 1:13; 4:7-11.

been inaugurated here in this world and is supposed to grow on earth, it challenges men by an intrinsic dynamic to commit themselves to the betterment of this present world, and not just to wait and prepare for the world to come. The kingdom of God and the final events are a permanent, urgent call to vigilance and sobriety, to responsible action in the world, to struggle against the destructive powers of evil, to living hope and commitment for the salvation of the nations.

c) Fundamental for the Christian communities is the experience of Jesus and of his way. Christians are those who "follow Jesus" (language of the Gospels) and "put on Christ" (language of Paul). It is the faith of the New Testament that the way of God is paradigmatically present in the way of Jesus. The following of Christ and the grateful devotion to him as friend and saviour has at all times exercised the greatest influence upon the Christian believers. "When all allowance is made for varying interpretation, the imitation of Christ remains the heart of the Christian ethic."[1] The moral life of Christians is more radically measured by the person of Christ than by general laws and principles. In him they find the most perfect model of a life in the service of the kingdom, which royal service is also their vocation.[2] Repeatedly Paul uses the example of Christ's love, forbearance and self-sacrifice as motive for his exhortations to love, faithfulness and disinterested service.[3] It should be quite clear that the idea of imitating and following Christ is not to be understood in the limited sense of an external imitation, but as a sharing in Christ's life, destiny and spirit of love.

d) The latter thought of a sharing in Christ's life and destiny is taken up by Paul in the phrase of "putting on Christ". The foundation for it is the new life Christians have received through faith and baptism. In baptism they have died to their old, sinful nature and have been raised to newness of life.[4] They have become children of God and children of

---

[1] R.E.O. White, *Biblical Ethics* (Exeter: Paternoster Press, 1979), 109.

[2] Mt 10:37f; 16:24 par; Mk 10:43-45 par; Lk 14:26f; Jn 8:12; 12:26; 13:13-15.34; 14:6; 1 Jn 2:6; 1 Pet 2:21.

[3] Rom 8:17; 15:1-7; 2 Cor 1:18f; Eph 5:1f; Phil 2:5-8; Col 3:13; also Heb 12:1-3.

[4] Rom 6:3-14; 2 Cor 5:17; Gal 6:15; Col 2:12.

the light.¹ They are a new creation, incorporated into Christ, who lives in them and they in him.² The Holy Spirit dwells in them and they are his temples.³ This new existence motivates the summons of the apostle to a holy life, worthy of the new status of Christians.⁴ Because believers have died with Christ and live in him, they ought to sin no more, walk in newness of life, put on the Lord Jesus and let him dwell in their hearts. Because they are temples of the Holy Spirit, they must live by the Spirit and glorify God in their bodies.⁵ So when the question is asked: "What ought we to be and do?", the answer of early Christians appeals to Jesus as pattern, teacher and example and to his continued presence in their midst in the Spirit.

e) Life in Christ and in the Spirit is however not a life in isolation. Since it is one and the same Spirit who lives in all, the believers are united by a common bond as one people. The early Church is characterized by a pervasive sense of being a new community in Christ. According to Paul, the Church is a body and those who belong to it are members of the body. Christians are built up into it by their baptism in the one Spirit. The head of the body is Christ, from whom the whole body receives life and growth, unity and control.⁶ The image of the body of Christ is completed by other metaphors. The Church is God's household and city. It is a building constructed by the Lord to be his holy temple. The believers are built into its structure as "living stones" with Christ as the cornerstone. Again, Christians are a chosen race, a holy nation, God's own people.⁷

From the concept of the Church as Christ's body it follows that believers ought to use their different gifts for the best of the whole body. In order "to maintain the unity of the Spirit in the bond of peace", they are urged to practise mutual respect, patience, concord, compassion, charity, sincerity and other social virtues. Christians cannot neglect these virtues

---

¹ Jn 1:12; 12:36; Gal 3:26; Eph 5:8; 1 Jn 3:1f.
² Rom 8:1.10; 2 Cor 13:5; Gal 2:20; Phil 3:8f.
³ Rom 8:9.11; 1 Cor 3:16; 6:19.
⁴ Rom 6:4.11-13; 13:14; Col 3:5-10; Eph 3:17; 4:24f; 1 Pet 1:23-2:2.
⁵ Rom 8:13f; 1 Cor 3:16f; 6:19f; Gal 5:25.
⁶ 1 Cor 12:12-27; Eph 4:1-16; Col 2:19.
⁷ 1 Cor 3:9; 2 Cor 6:16; Eph 2:19-22; 1 Pet 2:4-10.

without doing harm to each other. And vice versa, wherever these virtues are cultivated, they foster unity and strengthen the community.[1] Whether the community will be built up (or not) should be the criterion guiding whatever Christians do. "Build one another up!" This is a constant subject in Paul's exhortations.[2] The ethical life of Christians takes place not in isolated individuals but within a social organism. Christians do not exist for themselves. They are members of the body, like a hand or a foot. And it is their responsibility to be useful members of the community. The formation of right moral judgments is therefore likewise not a matter for the individual alone. "The examination and discernment of the divine will has its proper place only in the community and in the unity with the other members of the body of Christ."[3] Joined together by the same Spirit, each member will listen to the other members and each community to the other communities.[4]

II. The faith community as matrix of moral identity

"We cannot and do not muster moral insight for ourselves by ourselves apart from our communities, any more than we are or can be human beings apart from others. Everything we know about morality and the moral life, or anything else, for that matter, is finally a community enterprise and achievement. While it is true that individuals are not simply community clones, are unique, and may well rise above the moral level of their communities, it is true with equal force that even the most private decisions and achievements are the results of our social experience and could neither exist nor be understood apart from that experience."[5] Many moderns perceive society

---

[1] Rom 12:3-8; 1 Cor 12:26; Eph 4:1-3; Col 3:12-15.
[2] Rom 14:19; 1 Cor 10:23f; 14:12.26; 1 Thess 5:11.
[3] W. Schrage, *Die konkreten Einzelgebote in der paulinischen Paränese* (Gütersloher Verlagshaus Gerd Mohn, 1961), 174. "How strongly the community is considered a unity, a 'body', is shown by the continuous linguistic use of the apostle: 'we' resp. 'you'. Paul knows nothing of the ethical autonomy of the individual" (H.-D. Wendland, *Ethik des Neuen Testaments*. Göttingen: Vandenhoeck und Ruprecht, 1978, 65).
[4] Rom 12:16; 15:4; 2 Cor 13:11; Phil 2:1f.
[5] B.C. Birch and L.L. Rasmussen, *l. c.* 17f.

in largely atomistic ways as an arena for balancing the needs, desires and demands of various groups, while focusing most intensely on individual freedoms and rights. "Picturing society this way only reinforces the illusions of individualism. It is hardly a surprise that the more freedom we attain, the more we suffer from such social disorders as impersonal behaviors (some of them violent), isolation, alienation, emptiness, and loneliness; and the more we yearn for 'genuine community' and are attracted to groups which promise it."[1]

Community as a general subject of reflection has been notably absent in the literature of ethics in the West since the Enlightenment. Scholars have failed to see that as a practical matter there is no factor more influential for moral choice than the communities of which human beings are a part. The fact is that practical moral reasoning is not only a matter of how moral *ideas* work, but even more so of how moral *communities* do. Here the concern of the already mentioned ethical theory of communitarianism is justified, which calls attention to the important role of the community in the formation of moral judgments and norms.

Israel and the early Church conceived themselves as a people, i.e. as the people of God. Community is the commanding moral matrix for them. Morality exists as part of the community's vocation to be God's people and is the outcome of the community's faith. Christian ethics has never entirely lost its sense for the communal embodiment of faith so characteristic of its origins. The reason for it is, not least, that almost all the biblical images of religious identity are communal ones: God's people, covenant, family, kingdom, one vine with many branches, a body with many parts, a chosen race, temple of the Holy Spirit, the new city Jerusalem, etc. The faith community is the reference point for the moral life of Christians. To belong to the people of God means the formation of personal moral identity in keeping with the faith identity of the community.

Moral deliberation and moral formation are tied to the shared memory, mission, faith tradition and living experience of the Christian community. "Within its social world the Christian community has the task of forming perception and character in accord with this faith. The community is the

---

[1] *Ib.* 18.

socializing agent for the faith. A major part of this work consists of immersing members in the particular stories, traditions, symbols, and lessons (both positive and negative) of past and present faith communities. These become essential content as the community helps to define moral goodness."[1] The formation takes place in a prominent way in worship and in the liturgy of the Church. "Worship is crucial because it is the continual medium for those basic symbols, stories, images, rituals, and traditions, founded in the biblical tradition, that carry the meaning of the faith and serve to form Christian character. Worship has a direct impact upon the 'seeing' so central to the Christian moral life."[2] True, the significance of worship is more than its meaning for the moral life. But its consequence for morality should not be underestimated. Therefore the life of worship ought also to be governed by a concern for the Christian moral life.

Religious instruction in schools and the preparation for the sacraments of reconciliation, the Eucharist and confirmation contribute to the social location of Christians and fashion their social and moral world. Instructions at the occasion of marriage preparation and baptism of children are forms of religious education at a later stage. Many other Church gatherings and the activities of religious organisations likewise give occasion for forming moral identity.

The faith community however also has the task of integrating materials from the social worlds which lie beyond its boundaries. The social location of Christians in their communities is often so powerfully present that they identify it as the only real world and act accordingly. They assume that the reigning moral standards of their world are *the* standards and are inclined to treat them as though they were universal and absolute. Critical analysis must expose the possible narrowness of morality, expose its limited dimensions and prepare the way for the integration of new moral insights. This also extends to the diversity of traditions which belong to the different Christian communities and even other religions. They too can enrich one's own tradition. "The pluralism and cross-cultural diversity among Christian faith communities, and across subcultures within the same culture, can check the

---

[1] *Ib.* 78.
[2] *Ib.* 198.

persistent tendencies of a close community to be sectarian. The other check is openness to the wider world as a constant partner in conversation and a locus of the presence of God."[1] Openness of the local Church to the entire Church, of the particular Church to the other Christian Churches, and of the Christian community to the social worlds at large must become a corrective against a possible provincialism of mind and argument.

"Plural sources formed the biblical materials themselves, and the church has always grafted influences which were non-Christian in origin onto its own traditions (Augustine used Plotinus, Aquinas used Aristotle). So the question for any present community facing a moral choice is not whether the moral content is in the Bible, in the church's traditions, or in the Jesus story itself; the question is whether a center exists to which varied materials can be related, and whether a criterion exists which can take their measure."[2] The fundamental criterion for a Christian ethics is the harmony or disharmony of the materials with the prominent lines discerned in Scripture and in the Jesus story. That is, the materials from whatever source must complement, not violate, the ancient message of the Gospel. The process of critical separation, stimulation and clarification of moral contents and norms, taking place in this encounter, has been dealt with in the treatment of the distinctiveness of Christian ethics, and reference may be made to it here.

In conclusion and in practical terms, the formation of moral identity requires more than the mere transmission of norms and rational principles. Worship, Bible study and life with the Church must be grasped as essential to the empowerment to moral witness. Those who are concerned with moral issues in the Church must confront the long-term task of shaping moral values, virtues, obligations and vision in the Church, so that Christians may stand ready for meaningful and timely response. An important role here devolves upon the teaching office of the Church, to which, because of its particular responsibility in this field, there is a correlative and corresponding claim to attention and acceptance from believers. For the latter question, reference be made to the section "The

---

[1] *Ib.* 119.
[2] *Ib.* 126.

ecclesiality of faith" in the second volume of this moral theology. Correspondingly the members of the Church, who all have to face moral issues in one way or the other, must also on their part be concerned with the formation of their moral identity by the same means and resources.

B. Character formation

The reality of character, in this context, refers to moral elements which are considered internal to the person: motives, dispositions, attitudes, intentions, basic options. They belong to moral being and constitute part of a person's moral identity. Character is a totality of attitudes and motivations, on account of which a person usually prefers a certain moral conduct as against another one. It makes possible a well-founded, even though not infallible prediction of a person's comportment in certain situations. It comprises good as well as bad motivations, virtues as well as vices, positive as well as negative dispositions.

There are other uses of the word, which differ from the one meant here. Thus character can mean a person's inherited temperament; in this sense we speak of an introvert or extrovert character. Character as a moral reality on the other hand refers to attitudes and motives which a person can influence and over which he has a certain control. Just as a sculptor, although limited by the material of the stone which he hews, can nevertheless model it creatively, so in the moulding of the character a person is limited by his temperament or other elements, such as the social environment, yet is nevertheless the creative shaper of his character.

The word character can also refer to a certain habitual quality of a person, e.g. honesty, politeness or stinginess, of which one may say that this is his special character. Virtues and vices pertain to the character of a person. Yet in the sense understood here, character does not merely refer to particular qualities of a person, but to their entirety, and that in view of their imprint and inspiration by some basic attitude, which in the present literature of moral theology is commonly called existential decision. "The Christian life cannot be specified by a set of virtues to be achieved apart from their arising as a response to Jesus Christ; nor can it be interpreted solely as a pattern of rules to follow or good acts to do. It is first and foremost adherence to this man, Jesus Christ, as the bringer of God's order in his person and work."[1]

There is a growing awareness today that, beyond just laws and codes of ethics, society stands in need of the formation of the character of its members. Ethics not only inquires into which actions are morally good or bad, although this is certainly also its task. It must equally and even primarily be concerned with how the agent becomes a good person through his activity. The formation of character is by no means only the result of the insights of reason; it is equally the result of the aspirations and inclinations of a person's will and not least of the influence of his environment.

Inasmuch as a person's character and moral identity are greatly influenced by the beliefs, convictions and moral identity of his community, attention must likewise be given to the moral values and vision of the community at large. Every community has its moral legacies, which reside in the forms of culture and its institutions, in the memories and traditions, in the choice of heroes and in the songs people sing, in religious creeds and devotions. These legacies display what is valued in a society, what is esteemed as good and which are its moral priorities. They are absorbed by the members of the community and form them. If character is the chief architect of human decisions and actions, community is the chief architect of character. Indeed, "an ethic of character is open to subjectivistic perversion if the significance of the ethics of community is not properly appreciated".[2]

Character depends on the materials provided by the social world. Nevertheless their absorption is not an automatic and necessary process. Our internalizing of our social and moral values is selective. We integrate some, but not all, of them; some, but not all, of the images and other carriers of meaning present in our world; some, but not all, of the predominant commitments and perspectives. The materials and values thus acquired form the character and determine what a person perceives, values, accepts, ignores or rejects. Some horizons become the horizons of the person's interest or that of the group, and some never appear as matters of interest at all.

---

[1] Stanley Hauerwas, *Character and the Christian Life* (San Antonio: Trinity University, 1985, third printing) 182.

[2] *Ib.* 231.

"Some issues are deemed morally significant and others are not. Some fail to register at all as moral matters to us, while our neighbors regard them as issues of burning immediacy.... In short, who we are and are becoming, in accord with the faith we hold, largely determines what we see."[1]

To some extent of course a person can influence that process, and indeed he ought to do so in an effort to widen the positive dimensions of his personality. The process is sometimes referred to as conscience formation. But that is too narrow a view. While conscience informs man of his moral obligations and urges him to fulfil them, character includes fundamental dispositions, intentions, motives and above all his fundamental option, which shall be dealt with subsequently. Character includes a person's moral capacities as well as active moral options. Its formation is a continuing process, which is never entirely finished. Although there is a kind of permanence to character, it is subject to changes, just as the motives, intentions, virtues or bad habits are which belong to it. It is an enduring task of humans to oppose the negative elements in their personalities and to help the good elements in them to grow.

For Christians, biblical materials help in the formation of character just as does the moral world of the faith community. What has been said above about the Bible and the faith community as formative principles of moral identity is fully relevant for the formation of a person's character. The Bible and the faith community shape a person's moral existence, and they do so at the deepest level of his being. "To be a Christian is to have one's character determined in accordance with God's action in Jesus Christ. This determination gives one's life an orientation which otherwise it would not have."[2]

Character is the deeper ground for a person's concrete moral decisions and actions. Character informs actions. But this must not lead to an attitude of indifference towards concrete, good actions. Actions on their part also have repercussions on character. Aristotle rightly observes: "We become just by doing just acts, temperate by doing temperate acts, brave by doing brave acts."[3] The interaction between character

---
[1] B.C. Birch and L.L. Rasmussen, *l. c.* 77.
[2] S. Hauerwas, *l. c.* 227.
[3] *Nicomachean Ethics*, book II, chap. 1.

and concrete moral actions shall find greater attention in the following considerations concerning the fundamental option and in the section on the virtues in the last chapter, which are essential aspects of a person's character and determine it decisively.

C. Basic intention and fundamental option

In the preceding section reference has been made to the fundamental option. Closely related to it is the basic intention. The latter is a comprehensive and basic orientation of a person's life, which results from his or her existential choice. The existential choice is a matter of a particular moment in time and can be repeated. But it leaves in man an imprint of lasting duration. This imprint is the basic intention. It is obvious that it will qualify and mould a person's character in a decisive way.

Human actions do not constitute a plurality of isolated, disconnected good or sinful deeds, which can be sufficiently understood and judged each by itself. They usually have their roots in basic decisions which give purpose and determination to the whole of man's life. This is so because life is a coherent task, which man has to accomplish. Life is the creative moulding of one's personality and of one's environment. Such a creative task is not realized in many independent, separated decisions, but on the basis of a fundamental, existential blueprint and of a unifying design of one's life work. This basic design decides in principle which actions will be preferred, admitted or rejected.

The decision by which a person embraces this basic orientation can be termed fundamental option, existential choice or core decision. Only decisions of this nature constitute morally grave acts, apt to bring about that total commitment to goodness and holiness which Christians call the state of grace or that radical refusal of a person's true destiny which is called mortal sin. In the existential choice a person decides which value he will adopt as the supreme value for his life. On the basis of this fundamental decision he will henceforth make his preference choices.

To be distinguished from the existential choice are the particular choices or options (also called categorial choices, because they are concerned with the various categories of concrete actions). They are choices concerned with the concrete ways of conduct and actions, fit to express and realize a person's fundamental option in his day to day life. The fundamental option of course will have a decisive influence on the particular choices a person makes. A good fundamental option inclines to particular choices of a good nature and an evil one to corresponding choices of an evil nature. The difference between fundamental option and a person's concrete, daily acts is at issue when Scripture says that God looks not only at man's deeds but also at his heart and that he will recreate man by giving him a new heart (Ezek 11:19; 36:26; Joel 2:12f); or when Christians are exhorted to put on Christ and the new nature created after the likeness of God as the source of all virtues and good works (Rom 13:14; Gal 3:27; Eph 4:22-24; Col 3:10).

A middle position between fundamental option and particular choices is held by the predecision. It brings about a certain preference of the will in a certain sphere of action. Challenged, for example, by the value of truthfulness or by the realm of sexuality, man usually arrives at a decision of how he will behave in principle in these matters. Such a decision in principle is a predecision. "Predecisions always refer just to particular spheres of the moral world. One takes one's stand on *something*: in regard to the professional realm, to money, to the value of justice, to the place of children, etc. It is never - this is the fundamental difference with regard to the fundamental option - a decision for good and evil overall."[1] On the other hand the predecision is also distinguished from the particular choices, since it extends to an entire realm of activity and is also able to influence subsequent decisions. A predecision in one realm has the tendency to expand itself also into other realms. Whoever opts for truthfulness in speech, will by and large also desire to be just and fair. Nevertheless man is "too contradictory for his good attitude in one area always to expand in fact to goodness in another area, or even in all areas of his life. We are actually so thoroughly untalented at consistency and coherence that, time and again, predecisions to positive action on the one hand and stubborn tendencies and susceptibilities to behaving in an inglorious or even shabby

---

[1] H. Weber, *Allgemeine Moraltheologie* (Graz: Styria, 1991), 241f.

Moral Identity and Fundamental Option   225

and malicious way on the other are both found together."[1] The concept of predecision is therewith clearly more concrete than that of the fundamental option. True, it is less deep and less pretentious. On the other hand its greater concreteness more readily offers points of departure for concrete action.

Since in a person many different dispositions, inclinations and influences are at work, the particular choices will not always and necessarily be in harmony with the existential choice. The transforming force of the basic intention does not draw everything in its train. Much remains outside its influence and is not drawn along. In the concrete reality of life the existential blueprint adopted in a core decision always remains somewhat indeterminate and open to different possibilities. Since it is not clear from the very beginning which potentialities a person can and should develop and realize, and since one is confronted with a multiplicity of tendencies and attractions and desires, one will not always find the definite course right away. One will often try in directions which one later abandons, once one becomes fully aware of all the consequences they involve. So one may initially believe that the two goals to make as much money as possible and to treat all men fairly can be harmonized. But at a certain point one will be confronted with the decision to choose either the one or the other. At other times one will just experiment without deeper reflection or serious intent. This explains the possibility of wrong steps even where the basic choice is right, and vice versa.

There also exists the possibility of changing a former existential blueprint and basic design into a different one by continuous contrary decisions and acts, be it to the better as in conversion, or be it to the worse as in dereliction of God, which is the state of mortal sin. The time of transition will be characterized by tensions and contradictions until the decisive basic choice is made.

An existential choice is brought about by a profoundly good act or by a mortal sin. This does not mean however that once a person has made an existential choice, no further act of grave moral nature can be set, as long as the existential choice is not changed. Rather acts which repeat and renew the good or vicious option in a radical way are profoundly good acts or mortal sins again.

---
[1] *Ib.* 242.

As a rule an existential choice will be brought about by an act concerned with a grave matter, be it an act of great generosity, e.g. renunciation of a hateful revenge against an enemy, or of great evil, e.g. perversion of justice by bribery of a judge. Actions concerned with a light matter will usually result only in peripheral confirmations of a good or vicious core decision and therefore be good acts of a light nature or venial sins. The thievery of a person who is otherwise given to a good existential orientation will be a bad act of superficial nature, and the aid given to a poor man by a person with a basically selfish orientation a welcome inconsistency; but as long as these acts do not change the existential orientation, they remain bad or good acts of light nature only.

Moral theology was always aware that the gravity of the external deed and the intensity of the internal moral commitment do not necessarily run parallel. Especially in the treatment of sin this insight has been unfolded. Handbooks always caution that the externally grave or light matter is not necessarily the sign of an internally mortal or venial sin (because insight or consent of free will can be deficient). Today this insight is given still greater emphasis, and it is also more clearly applied to good actions. The external actions allow approximate conjectures as to the internal state of a person, but they do not give certainty about it. Particularly isolated, individual acts do not permit such conclusions as to the internal state of a person. "Accordingly the moral disposition of a man is not gathered from individual actions, but only from the succession of different actions, i.e. from the history of that person."[1]

Paradoxically that decision, which people resolve in their deepest freedom and which therefore is most properly their own, is withdrawn from a direct knowledge. Its subject matter is after all not a concrete object, as in the categorial decisions, but the global orientation of a person's life, which lacks a well defined object. According to Scripture therefore man is not only forbidden "to make absolute assertions about the real state of a person deep down and in the sight of God, but he also cannot and is not allowed to pass an absolute judgment on himself and declare himself to be either absolutely justified or an absolute sinner, in the sense of declaring that a justifying or sinful act has certainly taken place here and now. Thus,

---

[1] Hans Rotter, *Grundlagen der Moral* (Einsiedeln: Benziger, 1975), 80.

the constitutive sign on which such a judgment would have to be based, cannot be so absolutely unequivocal that it allows him to pronounce such a judgment before the divine tribunal."[1] This agrees with the declaration of the Council of Trent that no one has a certain knowledge of the state of grace (DS 1533f). The knowledge of the heart is reserved to God alone.[2] This however does not imply an absolute uncertainty about the ultimate orientation of a person's life. From the concrete, categorial actions one can approximately also infer a corresponding fundamental option.

The ultimate uncertainty about a person's state in the depth of his or her being does equally not exclude that a grave external offence be a sufficient basis for certain obligations concerning practical duties, as e.g. the duty to confess one's grave sins, to make restitution, and to comply with civil or ecclesiastical penalties.

A practical conclusion resulting from the significance of the good basic intention for the moral life is the necessity of cultivating it with particular care. "From the decisive significance of the basic intention for the moral life and for communion with God, it is immediately plain how much one has to attend to the preservation and consolidation of the good basic intention. The good fruits (particular acts) presuppose the good tree and good roots. If education and pastoral guidance unilaterally aim at the external action, at externally correct conduct, then the danger of justification merely by external works lurks, even of pharisaic self-righteousness."[3] On the other hand it remains likewise true that the good actions, insofar as they proceed from a personal decision and are affirmed by it, rebound on the basic intention. Care for basic intention and deeper motives is in a special way aided by meditation, in which a person reflects on himself and the real motives of his actions. In particular the theological virtues of faith, hope and charity are those inner dispositions through which the Christian, but also every person of good will, disposes of himself in his totality and answers the call of God.

---

[1] K. Rahner, *Theological Investigations*, vol. II, 1963, 276.

[2] Cf. St. Augustine: "Now what sins are trivial and what are grave it is for divine judgment, not human judgment, to decide" (*Enchiridion de fide, spe et caritate*, nr. 78).

[3] A. Günthör, *Anruf und Antwort*, vol. I (Vallendar-Schönstatt: Patris Verlag, 1993), 378.

Chapter V

REALIZATION OF THE MORAL VALUE IN HUMAN ACTS

Having acquired the knowledge of his moral responsibility and task, man must realize the guidelines and imperatives of the moral law in his actions. Accordingly the nature and characteristics of human acts must be studied next, which acts enable man to proceed towards or also to depart from his ultimate end and to attain or to miss it.

A. Concept and nature of the human act

I. Concept of the human act

Human acts (*actus humani*) are actions that proceed from insight into the nature and purpose of one's doing and from consent of free will; or shorter, they are acts which proceed from insight and free will. They can also rightly be called personal acts.

Human acts are to be distinguished from acts of man (*actus hominis*), which are performed without intervention of intellect and free will. They comprise all spontaneous biological and sensual processes, like nutrition, breathing, sensual impressions; all acts performed by those who have not the use of reason, like people asleep, lunatics, drunken people; all spontaneous reactions which precede the activity of intellect and will, like first reactions of anger or sympathy. Likewise distinguished from human acts are forced acts which, though effected with some insight and cooperation of the intellect, are carried out against a man's personal decision and will (e.g. coercion of a defeated enemy to destroy his citadels). Some authors subsume forced acts under the acts of man as well.

As the definition of the human act makes plain, there are two principles which constitute this act: an intellectual and a volitive constituent.

The intellectual constituent. The will can decide for something and seek it only if it is first known. Hence the human act is voluntary only if its different elements are sufficiently known. This requires as essential conditions for a human act knowledge of the aspired object, attention to the action with which the object is to be pursued, and judgment on the value of the act. The reason is that man cannot will without knowing what object he is concerned with, without being master and therefore conscious of the act he is to perform in order to realize the aim, and without evaluating the action in its concrete nature as a desirable good or undesirable evil, which appraisal also includes the judgment on the moral value of the act.

In order however that the latter judgment be experienced as a demand by a person, more is needed than merely a purely conceptual knowledge; an evaluative knowledge is needed, which touches and involves the heart of the person. This already relates to the volitive constituent of the human act; for the affirmation and acceptance of a value ensues from the will.

It is to be noted that an action is human, and therefore good or bad, only under those of its aspects which are known. If a man robs and strikes a person not knowing him to be a priest, he is guilty of criminal injury but not of a personal sacrilege. If a woman receives the gift of a pearl necklace, not knowing that it is stolen, she is not guilty of any offence, but a victim of ignorance which excuses her from guilt.

The volitive constituent. Every voluntary act of man includes a necessary element, the quest for good (the formal element of every desire), and a free element, the choice of the concrete object in which the good is sought (the material element of desire). It is because of this second aspect that we say that the voluntary act, and therefore the human act, is free.

If a man for some reason is not free to choose what he would like according to his insight and will, but has to act against his will, his action is not free and consequently not a human act. Suppose a psychologically afflicted person feels compelled to wash his hands again and again. He is clearly conscious of the object he is concerned with and of the action with which the object is pursued; and he is also aware that this act is of no real value and ought therefore not to be performed. In executing the act nevertheless, he does so under the pressures of his psychic compulsion, i.e. without consent of his free will. Since such an act is not voluntary, it is not a human act. The second essential condition for a human act, consent of the free will, therefore presupposes freedom from any external or internal compulsion.

The freedom from external and internal (psychic) compulsion secures a person freedom of action, but leaves the will neutral in regard to the choice of the rightful and good. The rational knowledge of a moral value (the intellectual element) presupposed, there is need for the assent of the will to this value. Intellectual knowledge alone is not sufficient. An evaluative knowledge is required, as already mentioned. "This kind of knowledge is not acquired nor altered through rational argument alone, but by personal experience, discovery, and appreciation of moral values."[1] Appreciation implies an affirmation of the value, a certain love for it, which is a volitive element. Identification with the parents and with other educators or esteemed persons as well as the whole world of the family and of the other communities in which a person grows up and to which he or she belongs plays an essential role in the practical experience of moral values. Every person however has also a personal influence on the possibility of value experiences or their exclusion.

II. Divisions of the voluntary act and effect

Human acts and voluntary effects are distinguished in many ways. Some of the more important divisions are the following.

1. *The perfectly and imperfectly voluntary act.* Perfectly voluntary is an act which is performed with full attention and full consent of the will. Imperfectly voluntary is an act if attention or consent of the will or both together are imperfect. Though imperfect attention and imperfect consent usually go hand in hand, full attention can nevertheless at times exist together with imperfect consent. Thus a person who acts under the influence of fear may act with full attention but with imperfect consent.

2. *The directly and indirectly voluntary effect.* The effect is directly voluntary if it is intended in itself as an end, e.g.

---

[1] R.M. Gula, *Reason Informed by Faith* (New York: Paulist Press, 1989), 87.

murder for the sake of revenge, or if it is intended as means for another end, e.g. murder for reasons of robbery and profit. The effect is indirectly voluntary if it is not intended but merely permitted as the inevitable result of an object directly willed. Thus the death of a foetus caused by the removal of a uterus affected by cancer is not intended as a means nor as an end, but only permitted as an indirectly voluntary effect. In the latter case, colloquial language commonly speaks of side-effect. For example a medicine against cancer may have the undesired, though foreseen (indirectly voluntary) side-effect of nausea.

3. *The positively and negatively voluntary effect.* The will effects something positively by exercising active influence on the causation of an object, as for instance injuring a neighbour by setting his house on fire (which, being an offence against justice, obliges to restitution). The will effects something negatively by voluntary omission of an act which could have averted an evil from another person or helped him to secure a good. Thus it is negatively voluntary not to extinguish a fire already started in a neighbour's house or, in the positive sense, not to prevent a bequest in the last will of one's parents in favour of an orphanage. Evidently in the one case the omission is sinful (but being an offence against charity only, it does not oblige to restitution), in the other on the contrary meritorious. The problem of negatively voluntary effects is of special concern today in the case of terminally ill patients, when the question arises whether to initiate, continue or discontinue treatments of life support.[1]

---

[1] At times this difference between an intending and a permitting will is identified with the above distinction between the directly and indirectly voluntary effect. But this has justly been contested. The two distinctions do not coincide. The indirectly willed effect of a castration, caused by the removal of cancerous testicles, is evidently not due to a mere omission and therefore not merely negatively voluntary. On the other hand the fact that a fire breaks out in the house and no effort is made by a neighbour to extinguish it, is negatively voluntary, but it is not indirectly voluntary, since no action at all is produced by the neighbour, to which the fire could be attributed as an indirect effect. Such an identification is made by R.A. McCormick (*Doing Evil to Achieve Good*. Chicago: Loyola Univ., 1978, 35f; 263) and B. Schüller (ib. 173-175). It is contested by C.E. Curran ("The Principle of Double Effect," in *Ongoing Revision: Studies in Moral Theology*. Notre Dame, Ind.: Fides Publ., 1975, 206f).

III. The presupposition of freedom

An essential condition of moral action is freedom of will. Without at least a minimum of freedom of decision, no moral act is possible. With great seriousness the theology of past epochs has discussed and studied the problem of the cooperation between God as the ultimate cause of all events and the free will of men. The question is dealt with in the treatise on creation in dogmatic theology, and it can be consulted there. As difficult as a satisfactory solution of the problem may be for the human spirit, Christian theology has always upheld the freedom of will. Onslaughts against free will from philosophy, from the strict causal thinking of the natural sciences and from behaviourism[1] have of late greatly subsided. It seems much more plausible to man of today that he is capable of free decisions. "The fundamentally high esteem for freedom apparently does not permit its denial in principle in the case of the human person."[2] Even matter is no longer regarded as strictly predetermined by physical and chemical laws, as in the time of the predominance of the mechanistic world-view.

Nonetheless one has become more conscious of the various impairments and restrictions to free will. One allows for the possibility that even where somebody believes he is acting in freedom, he may in reality be subject to subtle determinisms. "Hence the conviction of a 'moderate indeterminism' can be regarded as prevailing today: Freedom is considered a given fact on principle for man, but one reckons with various limitations in the individual case."[3]

Much more in the foreground today stands the claim for personal freedom of action, opinion and conscience. The granting of that freedom is insisted upon and is forcibly

---

[1] "The discovery that certain, especially criminal, ways of conduct are found in steady regularity in a certain population has been considered proof that moral behaviour is in principle not free, but predetermined by set patterns. The basic mistake in this was the generalisation and the disregard of the individual case; the fact that something often happens still does not say anything about whether it also *has to* happen that way in the individual case" (H. Weber, *Allgemeine Moraltheologie*. Graz: Styria, 1991, 220, Footnote 332).

[2] H. Weber, *l. c.* 220.

[3] *Ib.* 221.

demanded. It is a justified concern, that all pressures and compulsions which narrow down a person's freedom of choice be ever more reduced and that the scope of freedom be ever more enlarged. To be sure, these freedoms are only a vestibule to the proper freedom of conscience. They do not establish freedom of conscience (it exists also where these freedoms are not granted), they only enlarge or restrict its scope. The external impairment of freedom of conscience however can become a serious threat to free will itself, inasmuch as under strong external pressure a person often does not muster the strength to follow his conscience.

Two forms of freedom can be distinguished in the moral life: basic freedom or freedom of self-determination on the one hand and freedom of choice on the other. In basic freedom humans decide about their beings as persons, i.e. about who they want to be, in the freedom of choice on the other hand about their concrete actions, i.e. about what they are doing to realize their being. The two forms of freedom find their counterpart in the two forms of decisions already dealt with: the existential decision, wherein a person decides on the fundamental project of his or her life, and the particular ("categorial") decision, which concerns concrete, particular actions. In the particular decisions and concrete actions humans are much more conditioned and confined by their environment than in the decision about the basic project of their lives. "It is therefore legitimate to presume that a decision will be all the more withdrawn from conditioning and accordingly free, the more it has as its object an overall project."[1]

1. *Freedom of will in Holy Scripture*

Scriptures of the Old as well as of the New Testament evidence the conviction that man has the freedom to do what is good and to avoid what is evil, and that therefore he is responsible for his actions. This is the presupposition of the biblical teaching about divine retribution for good and evil through reward and punishment.

According to the *Old Testament* man is created in the image of God and possesses the freedom to decide by himself.

---

[1] G. Gatti, *Temi di morale fondamentale* (Leumann, Torino: Elle Di Ci, 1988), 168.

This freedom is the presupposition for the expulsion of Adam and Eve from paradise, called forth by their trespass of the divine command not to eat from the tree of knowledge in the middle of paradise (Gen 3). "It was he who created man in the beginning, and he left him in the power of his own inclination. If you will, you can keep the commandments, and to act faithfully is a matter of your own choice" (Sir 15:14f). Life and death, blessing and curse are set before the people of Israel in the fifth book of Moses: "therefore choose life" (Deut 30:15-20). Time and again the prophets exhort the people not to abuse their freedom and to remain faithful to the Lord (Is 1:19f; Jer 11:6-8; Ezek 18:21-28).

The *New Testament* likewise presupposes free will. "How often would I have gathered your children together..., and you would not!" (Mt 23:37), deplores Jesus in the sight of Jerusalem, whose destruction he foresees. Every man will be repaid "for what he has done" (Mt 16:27; cf. 25:31-46). The teaching of the early Church contains many references to a judgment according to the good and evil a man has done. "For we must all appear before the judgment seat of Christ, so that each one may receive good or evil, according to what he has done in the body" (2 Cor 5:10).[1] Time and again the Christian communities are warned that those who do evil will not inherit the kingdom of God (1 Cor 6:9f; Gal 5:19-21; Eph 5:5). "Whatever a man sows, that he will also reap. For he who sows to his own flesh will from the flesh reap corruption; but he who sows to the Spirit will from the Spirit reap eternal life" (Gal 6:7f).

Besides this kind of freedom Paul very decidedly emphasizes another one, the freedom of Christians from the "law" (Rom 7:1-6; 10:4; Gal 3:23-26). It is to be noted that, when Paul, being a Jew, speaks of "the law" or of "law" in general, without any further, explicit or implicit qualification, he means the Mosaic law. This comprises, besides the moral precepts, also many cultic, ritual and civil laws. The freedom of Christians from the law therefore signifies their liberation from the Jewish law then in force, which under many aspects was historically and culturally conditioned and dated by the conditions of time. The council of the Apostles in Jerusalem confirmed this freedom and approved of the practice of the

---

[1] Cf. Rom 2:6-11; Col 3:23-25; Jas 2:14-26; Rev 20:12-15; 22:12.

apostle Paul not to oblige the converts from paganism to the Mosaic law (Acts 15; Gal 2:1-10). This freedom is not free will, to be sure, but the liberation of free will from unnecessary burdens.

Already at the time of Paul an interpretation of Christian freedom had crept in which constituted another extreme and misunderstood the freedom in a libertarian way. "All things are lawful for me", its partisans argued, and on this grounds they felt justified not only to eat all foods, but also to enjoy relations with prostitutes. Paul unmistakably dissociates himself from such an understanding of Christian liberty. "All things are lawful", he resumes, "but not all things are helpful" (1 Cor 6:12; 10:23). Christians must shun immorality because they are temples of the Holy Spirit; they are not entitled to do what they like, but must attend to God's claim over them and glorify him also in their bodies (1 Cor 6:12-20).

If Christians are no longer subject to the Mosaic law, this does not mean that they are "without law toward God" (1 Cor 9:21). They are still bound by the duty of "keeping the commandments of God" (1 Cor 7:19). They too have a law, which is the "law of Christ" (1 Cor 9:21; Gal 6:2). Paul correctly realized that there were requirements of the law which were of lasting validity, while others did not have this value and were for the Christian useless. However he was not in the fortunate position of possessing the later, scholarly terminology, distinguishing between moral or natural laws on the one hand and positive legislation of cultic and civil laws on the other. But the difference itself was perceived by him. There is a law written on men's hearts which they know by nature; all men must live according to this universal law and are judged by it (Rom 2:12-16). This is the "law of God" which is set against the things of the flesh; it contains the "just requirement of the law" and continues to bind Christians (Rom 8:4-8). It coincides with the "law of Christ". Christian freedom therefore does not mean freedom from all obligations. That man is truly free who is no longer under the power of sin, but who is able, unencumbered by disordered desires, to live up to his true vocation and to fulfil the will of God (cf. Rom 6:15-23; Gal 5:13-26).

2. Theological reflection

"In the free act we encounter in a special way the secret of the human person. He determines himself, because he is in a certain way his own."[1] For his self-determination the person is responsible before God. Against all forms of divine predestination and philosophical determinisms, the Church has repeatedly defended man's capability to make free decisions of himself.[2] The Pastoral Constitution of Vatican II writes: God willed that man "might of his own accord seek his creator and freely attain his full and blessed perfection by cleaving to him" (GS 17).

Freedom here does not mean mere indifference towards good and evil, as often people think. Men of today, so the Council Vatican II notes, appreciate freedom highly, and rightly so. "Yet they often cherish it improperly, as if it gave them leave to do anything they like, even when it is evil" (GS 17). They consider freedom threatened not only by physical and psychical coercion, but also by the claims of moral norms and by the predisposition through habits good in themselves and through virtues. This leads to an inclination to assert freedom in the "no" to precepts and authority. In exaggeration of this attitude, anticonformism on principle is considered as a special realization of freedom. With this goes the tendency to view the binding orders of the community, the state and the Church from the start as a menace to one's own full freedom.

This understanding is contrasted with the other, which regards freedom as the ability to direct oneself abidingly towards what is good. Thus the gift of freedom includes for Vatican II the ability to use freedom correctly, i.e. by means of it to realize what is truly good and to devote oneself to God. Man comes up to this task when, "ridding himself of all slavery to the passions, he presses forward towards his goal by freely choosing what is good, and, by his diligence and skill, effectively secures for himself the means suited to this end" (GS 17). Freedom so understood consists in this, as already set forth in the explanation of the biblical teaching,

---

[1] A. Günthör, *Anruf und Antwort*, vol. I (Vallendar-Schönstatt: Patris Verlag, 1993), 359.

[2] DS 331; 685; 1486; 1521; 1965; 2002.

that man, unencumbered by impairments of any kind, be wholly free to answer his true calling and to comply with the task God has assigned to him within the scope of his plan for the world. This freedom is not a settled possession of man from the beginning, but must be gained through steady effort and always be confirmed again. Freedom accordingly is not always a constant point zero of indifference, but an aptitude for goodness, which ought to increase ever more through the steady diminution of all impairments. It is not primarily a right, but a duty.

For freedom thus understood, the law, its correctness presupposed, is not an opponent and an impairment, but a helper to direct as person towards what is good. This is true above all for the norms of the moral order, which disclose the value of the good towards which the person is ordered from within. But the positive attitude towards the law in principle also extends to the civil and ecclesiastical authorities, to the extent that their laws are legitimate and just. Even though the laws of the community often limit freedom of choice for men (for example through the regulations for traffic or worship), they facilitate a better realization of the common tasks as a whole. Therefore the limitations in the last analysis stand in the service of man's true freedom. This understanding of freedom is confirmed by the fact that no manual of moral theology ranks the moral or civil and ecclesiastical laws with the impairments of the freedom of will.

There are impairments of freedom which a person himself can remove or at least reduce, e.g. negative dispositions, such as inclinations to indolence and disorderliness, uncontrolled passions, submissiveness, unruliness. The overcoming of these impairments is an important moral task for the individual person himself or herself. There are other impairments which are caused by social conditions and structures, such as restrictions of the rights of freedom in a nation (e.g. freedom of religion and expression) or for certain groups in it (e.g. for women or ethnic minorities), lack of freedom to choose one's profession, inadequate access to scholastic education etc. The diminution and removal of impairments of this kind must be a concern of society and of the influential groups in it, not least of the Churches and religions. Christian ethics "must take the risk of increasing freedom and power among those who have been deprived of them. It is true that freedom itself is ambiguous, and it must be expected that some will abuse it. But it is an even more important truth that there can be no full humanity without the freedom to act and to exercise the creative capacity."[1]

B. Obstacles of human acts

The impairments of human freedom are realities with which ethics and jurisprudence have to reckon, today as much as in the past. Far from disregarding the issue today, the anthropological sciences have made man aware of the numerous factors which can inhibit truly human behaviour. Men are preconditioned in many ways. They are never totally free. This is no denial of a realm of genuine freedom in men, a realm which ought to be increased by pushing back the margin of ignorance and undue pressures ever farther. But certain limits of freedom will always remain, and at times unfavourable conditions can impair it grievously or even totally. Ethics and jurisprudence have to take these possibilities into account when judging the conduct of men.

Some obstacles do not impair the origination of a human act but only the voluntariness, and consequently imputability, of its effects by preventing a clear knowledge of the object of the act (the intellectual constituent), such as ignorance, error, forgetfulness, inadvertence. Other obstacles impair the coming about of a human act in its roots by diminishing or preventing the consent of free will (the volitive constituent), such as passion, fear, violence, habits and dispositions of temperamental or of pathological nature.

I. Impairments of required knowledge

The distinctions and principles to be drawn up for ignorance hold equally good for the other defects of knowledge, such as forgetfulness, error and inattention. The latter two still call for some supplementary remarks.

---

[1] John Macquarrie, *Three Issues in Ethics* (London: Harper & Row, 1970), 71.

1. Ignorance

Ignorance may be invincible or vincible. That ignorance is invincible which a man is not able to dispel by such reasonable diligence, as is commensurate with the issue of an act and with one's opportunities. In some situations reasonable diligence would mean considerable diligence, as when important issues are at stake, such as saving another person from dangers to health and life. Invincible ignorance is inculpable. It is also characterized as antecedent ignorance, because it precedes any voluntary act and is not willed by any consent of the will.

Ignorance is vincible if it could be removed by reasonable diligence but is not because of negligence or bad will. Vincible ignorance is culpable. It is also described as consequent ignorance, because it is admitted or willed either directly or indirectly, flowing thus as a consequence from a previous decision of the free will. According to the lesser or greater degree of negligence of which one is guilty, ignorance may be simply vincible, if some but insufficient diligence has been used in dispelling the defect of knowledge; it may be crass or supine, if no serious effort has been taken to remove the ignorance; or it may be affected, if one deliberately wills to remain ignorant.[1] The following principles apply to ignorance and its imputability.

(I) Invincible ignorance prevents the human act from being voluntary in regard to that which is not known. What namely is not known, cannot be voluntary in itself, as follows from the definition of the human act; and what is not known with invincible ignorance, is not voluntary in its cause either. Therefore if a cook should cause the death of some people by unknowingly serving them spoiled meat or poisonous mushrooms, which had been sold to him by careless merchants,

---

[1] The distinction between indistinct and distinct knowledge belongs in this context, since indistinct knowledge implies ignorance concerning the precise nature of an object. Distinct knowledge grasps the quality and gravity of a good or evil act clearly and accurately, while indistinct knowledge grasps this quality and gravity only vaguely. Thus if somebody steals a sacred object, conscious that this is a sacrilege, he acts with distinct knowledge; but if somebody steals the sacred object, conscious only that such theft is a graver sin than a simple theft, he acts with indistinct knowledge. With regard to the not clearly grasped aspects of an action or omission, indistinct knowledge may reduce imputability somewhat.

he is innocent of this calamity and excused from guilt. For the same reason, anxiety regarding actions one did years ago, not knowing their sinful character, is unreasonable.

(II) Vincible ignorance does not take away the voluntariness of what is effected by a human act or its omission, but it diminishes voluntariness, as long as the ignorance is not affected. Vincible ignorance does not prevent voluntariness, since the ignorance is voluntary in its cause, provoked by negligence or laziness or even bad will. Indirectly voluntary are consequently also the effects resulting from such ignorance. Making an application to ordinary life, this would mean that, e.g., a jurist, physician or priest who has seriously neglected his studies or further professional development, cannot be excused on the ground of ignorance if he blunders in the performance of his profession.

Nevertheless vincible ignorance usually diminishes voluntariness and guilt, since the imputability of an action essentially depends on the insight a person has of a matter, and this insight is deficient in this case; and simple negligence or laziness do not usually imply a full consent to all the possible evil consequences which may come therefrom. Of course the greater the neglect is, the greater is the guilt. Crass ignorance in a serious matter will generally make the sin grave, simple ignorance will reduce the guilt somewhat. A physician who endangers a patient's welfare and life because of crass ignorance is guilty of grave irresponsibility.

Affected ignorance however does not diminish guilt. Ignorance is kept up intentionally in this case, so that a person may not be bound by the law and have greater freedom to commit sin. There is full consent to the sinful effects which result from such ignorance, because there is no real effort and no intention to avoid them. For example inspectors of factories, sent by the government to investigate the implementation of labour contracts in the workshop place, who have been bribed and who choose to remain ignorant of any violations of the contracts by neither interrogating the workers nor seriously checking the records are guilty of affected ignorance.

Ecclesiastical law recognizes these principles concerning ignorance (CIC 1323, nr. 2). Civil law generally does not regard ignorance of the law or of the penalty as an excusing cause, but as a reason for a milder penalty. Ignorance of a fact however is also recognized by civil law fully as a cause excusing from guilt (e.g. ignorance of the fact that goods were stolen).

2. *Error*

The origin of errors, prejudices, false opinions and convictions may lie in deficient education, the influence of bad company, the reading of misleading books and papers, etc. Man is challenged to overcome the errors which hold him under their sway in personal search for truth, to escape the negative influence of those forces which misguide him, and to reach views based on sound reasons. For false convictions bring with them false attitudes to life.

One of the greatest hazards to freedom in our times is the insidious influence of mass suggestion, which often emanates from organizations like parties, ideological groups, nationalist and fundamentalist circles, liberalist and antireligious movements, or other powerful associations of citizens, and which above all avails itself of the far-reaching potency of the mass media: press, radio and television. Such suggestion not seldom affects the broad masses like an epidemic. Even morally mature men and women can be perceptibly hampered in the independent exercise of their moral responsibility. Pernicious outbursts of fanatic nationalism, hatred for minority groups, other races and nations, the rash of superstition (e.g. witch trials), lynch justice, all result therefrom.

The development of true moral freedom demands the gradual emancipation of the human person from the fraud of the masses. This demands a personal striving after truth, objectivity and justice. Yet the individual alone is often too weak to break the outrages of mass thinking on his freedom. He needs the support of the community of the good, who must bind together in order to resist a perilous climate and to defend the true values and rights of men against the infections of comfortable and pleasing errors. In the face of such prejudice and bondage of falsehood, the Church especially has an important role to play as the guardian and promoter of truth, right and genuine freedom.

3. Inattention

While ignorance and error are habitual privations of knowledge and true insight, inattention is an actual, momentary privation of knowledge. So far as inattention only extends to certain aspects of an action, the same principles apply to it as those drawn up for ignorance. However inattention can also extend to the action as a whole, and for this some additional norms come into play.

(I) If a person does not attend at all to what he is doing, he does not accomplish a human act. The absent-minded professor who is so absorbed in his scientific problems that he boils his watch instead of the egg does not perform an imputable human act in committing this error. Acts performed in a state of complete intoxication, fogging by drugs, and the like are not human acts either. But sometimes these acts may be voluntary in cause, as e.g. damage caused by a drunkard who had foreseen that such behaviour would possibly be the result of his drinking.

(II) If a person is only half-attending to what he does, the acts he performs are only imperfect human acts. Attention is imperfect if it is disturbed and diminished, though not completely extinguished, by some obstacle, e.g. if somebody is in a state of semi-wakefulness, partial intoxication, violent passion, distraction by other occupations. The convenience or inconvenience of the action is partially perceived, but not to its full extent. With this attention a grave moral act and therefore also a grave sin is excluded. A perfect human act is only performed when full attention is had to what one is doing.

II. Impairments of free consent

1. *Passion*

a) *Concept and nature.* Passion or concupiscence is a movement of the sensitive appetite which is produced by good or evil as apprehended by the imagination. Related concepts are affects and sentiments. The word affect rather denotes a momentary flush of the sensitive appetite. Lighter motions of the passions are often called sentiments. Passions are grouped into two classes by scholastic theology, the concupiscible and the irascible. The first class comprises love, hatred, desire, aversion, joy, sadness. The second class comprises anger, courage, fear, hope, despair. Movements of the passions are frequently also called feelings, especially if not vehement.

Concupiscence in the sense here defined has no connotation of evil. God has endowed men with these appetites, which pervade their whole sensitive life. They are instruments for self-preservation of the individual and the human race. Hence the concept of concupiscence is here not used in the Pauline sense of inclination to evil (cf. Rom 7:8), nor is it limited to the sexual desire. A man without them would be with no capacity for self-defence, growth, improvement and devotion. Therefore it is no surprise that we notice passions also in the lives of saints and of Christ himself. "My soul longs, yea, faints for the courts of the Lord; my heart and flesh sing for joy" (Ps. 84:2), prays the psalmist. And in burning anger Christ turns against the hypocrisy of the Pharisees and scribes, whom he calls blind guides, whitewashed tombs and brood of vipers (Mt 23:13-36).

The passions become destructive and evil only if their force is not controlled by reason. Since this is not a remote possibility, but on the contrary a common danger, man has the urgent duty to control and to check his sensitive appetites. In fact the whole process of moral education, both in the early and in the maturer years, is to a large degree a process of gaining command over the movements of the passions. Thus man has eventually to become master of himself.

b) *Division.* Passion or concupiscence may be antecedent or consequent. Antecedent passion precedes the action of the will and at the same time induces the will to consent. This takes place in involuntary movements. Thus delicious food served at table spontaneously causes appetite and the desire to eat it. Consequent passion follows the free determination of the will and is either freely admitted and consented to or deliberately aroused. If passion is freely consented to, it has first risen spontaneously, true, but afterwards the will accepts and fosters it by free decision. Passion is deliberately aroused if one purposely evokes and stimulates it, e.g. in an evil sense by reading immoral literature, or in a good sense by singing hymns of divine praise (e.g. in charismatic meetings).

c) *Principles.* (I) Antecedent passion always lessens voluntariness and sometimes precludes it completely. Passion lessens voluntariness because it hinders the reflection of reason and weakens its attention. At the same time it strongly urges to action and entices the will to consent. Furthermore, since the forces of the soul are limited, it holds that the stronger the activity of one psychic faculty is, the weaker becomes the activity of the others. The more intensive concupiscence is, the weaker are intellect and will. This explains why a very vehement passion can occasionally, though only seldom, overrule intellect and will in such a way that free choice and a voluntary human act are excluded.

If passion diminishes voluntariness, it increases on the other hand the inclination of the will. In other words, what is willed through antecedent passion is willed with greater intensity but less freely. But this does not preclude that a grave offence may be committed nevertheless. Moreover the passion is often willed indirectly, either because one exposes oneself to danger without adequate reason, or because one does not resist one's passionate disposition in spite of the awareness that one has an obligation in that regard.

(II) Consequent passion does not give rise to lessened voluntariness and is therefore good or bad. Consequent passion is freely accepted or even deliberately roused; for this reason it is voluntary in itself and voluntary in the passion as their cause are also the consequences flowing therefrom, i.e. the obfuscation of the intellect and the enticement of the will.

2. Fear and social pressure

a) *Concept and nature.* Fear is the shrinking back of the mind on account of an impending evil. This intellectual fear is to be distinguished from the fear of the senses, which is one of the passions and to which therefore the principles regarding passions are applicable. Intellectual fear does not generally escape the control of the mind and will, as the fear of the senses easily does, and leaves the person in principle free. The evil which causes the fear may threaten the affected person himself or his relatives, friends and others associated with him.

A very pervasive form of fear, mostly working in a subtle way, is social pressure. An instinctive need, rarely emerging into consciousness, for acceptance, competitiveness, esteem, safety, shelter, etc. pressurizes human beings to conform to prevailing opinions and behaviour patterns. Even so-called intellectuals are more susceptible to such influences than they like to think. Of course many of the fashions in ideas and life style are rather neutral from the moral point of view. Many others are entirely justified, as e.g. the sanctions attached to the written and unwritten rules and laws of social life. But where erroneous beliefs, prejudices or false ideologies are at work and recognized by a person as such, he ought to dissociate himself from them and stand up against them. Yet all too often the powers of fear and shame fetter a person's freedom and prevent him from doing what in conscience he ought to do.

b) *Divisions.* Fear may be grave or slight according to whether it is caused by a grave evil which one cannot easily escape; or only by a slight evil, or by a grave evil which one can however easily avoid. Fear is absolutely grave if it exercises a great deterrence upon the average person, like death, torture, unemployment for a father who has no other resources to sustain his family. Fear is relatively grave if the threatened evil is objectively only slight but frightens a particular person subjectively very much because of his timidity, as e.g. a child might dread to be locked up in a dark cellar. A frequent kind of a relatively grave fear is reverential fear, by which a person shrinks back from opposing someone to whom he is obliged to show reverence. Although it is usually accounted a slight fear, it can seriously impair freedom of decision especially of children or also already grown-up daughters with regard to their parents. At times reverential fear can be absolutely grave, if namely opposition against a person in authority would result in long lasting disfavour, quarrels and vexations.

Another division distinguishes between unjustly and justly inflicted fear. Fear is inflicted unjustly if it is not justified by any guilt or potential misbehaviour of a person or is out of proportion to them. Thus it is unjust to threaten a person with the loss of his job if he continues to be a practising Christian. Fear is inflicted justly if it is justified by a person's guilt or potential misbehaviour. Thus it is just to threaten a rapist with prosecution and prison, unless he pays compensation and alimony for the child. The punishments threatened by penal codes against offences and crimes in principle pertain to the category of justly inflicted fear. They are justified social pressures.

c) *Principles*. (I) Fear does not destroy the voluntary character of an action; but it usually lessens its guilt as well as its merit. According to the accepted principles of moral theology, no degree of fear, unless it hampers the use of reason, destroys voluntariness and excuses from sin or, on the other hand, takes away the merit of a good action. Even though the act has an involuntary aspect, it holds that a person who executes a certain action to avoid an evil which he fears, does so by decision of his will and therefore performs a human act. Thus in times of persecution the fear of death was never taken as an excuse for apostasy. Nor does the fear of death excuse a soldier from not remaining at his post till death. In the same way the imminent approach of shipwreck never justifies a crew to take to the boats and leave women and children behind to their fate.

Yet fear often diminishes guilt and merit, because there is an involuntary aspect insofar as fear makes a person will what otherwise he would not will. This is most obvious if the threatening evil is very great, like torture. Apostasy for fear of torture is accordingly a considerably lesser sin than apostasy for the sake of getting a promotion in office. On the other hand, if a soldier only continues to fight because he is afraid of court martial, his merits and virtue are almost null.

(II) Grave fear usually excuses from the obligations of positive ecclesiastical or civil law (unless they are at the same time precepts of the natural moral law) and of affirmative natural law. The reason is that moral impossibility excuses from the compliance with such laws (cf. the expositions on cessation of the obligation of the law and on epikeia). Thus grave fear exempts the faithful from assisting at Sunday Mass; or it releases from the obligation to restore ill-gotten goods. But fear does not excuse if a positive law is of such a nature that its violation would cause great harm to the common good. Hence under no circumstance is it lawful for a priest to reveal confessional secrets.

As to negative natural laws, such as the prohibitions of murder, blasphemy, denial of faith, etc., grave fear as a rule does not excuse from their observance. However if material goods are concerned, it may excuse from the prohibitions of theft and damage to other people's possessions. Thus under the threat of death, a bank employee may hand over the money of the cash-box to the robbers (cf. the rules for cooperation in the wrong deeds of others).

It is to be noted that ecclesiastical and civil law often invalidate actions rescindable at the instance of him who was influenced by fear. Ecclesiastical law invalidates the following acts from the very beginning, if undertaken as a result of grave fear unjustly imposed: matrimony, admission to the novitiate, religious vows, other vows, promissory oaths, resignation from office.[1] Holy Orders received as a result of fear are valid, but can be rescinded by the Church authority if petition is made by the affected party.[2]

3. *Violence*

Violence is a compulsive influence brought to bear upon one against his will by some extrinsic agent. Violence is not caused by moral force such as fear, but only by the compulsive force of some physical or psychic agent. Though this agent is extrinsic to the will, it need not necessarily be extrinsic to a person's body and psyche, since violence can also result from pathological conditions.

While internal resistance of the will is essential for violence, external resistance is not always called for. It is required if there is hope that the force can be repelled by counteraction; or if it is necessary to preclude the danger of internal consent, or if there is need to prevent others from thinking that consent has been given. Therefore if a state should unjustly expropriate Church property, the ecclesiastical authority ought to protest, even if there is no hope of getting back what has been taken away, to state clearly before the public and the law that the Church did not approve of this action. On the other hand, if a Christian is arrested because of his religious conviction, he need not refuse to make the way to prison on his own feet, since such refusal would not profit anything, but on the contrary only worsen the situation.

Violence is absolute if the will dissents totally and resists as best it can and is meaningful. Violence is relative if the will dissents only partially or weakly and is perhaps deficient in its external resistance. A person who is dragged to the

---

[1] CIC 1103; 643, n.4; 656, n.4; 1191, §3; 1200, §2; 188.
[2] CIC 125, §2; 1026.

altar of pagan gods and in whose hands is put incense as an offering, may be tempted to give partial consent to the force, since it will save him from torture and death. The following rules apply to the influence of violence on imputability.

(I) Absolute violence excludes any voluntariness from the forced action. The reason is that lack of consent precludes a human act and consequently imputability. If it is a question of juridical acts, the Church declares them invalid (cf. CIC 125, §1).

(II) Relative violence does not impair voluntariness completely but lessens it. Voluntariness is not completely taken away since there is a partial consent of the will. But voluntariness is lessened because relative violence makes a person carry out what otherwise he would not do.

4. *Dispositions and habits*

There are natural dispositions which incline one man more than another to certain ways of reaction and conduct and which have their roots in his character and inherited propensities. Education by one's family and environment plays an equally important role in the formation of attitudes and customs, which influence an individual strongly and which he cannot easily overcome. According to the findings of depth-psychology, a person's past experiences, especially the experiences of early childhood, build up unconscious patterns of behaviour and motivations, which can exert psychic pressure upon him, and sometimes a very powerful one, such as tendencies to disorder, aggressiveness, fear of social contacts, submissiveness. All these factors have an impact upon a person's free will and affect his decisions. They are apt to narrow a person's liberty and to diminish the voluntariness of his actions to a certain degree, although they cannot take it away altogether.[1]

The fact that education is so powerful in forming good or bad attitudes and habits makes it necessary that the child be gently trained from his early years to subdue evil inclinations,

---

[1] This also holds good for unconscious motivations and neurotic propensities. Although it cannot be doubted that these impulses of the dynamic unconscious exercise pressure on an activity, this does not signify that they compel it, as is sometimes claimed (cf. J.C. Ford and G. Kelly, "Imputability and Unconscious Motivation," in *Contemporary Moral Theology*, vol. 1. Westminster: Newman Press, 1958, 174-200).

to acquire good habits and to practise Christian virtues. For this reason it is totally wrong to leave a child uninfluenced by religion until he is able to make his own choice. The love of God, the appreciation of prayer, virtues and sacraments, the resistance against sin need to be impressed upon a child from his earliest age. This is an inestimable aid for the child's future confrontation with life. It spares him many struggles and mistakes and leaves his energies free for the positive tasks of love of God and neighbour.

When a person frequently follows out an inclination, he acquires thereby the power to perform the action easily. The inclination becomes stronger and finally grows into a habit. The habit is defined as a facility and readiness of acting in a certain manner acquired by repeated acts. Man is not without responsibility for the development and retention of his habits, be they good or bad. The following principles apply to the imputability of habits as well as dispositions and the actions flowing from them.

(I) A deliberately admitted habit does not lessen voluntariness, and actions resulting therefrom are voluntary at least in their cause. Although a person may not be free by force of his habit at the moment he acts, he is still responsible for his actions if he consents by free decision to the habit as such. For approval of the habit as such necessarily also includes approval of all the consequences which one knows will follow from the habit.

(II) An opposed habit lessens voluntariness and sometimes precludes it completely. The reason is that a habit weakens intellect and will in the concrete situation in a similar way as passion does. Hence in spite of a person's disapproval of his bad inclination, he is often overcome by the force of the habit. When a person earnestly strives to rid himself of a bad habit, he will frequently be excused from sin if he nevertheless yields to temptation. As long, for example, as a man who is in the evil habit of cursing and using profane language does not disapprove of his habit at all, his acts of cursing are fully imputable and sinful. If he shows dislike for his habit, yet counteracts only weakly, he is responsible for his bad acts to the degree of his tepidity and indolence. But should he resolutely fight against his bad habit, the evil words which still slip out in spite of his good intentions are no longer culpable, since they are no longer freely consented to.

With regard to *pathologic conditions* of psychiatric nature or mental deficiencies and their influence on the liberty of man, these conditions do not constitute impairments which are specifically different from those already mentioned. The psychic defects can ultimately be reduced to the other impairments of human acts and their freedom. At times mental illnesses prevent the origination of human acts altogether by depriving the afflicted person of the normal use of reason. This means that the required knowledge or insight is lacking, without which human acts cannot come about but only acts of man. At other times mental illnesses may cause psychic compulsion, which amounts to the impediment of violence. Or they may pressure a person in the line of dispositions and habits. Often psychic compulsions, such as kleptomania, agoraphobia or certain instances of scrupulosity, can considerably be reduced by a person's will and discipline, although not totally eliminated. In this they resemble inveterate habits. Also bodily illnesses can impair the freedom of will and inhibit initiative or lower the threshold of irritation with regard to negative stimuli. Although the sick person may not simply abandon himself to conditions of this kind, his surroundings ought to take those handicaps into account.

C. Sources defining the morality of human acts

The norm which determines or measures the morality of a human act is objectively the moral law and subjectively a person's conscience. Human acts are morally good if in agreement with these norms and morally evil if in disagreement with them. The question to be answered here is the question about the various elements in the human act which have to be measured against the moral norm and which determine its morality. These elements are called the sources of the morality of the human act, because the human act derives its morality from their agreement or disagreement with the moral norm.[1]

---

[1] Te be distinguished from the "sources of morality" are the "sources of moral theology", a terminology used by Mausbach/Ermecke. With this the authors of the manual refer to the loci from where moral theology takes its arguments. In detail these loci are Holy Scripture, the tradition of the Church and reason (*Katholische Moraltheologie*. Münster: Aschendorff, ^{9}1959, 43-50). Understandably the manual then avoids the expression "sources of morality" in the traditional sense, since that could easily lead to confusion. In its stead the manual speaks of the "elements of the moral action" and their morality (242ff). In the present text the question of the "sources of moral theology" is dealt with in the introduction.

Traditionally moral theology lists three sources of the morality of human acts: object, circumstances and intention. A human act is good if all these three elements are in harmony with the moral norm. On the other hand a human act is morally evil if only one of these elements offends against the norm of morality. This is the meaning of the terse Latin principle: *Bonum ex integra causa, malum ex quovis defectu.*

I. The object

The object of the human act is that effect which an action primarily and directly causes (*finis operis*). It is always and necessarily the result of the act, independent of any circumstances or of the intention of the agent. Human language identifies the various types or categories of actions by certain words and descriptions, such as theft, abortion, lying, almsgiving, healing, worship, etc. Object of the actions thus identified is that effect which pertains to the essence of the act and without which the action would no longer be the same. Thus the object of a theft is always the appropriation of another person's goods against his will, whether it is taken from a rich or a poor man, whether its purpose is personal enrichment or alleviation of extreme need. The object of an abortion is always the forcible removal of the non-viable human being from the mother's womb, whether it is done to avoid public shame or for therapeutic reasons.

In order to have a clear idea of the object of the human act, it is necessary to determine as precisely as possible the primary and direct effects of the human act whose object is to be defined. The effect of the human act is first of all the physical, biological, psychological changes which an act brings about. Yet these changes alone do not yield much for the moral evaluation of the act. The transfer of goods from one place to another, the destruction of a human life, the event of a sexual relation, in themselves do not yet state anything about the moral qualification of the act which caused them. Also to be computed among the effects of the human act is the impact of the act on rights and claims of persons, whether of other persons or of the agent himself, and the changes the act brings about in this sphere, i.e. the dissolution, appropriation, suspension, creation or transfer of claims and rights.

Hence the object of a contract of sale is not only the physical transfer of goods from one place to another, but also the exchange of property rights attached to the goods. The object of an act of adultery is not only the physiological happening of intercourse, but also the assumption of marriage rights by partners who are not married with each other and the encroachment on the rights of a third person.

The object is generally regarded as the primary source for the judgment on the morality of an act. The most important aspect of an action seems to be the immediate effect which the action inevitably brings about in the objective order, independent of the intention of the agent and additional circumstances.

Catholic moral handbooks universally hold that the object of a human act can be morally good, evil or indifferent. Indifferent from the viewpoint of the object are, e. g., the taking of a walk or the playing of an instrument. But this does not mean that the entire action is morally indifferent; for its morality further depends on the circumstances and particularly on the intention of the agent. The circumstances and the intention also further modify the morality of an action with a morally good object, even to the extent of making the action in its totality evil, as shall be seen later.

Where the object of the human act is morally evil, as for example in a case of rape or of the killing of an innocent person, no purpose and intention of the agent, be it ever so good, can permit this act. This has been the common teaching of Catholic moral theology till now. It presupposes the existence of moral absolutes, a question which has been referred to already earlier. They are prohibitions of actions which exclusively on account of their object are considered absolutely and intrinsically evil. In this sense the encyclical *Veritatis Splendor* underlines that the object decisively determines the act of willing on the part of the acting person. The encyclical illustrates this by the following text from Thomas Aquinas: "It often happens that man acts with a good intention, but without spiritual gain, because he lacks a good will. Let us say that someone robs in order to feed the poor: in this case, even though the intention is good, the uprightness of the will is lacking. Consequently, no evil done with a good intention can be excused."[1] The encyclical adds as a reasoning: "The reason why a good intention is not itself sufficient, but a correct choice of actions is also needed, is that the human act depends on its object, whether that object is capable or not of being ordered to God, to the One who 'alone is good'."[2]

Indeed the good intention does not suffice in order to make an evil action good. Yet if the intention of the person were to save himself from starvation, the theft would be a permissible exception. It would be permissible food theft, as this is the common teaching of moral theology. Accordingly theft is in principle not lawful. The hurt for the common weal is such that not just any kind of good intention can permit an exception. Only a very significant value can justify an exception, such as the saving of one's life. Only in order to avoid a still greater evil, can the evil of theft exceptionally be permitted. In this case namely the act of theft can - as the criterion formulated by the encyclical runs - be ordered to God and "its object is in conformity with the good of the person with respect for the goods morally relevant for him".[3]

Theft wherefore is always an evil, but not absolutely and always a *moral* evil; in exceptional cases it can be morally permitted. On account of this observation, here as in other cases, more and more theologians have of late raised the question whether there are really any external actions which are absolutely evil and therefore can never and for no good purpose whatsoever be allowed. These authors admit of actions which by the nature of their object are most of the time evil. Nevertheless, if the object of the action is viewed in isolation from the agent's purpose, it has as yet no definite moral qualification. Only if weighed together with the purpose or intention of the agent, can an unequivocal judgment on the moral quality of the action be pronounced.

In the overall there are not many absolutes even in traditional Catholic moral theology, i.e. actions whose object is considered always and in all circumstances evil. Only those actions merit the qualification of absolutes with certainty which always contradict man's ultimate end, such as denial of faith

---

[1] *Veritatis Splendor*, 1993, nr. 78.
[2] Ib.
[3] Ib.

or seduction of others to sin. No good purpose or intention of the agent can permit them. But in most other cases it is very difficult to show that no exception at all might be compatible with the demands of the ultimate end.

The traditional distinction between good, indifferent and evil objects of the human act is certainly not without foundation. The object of an act of almsgiving is something good and the object of theft is something bad. But recent theologians correctly point out that these distinctions do not yet constitute moral qualifications, but rather pre-moral ones. If a person gives alms in an irresponsible way to the detriment of his family, it is after all not a morally good act. And if the purpose of a theft is to save one's family from starvation, it is a lawful act in spite of the harm caused. Accordingly one ought to distinguish not between valuable and harmful objects in a moral sense, but rather between valuable and harmful objects in a pre-moral sense. There is a presumption that valuable objects merit to be favoured and harmful objects ought to be avoided; for premoral evils, such as pain, hunger or death, remain evils, even if they have possibly to be tolerated. But a final judgment on the morality of the act is possible only under simultaneous consideration of the circumstances of the act and above all the intention of the agent.

II. The circumstances

The circumstances are particulars of the concrete human act which are not necessarily connected with its object. Alms may be given by a poor man or by a rich man, in private or in public. These circumstances can vary without modifying the object of the act of almsgiving, which always remains the same. Not all circumstances exercise an influence on the morality of an act. In fact most of them are morally indifferent, e.g. whether the alms are given on a Monday or Friday, on the road or in the house. Circumstances are morally relevant if they increase or decrease good or evil effects or bring about additional effects of evil nature or at least are apt to occasion such effects with some likelihood.

It is to be noted that a particular condition of an act which is at one time merely a circumstance may at another time pertain to the object of the act. This is then the case when this condition is the basis for a right or an obligation in justice. The fact that an action is performed by a married man or in a church is usually a mere circumstance. But in an act of extramarital intercourse, the fact that a man is married enters into the object of the act, since his married status is the grounds for rights and obligations in justice, which are affected and changed about in this act. Therefore the act is not qualified simply as extramarital intercourse but as adultery. Or if profane dances are performed in a church, then the circumstance that the place of the action is a church enters into the object of the act, since the consecration of this place to the worship of God establishes special claims of God over this place, which are tampered with in this act. Therefore the act is qualified as a sacrilege.

Commonly the following seven circumstances are enumerated: who, what, where, with what means, why, how, when.[1] The circumstances can alter the morality of human acts for better or for worse. In particular, circumstances can influence the morality of an action in the following ways:

(a) In the positive sense, a circumstance can make better an act good in its object. If a poor man gives alms, the act of charity is greater. A circumstance can make good an act indifferent in its object. The friendly manners of an employer in the relations with his employees impart to even his morally indifferent dealings with them a moral goodness. A circumstance can make less evil an act evil in its object. The denial of faith under threat of torture is less evil than the denial of faith for a promotion in office.

(b) In the negative sense, a circumstance can make worse an act evil in its object. To be guilty of detraction before several people is worse than to commit detraction before one person. A circumstance can make evil an act indifferent in its object. The playing of a radio may become evil if it is so loud that it seriously disturbs others. Finally a circumstance

---

[1] See *S. Th.* I-II, q. 7, a. 3. G. Stanke (*Die Lehre von den "Quellen der Moralität"*. Regensburg: Pustet, 1984, 47) judges that the inclusion of the purpose "why" in this list is inconsequent. In fact the circumstance "why" can be understood as the purpose or intention of the agent, and then the objection is valid. It can however also refer to an influence external to the will and nevertheless affecting the action, such as the influence exerted by error, violence, passion or inveterate habits. In this sense the why of the action is different from the purpose and a mere circumstance indeed.

can make less good or evil an act good in its object. Christmas carols, meant to cheer up old people, are a good work, but it is less good if they are badly prepared. The construction of a chapel is a praiseworthy work; but if it is done with materials that are stolen or a land title that is forged, it is ultimately evil.

III. The end intended by the agent

The end or the purpose (*finis operantis*) is the reason for which the agent undertakes an act. The agent performs the action for the sake of this end, which he expects or hopes to be the effect of his act. The end can therefore also be defined as that effect which the agent subjectively aims at in his action.

The end or effect aimed at by the agent in an action may be the same as the object of the action, in which case *finis operis* and *finis operantis* are identical. The immediate effect of the consumption of a greater amount of alcohol is drunkenness, i.e. a state of exhilaration and lessened concern. This object of the act can be the subjective end of the agent. But the agent may also aim at another, indirect or remote effect of his act, which in some cases may come about with certainty, yet which in other cases may only be possible and hoped for. A captured spy may kill himself in order not to betray any national secrets. The object of this act is suicide, and the end is prevention of betrayal of secrets. This end is an indirect effect of the act, which effect in this case will follow with certainty. Very often however the end aimed at by the agent is only hoped for and its realization is not certain. A bank robbery requires many preparatory actions, which all have the same remote end. But the successful realization of this end is only hoped for and not certain. This latter example also illustrates that very often several acts proceed from the same intention and have the same end.

In place of "end" the term "intention" is also often used to name the third source of the morality of human acts. Intention is the plan or determination of the will to bring about a certain effect. The term intention views an end as adopted by the will in order to bring it into existence, i.e. it views the end as a source of action, whereas the term end only views the reality of the effect in itself, independent of the motivating force it exerts upon the agent.

The end modifies the morality of an act in similar ways as circumstances do. A good end can make better an act good in its object, good an act indifferent in its object, and less evil an act evil in its object. A bad end can make worse an act evil in its object, evil an act indifferent in its object, and less good or evil an act good in its object. Yet if the good or evil end intended by the agent is identical with the good or evil object of the act, no further goodness or badness is added to the act. Thus the object of an alms is the relief of a fellow-man's need, and this is most of the time also the purpose of the agent.

It merits attention that not every defect of intention must entirely spoil an act whose object is good. "One helps another person, one stands up for the community, one strives hard in one's profession. But it comes from the not so nice intention to carry weight, it is accompanied by ambition, in all of it one thinks more of oneself than of the others." Clearly in all these cases a defect can be noted. But are they all necessarily bad intentions? "It might be closer to reality and more just to understand them as still imperfect and only initially good. They are still in need of purification, but also capable of it. The view that in this subjective sphere of intention and purpose everything could and should right away always and from the start be perfect, misjudges the true resources and possibilities of the person."[1]

In contrast to circumstances, which are often morally indifferent, the end is of relevance for the morality of every human act. Besides, the end frequently joins many diverse actions in one unity and imparts to all of them a common goodness or badness. Thus the end to help flood victims gives a common goodness to all the actions undertaken by the one who organizes a relief campaign.

In the moral evaluation of an act, the end therefore is of great importance. It has been stated that "the end is the primordial element of the structure of an action, because it is the proper object of the act of the will".[2] There is truth

---

[1] H. Weber, *Allgemeine Moraltheologie* (Graz: Styria, 1991), 319.

[2] Louis Janssens, "Ontic Evil and Moral Evil," in *Readings in Moral Theology No. I: Moral Norms and Catholic Tradition*, ed. by C.E. Curran and R.A. McCormick (New York: Paulist Press, 1979), 42.

to this assertion. Nevertheless some caution is in place. The proposition might lead to conclusions which underestimate the weight of the circumstances and particularly of the object in the moral evaluation of an act. Not what a person does is then considered important, but only the frame of mind in which he does it. Yet evidently a good intention alone is not sufficient. It cannot justify any means whatsoever.

There is one end indeed which, as the supreme criterion of the moral action, can justify any means. This is the ultimate end of man. However in his concrete actions man does not directly aim at the ultimate end, but rather at intermediate ends. Even if these ends are in harmony with the ultimate end, they do not on this account share in its character as an absolute norm and value. They constitute relative values. Therefore their realization is subject to conditions and limitations. The construction of a church is certainly in harmony with the great concerns of the ultimate end, i.e. the furtherance of God's glory and the unfolding of his creative designs. Nevertheless this does not justify acquisition of the land for the church by a forged title and procurement of the money for the construction by a bank robbery. Even though the construction of the church is in harmony with the ultimate end, the means used for this purpose are more damaging to this end than the good results gained by the construction.

Accordingly the immediate, relative ends people are aiming at in their actions are just one element in the evaluation of the morality of an action besides the object of the act and the circumstances. All the elements have to be weighed in their proportion to each other and their fitness to serve the ultimate end. If in spite of a person's good intention an action becomes counter-productive to the ultimate end because of the object and circumstances involved, the action as a whole is not good but bad. As a basic rule holds: The end which one wants to achieve must not be blasted by the means used and the mode of acting.

Even though many of the actions which men and women do throughout the day may seem very insignificant in view of the comprehensive goal of the ultimate end, all actions have to be measured by this supreme criterion. All of them must remain in harmony with this end and in some way serve it. Vatican II correctly asserts: the mandate to relate the world to God's glory and to contribute to the realization in history of the divine plan "holds good also for our daily work" (GS 34). If this harmony does not exist, an action is no longer good, it is morally wrong and, if not excused by invincible ignorance, sinful.

Time and again the importance of a good intention is emphasized in pedagogical writings. This is a valid concern. "Good intention" here refers to a more comprehensive motivation, such as the desire to serve God, to be faithful to Christ, to be a useful member of the community, etc. It surely is a strong inspiration for a person to do what is good in contrast to a selfish intention, which inevitably must result in many selfish and objectionable actions. Nevertheless a good motivation alone does not guarantee the moral rightness of all the actions motivated by it. Many offences and even crimes have been committed by the good intentions of religious fanatics of all colours. Here too the means used have to stand the test of the standards set by the ultimate end. Nor can a good intention dispense a person from the efforts to come to grips with the facts of reality, to know the nature of things and the rights of persons with which his actions are concerned, and to study the consequences which his actions entail.

A dispute exists concerning the question whether there are morally indifferent intentions and consequently *morally indifferent actions*, i.e. concrete human acts which are morally indifferent. (Note that this question only concerns human acts, i.e. acts which proceed from insight and free will, not acts of man, such as involuntary reactions, which are recognized as morally indifferent by everybody.) Many Fathers of the Church and the Franciscan School admit the possibility of indifferent human acts. But the majority of theologians, particularly the Thomists, reject the possibility of human acts which, taken in their concrete totality, are morally indifferent. For, thus they argue, a human act is directed either to an appropriate end and thereby is good, or to an inappropriate end and thereby is evil. There is no midway between these two alternatives. Certainly, for a full clarification of the problem a more comprehensive study would be required. However the question seems not of great practical importance. Even the Franciscan School will admit that most of the concrete human acts are either good or evil. And it does not matter much whether in fact there are some human acts which are morally indifferent, since they do not affect a person's final goal and eternal destiny.

IV. Moral significance of the external act

The question is posed whether the external realization of an act is an additional source of its morality, i.e. whether it increases the moral goodness or badness of an action; or whether the morality of an act exclusively and entirely results from the internal consent and approval of the will. Is the person who wants to give an alms, but has his money stolen from him, therefore less good? Is another person who wants to rob a jeweller's store, but is prevented from it by an accident, therefore less bad?

Already common sense spontaneously judges that in the two above examples the good or the evil determination to the act count for the deed, although the external realization of the intended action was prevented by circumstances beyond the agent's control. Per se the external act does not increase the morality of the internal act. This is confirmed by Holy Scripture, which judges the evil desire of the heart to be as bad as an already performed act. Thus our Lord declares: "Every one who looks at a woman lustfully has already committed adultery with her in his heart" (Mt 5:28).

The reason is that moral imputability is based on a person's free consent. This consent is an internal decision, and the external act does not involve any additional approval. Naturally the internal consent must be a firm and efficacious determination to proceed to external action if the opportunity lends itself. It may not be a mere volition, as is very often the case with good as well as with bad desires. The volition is only a liking and an inefficacious desire, which is not truly resolved to proceed to the external realization of its object. Mere volition indeed gains a new moral weight by the decision of the will to put an action into effect. But this additional moral weight results from a new, internal consent and again not from the external act.

Per accidens however the external accomplishment of an act may increase its moral goodness or badness. Through repercussion on the will namely the interior acts may be intensified, prolonged, renewed and multiplied. And by no means may a morality of pure inwardness be construed, which emphasizes the inner intention in such a way that little or no importance is given to its external realization. Neglect of the opportunity offered and disregard of the occasion for the inner act to express itself externally in action is the sign of a half-hearted will, not truly resolved to good action (nor, of course, to bad action either). Such kind of good intention is not on a par with the external good action.

From the preceding considerations on the moral import of the external act follows a further conclusion that neither do external success or failure determine the value of an action. The preaching and apostolate of a dedicated missionary is equally praiseworthy, whether he has hundreds of conversions, as in some regions of Africa, or whether he has only very few every year, as in Japan.

External success does not add to the morality of an act. But this does not mean that a man can simply remain unconcerned about the success of his good ventures. For the resolute will to use one's abilities to the best in order to secure success does indeed add to the morality of an action. A parish priest's lame appeal from the pulpit to clean the neglected cemetery and to beautify it, which does not meet with success, is not of the same moral value as the energetic involvement of a priest who approaches his parish organizations for this project, recruits volunteers, contacts individual parishioners to do something for their deceased relatives, etc. The determined striving after the successful accomplishment of a work and the earnest will to realize the objective are very essential to the moral value of an action.

D. Preference rules and problems of the lesser evil

The themes dealt with here concern questions of the just ethical decision in instances of alternative possibilities of acting or of persons obliged to a task. The subject is general orientations, which on account of their general character, applicable in various realms of life, are being treated in general moral theology. The preference rules give norms regarding the *greater good* to be preferred in cases of alternative possibilities of acting or the person primarily obliged to a certain task. The other themes deal with the problem of the *lesser evil*. The first, the admission of indirectly willed effects, essentially has to do with the actions and related effects of the acting person himself or herself. The other two, cooperation in the wrong deeds of others and the ethical compromise, imply a social dimension. The problems here result from a social entwining of human actions. Men find themselves confronted with the wrong deeds of others or with unjust legislations, which condition their actions in ways that contradict their true will.

I. Preference rules[1]

The preference rules give some fundamental orientations for moral norms on the basis of a hierarchy of values grounded in natural law and in man's ultimate end. They underlie many of the concrete norms elaborated by moral theology and ethics. Indeed it can be said that all ethical norms which order the relations between humans are ultimately based on a judgment of preference. "Norms are so to speak coagulated balances of values or preference rules."[2] The norm, e. g., that the right and duty of the education of children primarily pertains to the parents designates the higher good as against the education by other people or the state. The duty of alms implies that the relief of the plight of the poor is the higher good as against the retention of dispensable goods on the part of the better situated person.

A most fundamental rule and a presupposition for many of the other rules is the principle that values of more basic importance have to be preferred to values of lesser importance. However the hierarchy of values poses no small problem. Otto Schilling gives the following order of precedence: values which refer to eternal salvation, life, health, liberty, honour, and material goods.[3] But on occasion inversions are possible. A person may have to risk his life in order to defend the liberty of his country. A still more fundamental problem is

---

[1] A helpful compilation of preference rules is found in Hans Reiner, *Die Grundlagen der Sittlichkeit* (Meisenheim am Glan: Anton Hain, ²1974), 168-176. A collection of preference rules is also offered by Rudolf Ginters, *Die Ausdruckshandlung* (Düsseldorf: Patmos, 1976), 92-95.

[2] Alfons Auer, "Absolutheit und Bedingtheit ethischer Normen," in *Unterwegs zur Einheit*, ed. by J. Brantschen und P. Selvatico (Freiburg/Wien, 1980), 354.

[3] Otto Schilling, *Handbuch der Moraltheologie*, vol. I (Stuttgart: Schwabenverlag, 1952), 161.

the question: How does one arrive at this order at all? Here once again the supreme value of man's ultimate end is of decisive importance. The hierarchy and precedence of values is ultimately determined by man's ultimate end. Those values which are of greater importance for the realization of this end merit precedence. Definitely the order of precedence will vary according to the nature of the ultimate end a person adopts for himself. For some types of utilitarianism material goods will be of greater importance than the values of honour. Schilling's hierarchy essentially corresponds to the Christian order of values, arrived at in the light of the supreme value of God's glory and kingdom. But as the situations vary, the hierarchy will time and again need modifications and adjustments. - Besides this general rule, the following, concrete preference rules can be pointed out.

1. Particular goods of a person should be subordinated to the general good of the whole person, the goods of an individual person to comparable goods of a group or the community as a whole, the goods of lesser communities to comparable goods of broader ones. This includes the demand to prefer that mode of action which satisfies the more urgent needs of a person and serves his development more. Accordingly it will be more important for a youth to dedicate herself to her studies than to travel around and enjoy the world.

2. Whoever is the only one suited for a task whose performance is necessary or very desirable, is also the only one obliged to it; whoever is better suited for the task, has also the prior duty to it. Thus if a priest is the only one who can settle a precarious dispute between tenants and landowners, he has the obligation to mediate in the dispute. But it should be understood that if a person, who in the abstract is the one suited best for a task, is already occupied with other important tasks, he may in the concrete no longer be the one suited best for the additional task.

A special instance of the mentioned rule is the norm that ordinarily a person has the prior duty to care for his own needs, since in many regards he is the one suited best for this task and often even the only one. Thus the first duty to take care of an adult person's religious life rests with that person himself. For the same reason, parents usually have the first obligation to take care of their children, since they have the best qualifications for it.

3. An action or condition which offers greater probability of success is to be preferred to one whose success is less assured. The presupposition of course is that the actions are not morally objectionable. On this account, everything else being equal, a person is to prefer sufficiency to want, freedom to slavery. Here can also be counted the rule that an action which will only probably cause an evil effect is to be preferred to an action which will cause it with certainty.

4. An imperiled value whose safeguarding needs immediate action is to be preferred to an endangered value which can still be saved at a later time. Thus it is more urgent to reinforce dikes against a present flood than to save a building threatened by gradual dilapidation. Here also pertains the preference of goods of a lower rank vis-à-vis higher ones, if only in this way the ones of higher rank can be secured in the long run. "In this context one distinguishes between proximate and remote ends. Attention has to be paid that the temporary deferment does not lead to a sacrificing of the good of higher rank. Greater urgency stands in the service of the higher rank. The first step must always functionally be done in view of the last one, it must not block the way to it."[1]

5. Relief of a need that is certain, merits preference ove a need that, ceteris paribus, is only probable. A family father of frugal means who may need a coat for his children only after two years may have to give it to a relative who is in urgent need of it now.

6. Non-violation of existing values has priority over against the creation of new values. The duty to protect an existing life is by far higher than the right to give birth to a new life. However lower values may at times be sacrificed to give place to higher ones, if this is the only means to realize the latter.

These are some of the more important preference rules, although the list is not exhaustive. From of old traditional moral theology has developed a number of preference rules in the treatment of the order of fraternal love, be it preferences with regard to persons or be it with regard to the gravity of needs. They concern a concrete field of special moral theology

---

[1] K. Demmer, *Deuten und Handeln* (Freiburg: Herder, 1985), 184.

and are therefore dealt with there, i.e. in the chapter on love of neighbour.¹

H. Reiner calls attention to the fact that the application of the preference rules is by no means always simple and easy. The individual, left to himself alone, is often not equal to this task. He stands in need of the moral traditions of the communities to which he belongs and of the assistance of the competent moral authorities. Acquaintance with these rules provides helpful orientation, but it is no substitute for their concrete, detailed application in the various sectors of special moral theology.²

II. Imputability of indirectly willed effects

An effect is indirectly willed if it is not intended as an end or a means, but only foreseen as the result of a directly willed effect. The man who likes a glass of wine or brandy wants to enjoy the good taste of these drinks. But if he is a driver, who still has to drive his car afterwards, the alcohol may have the side-effect of reducing the reliability of his reactions in traffic, so that he endangers himself and others on the road. This side-effect is by no means intended by the driver as the purpose of his drinking. It is also not the means to obtain the pleasure of a good drink (as for example a theft may be the means to buy a bottle of brandy). It is an indirect effect of the action, which is not intended by the driver, but for which he is nevertheless held liable. A driver must know of the consequences of alcohol for his traffic discipline and is therefore obliged to abstain from it. If he nevertheless drinks and drives, the ensuing evil effects are indirectly willed.

It is to be noted that in order to be willed, the indirect effect must at least dimly be foreseen. A man who until now never experienced the influence of alcohol over him and who becomes violent when drinking for the first time is not guilty of this unforeseen reaction.

1. *Imputability of indirectly willed effects in general*

A distinction must be made between the imputability of indirectly willed good and indirectly willed evil effects. The

---
¹ Cf. *Christian Ethics* II, 2004, chapter VI, 214-220.
² Cf. H. Reiner, *l. c.* 178-184.

former are not imputed to the agent, while the latter are at times imputed and at other times not. This difference demonstrates that indirectly willed effects are distinct from directly willed effects, since the latter are always imputed to the agent, whether bad or good, while the indirectly willed effects are not.

a) An indirectly willed *good* effect is not imputed to the agent. The reason is that a human act must proceed from a man's internal consent, i.e. it must result from a decision of the will. The indirectly willed good effect is merely admitted by the will in a tolerating way, not intended or desired by it. A man who steals a typewriter may sell it cheaply to a poor student, who otherwise could not afford to buy one. This is a good side-effect of the thievery. But it is not imputed to the thief as a good work, even if he is aware of it, since this indirect effect did not motivate him at all when stealing the typewriter and selling it to the student.

b) An indirectly willed *evil* effect, on the contrary, is often imputed to the agent; then namely when he could have avoided it and when he should have avoided it. The reason is to be found in the fundamental moral principle that good is to be done and evil to be avoided. A man is obliged to avoid the evil effects of his actions as far as possible. If he permits an evil effect which he is obliged to avoid, he decides to disregard his obligation to avoid evil. Hence this evil effect owes its existence to a decision of his will, i.e. it proceeds from consent and is therefore imputable.

Everybody spontaneously judges actions and their effects according to this rule, even if he is not able to give a reflex justification of his evaluation. A drunken driver is considered guilty of the accident he causes. Factory owners are held responsible for the poisonous pollution of rivers. Mining industries are liable for insufficient safety measures. Producers of medicines have to account for evil side-effects of their products. None of these effects is directly willed, not as a means and much less as an end. They are merely indirectly willed, but they are nevertheless imputed to the agents because they could and should be avoided.

The question of when an indirectly willed evil effect should be avoided and when, on the other hand, it need not be avoided but can be admitted leads to the so-called principle of double effect, which shall be discussed in the following.

2. *The principle of double effect*

This principle spells out the conditions under which an indirectly willed evil effect is not imputed to the agent and therefore can be permitted. Traditionally four conditions are listed.

1.) The act may not be evil in itself, i.e. its very object must not be of an inadmissible, evil nature. Such objects according to Catholic moral theology are, for example, direct abortion, direct suicide, adultery, denial of faith, blasphemy, and a few others.

2.) The evil and the good effect must at least equally directly proceed from the act; or else the immediate effect must be good. It may never be evil. Thus, e. g., a haemorrhage in the uterus during pregnancy may be stanched by means of ergot preparations, which stop the bleeding through contraction of the uterus. The contraction of the uterus however also endangers the foetus, because in the course of this process the placenta may be sheered off. The same action results into two effects, a good and an evil one, both of which proceed equally directly from the act. More frequent are instances where the immediate effect is good, while a more remote, indirect effect is undesirable and evil. The direct effect of the anodyne morphine is alleviation of pain; but if taken for a longer period, morphine involves the risk of addiction, which is an indirect and remote effect of this medication.

The demand that the immediate effect must be good and may never be evil is, in the last analysis, the same as the demand of the first condition that the act may not be evil in itself. For the immediate effect of an action is its object, and if this is evil, then the act is evil in itself. Ultimately therefore this second condition is only a further explication of the first and not a specifically different one.

3.) The intention of the agent must be good; i.e. the agent may not will the evil effect. The bombing of military objects during wartime often also involves the death of some civilians. This is an indirect effect of the bombing, whose direct purpose and object is the destruction of installations and plants of military import. Yet the agent may only intend the destruction of the military object, not the death of the civilians. Therefore if the military object has been destroyed and some bombs are still left over, they cannot be dropped on the living quarters of civilians.

4.) A proportionately grave reason must be had in order to justify the admission of the indirect, evil effect. This requires that, first, a value at least equal to that sacrificed is at stake; second, no less harmful way of protecting the value here and now is at disposal; and third, the means used to achieve the value will not ultimately undermine it. The value pursued in a defensive war is the defence of the lives and the liberty of the citizens; if however in the defence of this value the lives of the civilians of the enemy nation are sacrificed indiscriminately, then the value of the defence of lives is ultimately undermined. The fourth condition is known today as the principle of proportionality or proportionate reason.[1] It is of a special weight. The reason for the admission of the evil effect must be all the greater,

a) the graver the indirectly willed evil is. A graver reason is required to run with one's car into a man than to run into a cow.
b) the more surely the evil will come about. The greater the possibility that an operation will not be successful but lead to death or to mental derangement, the more extreme the illness must be.
c) the more proximately the action leads to the evil. A graver reason is required to assist during an illicit operation (e.g. abortion) than to prepare the operating theatre before the operation. (In these instances we are at the same time dealing with the cooperation in the wrong deeds of others.)
d) the greater the obligation is to prevent the evil. A superior (bishop, religious superior) has a graver obligation to correct faults of his subjects than an ordinary fellow citizen.

As to the reason why, under the indicated conditions, evil effects can be admitted, moral handbooks generally point out that otherwise life would be unbearable. Much good could

---

[1] A helpful discussion of proportionate reason and proportionalism is found in R.M. Gula, *Reason Informed by Faith* (New York: Paulist Press, 1989), 272-279.

not be done because of possible evil side-effects of an action. Every electrical installation carries with it the risk of fire or death by faulty wires; every participation in traffic by land and air involves the danger of accidents; the benefits of big technology are accompanied by hazards to health and environmental pollution. If indirectly willed evil effects were never to be admitted, all these ventures could not be allowed, in spite of the good effects which they produce and which by far prevail. It would be unreasonable to subscribe to a moral tenet of such an extreme nature.

3. *Problems and controversies*

The principle of double effect has been the object of a lively controversy since the late 60's and early 70's. The question is raised whether the great importance attributed to this principle by Catholic tradition is justified and well-founded. With some surprise theologians have noted that the principle is the almost exclusive property of Catholic moral theology. A moral principle which is given so great importance by Catholic theology is widely unknown or even explicitly rejected as irrelevant by non-Catholic ethicists.[1]

Yet it is to be noted that even in Catholic moral theology the principle is not of so ancient origin as its wide diffusion in the manuals of the last hundred years might lead one to believe. There is a reference in St. Thomas, it is true, in his treatise on self-defence, that an action can have two effects, the one willed and the other not.[2] But he does not derive therefrom a universal principle for the solution of moral problems. Much less do we find in him a formulation of the four conditions for the principle of double effect, commonly listed in the more recent handbooks. The first clear and express formulation of the principle is attributed to John of S. Thomas

---

[1] Bruno Schüller notes that apart from Paul Ramsey and Philippa Foot he could not find any non-Catholic author who made use of this principle ("Neuere Beiträge zum Thema 'Begründung sittlicher Normen'," in *Theologische Berichte* IV. Einsiedeln: Benziger, 1974, 126, footnote). See also from the same author "Das Prinzip von der Handlung mit Doppelwirkung," in *Die Begründung sittlicher Urteile* (Düsseldorf: Patmos, ²1980), 181-196.

[2] *S. Th.* II-II, q. 64, a. 7.

(†1644).¹ But only since the moral theology of J. P. Gury in the second half of the 19th century do moral theologians universally give a sufficient explanation of the principle and apply it in a general way to the whole realm of moral theology.² Why is the principle controversial and what are the problems surrounding it?

A *first difficulty* results from the questions raised in view of the traditional teaching on moral absolutes. According to the principle of double effect, an evil effect is only then admissible if this effect is not the immediate result of the action, i.e. if the action is not evil in itself. This doctrine presupposes that there are certain actions which are always and absolutely evil, independent of any possible justifying intention of the agent. Among such absolute prohibitions are counted, for example, direct killing of the innocent, direct abortion, direct sterilization, lying, masturbation, contraception, bestiality, blasphemy, and some others. Catholic tradition asserts that they are intrinsically evil (*intrinsece malum*) and never permissible.

But recently, as already mentioned, doubts have been expressed, also among Catholic theologians, whether there are any external actions which are absolutely evil in themselves and therefore never permissible. These theologians "see how a specific kind of action could be condemned generally, that is, in most cases, because the action generally does serious harm and relatively little good... But it is the possibility of an absolute condemnation of any physical action, a condemnation applying in advance to all possible cases without exception, that leaves many a contemporary Christian ethicist uncomprehending."³ The moral judgment, argues C. van der Poel, is to be "made not so much about a human act in itself as a separate entity, but rather the individual human act should be evaluated insofar as it contributes to or destroys the building

---

¹ J. Ghoos, "L'acte à double effet. Étude de théologie positive," *Ephemerides Theologicae Lovanienses* 27 (1951), 51.

² Joseph T. Mangan, "An Historical Analysis of the Principle of Double Effect," *Theological Studies* 10 (1949), 59.

³ John G. Milhaven, "Moral Absolutes and Thomas Aquinas," in *Absolutes in Moral Theology?*, ed. by C.E. Curran (Washington/Cleveland: Corpus Books, 1968), 156.

of the (human) society."[1] Moral theology cannot be under the sway of several absolute values and imperatives. There is an absolute norm, but it is only one: the intent of God and the directedness of creation to him.

In fact, as already mentioned above, also traditional moral theology knows of only one supreme norm, absolute in its own right, just as there is only one ultimate goal of man. This supreme norm is the whole-hearted love of God and neighbour. The ultimate criterion for the moral value of an action is whether it contributes to God's creative and salvific plan or not; whether it promotes the human community in accordance with God's call or not. However traditional moral theology upholds that there are certain actions which are always opposed to this ultimate norm and which are therefore always and absolutely evil.

The problem therefore seems to boil down to the question whether it can be proven that certain actions always contradict the ultimate norm of love of God and neighbour or not. Each of the moral absolutes would have to be examined individually. Such an investigation would lead too far in this context and must be left to the respective treatises. Nevertheless, some general observations and remarks can be adduced here. One can notice that the number of moral absolutes has slowly decreased in the course of time. More precise studies repeatedly led to the admission of exceptions where before it seemed no exceptions were admissible. Among the traditional absolutes is the prohibition of lying. Moral handbooks commonly held that it is never allowed to tell a lie, not even in order to defend an innocent life. Yet especially in the last decades a considerable number of moral theologians expressed doubts with regard to the absolute character of this prohibition and admitted exceptions.[2] Another absolute is that of direct mutilation of one's body. It is asserted that one may permit such a mutilation only indirectly in order to save the health or life of the entire body. But at least in the case of organ transplants, this absolute has now been generally abandoned by Catholic

---

[1] C. van der Poel, "The Principle of Double Effect," in *Absolutes in Moral Theology?*, l. c. 192.

[2] For example A. Vermeersch, J. Ubach, Varceno-Loiano, Genicot-Salsmans, Tanquerey-Steven, and others (cf. *Christian Ethics*, vol. II, 2004, the historical summary concerning the lie, pp. 386-390).

theologians.¹ Again, direct abortion is judged as absolutely inadmissible. Yet some doubts have always persisted among moral theologians as to the admissibility of therapeutic abortion in extreme cases, and a growing number of Catholic theologians permit it.² And where a medical examination of the male sperm is needed, moral theology today hardly insists any longer on the absolute prohibition of masturbation and admits of an exception.

In view of such developments in moral insight, which repeatedly have shown the limitation of past moral judgments, G. Visser comes to the conclusion that it is extremely difficult to formulate moral norms of absolute character. "Doubtless in the past one was too easily inclined to believe that one could formulate them in notable quantity."³ Naturally, to the extent that the number of moral absolutes shrinks, to that extent the first and second conditions of the principle of double effect lose importance and become superfluous.

A *second difficulty* against the principle arises from the distinction between direct and indirect as morally relevant criteria for the unlawfulness or lawfulness of actions dealing with the traditional absolutes. According to the principle, directly willed evil effects are never permissible, while indirectly willed effects at times are. E. g., direct therapeutic abortion

---

¹ Cf. the instructive article by John Gallagher, "The Principle of Totality: Man's Stewardship of His Body," in *Moral Theology Today: Certitudes and Doubts*, ed. by the Pope John Center. Saint Louis, Mo., 1984, 217-242. Several statements of Pius XII seemed to exclude the possibility of organ transplants inter vivos, e.g. *AAS* 44 (1952), 782, 786f; 45 (1953), 747; 48 (1956), 461f; 50 (1958), 693.

² For example R. Troisfontaines, the Belgian Bishops, G. Visser, B. Häring, H. Rotter, L. Janssens, F. Böckle, and others (cf. Christian Ethics, vol. II, "The problem of therapeutic abortion").

³ Giovanni Visser "Aborto diretto sempre illecito?," in *Problemi attuali di teologia*, ed. by the Pont. Ateneo Salesiano in Rome (Zürich: PAS Verlag, 1973), 93. The author, who argues for the admissibility of certain types of therapeutic abortion, still refers to another absolute of the past which had to yield to new insights. For a long time the use of contraceptive sterilizing drugs was considered absolutely forbidden. But today many moralists grant at least one exception. Women who are confronted with an imminent danger of rape, e.g. in the event of military invasions, may use them in order to protect themselves against forcefully imposed conceptions (*ib.*).

is never permissible, while indirect therapeutic abortion is. What are the reasons?

The arguments which justify the permissibility of indirectly willed evil effects under certain conditions are - as already indicated above - the following. If it were never allowed to admit indirectly willed evil effects, life would become unbearable, much good could not be done, and it would be unreasonable to act in a contrary manner. These are valid considerations. But the question arises: would these arguments not hold true also for some instances of directly willed evil effects? If a mother who is in the fifth month of her pregnancy falls sick and if her life can be saved only by a therapeutic abortion, would it not likewise be unreasonable to let her die together with the inviable child? Does this not also mean that a great good is not done? True, one could argue that life does not become as unbearable for the human community as a whole as when indirectly willed evil effects were never permitted, because the instances in which directly willed evil effects might seem justified are much rarer. But is this difference in degree a conclusive argument? Is it not also morally unbearable for those concerned to let the mother die together with the child and not at least to save the mother?

Besides, it causes surprise that the entire reasoning limits itself to an argument of a posteriori, which justifies the principle of double effect only by the absurd consequences of the contrary. This argumentation seems rather scanty and does not fully satisfy. Is there no possible argument a priori which could be called upon? The argument which spontaneously offers itself is, that in a conflict between two evils one must opt for the lesser one. However this argument would also hold, even more manifestly than the above argument a posteriori, for some instances of directly willed evil effects, such as the mentioned example of therapeutic abortion. The directly willed evil effect of a therapeutic abortion is in terms of detriment to human life and to the good of God's creation a lesser evil than the death of mother and child together. In fact various authors hold that the problem of the admission of evil effects should, in the last analysis, be resolved by means of the principle of the lesser evil and by the use of proportionate reason.[1] In whatever way one judges the validity of such a procedure, the justification of indirectly willed evil effects presents problems which have not been satisfactorily settled and which need clarification.

On the other hand, the warning of Holy Scripture must not be forgotten but must be taken most seriously: that we should "not do evil that good may come" (Rom 3:8). The mere fact that the purpose of an action is good does not already justify any kind of means. If the evil caused by the means is greater than the good realized by the purpose of the action, then it can never be allowed.

Recent theologians who propose a *revision of the principle* of double effect, although not all with the same reasons, are P. Knauer, L. Janssens, J. Fuchs, B. Schüller,[2] C. van der Poel, F. Scholz, R. McCormick, T. O'Connell, R. Gula and W. Korff.[3] The permission of evil effects would be ruled only by the third and fourth conditions of the principle (or

---

[1] Against such a procedure the objection is raised that it can never be permitted to pursue a good end with evil means. Now the direct causing of certain evils (e.g. abortion) is evil in itself and can therefore never be a means for a good end, while this is not true of an evil which is indirectly caused. - But also this distinction and assertion demands a proof. Why are actions which cause certain evils directly evil in themselves, while the indirect causing of the same evils is permitted? The arguments here are once again the same as those which already have been given above in answer to this question: life would become unbearable, much good could not be done and it would be unreasonable to act in a contrary manner. And they have also in this context the same confusing result, that they do not only justify the indirect, but also at times the direct causing of the evil effect under discussion.

[2] *Readings in Moral Theology No. 1*, ed. by C.E. Curran and R.A. McCormick (New York: Paulist Press, 1979), 19 (Knauer), 68f (Janssens), 120-2 (Fuchs), 143f (Schüller).

[3] C. van der Poel, "The Principle of Double Effect," *l. c.* 197f; 205. F. Scholz, *Wege, Umwege und Auswege der Moraltheologie* (München: Don Bosco Verlag, 1976), esp. 124-126. R.A. McCormick in *Doing Evil to Achieve Good*, ed. by the same and P. Ramsey (Chicago: Loyola Univ., 1978), 262. T.E. O'Connell, *Principles for a Catholic Morality* (New York: Seabury, 1978), 170f. R.M. Gula, *Reason Informed by Faith* (New York: Paulist Press, 1989), 270-272. Wilhelm Korff, "Ethische Entscheidungskonflikte: Zum Problem der Güterabwägung," in *Handbuch der christlichen Ethik*, vol. 3, ed. by Anselm Hertz et alii (Freiburg: Herder, ²1993), 87f.

perhaps even only by the fourth one)[1], namely, that the intention of the agent be good and that a proportionately grave reason be had. In fact, as they advance as a further consideration in their favour, by far the greater portion of situations involving evil effects has been solved also by traditional moral theology with the help of these two conditions only; note the vast realm of damages to property or the areas of promise keeping, preservation of secrets, obedience to legitimate authority, etc.

In the context of the above discussions, the validity and moral relevance of the *distinction between directly and indirectly willed evil effects* has sometimes been questioned and denied altogether. But such a conclusion overshoots the mark and does not do justice to the facts. There is certainly reason to presume that a distinction which has so widely been used by Catholic moral theology is not without some moral significance. Rightly it has also been pointed out that common sense takes it for granted that such a distinction exists.[2] If a bombing raid on a military object causes the loss of some civilian lives as a side-effect, this is not imputed to the army men in the same way as if they had killed the civilians directly to undermine the morale of the enemy. Or if the brakes of a car fail and it dashes into a house in order to stop, this is not imputed to the driver in the same way as if somebody had destroyed the house deliberately in an act of sabotage.

There is indeed a morally relevant difference between directly and indirectly willed evil effects. Indirectly willed evil effects are more readily justified than those directly willed. The reason is that directly willed effects are aimed at with

---

[1] Some authors believe that the third condition, namely that the intention of the agent must be good, is already implicitly contained in the last or fourth one. But it still seems meaningful to state this condition expressly. A physician whose main objective is fame will much sooner find proportionate reasons to justify doubtful experimentation with human beings than another whose main objective is the good of his patients. And even if his external actions agree with the demands of objective morality, i.e. if they are morally right, the flaws of his intention make them morally defective; i.e. they are not morally good or they are less good.

[2] Cf. Augustine Regan, "The Accidental Effect in Moral Discourse," *Studia Moralia* 16 (1978), 102f.

deliberate purpose and definite determination, so that they come about with greater certainty. If civilians are killed in order to undermine the morale of the enemy, their death is deliberately sought out, with the result that they will surely die. The indirectly willed evil effect, on the other hand, is not pursued with the same singleness of mind and firm determination to bring it about. Therefore it usually comes about with lesser certainty and in a more accidental way. In a bombing raid which aims at the destruction of a military object, it is not at all certain how many civilians may die. Surely fewer will die than if the bombing had civilians as its direct aim. Or if a car dashes into a house because its brakes have failed, the damages caused are more accidental and usually less extensive than if the damage had been directly intended in an act of sabotage.[1] - A difference between directly and indirectly willed effects is also evidenced by the fact that in the case of good effects - as shown above - only directly willed ones are credited to a person as meritorious, not however indirectly willed ones.

As a rule of thumb, therefore, indirectly willed evil effects are more readily allowed. The reason is that they usually come about with less certainty and are pursued and aimed at with less determination of the will. Nevertheless the superior purpose of the ultimate end can also at times permit directly willed evil effects, more readily those of a material nature, but at times also those of a biological and psychological nature. (An evil effect of a psychological nature would be the deception caused by a lie.) But since as a rule they bring about greater evil than indirectly willed evil effects and are caused with greater freedom of will, it stands to reason that such instances will be much rarer.

---

[1] It is in line with these observations that R.A. McCormick expresses the view that the distinction between direct and indirect continues to retain a certain moral relevance, although the difference between the two be only a gradual one. Correctly he argues that "an intending will represents a closer relation of the agent to the disvalue and therefore indicates a greater willingness that the disvalue occur" (*Doing Evil to Achieve Good*, l. c. 263; cf. also B. Schüller, *ib.* 190f).

III. Cooperation in the wrong deeds of others

Cooperation in the wrong deeds of others is any physical or moral concurrence with a principal agent in an evil deed. Cooperator in this sense is the one who assists in the execution of an evil deed, who makes available the means, who gives advice and necessary information, etc. Cooperation does not give rise to the wrong deed of another, but it only assists a principal agent, who is already determined to the wrong deed previous to the cooperation.

1. *Kinds of cooperation.* Basic for the moral evaluation of cooperation is the distinction between formal and material cooperation in the sins of others. Formal cooperation obtains when one externally concurs in the sinful deed of another and at the same time internally consents to it. This kind of cooperation is always sinful.[1] Material cooperation is had when one externally concurs in the sinful deed of another without internally consenting to it.

Material cooperation may be immediate or mediate. It is immediate if one concurs in the evil act itself, as to help a burglar to empty the jewels that he is stealing into the burglar's

---

[1] Moral handbooks frequently distinguish between *explicit* and *implicit formal cooperation*. Explicit formal cooperation would be had if the sin of the other were directly intended, as e.g. the actors of an anti-religious stage-play may directly intend the derision of religion together with the stage-manager. Concurrence in the evil deed of another is considered an implicit formal cooperation if the assistance offered is of such a nature that it necessarily joins in the sinful deed of the other. Thus the actors in an anti-religious stage-play implicitly approve of the derision of religion by their participation in the performance, even if such derision is not their personal intention. Other authors (H. Jone, H. Davis) however more correctly regard the implicit formal cooperation as immediate material cooperation. For, although it is sinful in most of the instances, there are exceptions possible, while formal cooperation is always sinful. Thus under threat of death one may help a robber to break into a shop and carry the loot off for him. This kind of cooperation is, in spite of its close participation in the sinful act, not performed with real consent, which is a necessary condition for formal cooperation. Furthermore the fact that a cooperation necessarily joins one in the sinful deed of another is not an univocal criterion for its sinfulness. The scene designers and those who work the lights are also necessary for the presentation of an anti-religious play. Nevertheless the cooperation of one or the other group may at times be permissible material cooperation.

wallet. It is mediate if one provides means and other helps for the evil deed without joining in the evil act itself, as to supply the burglar with the keys to the house or with tools for his burglary. Mediate cooperation is often further subdivided into proximate and remote, according as it is more or less closely connected with the evil deed. Yet there is no strict, clear-cut separation between these two forms, and the transition from remote to proximate cooperation is fluid.

Helpful for the formulation of moral norms is the distinction between cooperation by means of actions which in themselves are not harmful to others, such as selling a bottle of whisky, giving a key, driving a car, preparing instruments for an operation, and cooperation by means of actions which by their own, internal finality cause harm to another, such as damaging another's property, condemning a person unjustly, beating or killing him. All the actions forbidden by the traditional absolutes belong to this second category.

2. *Norms for material cooperation.* Material cooperation in sinful deeds of others is in general illicit, since the evil of sin should not be supported by any means; on the contrary it should be opposed and suppressed. Yet on the other hand man often cannot escape some cooperation in the sins of others in order to avoid still greater evils. For example a clerk in a bank may hand over the money he holds in order to save his life. This leads to the following rules.

As a general rule holds that material cooperation is lawful in order to avoid a proportionately grave detriment to oneself or other persons close to oneself. In estimating the sufficiency of the reasons, one must take into consideration (a) the gravity of the other's sin; a greater reason is demanded for cooperation in a homicide than in a theft; cooperation in sinful deeds that will do great harm to Church or state (e.g. betrayal of national secrets) is never lawful; (b) the closeness of the cooperation to the sinful act; thus a graver reason is required to unlock the door of a safe to a robber than to lend him a car for his robbery; (c) the indispensability of the cooperation; the more certain the sin will be committed without one's cooperation, the lesser a reason is required for one's aid, e.g. when selling whisky to a drunkard; (d) one's obligation to prevent the wrong-doing; a night-guard in a factory has a greater obligation to safeguard the property of the enterprise than a simple worker.

Material cooperation by means of actions which by their own finality cause harm to others is most of the time not allowed and - if permissible - always requires a much graver reason than other kinds of cooperation. The reason is that in this case one does not merely indirectly make an evil possible, as in the previous category of cooperation, but one directly causes it. Therefore one also has a greater responsibility for it. In such instances a strict proportion is required between the damage inflicted on the one hand and the damage threatening the person who renders cooperation or a third person on the other. The damage inflicted upon the other person must be less than the evil threatening the person cooperating or a third one.

Accordingly it is lawful to cooperate in damaging another person's property in order to save one's own life, but it is not lawful to kill another person for the same reason. It is equally lawful to inflict a small material damage on another person in order to avoid a much greater one to oneself. Very probably it is also admissible to cooperate by a lie in bringing about some evil if by doing so one can avert a much graver one, e.g. the death of an innocent person. Likewise it should be considered lawful to beat a person in order to save him from still graver harm. When slavery was still extant, a slave-driver was allowed to whip a slave if otherwise the slave would have been killed by his master. Is it logical to conclude that it is equally lawful to beat a person in order to save the innocent lives of other people? But doubtless it is not lawful to beat another person for anything less than the value of his or another person's life or something truly equal to it, e.g. avoidance of a grave mutilation. Therefore one could not beat another person just in order to escape being beaten oneself.

Traditionally moral handbooks hold that immediate material cooperation in actions which are intrinsically evil, i.e. which pertain to the category of the forbidden absolutes, is not allowed, e.g. direct killing of the innocent, direct abortion, direct mutilation, etc. Doubtless also today presumption continues to stand in favour of these prohibitions. But where moral theologians arrive at the conclusion that exceptions from certain absolutes are possible, immediate cooperation of course also becomes permissible, as e.g. in certain cases of therapeutic sterilization.

In today's pluralistic society still another factor enters the picture. In some cases, for example in the field of medical ethics, the other person perhaps is not at all of the opinion that he is committing a wrong deed, rather the intended action appears to him or her as morally right or even obligatory (as in certain cases of sterilization, artificial birth control or experiments with embryos). If a physician and patient act in the honest conviction of behaving correctly, this could be considered a reason to render material cooperation more readily, even though not automatically in every case. The reason is that nobody can claim to possess the truth in its totality. The cases in question are mostly cases of conflict, where also the person who rejects a certain way of acting finds it difficult to reach subjective certitude about its immorality. This leads to the rule: "The lesser one's certitude, the more readily the lawfulness of a cooperation presents itself."[1] The opposite however also holds: the weightier the misgivings, the less readily a cooperation is allowed.

These are some general guidelines to give orientation in the thorny problem of permissible cooperation. The concrete instances of cooperation are very often complicated and therefore inevitably give rise to various opinions. They are a particularly difficult range of problems of moral theology.

3. *Advising the lesser sin.* Advising a lesser sin than the one a sinner is about to commit is ordinarily allowed, provided the sinner cannot otherwise be deterred from committing the greater sin. Thus it is allowed to advise an infuriated person to beat his enemy rather than to kill him; or to persuade a revengeful person to rob rather than to kill another. In such a case, it is even lawful to help the evildoer to perform the robbery, if he can thus successfully be restrained from killing his adversary.

But it is not lawful to advise the sinner to do a lesser evil which would result in injustice to a third person whom the sinner did not have in mind, in order to prevent him from committing the greater sin. Hence it is not permitted to

---

[1] K. Demmer, *Deuten und Handeln* (Freiburg: Herder, 1985), 200. See also there the noteworthy expositions to the theme on pp. 207-210.

advise somebody to commit adultery with his enemy's wife or to mutilate his daughter instead of killing him.

IV. The ethical compromise

Cooperation in the wrong deeds of another can, in a certain sense, be considered an ethical compromise, inasmuch as the one who cooperates makes cuts from what he regards the correct conduct on principle, although only in order to avoid still greater evil and injustice. All weighing of goods is a compromise in the sense that, for the sake of the realization of a more urgent good, the realization of a less urgent one is set aside. Hereto also the weighing of goods carried out by the principle of double effect pertains, which has been tackled above. Nevertheless according to its origin and in everyday usage compromise has a narrower meaning.

The concept of compromise originates in the juridical field. Thus one speaks of compromises in the context of procedural law. Each of the litigating parties reduces its legitimate claims, in order to reach a solution of the conflict. Of the same nature are wage agreements between entrepreneurs and employees and most of the compromises between coalition partners in the political realm. The present democratic and pluralistic society is not conceivable without the constant readiness for compromise. Compromise in this sense can be defined as a settlement for the partial realization of various contrary interests. Through partial renunciation by both sides of the full realization of their goals an agreement is reached. This is first of all a strategic compromise, whose contents in principle are morally neutral. The settlement for 25 days of vacation (instead of 21 or 28) in a wage agreement or the partial privatisation of the telegraphic system (instead of its full nationalization or privatisation) are in themselves not demands of the moral law. Insofar as the compromise has been negotiated fairly, it does not pose additional ethical problems.

Ethical compromises on the other hand are those which touch moral principles, values and actions. An ethical compromise is conceivable as a compromise an individual person makes with himself or herself between ends and resources (between desirable charitable aid and limited means) or between two tasks (between the demands of the profession and the needs of the family) or between two values (between truthfulness and the protection of secrets). Since however in these cases one is not dealing with two different partners seeking a common agreement, but with a balancing of limited possibilities within one and the same person, this is generally considered a compromise in the improper sense. This is even more plain in those instances where a lesser claim is set back in favour of a more important one (respect for alien goods set back in favour of preservation of one's life), in which cases we are not dealing with a partial realization of two claims, but with the realization of one under waiver of the other. An ethical compromise in the narrower sense then is the socio-ethical or interpersonal compromise, in which an accommodation is sought with the incorrect or culpable conduct or wrong moral conceptions of another. The latter is the type of compromise dealt with here.

The ethical dimension of the compromise demands a fundamental clarification. "The compromise concerns the correctness of the action, not the goodness of the acting person. One never chooses a lesser moral evil, at most one can admit its commission by someone else. Because a moral evil, as small as it may be, is no object of a choice."[1] This holds for an individual's compromise with himself as much as for the interpersonal compromise. If of two claims a person can fulfil only one or both only partially, he is not guilty for what he cannot comply with. For the impossible is not subject to the free will of a person and therefore is withdrawn from his responsibility. Whoever in a conflict between the right of private property and his life saves his life by a food theft, is weighing two goods against each other, preferring the greater to the lesser. The food theft is not a moral fault in this case. Catholic theology does not recognize moral guilt as inevitable. This would contradict justice and expose itself "to the suspicion of playing down guilt, an inevitable guilt is already no guilt any more. What sense then would there be in moral effort?"[2] Man becomes guilty only by a "foul" compromise, whereby he rashly fails to live up to his better possibilities.

---

[1] K. Demmer, "Kompromiß," *Neues Lexikon der christlichen Moral* (Innsbruck: Tyrolia, 1990), 383.

[2] *Ib.* 383.

The problem of the socio-ethical or interpersonal compromise arises above all at the level of the difference between moral convictions and legal norms which have come about as a social compromise, e.g. in the domains of abortion, divorce, prostitution, religious tolerance. Christian conviction e.g. rejects abortion, and it wants the human being protected from its earliest days. But if in parliament no majority can be obtained for this position, as often is the case, the Christian representatives could agree to the compromise of a law legalizing abortion within 12 weeks after conception, if the alternative is abortion within 22 weeks. By this they do not approve of the evil of abortion, they only tolerate it, and that within the limits of that minimum for which alone a majority can be gained. The ethical compromise does not mean that the Christian parliamentarians partially extricate themselves from the prohibition of abortion, they only tolerate it with those who are not of their conviction. They themselves as well as those whom they represent are at liberty, indeed they are expected to hold fast to the objective ranking of the moral values.

Compromises of the sort mentioned are time and again also necessitated by unjust dictatorial systems. Unjust laws essentially pertain to such systems, e.g. the prohibition of oppositional or ecclesiastical mass media, of opposition parties, of religious associations, etc. Correspondingly the courts are bound to prosecute violations of these laws. Honest judges will find themselves confronted with the alternative of resigning or of affording at least a partial cooperation. Up to a certain limit compromises are not only possible, but can be a demand of the higher values.

The foregoing exposition has shown that ethical compromise can be morally justified. "Compromise in moral matters is not something objectionable in itself or even a betrayal of the good. Rather it is the attempt to bring about the good as far as this is *possible*... From there its qualification is to be defined: The compromise is the better, the less the loss in goodness and the share of the negative; it is still permitted, as long as the positive outweighs the evil; it loses its legitimacy where the negative prevails."[1] One must also

---

[1] H. Weber, "Der Kompromiß in der Moral," *Trierer theologische Zeitschrift* 86 (1977), 114f.

take into account that humans are subject to misapprehensions, which may predominate in the society or group they are living in. This reinforces the necessity of the readiness to compromise, joined with the will to reconsider one's own position and, if need be, to correct it.

Of course the readiness to compromise can also be a sign of indolence, cowardice, escapism from personal efforts and plain opportunism. This is the case if in the compromise the higher values are sacrificed to the lesser ones. There are compromises which should not be made and could not be made. "The Church proposes the example of numerous Saints who bore witness to and defended moral truth even to the point of enduring martyrdom." For "there are truths and moral values for which one must be prepared to give up one's life."[1]

Nonetheless ethical compromise in principle is a morally legitimate possibility. If it is made according to the aforesaid rules and the rightly understood axiom of the lesser evil, it is morally good. Since however ethical compromise is only a partial realization of the good, it always demands re-examination. In this it differs from the strategic compromise in law, economy, politics, etc., which does not necessarily demand revision. Ethical compromise is like a wound, which cannot be the final condition, but calls for healing. The intention behind the given norm and the conception of a felicitous life contained in it must not get lost, but must be reconsidered always afresh in view of their best possible realization.

---

[1] *Veritatis Splendor*, 1993, nrs. 91 and 94.

Chapter VI

THE MORALLY BAD ACTION: SIN

Men are bound to strive after the ultimate end and not to offend in any of their actions against it. Therefore they ct badly if they disregard the obligations of the moral law and the commands of their conscience, which are meant to ensure the attainment of this end. Such a bad human act is sin. It is the freely willed infringement of the moral order. Since biblical and Christian thinking considers God as the author of the moral law, the disregard of the moral order is always at the same time an injury against God. From this point of view sin can be described as disobedience against God's will and as an offence against him (cf. SC 109).

The infringement must be freely willed, i.e. it must occur knowingly and with free consent. Only then is wrongdoing a formal, imputable sin. An unintentional, involuntary offence against the moral law is not sufficient to constitute a subjective, imputable sin. In pagan antiquity it was held that a person could be guilty without knowing it (cf. Oedipus and Iokaste).[1] Even animals could sin by violation of sacred taboos. This fatalism of sin and guilt was lifted off men's shoulders by Christianity. Although an involuntary offence must still be considered as a disorder which ought not to be and which therefore ought to be remedied, it does not constitute an imputable fault for the individual and is only a material sin.

---

[1] Laios, the king of Thebes, received the oracle that he would be killed by his son. Therefore, when his son Oedipus was born to him, he had the child exposed. Shepherds found the child and brought him to Corinth, where he grew up. In the search for his true parents, he unknowingly killed his father in a fight. Having solved the riddle of the Sphinx, his mother Iokaste, queen of Thebes, was given him in reward to be his wife. When a pestilence broke out in the town, the seer Tiresias revealed the involuntary guilt. Iokaste hanged herself and Oedipus blinded himself in expiation for their "sin". Traces of such a mentality are also found in the Old Testament. Lev 4-5 and Num 15:22-29 prescribe guilt offerings for unwittingly committed sins. And Uzzah, who put out his hand to prevent the ark from falling, was smitten for his unintentional sacrilege and died beside the ark (2 Sam 6:6-8).

Since there can be no guilt without a free human act, the notion of collective guilt must be rejected. Guilty are the members of a community to the extent that they were drawn in an injustice through their own choice or at least through their negligence and indifference. The individual person is called to work for the removal of the structures of injustice and to resist them according to his possibilities. If he does not do this, he in some way joins in the guilt.

Among modern men a dwindling of the consciousness of sin can be noticed. Especially the sense of sin as an offence against God wanes. For where the faith in God as creator and redeemer vanishes, the awareness of sin as injury against him must vanish as well. And where autonomous man becomes the measure of all things, sin as an offence against a superior divine authority is irrelevant. Still other facts contribute to dull the sense of sin and moral fault, such as the determinist theories of certain sociological and especially psychoanalytic schools and the absorbing force of the anonymous masses. Finally theology itself has disqualified the concept of sin by a too inflationary use the same. The frequent phenomenon of scrupulosity connected with this could only increase the rejection of such a type of morality.

On the other hand there are also factors of a positive nature. The whiles of evil and the misery of sin and guilt occupy a large place in modern literature and philosophy, which trace human wretchedness, depravity and malice down to their most secret roots and unmask their intrigues in the conscious and unconscious depths of the human soul. Wrongdoing and human malice are too obvious phenomena as to be simply disavowed. The call to morality is at present clear and plain. "For even if people do not like to hear of demands and even if norms and laws are little appreciated, morality as such is at present beyond all discussion. On the contrary, even where people think in an entirely secularized way today, they consider morality as something which cannot be renounced. No doubt, man should be moral and behave in a moral way."[1] Of course, a morality without guilt and sin is desired. Yet the unconditional character of the moral demand ultimately ceases to exist if there is no possibility of guilt.

---

[1] H. Weber, *Allgemeine Moraltheologie* (Graz: Styria, 1991), 259.

On closer examination one can observe not so much an end as a shifting of the sense of guilt. "Thus clearly a greater sensibility for patently social misbehaviour can be noticed as compared with former times. One senses something negative in ways of conduct which formerly remained unnoticed, such as intolerance, discrimination of persons of different opinions, denial of political and social liberties, disregard and disparaging treatment of other races etc."[1] There is a notable increase in sensitivity towards ecologically irresponsible behaviour. Joint guilt in structural injustice likewise finds greater attention, injustices consisting in passivity towards evil in society, easy accommodation with current behaviour patterns, indifference towards the fate and misery of others and withdrawal into private life.

Together with the greater attention to structural injustice however a tendency makes itself felt to shift guilt to structures and to "others" who have created them. Christianity resists that "unhealthy illusion of innocence that has become so widespread in contemporary society and to the practice of attributing guilt and failure, if their presence is acknowledged at all, to others and other causes... We attribute successes and victories to ourselves, but for the rest, we cultivate the art of denying our human condition" and are always in search of new alibis.[2] Change of heart and healing is possible only through honest recognition and admission of guilt.

A. Nature of sin

The concept of sin is very closely related to that of guilt. Sin and moral guilt designate the same reality, though under different aspects. Sin always involves moral guilt, and moral guilt always presupposes sin. Both always exist together. Sin expresses the truth that a wrongful act is morally evil and an offence against God. Guilt on the other hand denotes the fact that a person is liable for the evil he has done and that it is attributed to him as the responsible agent.[3]

---

[1] *Ib.* 261.

[2] Gemeinsame Synode der Bistümer in der Bundesrepublik Deutschland, *Beschlüsse der Vollversammlung*, I (Freiburg: Herder, 1976), 93.

[3] Cf. Hermann Fischer, "Der Schuldbegriff im Kontext heutiger theologischer Anthropologie," in *Handbuch der christlichen Ethik*, vol. 3 (Freiburg: Herder, 1993), 166.

Moral guilt must be distinguished from guilt feelings. Depth-psychology in particular has called attention to this fact. Guilt feelings can also be the result of unwarranted prohibitions of the superego, resulting from wrong education and social taboos, or of morbid psychic dispositions. They are therefore not unequivocal signs of moral offences. On the other hand not every feeling of guilt is morbid. The more tender a person's conscience, the more readily will it react with guilt feelings at a person's sins. Nevertheless not every moral guilt is accompanied by guilt feelings, especially if a person's conscience is dull. This however could hardly be elevated to an ideal. To the extent that guilt feelings are irrational, they call for treatment indeed. It is here that psychotherapy has a genuine task. But authentic guilt feelings definitely have a positive function, and it cannot be the aim of psychotherapy also to eliminate them.

Moral guilt must finally be distinguished from juridical guilt. Juridical guilt is incurred by a merely factual offence against the existing legal order. It is imputed to a person even if he has violated the law out of forgetfulness, distraction or ignorance. For moral guilt on the other hand the mere fact of the transgression is not the decisive criterion; it presupposes insight into the evil of one's doing and consent of free will.

I. Biblical delineation of sin

Guilt and sin play a significant part in Holy Scripture, although it does not present an explicit nor a complete theory of sin. The Bible always conceives of sin in the framework of man's relationship to God. Its deepest nature appears as refusal to respond to God's salvific will. For the Greeks, sin was an error, an ignorance or a foolishness, by which a person harms himself. Their understanding of sin is entirely different from that of the Bible. For the latter, sin is an offence against God and unfaithfulness to him. The history of mankind is seen precisely as the history of a falling away from God through sin and, thanks to God's mercy and grace, a turning home to him. Sin therefore is a primary presupposition of the Old Testament, especially of the prophets, and the Gospel of Jesus Christ.

a) *The Old Testament* often looks upon sin as a transgression of God's law and will. The root most frequently used for sin (*hata*) expresses the idea of missing an aim or of falling away from a known path. Sin then is the by-passing of a rule, its transgression. It is disobedience against the commandment of the Lord (Lev 26:14-39; Deut 11:26-28; 28:15ff). Some early texts speak of a solidarity in evil which suggests a collective guilt. On this question see below for specific treatment of the issue.

The third chapter of Genesis describes Adam and Eve's sin in paradise as the deliberate transgression of a divine order. Internally their rebellion against God proceeded from the presumptive desire to have and to be more than God had conceded them. The result was a rift between God and men (cf. also Is 59:2). The result of the rift however does not have consequences only for Adam and Eve; it also becomes a source of evil for all of mankind. Toil, suffering and death of humans have their origin in sin. It is noteworthy that already the sin of the first parents was mitigated by the fact that they had been tempted and seduced by an evil power (as is typical of man's situation in this world); nevertheless Scripture regards the offence in principle as a free, imputable act. On other occasions, sin is regarded as hatred towards God. The sinner is one "who hates" Yahweh (Ex 20:5; Deut 5:9; Ps 139:21)

The most characteristic outlook of the Old Testament on sin results from the covenant relationship, which Scripture sees established between God and man. Sin is considered as forgetfulness of the God of the alliance, as turning away from him and as ingratitude.[1] God offers man his benefits and his grace again and again. In response he expects man to be faithful to his commandments. Yet man does not live up to this expectation. He disobeys God's commandments and breaks the covenant. Thus he sins against Yahweh and provokes his anger and punishing wrath. Yet the Lord is always ready for mercy and reconciliation if man repents of his evil ways. This is a constant theme in the history of salvation. It finds its continuation in the New Testament and culminates in Christ.

---

[1] Is 1:2-4; Jer 3:19-25; 16:10-13; Hos 1-3; Ezek 16:59

b) *The New Testament*, in contradistinction to the Old, prefers *one* term for the concept of sin, the word *hamartia*, which originally means 'not to hit a mark', 'to miss'. In all its books the New Testament calls upon men to repent of their sins and to convert their hearts and ways. Jesus purifies and deepens the concept of sin inasmuch as he recognises only moral and not cultic transgressions. The heart is the place where evil is wrought. It is not purification of vessels but interior purity that is required (Mk 7:1-23; Mt 23:25f).

In the parable of the lost son, sin is considered as ungrateful desertion of the Lord. Such headstrong separation is of no avail to the sinner. He rather brings harm and ruin upon himself. Here as in other parables sin is represented by the loss of the very meaning of existence and by separation from God. The lost sheep is perishing in isolation and the lost drachma foils the meaning of its existence to be of service to men (Lk 15). He who separates himself from the saving will of God is lost and frustrates the very meaning of his existence.

At other times sin is presented as the antithesis to charity and an offence against love, i.e. as selfishness and hatred (Lk 7:47; 1 Jn 4:7f.20f). In the writings of John and Paul, sin is regarded as refusal of the light (Jn 3:19f; 1 Jn 2:8-11; Eph 5:8-14) and of the truth (Jn 8:44; Rom 1:18.25), and therefore as darkness and lie. It is lawlessness (2 Thess 2:3.8; 1 Jn 3:4) and disobedience against God (Rom 11:30-32; Eph 5:6).

The epistles of Paul add further aspects to the biblical concept of sin. He sees in man's wickedness a denial of the glorification due to God and the presumptive attempt to be one's own lord (Rom 1:18-32). The sinner lives in enmity against God. "For the mind that is set on the flesh is hostile to God; it does not submit to God's law, indeed it cannot; and those who are in the flesh cannot please God" (Rom 8:7f; cf. 5:10-12; Eph 2:1.4; Col 1:21). Therefore sinners are excluded from the kingdom of God (1 Cor 6:9f; Gal 5:19-21). If the state of grace is characterized by the presence of the Holy Spirit, the state of sin is a life in the flesh deprived of the Spirit (Rom 8:1-17). The Christian ought to be a temple of the Holy Spirit, but sin desecrates it, and that is why it is so abject (1 Cor 3:16f; 6:19f).

A particular aspect in the Pauline writings is the use of the term *hamartia* in the singular. "Here sin is understood either as a comprehensive condition in which human beings exist (Rom 6:1), or as the demonic power which dominates man and keeps him imprisoned" (Rom 3:9; 5:12; 6:20; 7:8f).[1] Besides this type of sin Paul equally knows a great number of individual sins, for example in the catalogues of vices (Rom 1:29-31; 1 Cor 6:9f; Gal 5:19-21; Col 3:5-9). Also the Johannine writings prevalently speak of the one sin (Jn 1:29; 8:21). "According to the Gospel it consists in unbelief towards the messianic mission of Jesus (cf. 3:18; 12:37-50; 16:8-10), according to the letters more so in hatred of the brethren (1 Jn 3:9-11; 3:23)."[2]

The teaching of the New Testament about sin is always accompanied by the idea of forgiveness. Indeed one can say that this thought stands in the centre of its teaching. Christ came to save men, to offer them divine forgiveness and to make of them children of the kingdom. The life and passion of Christ is the combat of the servant of Yahweh against the power of evil. He reveals himself as the saviour of sinners (cf. Mt 9:13; Lk 15; 19:10) and is "the lamb of God, who takes away the sin of the world" (Jn 1:29). Through faith and baptism men participate in the conquest of sin by Christ, if they let themselves be guided by his Spirit. Christ calls to conversion and to faith in the Gospel, and charges his Church to continue the forgiveness of sins on earth. The battle between Christ (and now his Church) and Satan, between light and darkness, good and evil is to continue to the end of time. But the evil spirits and the power of sin are wounded mortally in the death and resurrection of Christ.

II. Threefold dimension of sin

Holy Scripture gives expression to its lasting conviction that man can sin and become guilty before God. This is the permanently valid truth in its teaching and a reality which cannot be given up vis-à-vis tendencies in the secularized world to ignore sin and deny it. The possibility of sin lies in the character of man's free will during his earthly pilgrimage. In all his free activity, man necessarily strives after goodness. The attraction and impulses emanating from the beauty and

---

[1] H. Weber, *l. c.* 281.

[2] *Ib.* 282.

felicity of goodness in general is the enabling principle of all human activity. This is apparent from man's incessant and overmastering search for fulfilment, happiness, value, for all that is good. Indeed man is so bent on this good that even where he wants to do evil he can do it only under the appearance of good.

The possibility of declining the true good and of deciding for the illusory good of sin results from the fact that the finite reason and will of man can never grasp the infinite good fully and completely. In concrete reality, good in general is always encountered in particular goods, towards which a certain indifference is possible. So man can deceive himself. He can regard the true good as less valuable and prefer a lesser or illusory good, even while he knows in the depths of his conscience that it is only a transitory, evanescent value and not the real, lasting good. This is the contradiction inherent in sin.

Every sin contains a triple injury: an injury against the sinner himself, against fellow-men, and against God. This does not signify that in each sin man has the psychologic experience of this triple offence. But on the objective level, this triple injury is always effected.

1. *The personal dimension of sin*

Although the sinner "seeks himself" in his sin and although for the present he chooses the easier way, which demands less sacrifices from him and promises him more gratification, on a deeper level he suffers from an insidious, spiritual sickness and abandons his true happiness and fulfilment.

Man cannot find his happiness and fulfilment in goals for which he is ultimately not meant and created. By sinning a man misses his proper destiny, and this failure must inevitably result in disharmony and frustration (cf. GS 13). The sinner deprives his life of its meaning or at least gives it less meaning. It therefore "is not to be wondered at if sin, as the loss of meaning and purpose of life, produces a deep-seated anguish of existence, which goads people on to ever new repressions, attempts at appeasement and self-justification".[1]

---

[1] K. Demmer, "Sünde," *Neues Lexikon der christlichen Moral* (Innsbruck: Tyrolia, 1990), 754.

The sinner gets caught in a vicious circle of self-produced bondage, anxiety and guilt.

The writer of the book of Proverbs is conscious of this correlation, when he lets wisdom say: "He who finds me finds life and obtains favour from the Lord; but he who misses me injures himself; all who hate me love death" (Prov 8:35f; cf. also the parables of the lost sheep and the prodigal son, Lk 15). Man has been created by God according to certain structures and orders for a definite task. If he disregards the structures of his existence, he will finally destroy his spiritual personality through sin.

Viewed from another aspect, sin is the refusal to grow up to one's full stature and maturity. Man is not complete from his birth in any respect. He must slowly become what he has been called to. But the person of an unauthentic life flouts his calling. Depth psychology and existentialism see guilt precisely under this aspect of the personal dimension. The guilt of man (the term sin is rather avoided) consists in his remaining enthralled by his unauthentic existence and not being willing to progress further; he deviates in his development and falls short of what he should be. He refuses to become his true self, even though the authentic self is differently conceived by the different schools.

Sins are the symptoms of a sick personality and of a spiritual disorder and disease. Very aptly therefore Holy Scripture calls Christ the one by whom we have been healed, because he came to take from us the sickness of our sins (Is 53:5; 1 Pet 2:24)

2. *The social dimension of sin*

The sense of the social aspect of sin is rather alert among modern man, although there is often a need to deepen and to complete it. St. John writes: "If any one says, 'I love God,' and hates his brother, he is a liar; for he who does not love his brother whom he has seen, cannot love God whom he has not seen" (1 Jn 4:20). And "if we love one another, God abides in us and his love is perfected in us" (1 Jn 4:12).

Many sins affect our fellow-men more or less directly by causing harm to them. This is true for all the sins of lovelessness and injustice, of scandal and evil cooperation. To this category also belong the promotion and perpetuation of deficient conditions and of a bad public climate, or even the neglect to fight against an environment contaminated by evil. The theme of unjust, sinful structures must still find more attention further below.

Yet all sins, even those of most personal character, have a social dimension, although of a more subtle, indirect nature. Above all every sin constitutes an impairment of the realization of the common ultimate task. For the sinner refuses in every sin to work for this task and instead strives after different goals of his own liking. Laziness or addiction to narcotics, e.g., need not necessarily harm one's fellow-men directly, if somebody is rich enough or unmarried. But the human community will nevertheless suffer from these defects, because they hamper man in contributing as efficiently to the welfare of society and to the common tasks as he should and could.

Insofar as merely inner sins of thought and desire are concerned, their social impact is not yet activated at the moment they occur. But every inner disorder has the tendency to embody itself in action, e.g. thoughts of revenge. By such inner sins, therefore, man offends against neighbour and society inasmuch as he permits dispositions to develop which by their nature have the perilous proneness to reactions and effects detrimental to society.

Another reason for the social dimension of sin is revealed by the teaching of St. Paul on the mystical body of Christ. According to Paul, Christians "are the body of Christ and individually members of it" (1 Cor 12:27). All the members of a body depend upon each other, and if one member is sick or does not function, all the others suffer from it (1 Cor 12:26; cf. 5:6f). Therefore no one lives for himself alone. A member that is taken ill by sin impairs the transmission of the life of grace. It lessens the irradiation proper to goodness and holiness and thus deprives the Church and fellow-men of graces and helps they can expect from him. That is why we confess our sins daily before the altar not only to God but also to all our brothers and sisters.

Finally, insofar as Christians are concerned, their unfaithfulness to their vocation questions the vitality of their religious convictions before those who live with them. In this way they darken the image of the Christian religion and make the light of faith shine less brightly, especially among those who are still far from Christ.

3. *Sin as rejection of God*

Sin is ultimately and essentially rejection of God and his divine plan. This needs special emphasis today, because people have largely lost the sense of the religious dimension of sin and are inclined to deprive sin of it and to ignore it. More readily they have an understanding for the personal and social dimension of sin. These are valid points of view, but they are incomplete. The personal and social dimension must not be separated from the deeper religious dimension, which is the basis for the other dimensions and from which they lastly derive their genuine standards of value. Before anything else, there exists God, and every other being only exists because he wills it. He has created the world and man. He has set him his task and goal. The sinner's attempt and undertaking is to ignore and to reject the structures established by God and to draw up goals for his life according to his own liking. The injury against God contained in sin results from this defiance.

The rejection of God and his aims by the sinner disturbs and breaks a fundamental relationship. This rupture can be viewed under different aspects. God created the world to manifest his glory and to make man share in the riches of his divine life. Sin as refusal to cooperate with God's plan is impairment of the divine glory and loss of the participation in the divine life. In sin man refuses to accept his dependence on God, which demands that he orientate himself with unwavering determination towards the divine goals. Disregarding God's will, he denies the honour and obedience due to the supreme Lord, although he completely belongs to him. Man's turning away from the divine will must naturally result in separation from the love and communion with God. The experience of God, who gives peace and joy, consolation and security, is for the sinner no longer a reality of life.

If, as in the foregoing, sin is conceived as injury against God, the question arises whether those who do not know God or who profess themselves to be atheists can sin against him. In other words, it is asked whether their offences are theological sins committed against God or merely so-called "philosophical sins", which are moral offences against right reason but not offences against God. According to Catholic theology however, there is no such thing as a merely philosophical sin (cf. DS 2291). The reasons are the following. (1) No man in use of his reason is completely without knowledge of his ultimate end; at least in an implicit and unreflective way he knows about it. A human person who would completely lack this knowledge, would be in an absurd existence in this world. But since man's ultimate goal is inseparably linked with God and his glory, the knowledge of this goal implies some knowledge of God as well. Consequently even the atheist sins against God if he offends against his ultimate end, which is made known to every man through his conscience. (2) Further, if a man experiences his actions against right reason as morally wrong, he must be aware of an instance which forbids such contradiction against reason with absolute authority. In acknowledging the verdict of this authority, man admits an absolute claim upon him and implicitly acknowledges an absolute being. Hence a philosophical sin is not possible. The denial of God by atheists then either concerns a wrong concept of God, while in their hearts they are aware of some truer idea of God, or they culpably suppress their knowledge of him.

III. Mortal, grave and venial sin

Common sense spontaneously makes a distinction between light sins and grave sins, between shortcomings, minor offences and crimes. In the practical judgment, everybody knows that not all sins are of the same gravity, and he acts on this basis. Nevertheless the theological explanation of the different gravity of sins includes some controversies and problems.

1. *Different gradations of sins*

In the Old Testament some sins are said to bring about a radical break with God and loss of the divine favour. This is the case with the crimes listed in the curses of Deut 27:15-26 or with certain sins enumerated by the prophets and accompanied by divine menace: "He has done all these abominable things; he shall surely die; his blood shall be upon himself" (Ezek 18:10-18; cf. Lev 18:6-23). Other sins and offences receive a milder judgment and can be atoned for by rites of purification or good works (Lev 4f).

The New Testament knows certain serious sins and baneful ways of living which deserve death (Rom 1:28-32; 1 Jn 3:14f) or which exclude from the kingdom of God (1 Cor 6:9f; Gal 5:19-21; Eph 5:3-5; Rev 22:15). The synoptics speak of the sin against the Holy Spirit (Mk 3:29 par) and John of "a mortal sin" (1 Jn 5:16f), which probably refers to the hardening of the heart against the offer of salvation and to the refusal of faith (in Christ). On the other hand the New Testament is also aware of lighter sins, which are not of the same fatal consequences. Such are the sins committed even by the just man. Thus the petition of the Our Father "forgive us our sins" (Lk 11:4 par) primarily refers to the small transgressions of daily life. The same is true of the words of James: "For we all make many mistakes, and if any one makes no mistakes in what he says he is a perfect man" (Jas 3:2; cf. 1 Jn 1:8-10). In 1 Cor 3:10-15 Paul makes the distinction between two groups of Christians, which both build on the true foundation, that is Jesus Christ. Some build with gold, silver, precious stones, and their work will survive. Others build with wood, hay, stubble. When their work is tested by the fire, they will suffer loss, though they themselves will be saved. This points to sins for which one is not condemned, but from which one is to be cleansed. Finally John distinguishes two kinds of sin: sins which are unto death and others which are not unto death. "All wrongdoing is sin, but there is sin which is not mortal" (1 Jn 5:17). Hence, although the New Testament does not know the specific concepts and terms of what is nowadays called "venial" and "mortal" sin, it prepares these notions and has indications of this difference.

The teaching of the Church has always distinguished between grave offences against God and the Church community and smaller faults. This is especially obvious in the history of the sacrament of penance. Ecclesiastical and sacramental penance was required for serious sins, while forgiveness of lighter sins might be obtained by means of private practices of penance, such as prayer, fasting and almsgiving. This is not contradicted by the fact that within that constant conviction there have been variations in the opinions about which offences concretely constituted a serious sin. The present distinction between mortal and venial sin is expressly taught by the

Council of Trent. It declares that all mortal sins must be confessed, because those who are guilty of such sins are "children of wrath" (Eph 2:3), while venial sins need not be confessed, although it is recommendable to do so (DS 1680). For venial sins do not destroy the state of grace (DS 1537). Consequential and regrettable was the extension of the concept of mortal sin to ever new frailties in the post-tridentine period, which has lead to that erosion of sin which has strongly contributed to the present crisis of its understanding. The inclusion of quite minor transgressions in the category of mortal sin, especially in the realm of the rubrics and the precepts of the Church, but not alone there, has stripped the concept of its seriousness.

Recently attempts have been made to differentiate further the traditional division of sin and to distinguish between three categories, namely mortal, grave and venial sins.[1] While mortal sin, according to these theories, is a complete aversion from God, grave sin is a serious offence resulting from a certain weakness, be it a deficient sense of value or a lack of moral strength, and venial sin is a transgression in unimportant matters. However a correct understanding of the two traditional categories of sin does not seem to leave room for a third category which is substantially different from the two others. More realistic is a subdistinction of venial sins in grave and light ones.

For the practical study and classification of sinful actions the following distinctions are fundamental and must be kept in mind. Mortal and venial sin are gradations in view of the subjective condition of the sinner, namely whether he has separated himself from God in a sinful act and lost the divine life of grace, or whether he has only diminished the force of divine life in himself without causing its loss. Grave and light sin are gradations taken more in view of the detriment caused in the objective order to the realization of the ultimate goal. The objectively grave disturbance of the moral order is usually the sign of a mortal sin, but not necessarily, since lack of full insight or lack of free will can subjectively prevent the

---

[1] Cf. H. Boelaars, "Ist jede schwere Sünde eine Todsünde?," *Theologie der Gegenwart*, 6 (1963), 142-148. F.J. Heggen distinguishes between mortal, serious and venial sins (*Confession and the Service of Penance*. London: Sheed and Ward, 1967, 70-77).

origination of a mortal sin. Equally a light offence against the objective moral order is usually a sign of a venial sin, although an objectively light offence may sometimes be occasion for a deliberate rebellion against God and hence a mortal sin.

When Christian ethics in special moral theology investigates the gravity of certain offences, it does so only in view of the objective detriment they cause to the realization of the ultimate goal, that is to say in view of the question whether this detriment is great or light. The judgment on the subjective state of the sinner always depends on his or her *inner* state of mind, and the judgment about it is always difficult and accompanied by great uncertainty.

2. *Mortal and venial sin defined*

Theologians find themselves confronted with the problem: every sin is refusal of God's will and therefore a breaking with him. As it says in the letter of James: "Whoever keeps the whole law but fails in one point has become guilty of all of it" (Jas 2:10). How then can there be a second category besides mortal sin which does not constitute a breach with God?

The answers of theologians agree more or less in this that venial sins do not constitute a direct, complete refusal of God's will, as mortal sins do, but are only an insufficient, defective compliance with the same. But they differ in their explanation as to why venial sins merely constitute a deficient compliance with God's will.[1] Traditional moral theology sees the reason above all in the objective insignificance of the matter, although the subjective imperfection of the act is also taken into consideration as a secondary reason. The common doctrine of moral handbooks and, in their train, of catechisms can be summarized as follows:

---

[1] In the time of nominalism Occam and, in his train, Gerson and Baius taught that the difference between mortal and venial sin derives from the extrinsic decision of God, who decrees, in his sovereign will, to punish some sins with the loss of eternal life, while others draw only temporal punishment. This doctrine with its concept of God as an arbitrary tyrant was rejected by the Church, which dismissed the following assertion of Baius as wrong: "There is not a single sin which, of its nature, is a venial sin, but every sin deserves eternal punishment" (DS 1920).

"We commit a mortal sin when we transgress God's law in an important matter with full advertence and with a wholly free will; we commit a venial sin (1) when we transgress God's law in a small thing or (2) when we transgress God's law in an important thing, but without full knowledge or without full freedom of the will."[1]

Contemporary theological reflection however places the emphasis primarily on the subjective perfection or imperfection of the act as the explanation for the mortal or venial sinfulness of an offence. It stresses the fact that sin is first of all a disorder of the human will. The external sinful act is only an indication and a sign of the internal disorder, not however the certain proof for it. Beyond this, one can notice that the judgment on the gravity of transgressions is also subject to sentiments and evaluations conditioned by the times, and it is not conceivable that mortal sins are dependent on factors so very much human in nature. Recent theology avails itself especially of the doctrine of the fundamental option for the explanation of the two kinds of sins, which doctrine was developed precisely in order to gain a better understanding of the nature of sin.

Mortal sin accordingly is a morally wrong decision which is so intensive that it gives a wrong orientation to man's entire life. It is the option for a spurious, perverted blueprint of a person's life. Of course a person will not change a hitherto correct blueprint into a perverted one too often during his lifetime and vice versa. Does this mean that mortal sins are only very rare? They are probably rarer than traditional moral theology did assume. Nevertheless a person living in a state of mortal sin can still commit other mortal sins, if he makes morally wrong decisions of such intensity that they are apt to repeat and renew a vicious option. A ruthless politician with selfish motivation, who came to power by cheating, bribery and blackmail, may one day be confronted with the choice either to eliminate a competitor or to lose the grip on his power. If he were to opt for the assassination of his competitor, this would involve such a radical renewal of the evil option that it would amount to another mortal sin.

---

[1] So summarized by Piet Schoonenberg, *Man and Sin* (London: Sheed and Ward, 1965), 29.

Venial sin on the other hand is a morally wrong decision which either does not constitute an actual denial of man's true goal of life, but is only an inconsistent realization of his otherwise authentic blueprint; or, if the sinner already lives in the state of aversion from God by force of a previous wrong option, the sinful act is by its nature not apt to cause or to repeat the basically wrong orientation, but only superficially confirms it. Keeping these considerations in mind, the greater or lesser depth of the sinful decision is conditioned by the following two factors.

I. *Potency of commitment.* The potency of commitment in a morally wrong decision can be a broken one either because of lack of clear insight, which also includes insufficient awareness of the consequences involved in a sinful act; or because of imperfect consent of the will. In these instances the sin committed is a venial sin. Mortal sin on the other hand is a full commitment to an option which contradicts God's will and a person's authentic goal. It presupposes clear knowledge of the serious disorder of the sinful decision and full consent of the free will.

II. *Importance of the matter.* There are inconsequences and disorders which a man may consider as unimportant for the goal of his life and which in many cases are in fact also objectively small matters of minor import on the realization of man's true goal and God's eternal plan. As a rule they are not apt to evoke a fundamental decision against God's will, and this above all because objectively no such radical opposition to the divine plan is involved. Therefore they usually give rise only to venial sins (assuming they are committed with sufficient insight and consent of the will).

Mortal sin, on the contrary, is an intensive commitment, which is usually called forth by an important matter. Only in exceptional cases could a small matter also give occasion to a mortal sin. In questions of sin an important matter seriously opposes and obstructs the realization of the divine goals and of a person's genuine task of life in the objective order. Accordingly, if a person consents to a grave matter with full knowledge and a wholly free will, he will be involved in an existential choice. Hence there is a correlation, though not an absolutely necessary one, between important matter - intensive commitment, and small matter - superficial commitment.

By way of a conclusion, the essence and conditions of mortal and venial sin can be defined as follows: A *mortal sin* is a decision in radical contradiction to God's will, which always presupposes full knowledge and full consent of the will, and which is usually the case if we transgress God's law in an important matter. A *venial sin* is a transgression of God's will without complete commitment to the evil option, which is the case usually if we disobey God's will in unimportant matters or in important matters but with imperfect knowledge or imperfect consent.

Venial and mortal sin are essentially different. For this reason it is not the sum of many venial sins which finally could constitute a mortal sin. But there exists a dynamic relation between venial and mortal sin insofar as venial sin prepares the way for mortal sin. By committing venial sins, man disposes and readies himself to commit a mortal sin. The scholastic theologians compare this sometimes with the accidental modifications in a physical or chemical process which precede the substantial mutation. "The previous choices are an invitation and an inducement for a more profound choice in the same direction. Venial sin causes us to slacken in the love of God; it pushes us gradually into more serious sins. On the other hand, the «daily good actions» of him who lives in the state of mortal sin will make him slacken in his sinful attitude, thus inducing him slowly to accept the grace of conversion. Moreover there is a great similarity between the manner in which mortal sins lead us to final impenitence, complete loss of faith and hope, and the manner in which «basic moral acts» lead us to total self-donation and confirmation in love."[1]

3. *Criteria for the objective gravity of sins*

The objective gravity of a sin is determined by the gravity or levity of the objective disorder and injury a human action causes in the sphere of moral values. This objective disorder is called the "matter" of sin. The criteria for the gravity of a sinful matter are external if they are taken from the authority of Scripture, of Church doctrine and of theologians. They are internal if they are taken from the nature and effects of an offence.

---

[1] P. Schoonenberg, *l. c.* 38f.

a) *External criteria.* Holy Scripture is first among the external criteria. A matter is judged grave if Holy Scripture states of a certain sinful act that the person who does it shall be cursed; that it is abominable; that it cries to heaven;[1] that it deserves death or eternal punishment; that it excludes from the kingdom of God.

The criteria of Holy Scripture are however not always entirely clear and beyond dispute. For example among the abominations for which a person should be cut off from the people, the Old Testament also mentions intercourse during menstruation time (Lev 18:19). Although such an action may normally not be appropriate, no recent manual of moral theology qualifies it as sin and much less as a grave one. Likewise the Old Testament ordains that a person who does any work on the Sabbath shall be put to death (Ex 31:15), and this was applied even to a man who was gathering sticks (Num 15:32-36). Christian ethics could not classify the gathering of sticks on a Sunday as a grave sin.

At other times the Old as well as the New Testament include among the sins which deserve death or exclude from the kingdom of God offences which admit of degrees, e.g. thievery, greed, revilement, impurity, envy, anger, etc. (cf. Rom 1:29-32; 1 Cor 6:9f; Gal 5:19-21). It is evident that not every small theft or slight anger is a grave sin which could merit so serious a sanction as exclusion from the kingdom of God. Therefore here as much as in the determination of man's obligations in general, additional criteria have to be called upon in order to decide which matter is to be considered grave with regard to these sins and which matter light.

Further external criteria are the official doctrine of the popes and councils. Infallible definitions in matters of moral obligations are very rare, and there is perhaps none which explicitly defines the gravely sinful character of a particular offence. But also the other decisions of the magisterium of the Church enjoy great authority and have to be carefully adhered to by the faithful (cf. LG 25; GS 50; DH 14). General councils of course enjoy the greatest authority. Among papal

---

[1] Scripture speaks of four sins crying to heaven: murder (Gen 4:10), the sin of Sodom (Gen 18:20f; 19:13), oppression of widows and orphans (Ex 22:22f), and defrauding the hired servant of his earnings (Deut 24:14f; Jas 5:4).

pronouncements, encyclicals possess a particular weight, following by other statements and papal allocutions.

The common teachings of the Church Fathers and theologians are likewise important criteria for judging the gravity of a sin which merit adequate attention. Nevertheless new developments at times supersede former judgments and doctrines, as illustrated by the moral evaluation of interest on loans, the reasons justifying the conjugal act or violations of rubrics in the administration of the sacraments.[1]

b) *Internal criteria.* The internal criteria are of particular importance in the determination of the sinfulness of an act and its gravity. A sinful matter is grave if it constitutes a grave injury to a good of great value. And since in the moral order the values are determined and measured by the relation of a human action to man's existential ends and lastly to his ultimate end, a grave matter can be defined as a grave injury to man's existential ends and his ultimate goal. This means, more in detail, that a sinful matter is grave if, in view of man's existential ends and the ultimate goal, it results in a serious injury against God and the honour and reverence due to him; in serious harm to the state, the Church and the human community in general; in serious temporal or spiritual harm to one's fellow-men; or in serious temporal or spiritual harm to oneself.[2]

In many instances men are in common agreement as to what matter is to be considered grave in questions of moral obligations, e.g. serious bodily mutilations (such as destruction

---

[1] The following violations of rubrics, for example, were considered gravely sinful by the traditional Latin manuals prior to Vatican II: consecration of bread or wine not placed on a corporal; transfer of the blessed sacrament without sacred vestments; celebration of the Mass with a woman or even a religious sister as server or acolyte; anointing of the sick without surplice and stole (cf. K.-H. Peschke, "Die Sünde in den Traktaten über die Sakramente," in *In Verbo Tuo.* Festschrift. St. Augustin/Siegburg: Missionspriesterseminar, 1963, 235-246).

[2] If in Africa the gravity of a moral fault is also measured by the social status of a person or family, i.e. the higher the social status, the more serious the fault, then this criterion merits to be considered on a more universal basis when judging an offensive deed. Cf. M. Sebahire, "Faute, péché, pénitence et réconciliation dans les traditions de quelques sociétés d'Afrique Centrale," in *Schuld, Sühne und Erlösung,* ed. by K.J. Rivinius (Steyler Verlag, 1983), 151.

of a person's eye-sight), assassination, rape, robbery of goods of greater value (such as a horse or a car), seriously damaging calumnies, etc. But at other times opinions differ. Religious and social traditions can qualify certain actions as gravely sinful which in a neutral evaluation would not merit such a rating, e.g. certain violations of the Sabbath or Sunday rest, the eating of foods forbidden for merely ritual reasons, the touching of persons or items declared unclean, etc. At other times traditions or popular opinions can consider certain actions as lawful or morally less relevant which after all are serious offences of the moral order, such as human sacrifices, slavery or abortion. Judgments on the gravity of certain offences depend on the validity of the reasons which support them as much as moral judgments in general depend on the validity of their reasons. And just as scholars at times dispute the sinfulness of a certain action in principle, so their opinions also at times vary as to the gravity of a certain offence.

B. Division of sins

Handbooks prior to Vatican II usually paid much attention to the specific and numeric distinction of sins. The main reason for this is the demand of the Council of Trent that all grave sins must be confessed by species and number (DS 1679 -1681; 1707). This demand of the Council is of relevance insofar as confession is concerned. But since, apart from this more practical concern, these distinctions do not seem to yield much for a better understanding and comprehension of sin, it may be permitted to relegate their study to the treatise of the sacrament of confession, where these divisions are of immediate interest.

I. Different kinds of internal sins

Internal sins are sins which are consummated in the mind. They are sins of the heart, usually called "bad thoughts". Every sin is first committed in the heart of man. It arises in the evil dispositions and desires. "It is therefore only consequent and at the same time realistic to pay more attention to the sins of thought. For through them the terrain is prepared for the sins of action, tracks of feeling are entrenched, attitudes of expectation are built up and imperceptibly steer the course of events. The spiritual distance to sin gets lost, one has already leapt over the trench and compromised with the opponent."[1]

Tradition distinguishes three kinds of internal sins: sinful complacency, sinful joy in past evil deeds and evil desire. Inner stirrings of the same kind, of course, can also be directed towards the good. The mental pleasure in good deeds, the joy at the good done (by oneself or others), and the desire to imitate and to do the good are ways to ingraft the good in one's heart, just as evil imaginations and desires do the opposite. Just as the latter have to be banished from the mind, so it is the positive task of people to give room to good thoughts and desires in the heart and to let them bear fruit. To the three inner sins listed above a fourth kind shall still be added here, i.e. prejudice or bias.

1. *Mental complacency in sinful imaginations* takes pleasure in sinful fantasies and thoughts without the desire to bring them into act. It is to be distinguished from intellectual preoccupation with sinful modes of conduct, which are studied for the sake of gaining insight into their nature. The latter is indifferent and may even be a duty, e.g. in the case of a physician, counsellor or confessor, who need this knowledge to procure the necessary instruction and help to their patients and penitents.

2. *Sinful joy in an accomplished evil deed*, be it one's own or another person's sin, and *sinful regret* of not having performed an evil act are imaginations which imply an approval of the respective evil deeds. They are therefore sinful themselves. It is however not sinful to rejoice at the good effect of an evil deed, e.g. that by the murder of a corrupt government official a source of public injustice is removed, or at the manner in which an evil deed was executed, e.g. an ingenious forgery or bank robbery. Neither is it sinful to rejoice at something which was formerly lawful or will later become so. Thus a widow may reflect with satisfaction upon past marital relations with her husband; or the betrothed may think with joy upon the future fulfilment of the conjugal love.

3. *Evil desire* is the wish to perform a sinful action. The evil desire is inefficacious if one would like to carry out the deed, but does not really intend to do so, because of some

---

[1] K. Demmer, "Sünde," *Neues Lexikon der christlichen Moral*, 1990, 755.

reason one is ashamed or afraid to do so (e.g. one may not want to offend more seriously against God or to endanger one's good reputation) or because one perceives the vain or hazardous nature of such an attempt. People often happen to have strong desires and seem to be determined to do an evil deed..But if they are confronted with the possibility to put their wishes into action, they refrain from doing so. Their desire is not serious, but only an inefficacious volition. An evil desire is efficacious if it constitutes a firm intention or resolution. One is guilty of this desire even though some external circumstance may prevent its realization. "Bad will alone is a sin, even if the effect is lacking - that is, if there is no power to carry it out."[1]

The various kinds of interior sins bear, as to species, the same malice as the external act, yet not always also as to the degree. The efficacious desire however is always a grave sin if the desired evil is gravely sinful as well. The real performance of the external sin is merely an aggravating circumstance, as it further intensifies the bad attitude and disposition. Morally less sensitive people might sometimes fail to recognize the malice of purely interior acts which are not serious evil desires. But certainly a normal person cannot fail to perceive the malice of an evil resolution or intention, if he realizes that the action he plans to carry out is sinful.

4. *Prejudice or bias* is the tendency to eliminate from one's considerations and decisions data which are perceived to be a potential threat to one's well-being or to that of the group to which one belongs and to the accustomed ways of viewing the world.[2] Obviously the failure to account for significant data will have negative effects on the development of the individual and on the just ordering of society. Prejudice may be individual bias or group bias. Individual bias induces a person in a short-sighted way to pay attention to the satisfaction of personal needs and desires, while eliminating from consideration the consequences the action has on the needs of others and the common good. Group bias strives to protect the well-being of a group. The "decision-making be-

---

[1] Augustine, *De spiritu et littera*, c. 31, nr. 54 (Migne PL, vol. 44, 235).

[2] Attention has been drawn to this type of internal sin especially by B. Lonergan, *Insight: A Study of Human Understanding* (London, 1957; reprint ed. New York: Harper & Row, 1978), 218-242.

comes biased when there is a refusal to consider the effects which such decisions may have on people who do not belong to that particular group and on other groups.... Those in the dominant group become «blind» to the suffering of others and its causes and become unable to conceive of new possibilities for a more just social ordering."[1] Racism, imperialism and sexism are examples of group bias. Biases of this kind are the source of unjust social structures. To the extent that one is in some way, even indistinctly, aware of one's biased conceptions and refuses to overcome them, one is engaged in sin. Group bias however is often so deeply rooted that the individual takes it simply for granted without any inner hesitations. This is the problem of unjust sinful structures, which has to receive more attention further on.

II. Sins of omission and commission

A sin of commission is the performance of a forbidden act. It is an offence against a negative precept, such as "You shall have no other god before me;" "You shall not kill;" "You shall not steal." A sin of omission, on the other hand, is the failure to perform an obligatory act. It is an offence against a positive precept, such as "Remember the Sabbath day, to keep it holy;" "Love one another as I have loved you."

Although sins of commission are usually of a graver nature than sins of omission, the latter sins nevertheless constitute a great peril for the kingdom of God. Sins of omission remain more easily unnoticed, and that is why they are particularly dangerous. It is of course more difficult to discern what is positively just and therefore to be done, than to know what is unjust and therefore to be omitted. Only to a very limited extent the good to be done can be defined in general laws, because these duties of a person depend much on the individual aptitudes, talents and concrete conditions of life. Here in particular it becomes plain that the paradigm of sin does not simply consist in the trespassing of norms. It is therefore easier to avoid sins of commission than to do all the good which one ought to do. Not to sin by omission presupposes a greater degree of perfection.

---

[1] Mark O'Keefe, *What Are They Saying About Social Sin?* (New York: Paulist Press, 1990), 78.

The possibilities of omissions are manifold: neglect of one's professional, social or religious duties; neglect to reform oneself; neglect to fight deficient and evil public conditions; neglect to show concern and fraternal love for one's neighbour, etc. Of course an omission is only culpable if one has realized the duty to act. This duty is not always seen. Yet often enough a person is more or less aware of his obligation to do some good, but he shrinks back from the effort and leaves it undone. That is why Catholics at the beginning of the Mass ask pardon from God and their brothers not only for the evil they have done, but also for the good they have left undone. Sins of omission are real offences, the sources of much injustice, suffering and abandonment.

III. The capital sins

Christian tradition from the time of the Fathers put together a catalogue of main sins, denominated capital sins. They are called "capital" not because they are always necessarily grave, but because they easily become vices and sources of many other sins. Gregory the Great (†604) drew up a list of seven:

Pride or vainglory is an inordinate desire of honour, distinction and independence. It is opposed to the virtue of humility.

Avarice is the inordinate pursuit of material goods and is contrary to the virtues of liberality and equity.

Envy is discontent over the good of one's neighbour, which is considered as a detriment to one's own person. It offends against brotherliness and magnanimity.

Lust is the inordinate craving for sexual gratification and is against the virtue of chastity.

Gluttony is excess in the enjoyment of food and drink; the opposite virtues are temperance and sobriety.

Anger is the intemperate outburst of dislike with the inordinate desire for another's punishment. It is contrary to patience and meekness.

Sloth in the wider sense is laziness and is opposed to diligence. In the narrower sense it means spiritual sloth, a turning away from spiritual things because of the effort which they require. It contradicts the virtues of piety and love of God.

Parallel to the seven capital sins, tradition also lists seven main virtues: the three theological virtues faith, hope and charity, and the four cardinal virtues prudence, justice, fortitude and temperance. It is striking that there is very little correspondence between these main sins and virtues. The virtues opposed to the capital sins are different from the seven main virtues and vice versa. In fact the tables of the capital sins and of the cardinal virtues are not the result of systematic analysis and logical deduction, but stem from a popular ethics and have something of accidentalness. They are not so much aids in the scientific study of moral theology as helps to spiritual incitement and ascetic reflections.

C. Sources of sin

This section deals with the sources of sin by which men are tempted or by which they themselves become a temptation for others, i.e. temptation, seduction, scandal and structures of evil in the world.

I. Temptation

1. *Concept and nature.* Temptation is the incitement acting upon a person to do evil. It is the attraction by a good which in the larger context of the entire hierarchy of values constitutes an evil. The following example can illustrates this. Let us say that a certain food tempts me; it tempts me because it tastes good, which means that it satisfies my appetite. Yet it is a food that will do me harm; it will make me ill, and I am aware of this. I thus hesitate between the immediate satisfaction that I will experience if I eat it, and the prospect of becoming ill. In other words, the satisfaction of my appetite, considered independently of all other elements, is a good in itself. But taken in the context of my entire life, and considered in terms of my health, this good leads to disorder and becomes an evil. The possibility of being tempted by evil thus comes from the fact that the same object is good and evil from different points of view.[1]

---

[1] Taken from J. Leclercq, "Temptation," in *Pastoral Treatment of Sin*, ed. by Ph. Delhaye (Tournai: Desclée, 1968), 40.

Hence the tempted man is a divided man. He is divided between two goods, one of which is at the same time an evil. He knows that one of the alternatives is evil, but he hesitates whether to opt for it or not, because he is sensitive to the good which it also contains. Therefore temptation is a state of hesitation where no definite decision for good or for evil has yet been made, and where the final consent is still withheld.

Since man is a multiple being, besieged on all sides by multiplicity, temptation is a most natural phenomenon, which should cause little surprise. Man finds himself in the presence of many goods. "Each one satisfies one tendency; no single good satisfies man entirely and from every point of view. Having in mind the idea of the absolute good and the absolute happiness, man attempts to construct his good and happiness in the concrete. This construction of one's life demands a perpetual choice, and a perpetual renouncement of certain goods for the purpose of possessing others.... I can exercise one profession only if I renounce the exercise of still others; I can find happiness in marriage only if I remain faithful to one person; and I can aspire to the perfection of the religious life only on the condition that I forego the perfection which I would find in marriage."[1]

In addition the good a person does not possess and whose want he suffers seems to promise the fulfilment of what he is lacking in happiness. And this greatly increases the tempting attraction of a forbidden good. Man has the impression that once he obtains the good he is longing for, but which he is denied for some reason, he will be perfectly happy. A man who desires a house of his own but has none may feel that he will be fully content once he has a house. But as soon as he really owns one, he will fast discover other needs and unfulfilled wishes which deprive him of complete happiness. For there is no created good that can make a person so perfectly happy that there would be no more room for any want and nothing remain to be desired.

2. *Provisions against temptation.* According to traditional asceticism, the two principal means for combatting temptation are prayer and penance. Prayer is understood in a broad sense

---

[1] J. Leclercq, *l. c.* 46.

as including the sacramental life as well. Although prayer is not of great help once temptation becomes strong, it is certainly of importance as a provident measure. If somebody is assaulted by temptations against faith, chastity or charity and at the same time neglects prayer life, he is not free of guilt for this state of affairs. He has not done what is in his power to strengthen himself against temptation; on the contrary, he has prepared the ground for it by his negligence.

Penance is not so strongly emphasized today as in former times. Yet one should not conclude that it is no longer important at all. At a time when comfort has become an idol, it is sometimes necessary that an act be posited which runs contrary to an easeful life. This also includes the sacrifice of some satisfaction in order not to become a slave of comfort, but to retain the necessary freedom and openness to spiritual values. To penance one must add in our day physical exercise, hygiene and sports. Physical exercise has been discovered as a most apt means of bodily hygiene. The body must be disciplined if one is to become its master. Formerly this has been done by physical penance. Today this "is induced by exercises which have little to do with mortification, but the principle remains the same".[1]

Traditional asceticism likewise insists on the avoidance of idleness as preventive means against temptation, and in this it is certainly right. The obligation to serve God and the community through useful work is a general task and duty. At the same time it keeps the mind away from idle thoughts and harmful wishes and gives a man the satisfaction and joy of doing a useful work. Healthy social relations act in a similar way. The dissatisfaction caused by an isolated life easily becomes a source of temptation. Good friendships will help to dispel them. They give the mind new impulses, they broaden its horizon and present a person with challenging demands.

The avoidance of occasions of sin is a means against temptations no less needful today than in times past. It will not be the means against all temptations, because not all occasions can be avoided. But if an occasion to sin is serious, as e.g. the temptation for a married man is to be unfaithful and to endanger thereby the happiness of his family, and if

---

[1] J. Leclercq, *l. c.* 61.

the occasion can be avoided, although only with renunciations and sacrifices, one is obliged to do so. In the same line lies diversion from evil thoughts by distraction and by turning to other absorbing thoughts and occupations. This however should not be made an excuse to escape any sincere confrontation with troublesome thoughts. Although, e.g., desires of hateful revenge must be dismissed, a careful examination of one's reactions of anger and aversion will often be in place to gain clarity about their sources (which can also lie in the person harassed by such thoughts) and to procure possible remedies.

Finally a person must try to purify ever more the intentions and aspirations of his or her heart. In the Gospel we read that it is the good tree which bears good fruit, and that it is from the heart that evil thoughts arise. The attention must be directed to the roots of the tree, and it is the heart which must be purified. Above all one must endeavour to gain a clear and lucid notion of one's personal calling and of one's task in the service of God and of Christ's kingdom.

3. *Moral finality of temptation.* All authors agree: God does not tempt men, for God does not lead men into evil. Temptation arises from the fact that evil presents itself as desirable. Ultimately the possibility of temptation is rooted in the gift of freedom, with which God has endowed men. The gift of freedom inevitably includes the risks of temptation and sin. But at the same time freedom is also the necessary prerequisite for any creative activity on the part of men. Evidently the creative powers of men are of so great a value within God's plan of creation, that they are worth the risk of sin which goes along with them.

Moreover temptations are not just evil under every aspect. They also have a positive role to play in human life. Both, Christians and non-Christian moralists, are aware of the educational·value of trials in moral life. It is through struggles that men learn to know themselves and form themselves. Therefore Holy Scripture says: "Count it all joy, my brethren, when you meet various trials, for you know that the testing of your faith produces steadfastness" (Jas 1:2f). Trials have an invigorating effect, and they provide men with the opportunity to grow to maturity. Nevertheless men should not look for temptations. Such would be temerity, for if the temptation is effective, one cannot be certain that it will be overcome. It is for this reason that Christians pray: "And lead us not into temptation, but deliver us from evil" (Mt 6:13). Therefore spiritual writers tell us not to seek temptations, although not to fear them either. For if sent by God, they are instruments in the school of virtue and perfection.

II. Seduction and scandal

All negligence in the resistance against evil is indirectly a source of sins to others. Those, e.g., who do not fight an evil public atmosphere or morally evil conditions in an institution, although they could and should do so, are indirectly the source of sins provoked by such conditions. Likewise the negligent and unnecessary exposure of somebody in one's care to enticements to evil makes a person jointly responsible for the sins which may ensue. A particularly serious form of participation in the sins of others is the promotion of an unworthy candidate to an office and a position of authority. For this reason the first letter to Timothy admonishes: "Do not be hasty in the laying on of hands, nor participate in another man's sins" (1 Tim 5:22). Special treatment require seduction and scandal.

1. *Seduction*

Seduction is the deliberate effort to lead others to sin. It constitutes a twofold sin, first a sin against charity, and second a sin against the moral duty whose violation is caused. However one cannot speak of seduction in cases in which a person suggests to somebody a sinful deed to which he is already disposed prior to the suggestion. A thief who has made out a new plan for a robbery and invites an accomplice of former deeds to join in the delinquency cannot be called a seducer. Seduction presupposes that the seduced person is led to an action which stands in contradiction to his or her original personal intention and mind. A common instance is the persuasion of a companion to attend a bad movie or to read a pornographic magazine. A most vile example of seduction is the alleged recruitment of girls as housemaids and waitresses, or worse even their plain abduction, with the intent to seduce them, often under application of some pressure, and to use them for commercial prostitution.

In great wrath Jesus turns against those who seduce the innocent and guileless believer. "Whoever causes one of these little ones who believe in me to sin, it would be better for him to have a great millstone fastened round his neck and to be drowned in the depth of the sea" (Mt 18:6). Subsequently this woe is extended to all seduction and scandal. "Woe to the world for temptations to sin! For it is necessary that temptations come, but woe to the man by whom the temptation comes!" It would be better for such a man to cut off his hand or foot or to pluck out his eye than to be the cause of sin (Mt 18:7-9).

Note that it is permissible to make a request which can be granted without sin, but which one foresees will be sinfully granted, provided one has a serious reason to make the request. Thus one may ask a person to take an oath in court, although one knows that he will commit a perjury.

2. *Active and passive scandal*

At times the concept of scandal is taken in such a general sense that also the incitements caused by sinful structures are included in it. Usually however scandal is understood as conduct of individuals or groups by which they tempt others to evil more or less imputably. The influence of a sinfully distorted world will be dealt with separately below. Nevertheless the difference between scandal caused by communities and the temptations caused by sinful structures is not entirely sharp.

Scandal is distinguished as active or passive scandal. Active scandal is a conduct which gives rise to the sin of another. Passive scandal is the taking of scandal at the provocative action of another, be this action unbecoming and sinful or be it lawful and good.

a) *Active scandal in the strict sense* is an unbecoming conduct that gives occasion of sin to others. While seduction intentionally causes another to sin, scandal in the proper sense only gives an occasion to sin and permits the sinful deed following therefrom.

The unbecoming conduct can be a sinful deed, but it can also be an objectively correct action which however ought to be omitted because of the weakness or ignorance of those who witness it without sufficient understanding. It is for this reason that Paul exhorts the Roman Christians to avoid scandalizing those converts, yet weak in faith and understanding, who believe themselves still bound by certain prescriptions of the Jewish ceremonial law and not allowed to eat meat or drink wine. Although in principle no food is unclean for a Christian, those strong in faith should not provoke the weaker Christians by their conduct to act against their conscience and to eat or drink what they think is forbidden (Rom 14:13-23). The same holds for the eating of food offered to idols. According to Paul, Christians may eat such food, since there are in reality no idols. Yet if this gives occasion to Christians who do not have this knowledge of acting against their conscience, then those with a "strong" conscience rather must abstain from such food (1 Cor 8:10-13).

Active scandal in the wide sense is any conduct which gives rise to another person's sin, even if this conduct is lawful and justified. In this sense the New Testament speaks of the scandal of Christ and the Gospel. According to the prophecy of Simeon, Christ is the great scandal for Israel. "This child is set for the fall and rising of many in Israel, and for a sign that is spoken against" (Lk 2:34). He is the stumbling stone "that will make men stumble, a rock that will make them fall" (Rom 9:33; cf. Is 8:14f; 1 Pet 2:7f). Christ does not attempt to avoid the scandal caused by his teaching to the Jews. When they are provoked at his saying that it does not defile a man to eat without having his hands washed, and when the disciples caution him: "Do you know that the Pharisees were offended when they heard this saying?", he does not try to lessen the scandal. "Every plant which my heavenly Father has not planted will be rooted up. Let them alone; they are blind guides" (Mt 15:1-14). Christ must preach the truth and open the eyes of men, no matter whether the result will be that some turn away from him or are still hardened further (cf. also Jn 6:60-69).

The apostles equally do not try to avoid the scandal of the Gospel and of the cross. They are firmly determined to "preach Christ crucified, a stumbling block to Jews and folly to Gentiles, but to those who are called, both Jews and Greeks, Christ the power of God and the wisdom of God" (1 Cor 1:23f; cf. Gal 5:11). The Christian as the disciple of Christ must not be afraid of being such a scandal either. For in a world hostile to God, the message of the Gospel and the fellowship of Christ will continue to be a frequent stumbling block and scandal.

Churches and Christians must however beware of interpreting every criticism on the part of the world as a sharing in the cross of Christ and therewith close their minds to it form the start. Such a distance to the world "can too easily become a self-righteous defensive reaction against the God-given signs of the times and lead Church and Christian to rejection of the wider divine call embodied in current history in defence of narrower ecclesiastical interests."[1] Although it is true that the Church often shares the fate of Christ, she is not identical with him. She can be subject to deficiencies to which Christ was not. The criticism by the world must therefore move the Church to examine herself always anew whether there is a justification to it.

b) *Passive scandal* can be due to bad example, or it can be a scandal of the weak, or a pharisaic scandal.

The *scandal due to bad example* is the most frequent one. It is caused above all by sinful, evil deeds; thus the dishonesty of an official in money matters or his sluggish indolence in his work will induce the subjects to a similar usage and behaviour. This kind of scandal can also be caused by neglect of love and lack of true piety of those who should know better. This is the scandal of a specific legal minimalism and formalistic piety which hinders men to find the way to Christ or which makes them scorn the Church. Not only individual Christians but also Christian communities can darken the witness for the Gospel through their spiritual mediocrity.

The *scandal of the weak (scandalum pusillorum)* is caused by objectively lawful actions which however have the appearance of evil and are apt to disturb a weak conscience. The two examples from Paul's letters related above pertain to this category (Rom 14 and 1 Cor 8). A current example is the case of a priest or educator who wishes to see a controversial movie or show for the sake of information and in order to form for himself a judgment of its moral character. But since the parishioners or subjects may not understand his true motive, some may be scandalized by his action. For this

---

[1] Enda M. McDonagh, "The judgement of scandal," *Concilium*, nr. 107 (New York, 1977), 90.

reason he will at times have to omit attendance at the show in spite of his otherwise reasonable motive or rather attend it in a place where he is not known.

Pharisaic scandal is caused by rightful and even necessary actions whose provoking effect is due only to the malice of the person who is incited to sin. Since such was the nature of the scandal which the Pharisees took at the teaching and life of Jesus, it is called 'pharisaic scandal. Although not all scandal taken at great Church possessions is pharisaic scandal, the indignation at the possessions of the Vatican state is of this nature, if one takes into consideration the expenses the Vatican has in Rome and in the world at large. And the indignation of certain people at the construction of beautiful, solemn churches and the use of more valuable garments and implements for the liturgical service is of the same nature.

3. *Moral evaluation of scandal*

a) *Sinfulness of scandal.* Scandal in the strict sense is an offence against the love of neighbour. Although the scandal does not intend the sin of the neighbour directly, as this is the case with seduction, one nevertheless allows the temptation to sin, although one could and should avoid it. The scandal is likewise an offence against the good of the community, because it can weaken the consensus in it, e.g. in a parish. The gravity of the sin of scandal depends on the gravity of the evil to which it gives culpable occasion. Hence if the circumstances are such that only a light scandal is justly to be expected, the unbecoming action is not more than a venial sin even if somebody, because of his particular evil disposition, takes it as an occasion for a grave sin. No scandal at all is had if those who witness an unbecoming action are either so good or so corrupt that they cannot be depraved by it.

Accordingly scandal is always of a relative nature. Whether an action is a grave or a light scandal or no scandal at all is relative to the circumstances in which the sinful or uncommon action takes place. In principle it holds that a scandal is the greater, the greater the dignity or esteem a person enjoys; the greater the actual influence that an unbecoming action has on the sin of the other; the graver the sin which is occasioned; the greater the number of people who are scandalized.

Scandal culpably caused demands *reparation*. This is an obligation incumbent upon all who have scandalized, and of course especially upon those who have seduced others. Ordinarily this is done by avoidance of the scandal, by good example, by repentance in the sacrament of penance. Yet scandal caused by public statements, e.g. statements hostile to religion or destructive to morality, must be corrected by public revocation or correction of such utterances. Furthermore justice demands a special compensation for the damage caused by seduction which obtained consent by use of unjust means, such as fraud, intimidation, force.

b) *Permissible admission of scandal.* Not every admission of a scandal is devoid of justification. An obvious example is the fate of Christ. For the scandal can have its source in the sinful disposition and obduracy of those who take the offence or also in the moral weakness culpably brought on by the person scandalized. The following norms give orientation for the lawful admission of scandal.

(1) Rightful actions which do not have the appearance of evil, but which nevertheless give others occasion to sin, need not be omitted if one has a reasonable cause to act. Otherwise, for the sake of charity, one should refrain. Hence a priest should avoid going in priestly attire through certain streets of a town where people are known to be hostile to the Church, lest he provoke them unnecessarily to curses and blasphemies by his passing by. Yet if he has any good reason for going there, e.g. for the sake of visiting a sick parishioner, he can do so without hesitation. It would be likewise unreasonable to be compelled to give a large alms to a beggar in order to prevent his cursing, since others would soon imitate him.

(2) Lawful actions which have the appearance of evil and give others occasion to sin ought to be omitted if one can easily do so. However as a rule the obligation to omit such an action ceases after an explanation of the lawful nature of one's conduct has been given. In the same way, if the omission of the act would result in an unproportionately grave detriment and hardship, the risk of the scandal can be permitted. Nor may "consideration for human frailty in others be carried

to the extreme of jeopardizing our capacity for essential decision and joyful effort for the kingdom of God".[1]

Good works that are likely to be misunderstood should usually be omitted or deferred. Missionaries, e.g. in New Guinea, sometimes run little stores to provide their people with cheap goods for their daily needs, for which goods they must otherwise pay very much. But if this is misunderstood by the people as if the missionary were out for business and if this darkens his priestly mission, he rather ought to desist from the project and close the store.

(3) The observance of a positive law may be omitted to avoid scandal. Ordinarily however one is not obliged to do so. A wife or children may miss Sunday Mass if they can thus prevent an outburst of fury of the husband or father. For the same reason a man would be excused from going to Sunday Mass after a recent fight with some companions, if he knows that his presence at the Church would inflame the brawl again.

(4) For a proportionately grave reason it is lawful to afford an occasion of sin, if the action itself is either good or indifferent. Employers may leave money lying about in order to test the honesty of their employees. The same is permitted to parents who want to test and to correct their children. As a general rule it may be said that the more urgent the need is to test a person (e.g. army personnel or public officials), the more serious the means may be which are employed to carry out the test (e.g. offers of money in return for national secrets).

III. Impact of a sinfully distorted world

1. *Solidarity in evil according to Holy Scripture*

The Scriptures of the Old Testament see a solidarity of human groups (family, tribe, nation) in good and in evil. For according to the Semitic mentality the community is as primary as the individual. In a rather crude form this law of solidarity

---

[1] B. Häring, *The Law of Christ* II, 1963, 480. A Catholic private school may have common Mass and devotion for all Catholic children and give them common preparation for confession, notwithstanding possible protests raised by some people on the wrongly understood principle of religious liberty.

The Morally Bad Action: Sin 321

is expressed in a certain number of old texts which speak of collective and hereditary sanctions (cf. Num 14:18; Josh 7:19-26). An example of this is the menace which follows the prohibition of idolatry in the decalogue: "You shall not bow down to them (i.e. the graven images) or serve them; for I the Lord your God am a jealous God, visiting the iniquity of the fathers upon the children to the third and the fourth generation of those who hate me, but showing steadfast love to thousands of those who love me and keep my commandments" (Ex 20:5f). At a later period, the Bible itself will undertake the criticism of this older view. Jer 31:29f and Ezek 18:2-4 insist that the teeth of the children will not be set on edge because their fathers had eaten sour grapes. Every one shall die for his own sins. Still it is only the extreme presentation of this theory, a sort of blind automatism, which they reject, and both prophets insist on collective influences of sin (Jer 2:2-9; 16:10-13; Ezek 16; 20). The same is true of Isaiah who speaks of unfaithful Israel in a joint sense as a daughter of Babylon (Is 47). Hosea compares the Hebrew nation to an adulterous wife (Hos 2-5) and a disobedient son (Hos 11), whose sins will be punished by the Lord.

For the New Testament the world is so much distorted by sin that Christians are exhorted again and again not to live according to the norms of the world. For Paul the world stands opposed to Christ.[1] Sin reigns in the world (Rom 5:21; 6:12-14) and enslaves humanity (Rom 6:6.17.20). Christians should "not be conformed to this world" (Rom 12:2), so that they "may not be condemned along with the world" (1 Cor 11:32). To John the world has been judged because it does not accept the Son but hates him.[2] And James warns: "Do you not know that friendship with the world is enmity with God? Therefore whoever wishes to be a friend of the world makes himself an enemy of God" (Jas 4:4). That is why the Christian must "keep himself unstained from the world" (Jas 1:27).

Hence sin depraves not only the individual but depraves also the community to which he belongs and the world in general. That is not to be understood in the sense that the guilt of one person simply passes to the other members of a

---

[1] 1 Cor 1:26-28; 2:12; 3:19; Gal 6:14; etc.
[2] Jn 12:31; 15:22-24; 16:8-11; 1 Jn 5:19.

community. This conflicts with the principle that God "will render to every man according to his works" (Rom 2:6; cf. Mt 16:27; Rev 22:12). But sin "becomes incarnate in social structures, in value systems, in ideologies, in traditions, in habits, in collective behaviour, and in the mentality common to a group of individuals who compose a given society."[1] This leads over to the following reflections.

2. Man's situation in a sinfully distorted world

The modern behavioural sciences make us realize to what extent the decisions of the human will are influenced by a person's whole education and environment. This insight has also found entry in the documents of Vatican II. It notes down that man "is often turned away from doing good and urged to evil by the social environment in which he lives and in which he is immersed since the day of his birth" (GS 25). Social conditions affected by sin, also termed "social sin", induce those who live in them to choose lesser values and to act against authentic values - a tendency already present in humans due to original sin. Naturally deficient social attitudes towards values will also have negative repercussions on a person's fundamental option, just as of course constructive attitudes will have positive ones. This influence takes place in several ways.

There is first the impact of a demoralizing public atmosphere. Moral values are called into question and sinful ways of conduct approved or even recommended, if not theoretically then at least practically. This deprives men of the encouragement to do good; an encouragement which not only children but also adults need. Not seldom the example of the others equals an invitation to do likewise, e.g. to make profit by dishonest means or, among government officials, to seek bribes for services to be rendered.

The force of evil is intensified if it is accompanied by group pressure. In that case doing the good excludes a person from the group, which is hard to bear. The others, even though unconsciously, do not consider one any longer as a fellow member. The duty which a person believes must be

---

[1] Albert Gelin and Albert Descamps, *Sin in the Bible* (Tournai: Desclée, 1964), 27.

performed, does not belong to the current style of life. He is threatened with exclusion from the group and its support if he does not conform to its evil attitudes and demands. A youth who does not participate in drinking parties and join in watching bold movies will be shut out from the gang. A faithful religious life with weekly assistance at Sunday Mass will bar a person not only from antireligious circles, but readily even from circles who display religious indifference. Group pressure is of course strongest when the leading party of a country favours certain attitudes and principles which contradict justice and faith, like oppression of religion in countries hostile to the Church. Fidelity to one's convictions then includes serious deprivations in the amenities of life and in professional and social development. The extreme of such pressure is the threat of incarceration and death if a person should refuse to comply with the antireligious and immoral demands of those in power. This is the situation of martyrdom.

Finally there is the unconscious but all the more far-reaching impact of unjust social structures and mentalities. They precede a person's existence and encompass it. He is born in a situation where certain moral values and norms are obscured to the degree that they are no longer (or not yet) perceived by the community as a whole. The opposite, wrong attitudes and principles appear to be natural and a matter of course. This was true of slavery and the degradation of women in the Greek and Roman world. Caste systems, suppression of weaker or outlawed population groups, religious intolerance, conditions of economic and social injustice can affect whole nations and cultures. Nature itself is damaged by disrupted environmental structures. In many cases unjust and distorted conditions of this kind can be traced back to sinful choices of individuals and groups. Yet "to a certain degree, the changing of historical situations can create a situation of injustice where one had not previously existed, even without the apparent choosing of individuals involved in the structures through history".[1] Presently unjust structures, therefore, must not necessarily have their roots in sinful choices of men. But people may choose to perpetuate such structures for reasons of the benefit they gain from them at the expense of the less

---

[1] Mark O'Keefe, *What Are They Saying About Social Sin?* (New York: Paulist, 1990), 61.

privileged ones. Then these structures not only become unjust but sinful as well.

"It has become increasingly clear that efforts to help the poor and oppressed are blocked not so much by the ill-will of greedy individuals but by the embodiment of evil and its effects in established relationships and structures."[1] Especially the development of liberation theologies has advanced the recognition that sin and its effects become embodied in social structures, institutions and even worldviews. The need for liberation from oppressive structures was a major focus of the Latin American bishops at Medellín, Colombia, 1968, as well as at Puebla, Mexico, 1979. Structures of sin are likewise identified by John Paul II as roots of evil in today's world and obstacles to development.[2] Christian activity in the world must necessarily aim at the rectification and transformation of those sinful structures and mentalities.

Sinful social structures and conditions are sources of much injustice and evil. Modern men have become increasingly alert to them. The summons to fight them is a battle cry now frequently heard. There is need to expose such conditions and to correct them. However there is also the danger of shifting the cause of evil ever more to external, social conditions and to forget about the evil in man's own heart. All guilt is attributed to impersonal structures. "Accordingly one expects improvement and salvation not from the change of man but from the change of hardened structures and institutions, from a revolution of society."[3]

There is a partial truth in both positions. The failures and sins of men have created traditions and institutions depraved by sin, which now have their own existence and working mechanisms. Those born into them are exposed to them by force of the circumstances and influenced by them. This shows that the phenomenon of failure and sin is not sufficiently explained by personal guilt alone. Failure and sin have also features of doom and fate. Behind many a criminal there stand a social environment and a society which predispose

---

[1] *Ib.* 13.

[2] *Sollicitudo Rei Socialis*, 1987, nr. 36f.

[3] J. Gründel, "Das Verständnis von Sünde und Schuld in geschichtlicher Entwicklung," in *Handbuch der christlichen Ethik*, vol. 3, ed. by A. Hertz et alii (Freiburg: Herder, ²1993), 152.

and work upon the sinner. In order therefore to fight evil, it is not enough to turn against the sinner alone. It is equally necessary and urgent to work for a better public climate and more humane conditions of life (cf. GS 25f).

On the other hand it is an undeniable fact that social institutions are creations of men and upheld by them. Their existence is not simply fate; they can be changed by men. This presupposes a change of mind. But people may resist it for reasons of inertia or also for the advantages they gain from the status quo, even though at the expense of others. And as in the past, selfishness, greed, pride and desire for domination have been able to influence the institutions of society, so they remain operative also today. At all times therefore the reform and recreation of social institutions must go hand in hand with the reform and healing conversion of man's own heart.

Yet human exertion and good will alone are not always sufficient to discern and to counter sinful social conditions. There are limits to man's powers, which at times can only be overcome by superior intervention. "We see in the history of mankind certain thresholds beyond which a community seems unable to proceed by itself alone.... But we also see that the boundaries are broken and the thresholds crossed through the blossoming and expansion of moral feeling and of love which frequently derive from Christ and his message."[1]

---

[1] Piet Schoonenberg, *Man and Sin* (London: Sheed and Ward, 1965), 118. See there the entire chapter "The Sin of the World," 98-123.

Chapter VII

CONVERSION, VIRTUE AND PERFECTION IN HOLINESS

Sin in its multiform appearances is a frightful, threatening reality. Its vanquishing seems an almost insurmountable task. Inescapably people, whether believers or not, see themselves confronted with the power of evil and the question how to overcome it. "The question of perdition and salvation is the basic human question pure and simple; every philosophy and every religion together with its concomitant theology therefore attend to it fundamentally and in principle."[1]

The power of sin is clearly perceived by Christianity, just as before by Judaism. Human prowess is not up to the powers of evil. The biblical faith however sees the power of sin broken, and that through the salvific will of God and the redemptive work of Christ. The doctrine of God as the saviour of his people and of the redemption wrought by Christ pertains to the essential elements of the Christian religion. "The Christian proclamation is handing on the joyful message of the salvific will of God, manifested and turned concrete in Jesus Christ. In the sacraments the Church celebrates the salvation definitively dawned in Jesus Christ. In the daily activity the Christian is requested to live entirely in the light of this inconceivable gift."[2] In the encounter with Jesus the disciples witnessed how he went after sinners, preached God's pardon to them and through his mighty deeds and saving word overcame the powers of evil. Moved by this experience they began to proclaim with great confidence that in the life and death of Jesus the salvific will of God has conclusively been made manifest and become effective among men. The effect of the deliverance from the serfdom of sin is described in various

---

[1] W. Beinert, "Jesus Christus, der Erlöser von Sünde und Tod. Überblick über die abendländische Soteriologie," in *Schuld, Sühne und Erlösung*, ed. by K.J. Rivinius (Steyler Verlag, 1983), 197.

[2] Mauro Jöhri, "Vom Bösen erlöst?," in *Wie Böse ist das Böse*, ed. by H. Halter (Zürich: Benziger, 1988), 105f.

images and concepts, such as new creation, new life in Christ, divine sonship.

Salvation is a divine gift bestowed by God's grace. But it always also becomes a serious task. "In its roots evil accordingly has definitively been vanquished, sin forgiven, peace bestowed, yet now it is up to men to accept God's gift and to give way to it."[1] Reconciliation is offered and granted to men. The challenge now is to respond to and partake in it.

A. Conversion[2]

Man, who is estranged from God and from his true calling, receives the earnest yet joyous invitation to turn away from his evil ways and to convert himself to God's salvific will. "Repent, for the kingdom of heaven is at hand" (Mt 4:17). Although conversion necessarily entails sacrifices and renunciations, it is essentially not a dire must, but rather a joyful message to the sinner: the invitation to return to the home of the Father, the means for recovery from the sickness of sin, the way to salvation.

I. Man's need for conversion

1. *The call to conversion in Holy Scripture*

The *Old Testament* leads the sinner to atonement for his sins and prepares the way to conversion by various forms of cultic-ritual repentance. There were fasting (1 Sam 7:6; 2 Sam 12:16; Jonah 3:7), wearing of sackcloth and sitting in ashes (2 Kings 19:1f; Is 22:12; 58:5; Jonah 3:5-8), washings (Num 8:7; 19:7-10) and other expiatory rites (Lev 4; 16:20f).

However the external rites of atonement frequently drew upon themselves the criticism of the prophets, since the most important element in it, the interior change of heart, was for the most part left to one side.[3] This need of interior conversion

---

[1] *Ib.* 114.

[2] The theme of conversion has received special attention in the moral theology of B. Häring. For the history of the theme in moral theology, see Richard Bruch, "Die Bekehrung als Grundvoraussetzung christlicher Existenz," in *Moralia varia* (Düsseldorf: Patmos, 1981), 199-230.

[3] For example, 1 Sam 15:22f; Is 1:11-17; Jer 6:19f; Amos 5:21-24; etc.

is implied in the word *schub*, which is the term most commonly used for the reality of conversion. It has the meaning of changing one's route, turning about. "In a religious context, it means to be turned away from what is bad and to be turned toward God. That implies a change of conduct, a new orientation of the whole being."[1] The sinner is invited and urged to return to the Lord in order that he may be healed and live before him.[2]

The psalms return more than once to the theme of conversion, confession of sin and divine forgiveness (Ps 32; 38; 103). "The most perfect expression of these sentiments is the Miserere (Ps 51) where the prophetic teaching of conversion runs through as a prayer, in the form of a dialogue with God (cf. v 6): an admission of faults (v 5ff), a demand for interior purification (v 3f.9), a plea for grace which alone can change the heart (v 12ff), an orientation toward a fervent life (v 15-19)."[3]

Besides the demand of a personal conversion, there is also a call to communal conversion, addressed to the people as a whole. The prophetic preaching repeatedly refers to collective blindness, unfaithfulness to Yahweh and forgetfulness of the covenant. Therefore Israel as a whole is demanded to turn about and be converted to the Lord.[4] "Later prophecy interprets the whole history of Yahweh's dealings with his people as God's call to repentance and conversion."[5]

In the *New Testament*, conversion is one of the basic demands. The summons to conversion is at the heart of the preaching of John the Baptist. He calls upon his listeners to turn away from sin, to obey the commandments and to do works of brotherly love. By this change of hearts they are to prepare the way of the Lord and to straighten his paths. John's baptism is the outward expression of the inner readiness and desire for conversion. The Gospels describe

---

[1] "Repentance-Conversion," *Dictionary of Biblical Theology*, ed. by X. Léon-Dufour, 1988, 486.

[2] See Is 30:15; Jer 3:22f; Hos 6:1-3; Joel 2:12-14.

[3] "Repentance-Conversion," *l. c.* 489.

[4] See Is 29:13f; Jer 4:1-4; 31:31-34; Hos 14:1-4; Ps 81:8-14.

[5] Karl Hermann Schelkle, *Theology of the New Testament* III: *Morality* (Collegeville, Minn.: The Liturgical Press, 1973), 74.

it as "a baptism of repentance for the forgiveness of sins" (Lk 3:3 par).

The call to conversion equally stands at the very beginning of Jesus' preaching, though at the same time linked with the other demand of faith in his message and person. "Repent, and believe in the gospel" (Mk 1:15). The wedding garment that has to be brought to the heavenly banquet is nothing else than this interior conversion (Mt 22:11-13). Conversion is the condition for entering the kingdom of God. Jesus' call goes out to everyone, sinners and just alike, but especially to sinners (Lk 5:32). Two concrete examples of conversions of sinners are given in the stories of the penitent woman (Lk 7:36-50) and the publican Zacchaeus (Lk 19:5-9).

The parable of the prodigal son and other parables illustrate how ready God is to forgive (Lk 15). "Different from the Baptist, whose preaching is stamped with sombre earnestness, Jesus speaks constantly of joy in connection with conversion (Lk 15:7,10,32). It is, of course, true that Jesus also announces an unmitigated, hard judgment on those who reject this call to conversion (Mt 11:20-4; 12:41). Nevertheless God comes half way to meet the repentant sinner of good will."[1] Grace has a decisive part to play in the conversion of the sinner.

The apostles continue the preaching of the Lord on conversion, as can be seen from the Acts of the Apostles. "Repent therefore, and turn again, that your sins may be blotted out, that times of refreshing may come from the presence of the Lord, and that he may send the Christ appointed for you, Jesus" (3:19f; cf. 2:38; 26:20). Paul puts conversion at the beginning of the Christian life (2 Cor 5:20f). The Christian ought to detach himself from sin. He is led and requested to do so by the spiritual death and rebirth he undergoes with Christ in baptism (Rom 6; Col 2:12f). The idea of conversion is also evident in the demand to become a new creation and to live a new life. "You have died with Christ; put to death therefore what is earthly in you! You have been raised with Christ; seek the things that are above! Once you were darkness, now you are light; walk as children of the light! You are a new man now; put on the new nature

---

[1] J. Bauer, "Conversion," *Encyclopedia of Biblical Theology*, vol. I, 1970, 139.

created after the likeness of God."[1] Also for the Christian conversion remains a constant need.

The repeated call to conversion in the letters to the seven Churches in the Book of Revelation is bound up with the threat of tribulations, meant to induce even the most hardened evil-doers to repentance and make salvation possible for them (2:14-16; 2:20-23; 3:1-3.19f).

2. *Universality of conversion and its continuous need*

The whole history of salvation since the sin of Adam lies under the sign of conversion. The reign of darkness and the reign of light combat each other, and the struggle takes place in the very hearts of men. Yet after the redemptive death and the resurrection of Christ and the communication of the Holy Spirit, the battle is no longer undecided, in spite of the agitation and the malice stirred up by the demonic powers in the world. The struggle against the evil powers is accompanied by the optimism of Easter Day and of the victory of the resurrection of Christ.

The summons to conversion extends to every man, though not to everyone in an equal manner. It addresses in one way those who live far off from God and are caught in the alienation of mortal sin, and in another those who are basically on the right path, yet who still have need to correct more or less numerous shortcomings and imperfections. The conversion of those who set themselves goals of their own liking in contradiction to God's will and who imparted to their lives a wrong orientation must be a radical one. Their state requires a fundamental reorientation of their whole life and a new beginning. The persevering Christian is not in need of the same radical change of heart, nevertheless also he must harken to the call of conversion. That which began in baptism must attain an always greater depth and purity. The invitation to an ever greater generosity in the service of God and a more profound holiness accompanies the Christian throughout his life. The Vatican Council II accordingly declares that not only unbelievers are to be led to conversion, but that "to believers also the Church must ever preach faith and penance; she must prepare them for the sacraments, teach them to observe all

---

[1] Rom 6:4; 2 Cor 5:17; Eph 4:22-24; 5:8; Col 2:20; 3:9f.

that Christ has commanded, and encourage them to engage in all the works of charity, piety and the apostolate" (SC 9). The Christian wanders a spiritual journey from the imperfection of the beginning to the perfection in charity and holiness.

The necessity of conversion is however not limited to individuals alone. Often enough also communities and nations stand in need of it. Conversion "can happen to many and they can form a community to sustain one another in their self-transformation, and to help one another in working out the implications, and in fulfilling the promise of their new life. Finally, what can become communal can become historical. It can pass from generation to generation."[1] Many value judgments and attitudes to life of the individual are determined by the community, and in many instances the individual person is not able to change them, if they are wrong, unless the community as a whole supports such a change and undergoes a conversion itself.

II. Nature of conversion

Spontaneously conversion is seen as a change of heart and life by the individual person who has been in the wrong. But, as has been said, also communities may be called upon to show sorrow over injustices committed in the past, to detest them sincerely, to renounce them effectively and to promote God's royal dominion over all the realms of their common life. This likewise holds for religions and Churches, which may have reason to examine some of the traditions they hold or their attitudes towards each other (cf. UR 3f). Indeed, they even ought to be examples of continuous conversion. A study on the nature of conversion must pay attention to both aspects, the individual and the social one.

1. Repentance of past evil deeds

Sin as the contradiction to man's true calling, as alienation from the community with God and his people, and as endangering of one's salvation leaves the sinner in a state of forlornness and misery, at least in the long run. It affects him with humiliating distress of soul and dismal desolation.

---

[1] Bernard Lonergan, "Theology in Its New Context," in *Conversion*, ed. by W.E. Conn (New York: Alba House, 1978), 13.

This is pertinently described in the parable of the prodigal son, who left his father's house to live a dissolute life. But he ended up as swineherd, more miserable than the hired servants of his father. This pitiable situation caused him to repent of his sins, to return to his father and to ask for forgiveness (Lk 15:11-24; cf. Dan 9:4-19).

The state of misery, caused by sin, is most clearly made manifest in the dire passion and death of Jesus Christ. The cross of Christ confronts the sinner with the abyss of sin, but at the same time also with the infinite mercy of God, who wants to lead men to conversion through the death of his son and open to them the way of reconciliation.

The perdition in the state of sin, the loss of salvation and holiness, the alienation from God and from the community of his people are motives of true and wholesome sorrow. The sorrow over sin and over its bitter consequences results in detestation of sin as the woeful source of desolation and misery. The sinner pronounces the verdict of condemnation over his evil-doings and over his life of sin. Thus he anticipates the judgment of God and gives room to the divine forgiveness. "If we judged ourselves, we should not be judged" and condemned with the world (1 Cor 11:31f).

Sincere repentance over sin will necessarily lead to renouncement of sin or at least to the proposal and will not to sin anymore and to avoid it to the best of one's ability. This implies a breaking away from the state of perdition and the false mode of existence resulting from the wrong orientation of one's life towards selfish, sinful goals. The repentant sinner dismisses all lawlessness and injustice and submits entirely to God's commandment as the manifestation of his salvific will. Renouncement of sin is a conversion to the path of truth. The convert says "yes" to the truth of God, regardless of what it may tell him or demand of him. This leads over to the positive aspect of conversion, the renewal of one's life in love and holiness.

Decisive for a truly salutary repentance is the motive from which it proceeds. Contrition merely out of fear of being compromised and exposed to human sanctions is not a sufficient motive of effective conversion. Two motives of genuine, salutary repentance are distinguished by theology. Imperfect contrition, also called attrition, is that sorrow which proceeds from detestation of the moral disorder that has caused injury to a person's deeper self, from fear of divine punishment and from the desire for salvation. This kind of contrition has been admitted as legitimate by theology after lengthy altercations, but is considered - as the expression imperfect contrition already indicates - as less valuable. Perfect contrition on the other hand proceeds from a motive of love. "One is sorry for the past because people have suffered from it and because one has offended God. Such a contrition does not come from looking at oneself, but fully and entirely from looking at the other."[1] It is considered as that contrition in which full forgiveness is granted while, according to the sacramental theology of the Catholic Church, imperfect contrition (in the case of grave sins) essentially is in need of the sacrament of penance.

2. Return to God's salvific will

The Lord's call to conversion is misunderstood if one sees in it only or even first of all a demand for works of penance. Of course the sinner must renounce his sins and must possess the spirit of penance, which also disposes him to works of penance. But the very heart of the invitation to conversion is glad tidings, a message of good news. Conversion is the restoration of the first love for the God of the alliance (cf. Jer 3:12-14). It is the setting-out for the house of the father. "I will arise and go to my father" (Lk 15:18), says the prodigal son in his forlornness in the foreign land. And when he arrives home, he is accepted in joy and gladness by the father, and a feast of welcome is celebrated on his behalf.

The sermon of repentance as found in the New Testament, both in the preaching of John the Baptist and of Christ himself, is most intimately related to the coming of God's kingdom (cf. Mk 1:15). True conversion means to "seek first his kingdom and his righteousness" (Mt 6:33). Conversion brings about the restoration of God's regal authority over all domains of life and disposes the convert to work and to battle together with all men of good will for the victory of the divine reign. To be converted consequently means adherence to God's plan for mankind and for the world.

---

[1] H. Weber, *Allgemeine Moraltheologie* (Graz: Styria, 1991), 309.

Although conversion cannot be realized without sacrifice and efforts, its purpose and goal is a most positive one: the community and friendship with the Lord, the coming of his kingdom, the salvation of mankind. It is perfectly true that repentance is necessary in order that conversion becomes possible. But the painful and laborious element ought not to receive unilateral emphasis. "Fruits worthy of repentance" cannot be hoped for without sowing the seed of the gladdening joy of the return to God and the rebirth into a new life.

3. Conversion as social event

Conversion does not only signify a change in the inner attitudes, but also transmutation of the world in harmony with the reality of the kingdom of God. "For just as guilt and sin have social repercussions, so reconciliation and conversion must have implications for changing those conditions which render human life and coexistence more difficult or even impossible."[1]

Social conversion requires an awareness of the structures of injustice, which generate disadvantaged and oppressed sectors of society. This presupposes a process of conscientization. Liberation theology in particular has called attention to this need. "The more fortunate must have their eyes opened to the suffering of the poor through education and through solidarity with the poor which will sensitize them to problems they face."[2] The change of ingrained unjust structures will often involve confrontations between the old ways of thinking and the new ones. Yet the means used in the confrontations ought to be those of conviction by the spoken and written word, of protests and similar means of a non-violent nature. Violent resistance against the lawless tyranny of a totalitarian government can only be justified as a rare exception.[3] The

---

[1] A. Elsässer, "Sünde und Schuld - Umkehr und Versöhnung," in *Leben aus christlicher Verantwortung*, vol. 1, ed. by J. Gründel (Düsseldorf: Patmos, 1991), 182.

[2] O'Keefe, Mark, *What Are They Saying About Social Sin?* (New York: Paulist Press, 1990), 88.

[3] For the conditions of legitimate violent resistance, see *Christian Ethics*, vol. II, 1992, "The right of resistance against unjust state authority" in chap. X.

Churches are called upon to be a prophetic witness for the authentic values in a society blind to them.

The injustices rooted in social institutions must however not obscure the fact that structures are ultimately maintained by persons. They cannot be rectified, at least not in a lasting manner, without changing the hearts of persons. For Jürgen Moltmann a personal transformation without a change in conditions and structures is "an idealist illusion"; it ignores the fact that human beings are conditioned by the realities of the social world. On the other hand a change of external circumstances without an inner transformation is "a materialist illusion"; it sees in the human being nothing else but the product of social conditions.[1] The truth is to be found between the two extremes. "As there is a dialectical relationship between person and society, personal and social sin, so there exists a dialectical relationship between personal and social conversion."[2]

III. Conditions of conversion

1. *Admission of sin and guilt*

Humility is prerequisite to true knowledge of self, to true penance and conversion. Only the humble man has the courage to admit his guilt. Pride suppresses the humiliating fact of sin and guilt in order to appease and justify itself. "«This I have done», says my memory. «This I cannot have done» - says my pride and remains unbending. Finally - memory yields" (Nietzsche).[3]

Saint Augustine, the great psychologist among the Fathers of the Church, says very forcibly that the first step towards liberation from sin is "humility, and the second step is humility again, and third step is humility; and as often as you may ask, I would give the same answer, humility."[4] Humility enables men to perceive their true status in the presence of

---

[1] J. Moltmann, *The Crucified God* (London: SCM Press, 1974), 23.

[2] M. O'Keefe, *l. c.* 93.

[3] *Jenseits von Gut und Böse*, in *Werke* II, ed. by K. Schlechta (Darmstadt: Wissenschaftl. Buchgesellschaft, 1966), 625.

[4] Augustine, *Epistola* 118,22; PL 33, 442.

the all-holy God and to see themselves as they really are with all their defects and all their need of healing.

The Bible teaches the same lesson of the importance of humility for true conversion. In the parable of the Pharisee, who vaunted his virtues, and the humble publican, who with a contrite soul prayed: "God, be merciful to me a sinner," the publican is justified and pardoned by God, not however the Pharisee. And Christ concludes with the words: "Every one who exalts himself will be humbled, but he who humbles himself will be exalted" (Lk 18:9-14). The woman known as a sinner in the town is forgiven because she weeps over her sins in humble self-accusation at the feet of our Lord, washing them with her tears and wiping them with her hair (Lk 7:36-48). Humble contrition characterizes the prodigal son. He does not make excuses. He does not try to extenuate his guilt by pointing out that his older brother was not kind to him or that others are also not better than he or possibly have seduced him. He casts himself before his father and plainly confesses: "I have sinned against heaven and before you; I am no longer worthy to be called your son" (Lk 15:21).

Humility is indispensable for moral health of conscience and for moral growth. It does not lose its relevance even for those who are advanced in virtue and perfection. This is illustrated by the example of the saints, who in their deep humility still call themselves great and ungrateful sinners. The further a person progresses in love and holiness, the more exalted does the ideal of perfection loom up before him, the greater appears the distance between God's holiness and man's imperfect accomplishments. Yet this awareness of the distance from the ideal at the same time leads a person always further beyond himself. This is why the humble man is exalted, besides the favour he gains in God's eyes. "Whoever humbles himself will be exalted" (Mt 23:12). "God opposes the proud, but gives grace to the humble" (1 Pet 5:5). Such is the paradox that self-exaltation by pride drags a man down to that which is below and humility draws him up to that which is above. Pride abases the heart, but humility elevates the soul to greater perfection.

2. *Openness to the gift of grace*

Although conversion will not be wrought without a person's willing cooperation, it is at the same time and even primarily a gift of grace by God. It is a basic Christian dogma that every step to conversion is preceded by the interior enlightenment and movement of divine grace.[1] Of course the call of grace takes different forms and may proceed from external events or internal emotions. But lastly it must always touch and move the very heart of man.

In spite of the great importance of grace in the conversion of a sinner, its call is not compelling. The sinner can ignore God's gift and leave the invitation of grace unanswered. There is however no doubt that he exposes his salvation to great danger if he does so. Since "grace is God's gift, and not man's own property of which he can dispose as he chooses, the sinner must fear in each instance that the grace rejected may be the last. He must fear that God will offer no further grace of conversion, that He will withdraw from him, will not enlighten him so clearly, will not knock again at his heart so loudly and perceptibly."[2] Besides, rejection of the offer of grace is a defect of love and gratitude towards God. Hence to the psalmist's warning ear should be given: "O that today you would hearken to his voice! Harden not your hearts" (Ps 95:7f).

Even if touched and urged by divine grace, conversion has nothing of the automatic about it nor is it like the spontaneous growth of a plant. Conversion entails personal effort and combat against the powers of evil and against everything that may be described as "the lust of the flesh and the lust of the eyes and the pride of life" (1 Jn 2:16). "He who does not take his cross and follow me is not worthy of me" (Mt 10:38; cf. 10:34-37). Admission of sin and grief of soul remain sterile and ineffective if not combined with the sincere prayer "thy kingdom come" and with the readiness to struggle for the coming of this reign, first in one's soul, but also in one's environment and in the world at large.

3. *Spirit and fruits of repentance*

One of the signs of life is the fruit which it produces. Genuine conversion too must prove itself by the good and holy works it brings forth. The repentant sinner is expected

---

[1] Cf. DS 373-375; 1551-1553.
[2] B. Häring, *The Law of Christ*, vol. I, 1966, 399.

to "bear fruit that befits repentance" (Mt 3:8; Acts 26:20). It pertains to the essence of conversion, "that there is no repentance without acceptance of suffering for the guilt committed and the history resulting from it".[1]

Although works of penance should not be conceived as the soul of conversion, fruits of repentance ought not to be entirely lacking. According to tradition, the grand categories of penance are fasting, almsgiving and prayer. Fasting is one kind of mortification to which many other forms of renunciation can be added which a person takes upon himself for the purpose of saying no to indolence and disordered desires. Almsgiving stands for all works of brotherly love, without which the other forms of penance would remain insipid. Prayer is an authentic work of satisfaction if it comes from the heart. It includes the encounter with God in the sacraments and other forms of worship as well.

Parallel to the penitential works and in many ways surpassing them is the prompt willingness to say yes to the divine visitations in the spirit of atonement. In many instances the patient endurance of afflictions requires a much greater spirit of penance than penitential works. The remembrance of Christ's suffering will be an important source of strength for those visited by God.

Genuine spirit of penance will induce the repentant person to do everything necessary to repair the evil done to his neighbour and the community, a task which at times demands great sacrifice. Reparation must be made for the violation of love, for the scandal caused, for damage to our neighbour's honour or to his property. True conversion cannot be reconciled with the will to hold fast to unjust gain or any other profit of the injustice committed (cf. Lk 19:8).

The most important fruit of conversion is of course a new life according to the Spirit. According to Scripture, a person's faithfulness and love for God manifest themselves in fulfilment of his commandments (cf. Ex 19:5; Deut 10,12; Lev 18:5; Prov 4:4). "If you love me, you will keep my commandments" (Jn 14:15; cf. 14:21; 1 Jn 2:3-5). The convert is expected to show the fruits of ready faithfulness towards God's will and precept. This expectation is not contradicted by the fact that those converts who have returned from long

---

[1] K. Demmer, *Deuten und handeln* (Freiburg: Herder, 1985), 237.

estrangement from God or who live in dechristianized surroundings may still fall from time to time. Nonetheless the external conditions of a person's life are likewise not withdrawn from his or her responsibility. It is a demand of sober realism to shape them, as far as possible, in harmony with one's faith. There is an interdependence between the personal growth in Christian charity and liberty and the transformation of the community in the spirit of the Gospel.

The spirit and works of penance are necessary fruits of conversion. Yet the sinner also realizes that he can never fully atone for the offence committed by sin against God. Therefore he will take refuge in the cross of Christ, who offered the great expiatory sacrifice. In isolation the sinner can never give full satisfaction to God by his works of penance, but he can do so in union with the sacrifice of Christ. The leads over to the realization of conversion in the sacraments of the Church.

IV. Sacramental enactment of conversion

Conversion is a spiritual occurrence that takes place in a person's soul. Yet humans are also corporeal beings. Wherefore the inner happening of conversion tends to express itself in external signs, and is on the other hand also called forth and intensified by external signs. "In accordance with the corporeal-spiritual, historical and social nature of man, conversion has always, though in very varying degrees, a liturgical and social aspect in all religions."[1] In Christianity, the social dimension of conversion finds expression in the liturgical rites of the sacraments, which are manifestations of the spiritual events of conversion and sanctification and are the effective means of pursuing them.

The characteristic sacrament of conversion for Christians is the sacrament of penance. It is the sacrament of conversion for those who have gone astray and live in a state of grave sin. But it is at the same time the sacrament of the continued conversion for all Christians who are basically on the right path, yet still in need of greater purification. Conversion in this sacrament takes the outward form of a judgment by Christ, who is represented by the priest absolving. The sacra-

---

[1] Karl Rahner, "Conversion," *Sacramentum Mundi* II, 1968, 4.

ment requires on the part of the sinner repentance, confession of his sins and satisfaction. The penance of the sinner together with the saving cross of Christ bring sin to judgment.

The forgiveness through God signifies a thorough overcoming of guilt. This forgiveness is described in the Bible in a variety of ways. The sins become white as snow (Is 1:18); they are cast into the depths of the sea (Mic 7:19); God moves them far away (Ps 103:12); he sweeps them away like a cloud (Is 44:22); he blots them out (Ps 51:1); he does not remember them any more (Is 43:25). "What has been done, cannot be made undone, equally not all negative consequences are halted or annulled. But the very fatefulness of guilt, the abandonment to what is destructive and negative, finds an end and is turned to the possibility of a new beginning."[1] True, the forgiveness of God is not exclusively bound up with the sacrament of penance. But the sacrament helps in a significant way to attain conversion by arousing faith in the forgiveness of sins and by giving it expression. "The fact that the confession of guilt in the sacrament is bound up with the faith that God is a merciful God and ready to forgive lets conversion attain its goal and profoundly distinguishes such a confession, for example, from a talk with a psychiatrist or from self-communication in a group."[2]

If inspired by sincere sorrow and embraced as an event of God's holiness and mercy, confession is a genuine act of worship and adoration. It prevents harmful repression of sin and guilt. By its very nature sin tends to hide in darkness and to disguise itself as something good. But this is not a neutral process. Rather it is a source of spiritual disturbance, conflict and illness. Sincere confession brings the sin into the light. The sinner acknowledges it before God, before the community represented by the priest and, not least of all, to himself. This brings clarity to soul and mind and makes for internal peace. The personal encounter of the sacramental event is most deeply experienced in individual confession. Penitential services of the community on the other hand are suited to call attention more strongly to the ecclesial dimension of confession, conversion and forgiveness. They complement

---

[1] H. Weber, *l. c.* 312.
[2] *Ib.* 315.

individual confession in a fruitful way, although they cannot substitute for it entirely.[1]

The sacraments are means of sanctification, signs of the visible Church and acts of worship. As effective signs of grace, they complete and sanctify the efforts to conversion and to a more perfect life by the merits of the passion and resurrection of Christ. As signs of the Church, they are attended to by the Church community, incorporate into it, build it up and strengthen it. Finally, by their intimate relation to the redemptive work of Christ, they are essentially religious and cultic acts. They revere God's holy majesty, praise his mercy and are prayers for his graceful help. Their final goal and perfect fruit is a person's transformation into a child of God, the consummate community of the divine kingdom and God's eternal glory.

B. Virtue

Moral handbooks usually conclude the section on the general principles of moral theology with the treatise on virtues. Virtues constitute an essential part of a person's character, just of course as do bad habits. Indeed, depending on the right or wrong basic attitude of a person, the same per se good and helpful habits can serve good or evil ends, such as diligence, accuracy, orderliness, prudence, patience, self-control, courage. Admittedly habits of this kind remain psychically good qualities even if placed in the service of evil ends. Virtue however in the sense of a *morally* good quality must be directed towards what is morally good and as such presupposes the right fundamental option.

The word virtue comes from the Latin *virtus*, manliness. Already in antiquity virtue is a theme, and the word was always an important concept in the whole of occidental ethics. At present, though, the word hardly finds an echo. Just as the word sin, so also the word virtue has worn out. It is true that ethics of values and phenomenological philosophy have "been able to ensure that the idea of virtue did not completely disappear from discussion, but a reverberation of it in the

---

[1] See Alois Müller, "Die Befreiung zur Hoffnung. Wege der Metanoia," in *Handbuch der christlichen Ethik*, vol. 3, ed. by A. Hertz et alii (Freiburg: Herder, ²1993), 190-194.

general mentality is in practice not noticeable".[1] In recent times new endeavours towards the theme appear in theology and philosophy;[2] impulses also emanate from behavioural research and psychology. One discovers anew how much human beings are by nature inclined to the formation of constant modes of acting and how much they need them, and once again pays attention to the importance and vital value of habits and consuetudes, qualities realized in the virtues.

But, as already mentioned, good and useful behaviour patterns can also serve evil ends, depending on a person's fundamental option. This observation has probably contributed to scepticism towards the concept of virtue. Yet a general rejection of virtues and their formation certainly does not do justice to their value and need either. Even if certain useful habits can be placed in the service of evil ends, they remain useful and good in themselves. Their abuse is not met by discarding them, but by taking care to place them in the service of morally good ends.

In Scriptures, the concept of virtue is not a dominant idea however. Biblical ethics do not centre on the Greek and humanistic ideal of a virtuous personality, which aims at the perfection in virtues as the highest summit of moral excellence. Christian perfection consists in conformity to the image of Christ and in the new nature created after the likeness of God in true righteousness and holiness (cf. Rom 8:29; Eph 4:24; Col 3:10).

Nevertheless the notion of virtue is not alien to Holy Scripture. Although the word virtue is hardly ever used in the Bible (Wis 5:13; 2 Mac 6:31; Phil 4:8; 2 Pet 1:5 are the few places where it occurs), concrete virtues are mentioned and recommended everywhere. Justice, obedience, faithfulness, mercy, patience, trust in God, fear of the Lord are some of

---

[1] H. Weber, *l. c.* 323.

[2] Stanley Hauerwas, *Vision and Virtue* (Notre Dame, Ind.: Fides Publ., 1974). N.J.H. Dent, *The Moral Psychology of the Virtues* (Cambridge: Cambridge University Press, 1984). Gilbert C. Mailaender, *The Theory and Practice of Virtue* (Notre Dame/London: University of Notre Dame Press, 1984). Alasdair MacIntyre, *After Virtue. A Study in Moral Theory* (London: Duckworth, ²1985). Vukan Kuic, ed., *The Definition of Moral Virtue* (Bronx, N.Y.: Fordham University Press, 1986). Romanus Cessario, *The Moral Virtues and Theological Ethics* (Notre Dame/London: University of Notre Dame Press, 1991).

the virtues frequently mentioned by the Old Testament. They all appear again in the New Testament, complemented still by other virtues. Against the legalistic attitude of the Pharisees, Christ emphasizes the greater importance of the virtues of justice, mercy and love (Mt 23:23; Lk 11:42). The catalogues of vices in the letters of the apostles are paralleled with contrasting catalogues of virtues. The believers are exhorted to put on, as God's chosen ones, love, gentleness, peacefulness, patience, meekness, compassion, forbearance, self-control, sincerity, godliness.[1] In accordance with the eschatological character of the Christian message, virtues like vigilance, joyful readiness, sobriety, temperance, steadfastness are brought to the foreground. Yet above all "faith, hope, love abide, these three; but the greatest of these is love" (1 Cor 13:13).

I. Nature of Virtue

Virtue is a habit that gives both the inclination and the power to do readily what is morally good. Hence it is not enough to be inclined towards the moral value and to love it, although this is a very essential and indispensable element of virtue. One must also possess the dominion over one's spiritual and sensual drives and passions, so as to be readily able to do the good which one esteems and loves. The virtues are therefore qualities which benefit the person and increase his or her capabilities. "Not rarely one even sees in this the only content of virtue and its precarious limit: it is too much a matter of the subject and therewith the expression of an individualistic morality."[2] This danger exists indeed if the virtues are cultivated and developed too much in isolation from each other. They are in need of a common, deeper root stock.

Genuine virtue flows from the correct fundamental option. It must be grounded in the unequivocal and definite orientation towards the supreme goal, which is the glorification of God and the realization of his salvific plan for men and the world. Or more briefly, virtue must centre in the love of God. This orientation places the whole life of the soul in order. All the particular virtues are veritable only insofar as they are rooted

---

[1] Gal 5:22f; Eph 4:2f; Col 3:12-14; 1 Tim 6:11; Jas 3:17f; 2 Pet 1:5-7.

[2] H. Weber, *l. c.* 333.

in the true option and existential choice, which consists in the unwavering love for God and his will.

Just as the life of nature is elevated by the life of grace, so are the good natural dispositions and powers elevated by infused supernatural virtues. This is the common teaching of the Church. The Council of Trent says that in justification faith, hope and charity are infused.[1] According to the common opinion also the moral virtues are infused.[2] The infusion takes place together with the imparting of sanctifying grace.

What the soul and the powers of the soul are in the natural sphere, sanctifying grace and the infused virtues are in the supernatural. However the term supernatural "virtues" seems not to be the most appropriate and precise one. For not virtues in the strict sense are infused, but supernatural dispositions and powers, which correspond to the natural dispositions and powers of the soul. They do not give facility of action. They must still be developed through practice, in the supernatural as well as in the natural sphere, and acquire that facility which is distinctive of virtue.

Since through Christ's salvific work the whole person is redeemed and placed into the supernatural order, it is actually a matter of course that a person's whole being with all its faculties receives a new orientation and qualification for the supernatural life as child of God and as cooperator in his salvific plan. Karl Rahner is therefore quite right when he states that a concrete Christian ethics need not trouble about the distinction between natural and supernatural virtues. In the actual order of God's universal salvific will, it stands to reason that the natural virtues have a supernatural finality.[3]

Nevertheless the doctrine of the infused supernatural virtues points out an important truth. Virtue does not centre in the human person and is clearly distinguished from any ethics regarding self-perfection as the *ultimate* purpose of the moral effort. Christian virtue takes its orientation from Christ and finds in him its fulfilment. The doctrine on the infused moral virtues clearly reveals the source and goal of Christian virtue. The source is the Holy Spirit with his transforming grace;

---

[1] DS 1530; 1553; 1561.
[2] Cf. the Council of Vienne, DS 904.
[3] "Virtue," *Sacramentum Mundi* IV, 1970, 338.

the goal is the glorification of the Father and the imitation of Christ.

II. The prime virtue and the many virtues

1. *Primacy of charity*. All the great ethical systems conceive of one virtue as the principal one, which contains all the other virtues in itself. Whoever possesses this virtue in a perfect way, possesses with it all the others. According to Socrates, insight or wisdom is the principal virtue. Plato regards justice as the all-embracing virtue; and Aristotle, prudence. St. Augustine considers love of God as the queen of virtues. St. Thomas places prudence at the summit of the natural moral virtues, whilst he gives prominence to charity as the fundamental theological virtue. Kant proposes that the universal sense of duty is the basic moral attitude.[1]

In spite of the prominent place which prudence holds in the retinue of virtues, Christian ethics never failed to exalt love or charity as the most fundamental and universal. This corresponds to the clear teaching of Christ and the New Testament. According to the New Testament, the commandment of love is the first commandment, in which the whole law and the prophets are fulfilled (Mt 22:34-40 par; Jn 13:34f). Love is the greatest of virtues (1 Cor 13), "which binds everything together in perfect harmony" (Col 3:14). Vatican II takes up and continues this biblical teaching when it affirms that "the first and most necessary gift is charity, by which we love God above all things and our neighbour because of him" (LG 42). The all-embracing virtue assigns to all other virtues their proper place and prevents a unilateral and exaggerated emphasis of single virtues, such as unconditional obedience or uncompromising justice.

As true as these affirmations are, they still are in need of a further clarification. The critical question is, in what does this love consist or what is its aim? Is the purpose of this love the worship of God in prayer and religious rites, or is it the temporal happiness of the neighbour, or a person's self-realization, or the promotion of economic or cultural values? This question is often not given explicit attention.

---

[1] J. Gründel gives a good historical survey of the doctrine on virtue in the article "Tugend," *Lexikon für Theologie und Kirche* X, 1965, 395-399.

Nevertheless it needs to be answered clearly. Evidently the virtue of love may not aim at lower values to the neglect of superior ones. It must aim at those values which merit man's best efforts. Which are those values? They are the value of man's ultimate end and all the other goods by which this end is served and promoted. In harmony with the definition of the ultimate end, as given in an earlier context, the content and goal of the virtue of love must accordingly be God's glory and kingdom, the unfolding of his work of creation and man's salvation.

The principal virtue is perfect only if a person also possesses all the particular virtues comprised in the principal one. Charity is perfect only if a person is not only just, helpful and honest, but also patient, merciful, docile, grateful, etc. The perfect virtue of charity cannot coexist with any bad habit. In this regard, the Stoic proposition is true: A man has either all virtues or none at all. Still, true charity is nonetheless quite possible - though imperfect - alongside partial or even almost complete failure in some particular virtue, as long as this failure results from weakness and not from a perverted will. This finds its explanation in the wounded condition of fallen man. A person may suffer from certain psychic frailties, conditioned perhaps also by bodily defects, which render the exercise of the free will difficult. For this reason he may often not succeed in the mastery of his passions and drives and may succumb to bad inclinations. Nevertheless in the depth of his soul he can be dedicated to the good and dislike his failures and therefore possess genuine love for God. Wrong attitudes which result from deficient insight into the real demands of the moral value can of course also coexist with a basically correct fundamental option.

Totally incompatible however with the virtue of charity, even with imperfect charity, is a fully deliberate adherence to a serious vice. Such attachment would betray a mind which is not really concerned with the will of God and his goals. What has the likeness of virtue in such a case, e.g. diligence or thriftiness, is only a useful means in the pursuance of disordered, selfish goals, wealth or power for example, and therefore disordered and selfish itself.

2. *Diversity of virtues.* The distinction among the virtues arises from the fact that the principal virtue of charity has

to be applied to different objects, e.g. speech as means of communication, which demands truthfulness, or to commercial exchange of goods, which demands commutative justice.

According to whether a virtue has as its immediate object God and the divine realities or human beings and the realities pertaining to the created order, distinction is made between theological virtues and moral virtues. Tradition lists three theological virtues, which are grouped together already by St. Paul: faith, hope and love of God (1 Cor 13:13 and elsewhere). There are however still other virtues which have God as their immediate object and are therefore to be called theological virtues as well. This is above all true of the virtue of religion, but also of the virtues of piety, the fear of the Lord, and others.

Among the moral virtues four important basic attitudes have been singled out from ancient times: prudence, justice, fortitude and temperance. This quadruplet can be traced back to Greek philosophy (Plato, Aristotle), and the Wisdom Book of the Old Testament mentions it (Wis 8:7). They are called cardinal virtues.[1] St. Thomas groups around them as supreme species all the other moral virtues. However this scheme does not prove fully satisfactory, since certain basic virtues do not appear in this scheme, which cannot be reduced to the four, e.g. fraternal love, mercy, humility, obedience, gratitude. Hence the scheme of the cardinal virtues ought to be supplemented by still other virtues.

III. Fundamental requirements of virtue

1. *Moral knowledge and prudence*

A person's decisions can reach no further than the light of the knowledge he has of the moral values. He cannot develop a virtue unless he has at least some unreflective insight and knowledge of the value it endeavours to realize (*nihil volitum nisi praecognitum*). If orderliness, neatness, thriftiness, comradeship, godliness are not apprehended as values, no corresponding virtue can develop. Of course the neglect of these values in default of insight will not be a vice in the strict sense either, because where understanding

---

[1] St. Ambrose has given the four virtues this name, because they are considered as hinges ("cardines") on which the whole moral life turns.

is absent, responsibility is also lacking. Nevertheless absence of these values is a deficiency which is to be deplored and which ought to be remedied as far as possible.

Hence arises the need of proper education, instruction and formation. The child must be guided by his parents and educators to perceive the moral values and to gain an understanding as to why certain things are good and therefore ought to be done. Yet also in later years the need for such instruction continues. Entire communities may stand in want of education in certain values, e.g. fraternal acceptance of minorities, tolerance, industry, corresponsibility in public life, etc. An important role in the extended education falls to the Church. One of her prominent tasks is precisely the accomplishment of this mission in the preached and written word. Finally, individuals themselves are obliged to perfect their insight into the values of the moral order and to continue the formation of their conscience. For ignorance is an excuse only if it is not the result of superficiality, indolence or even bad will.

For the practice of virtue it is further imperative to apply the demands of the moral value rightly to the concrete situation. This is the task of prudence. Prudence disposes a man to discern correctly what measures he must take to realize the exigencies of a virtue as well as possible in the concrete circumstances. Prudence is concerned with the means proportionate to the end, as St. Thomas says. Again, this is a question of the right insight into the demands of the moral values. If this insight is lacking without one's fault, no sin is committed; but on the other hand neither can the practice of the virtue be considered as perfect. Because of this general importance of prudence for the practice and perfection of virtue, prudence is not to be regarded as one virtue besides many others, but as an integral element in the structure of every virtue.

The formation and cultivation of prudence requires first of all acquisition of practical knowledge, which is gained by the study of history and concrete situations (*memoria praeteritorum*) and obtained from the lessons of personal experience. Furthermore a man must learn to look carefully into the concrete circumstances, to appreciate the importance of cautious deliberation, and above all to accept advice. Nature has not been equally generous in bestowing the gifts of clear insight and good judgment on various individuals. Not all have sufficient common sense, even with the best of effort and good will. But all can accept advice. Those who are less provided with the gifts of insight and reason ought all the more to possess the docility which knows to profit by the counsel and experience of others. The more prudent one is, the less likely will one spurn the counsel of others.

All the valuable excellences of prudence, like practical insight, circumspection, cautious deliberation, docility, can also be placed in the service of evil, sinful goals. In this case we are confronted with the prudence of the flesh. Obviously, then, it depends on the love which prudence serves whether it is spiritual or carnal. Hence endowment with the good qualities of prudence alone by itself is not yet the certain mark of a virtuous personality.

However this cannot equally be said of prudence perfected by the gift of counsel. It makes a person attentive to the voice of God and docile to the guidance of the Holy Spirit. Wherefore this prudence is the sign of a spiritual person. It is already invested with love for the true values.

2. *Love of moral value*

There is a profound difference between the conceptual knowledge of the moral good and the devoted, effectual love for the moral value. The abstract cognition of something as good and the perception of the intrinsic reason why it is good does not arouse personal enthusiasm and does not yet beget virtue. The beauty and goodness of the moral value must be deeply sensed and truly loved, if a virtue is to develop. This existential awareness and active love of a moral value is much more decisive for the formation of virtue than the clear conceptual comprehension of the moral good. A simple peasant, with his simple understanding but deep love of God and of good, may possess the virtue of a saint, while theoretic moral knowledge is by no means yet the guarantee of a virtuous, holy life.

Love for the moral value is attained and fostered by the deepening and faithful pursuance of the right existential choice. Consequent continuation of the option for God's glory and salvific reign will necessarily lead to growing love for the good and to discovery of ever new values. Thus the existing virtues will be strengthened and the growth of new ones brought about. A further important means to attain to love of virtue is the concrete experience of its beauty and amiability, be it in the example of another person or a winning ideal in literature, theatre and film, or be it, usually at a later stage, through personal practice.

The greatest and most influential example for the Christian is the person of Christ. "This is Christianity's unique contribution to ethics: the identification of the moral ideal with a historical person; the translation of ethical theory into concrete terms in a real human life; the expression of moral obligation in the language of personal loyalty; and the linking of the highest moral aspiration with the most powerful motives of personal admiration, devotion, gratitude, and love."[1] Instead of the abstract rule, often offered by philosophers, "to act in accordance with reason", Christianity teaches its believers the concrete norm of the imitation of Christ. All through the centuries it has been a great moving force on the way to virtue and holiness for innumerable Christians.

Still it remains a mystery why the human will in some instances finds the strength to love the true values and to make the right existential choice, and why in other instances, in spite of sufficient knowledge and incentives, it does not find the strength and decides instead to follow the course of evil. One truth however must still be considered. The master of the human heart is God. It is in his power to change it. Men ought therefore to turn to him in humble prayer for his transforming grace and for the necessary help in attaining to the right love. Confident and persevering prayer is not the least of the means to be used in the pursuit of true values and in the education in love for goodness.

3. *Dominion over passions*

Traditional theology stresses repetition of virtuous acts as the means to acquire facility in doing good as the characteristic of the habit of virtue. Knowledge and love of value are certainly most essential conditions for the acquisition of virtue, but the realization of the moral value can still be impaired by insufficiently controlled passions. They can even

---

[1] R.E.O. White, *Biblical Ethics* (Exeter: Paternoster Press, 1979), 231.

suffocate the very love for virtue. Hence virtue presupposes dominion over the passions, and this dominion is to be acquired by repeated practice of moderating restraint or strenuous engagement.

Dominion over passions does not constitute the essence of virtue. The essence of virtue consists in love for the true values, which is the most decisive element. A person who adheres to this love is basically good, although not yet virtuous if he or she should still lack much in the control of the passions. On the other hand, a sincere love of virtue will always keep trying to gain mastery also over the passions.

The initiative in the bridling of passions may be taken by educators, especially in younger years, or by the individual himself. Parents doubtless render their children a great service if they urge and train them to dominate their drives and inclinations in a habitual way, e.g. to keep order in their belongings, to give precedence to visitors at table, to behave reverently in religious places, etc. The same is true for all educators of youth. Such training will spare the grown-up many troubles and additional efforts, since the acquisition of good habits becomes more arduous in later years. Nevertheless in every case adults have still to complete the work of the educators of their youth by the work of self-education.

The stress on repetition, mechanical exercise and consuetudinary habits is not seldom criticized, because it would favour superficial routine, bare of the qualities of real virtue. This criticism contains some valid truth. Good behaviour patterns are not to be identified with virtue. The essence of virtue does not consist in them but, as has been said before, in the love for true values. Yet the criticism is very wrong if it belittles and even ridicules the educational training and exercise in good habits. The habitual control over passions renders the practice of virtue easier and more efficient. No perfect virtue can exist without it. Habitual dominion over passions, too, is an integral part of virtue.

C. The universal call to perfection and holiness

The moral teaching of the past not seldom left the impression that striving after perfection was only the concern of a few more generous souls, especially of the religious insofar as they belong to the "state of perfection". It was assumed that the greater number of Christians would content themselves with a life according to the commandments without higher aspirations, and that indeed no more was required of them. Good deeds and obligations that go beyond the demands of the commandments were considered "works of supererogation". This understanding is above all based on the conversation of Christ with the young rich man (Mt 19:16-22 par). In answer to the question of the young man: "Teacher, what good deed must I do, to have eternal life?", Christ merely lists the commandments. Only when the young man replied that he had observed all these from his youth, Jesus added: "If you would be perfect, go, sell what you possess and come, follow me." Hence it was concluded, the observance of the commandments is sufficient for the attainment of eternal life. Further demands concern only those who want to be perfect.

This distinction and separation was also encouraged by the traditional approach to moral theology, which as a rule limited itself to the strict obligations and duties of Christian life and left the ideal of perfection and holiness to ascetical and mystical theology. For this reason moral handbooks usually do not include a chapter on the perfection of the Christian life.[1]

The express wish of Vatican Council II however is that moral theology should also "throw light upon the exalted vocation of the faithful in Christ and their obligation to bring forth fruit in charity for the life of the world" (OT 16). The Dogmatic Constitution on the Church furthermore dedicates an entire chapter to "the call to holiness" (LG 39-42). Basing itself particularly on Holy Scripture, the Council concludes: "It is therefore quite clear that all Christians in any state or walk of life are called to the fullness of Christian life and to perfection of love" (LG 40).

Since, then, the call to perfection is a universal one and since it represents not only a counsel but an obligation, it is certainly suited, if not imperative, to give some consideration to it in a systematic treatment of moral theology.

---

[1] Exceptions to this are Fritz Tillmann, *Handbuch der katholischen Sittenlehre* III: *Die Idee der Nachfolge Christi* (Düsseldorf: Patmos, 1949), 190-205; and Mausbach/Ermecke, *Katholische Moraltheologie* I (Münster: Aschendorff, 1959), 310-318.

I. Defective ideals

Popular opinion frequently conceives of holiness as the performance of more and more good works, zeal in religious practices, conscientious participation in parochial organizations and abstention from any vices. "Many today think of the christian life as meaning, first, a certain amount of church-going, saying of prayers, pious practices, and secondly, not breaking the commandments, which in practice boils down to not breaking the sixth commandment and the commandments of the Church.... Further, growth in holiness may easily be taken to mean piling up more and more prayers and pious practices and becoming more and more free of any sense-entanglements."[1]

Seen from this point of view, holiness becomes conformity to what is commonly accepted as good and pious in a religious community. The stress is then placed on exterior signs of piety and respectability. Certainly this exteriority must not automatically be dismissed as pharisaism. There may indeed be much real moral goodness in this kind of religiosity. "However, there will always be a certain lack of depth and a definite one-sidedness, an incompleteness that will make it impossible for such persons to attain to the full likeness of Christ, unless they can transcend the limitations of their social group by making the sacrifices demanded of them by the Spirit of Christ."[2] In persons with neurotic and scrupulous propensities, the emphasis on external conformity to social norms and ideals may result in types of moral perfectionism which psychologists often feel compelled to oppose on behalf of a person's spiritual health and authentic maturity.[3]

The misunderstanding here is the same as the one to which moral handbooks and rules of religious orders are frequently exposed. Their norms and guidelines are often taken as the sum total of what a faithful moral or religious life

---

[1] Gerald Vann, "Holiness and Humanness," in *Moral Dilemmas* (London: The Catholic Book Club, 1965), 32.

[2] Thomas Merton, *Life and Holiness* (New York: Herder and Herder, 1963).

[3] Josef Rudin, *Psychotherapy and Religion* (Notre Dame/London: University of Notre Dame, 1968), 203-228 (c. X: "Neurosis - Perfectionism - Piety").

requires of a person. In reality however they are only able to outline a general framework of the moral and religious life. Doubtless these norms and rules are truly obligatory for those for whom they have been laid down. But since every man or woman is not merely an instance of the general category of man or religious, but has also been gifted with his or her individual talents and charisms, they have also to attend to their particular vocations within the universal calling of all mankind. Being unique and unrepeatable, this personal vocation cannot be found in any general book of moral and spiritual theology. It can only be discerned by personal faithfulness to the promptings of the Holy Spirit in a person's heart. A holy person therefore is one who is guided by the presence and action of God and who lives up to his personal call.

The popular idea of perfection and sainthood is often still further corroborated by the conventional descriptions of the lives of saints and the works of pious art. They tend to idealize the saints, to retouch their weaknesses and to conform them to the popular concept of a holy person. Since the saints have the approval of the Church, her commendation is usually also extended to their biographies. "In this way, the Christian who devotes himself to the pursuit of holiness unconsciously tends to reproduce in himself some features of the popular stereotyped image."[1] He imagines himself in some sense obliged to follow this pattern.

Yet in order to become a saint, a man or a woman must first live a life in all the humanity and fragility of men's actual condition. "This implies a greater capacity for concern, for suffering, for understanding, for sympathy, and also for humour, for joy, for appreciation of the good and beautiful things of life."[2] To be in love with God is to be in love with his creation. Seeking the glory of God, the saint wishes himself to be nothing but a pure instrument of the divine will. That is the Christian ideal.

The striving after holiness is a kind of dialectic between ideals and reality. Ideals, which are generally based on universal ascetic norms intended for everybody, "cannot be realized in the same way in each individual. Each one becomes perfect,

---

[1] Thomas Merton, *l. c.* 18.
[2] *Ib.* 21.

not by realizing one uniform standard of universal perfection in his own life, but by responding to the call and the love of God, addressed to him within the limitations and circumstances of his own peculiar vocation."[1] Of course each one is called to serve God and praise him within the scope of the universal destiny of the entire human family. But he is called to do so according to his own, personal vocation and the requirements of his own, unrepeatable task.

II. The call to perfection in Holy Scripture

The call of the people of God to holiness and perfection is a doctrine characteristic of the Old as well as of the New Testament. "Be holy, for I am holy" (Lev 11:45; 19:2), the Levitic command enjoins in the Old Testament. In the New Testament this precept has its parallel in Christ's mandate: "Be perfect, as your heavenly Father is perfect" (Mt 5:48). What these two precepts summarize in brief formulas, shall be made more explicit in the following.

1. *The Old Testament.* The Hebrew words that are mainly used to express human perfection are *tom, tam, tamim*. Their chief connotation is sinlessness, completeness, blamelessness. It is to be noted that the Old Testament does not ascribe the attribute of perfection to God. God is holy; that is to say, he is of a completely other order than the beings of this world. One does not qualify him as "perfect". In Hebrew the word applies only to created, limited beings. If the Old Testament speaks of perfection in God's works (Deut 32:4), his laws (Ps 19:7), his ways (2 Sam 22:31), this remains in basic agreement with this usage.

When the God of holiness chooses a people for himself, this people becomes holy in its turn, i.e. consecrated and separated from the profane. At the same time a demand for perfection is imposed on it (Lev 11:44f; Deut 7:6). What is consecrated must be whole and without defect. The wholeness required from men consists in their religious and moral integrity. Yahweh must be served with a perfect heart in all sincerity and fidelity (Deut 6:5; 10:12; 1 Kings 8:61).

---

[1] *Ib.* 29.

The upright Israelite must be "blameless" before the Lord (Deut 18:13), which means to belong to him whole-heartedly, without practising idolatry, sorcery and other abominations (Deut 18:9-14). Of Noah we read: "Noah was a righteous man, blameless in his generation; Noah walked with God" (Gen 6:9; cf. 17:1; Sir 44:17). Exemplary conduct could be described in these terms. The righteous, God-fearing man "walks in integrity" (Ps 101:2.6; Prov 11:20; 20:7; 28:18). "To walk blamelessly" and "to do what is right" is the same thing (Ps 15:2; Prov 2:20f).

On the basis of the covenant, men are above all expected to keep God's commandments and to serve him whole-heartedly. "Take good care to observe the commandment and the law which Moses the servant of the Lord commanded you, to love the Lord your God, and to walk in all his ways, and to keep his commandments, and to cleave to him, and to serve him with all your heart and with all your soul" (Josh 22:5; cf. Num 15:40; Deut 10:12; 11:13).

In a particularly prominent way the demand for an entire, complete dedication to God is expressed in the great commandment of the love of God. "You shall love the Lord your God with all your heart, and with all your soul, and with all your might" (Deut 6:5). This love is a matter of the whole person. It demands a total gift of a person to the service of God. In short, it demands a perfect love.

As already indicated in some of the earlier scriptural references, the idea of perfection is often associated with "way" and "walking". The demand "to walk humbly with God" is a most eloquent expression of the covenant ethos of the Old Testament. "It contains echoes of the memory of the exodus when Israel set out on the way not only into the promised land but also into her own history with Yahweh as her leader."[1] Our minds must be open to this association when we meet such expressions in the Old Testament as "walking with God" (Gen 6:9; Mal 2:6), "walking in his ways" (Deut 19:9; 28:9; Ps 81:13) or "walking before him" (Gen 17:1; 48:15; 1 Kings 9:4). A person is perfect when he walks with God or in God's way, and avoids any way which

---

[1] A. Deissler, "Perfection," *Encyclopedia of Biblical Theology*, vol. II, ed. by J. Bauer, 1970, 661f.

is sinful and so leads him away from God. From this viewpoint, human existence before God acquires a dynamic quality and openness to the future.

In summary, the OT concept of perfection can be defined as whole-hearted service of God through obedient fulfilment of his commandments and faithful, undivided love. This ideal envisages the covenant people as a whole. It is therefore marked by a universal character and meant as a goal that can and should be aimed at by every member of the covenant people.

2. *The New Testament.* So far as the term goes, there are only two passages in the Gospels in which Jesus makes explicit statements about perfection. Once in the Sermon on the Mount we find the exhortation: "Be perfect, as your heavenly Father is perfect" (Mt 5:48; cf. 1 Pet 1:16). Since the preceding logion exhorts to selfless love of neighbour and enemy according to the example of the Father in heaven, who makes his sun rise and who sends his rain upon the evil and upon the good, it is possible to recognize that the perfection for which the disciples of Jesus must strive consists above all in whole-hearted love which takes its measure from God. How much this love exceeds the normal measure is shown by the fact that it is extended even to enemies.

The other text is the pericope of the rich young man according to Matthew's version (Mt 19:16-24). Perfection as understood here adds to the OT concept of perfection the demand of close, generous discipleship of Jesus, which prepares a man even to total renunciation of all possessions. As has been mentioned before, it has often been concluded that Jesus admits two standards of Christian life in this pericope: the state of the commandments alone, which is sufficient for eternal life, though not for the closest friendship with God, and the state of perfection, which is optional and reserved for more generous souls. Yet such an interpretation encounters the difficulty that in the general teaching of Holy Scripture perfection is considered as a goal to be aimed at by all. Furthermore, by the fact that the rich young man refuses to give up his riches, participation in the kingdom of heaven is gravely endangered for him (Mt 19:23f). Hence it seems that for the rich man observance of the commandments was not simply sufficient to attain eternal life.[1] Obviously not everybody is called to a life according to the counsels. The invitation to a life of poverty in closest fellowship with Christ addressed to the young man was a special call. The observance of the commandments mentioned by Jesus constitutes the universal condition for the attainment of eternal life. Everybody is supposed to fulfil them. But according to his individual gifts, each person has still his personal vocation. For some Christians this special vocation consists in the life according to the three evangelical counsels, for others in the adherence to other counsels, for others in the married state, etc. No universal ruling and law is possible with regard to the personal call. Only this universal rule can be deduced from the pericope of the rich young man, that everybody is expected to follow Christ in generous discipleship, ready to renounce everything that would hinder him to reach the perfection proper to his vocation.

Another text of fundamental importance for the idea of perfection in the Gospels is - as already before in the Old Testament - the great commandment of love, now enlarged by the inclusion of the love of neighbour. Even though the term perfection is not mentioned in this text, its formulation demands nothing less than a love which is perfect. The commandment to love God with one's whole heart and to love one's neighbour as oneself sums up the whole law. It is its perfect fulfilment (Mt 22:37-40; Mk 12:30f; Lk 10:27f).

According to John, love of God and of Christ manifests itself in the observance of the commandments, especially of the new commandment of fraternal love according to the example of Christ. "He who has my commandments and keeps them, he it is who loves me; and he who loves me will be loved by my Father, and I will love him" (Jn 14:21; cf. 14:15.23f; 15:10). The first epistle of John completes the thoughts of the Gospel and states explicitly that perfection in love of God is shown by keeping his commandments and by love of one another. Whoever obeys God's commandments

---

[1] With this agrees that the wording in the parallel texts of Mark 10:21 and Luke 18:22 has, instead of Matthew's "if you wish to be perfect", the phrase "one thing you still lack". The "thing" is the interior freedom in regard to riches, a freedom which would have permitted the young man to follow Christ unconditionally.

and "keeps his word, in him truly love for God is perfected" (1 Jn 2:5). And "if we love one another, God abides in us and his love is perfected in us" (1 Jn 4:12). John thus continues the teaching of the Old Testament with regard to faithful observance of God's commandments as the way to perfection; but he also goes beyond it by the emphasis on the new commandment of love according to the example of Christ, who is its model and measure. "A new commandment I give to you, that you love one another; even as I have loved you, that you also love one another" (Jn 13:34; cf. 1 Jn 2:6).

Here as also in other texts the person of Jesus Christ himself, whose life story is the object of the Gospels, becomes a new revelation of the meaning of holiness. By repeated demands to close fellowship with him, holiness becomes a challenge for all Christians.[1] "The stories of Jesus and about Jesus portray most explicitly what life looks like for one who is whole-heartedly committed to God. These stories show how the whole of one's life can become a response to the gift of divine love."[2] The life resulting from it is concerned not in the first place with self-perfection and humanistic altruism, but with the glorification of God and dedication to his kingdom.

For the apostle Paul, too, the will of God is directed primarily towards the perfect. "Do not be conformed to the world but be transformed by the renewal of your mind, that you may prove what is the will of God, what is good and acceptable and perfect" (Rom 12:2). "The standard of christian perfection may be considered from two aspects. On the one hand it is for Paul (as for Jesus) love, which binds all the other virtues together into one (Col 3:14).... From another point of view the standard of christian perfection is to be found in the glorified Christ himself; for in him is that goal which is to be set before the eyes of every man as 'perfect'."[3] The perfect Christian is the man or woman who attains "to mature manhood, to the measure of the stature of the fullness of Christ" (Eph 4:13). Paul is aware that perfection is a goal

---

[1] See Mt 10:38 par, 16:24 par; Jn 12:26; 13:15.34.

[2] R.M. Gula, *Reason Informed by Faith* (New York: Paulist Press, 1989), 186.

[3] F. Mussner, "Perfection," in *Encyclopedia of Biblical Theology*, vol. II, 1970, 664f.

which lies before him and which neither he nor his Christians have reached yet. "Not that I have already obtained this or am already perfect; but I press on to make it my own, because Christ Jesus has made me his own" (Phil 3:12). And he wishes that his Christians be equally minded and keep striving after the goal of perfect manhood in Christ (Phil 3:14f; Col 1:28f; 4:12).

The letter to the Hebrews regards the Christian life as the life of a wanderer with Jesus and to Jesus in heaven. "Let us run with perseverance the race that is set before us, looking to Jesus the pioneer and perfecter of our faith" (Heb 12:1f). Perfection is understood as a goal towards which the Christian wanders with Jesus as long as he lives.

III. Essence and universality of the call to perfection

1. *Nature of perfection*

The study of Holy Scripture has brought forth several aspects of the concept of perfection. Perfection is conceived as whole-hearted service of God, as faithful fulfilment of God's precepts, as selfless, dedicated love for neighbour, as close discipleship of Jesus.

Theological reflection further unfolds the concept of perfection in the light of man's ultimate end and the fundamental option for it. Under this aspect perfection can be defined as the most consequent realization possible of the whole-hearted option for God's creative and salvific will.

Option for God's will is a person's assent to God, by which he makes his own the plans God has for creation as a whole and for mankind and each person in particular. The concept of perfection can therefore be further unfolded as dedicated, whole-hearted service to the greater glory of God, to the establishment of Christ's kingdom, and to the universal welfare and development of fellow-men. Perfection finally consists in the thorough development of the personal abilities and graces required for the efficient fulfilment of one's role in the Mystical Body. All these aspects and dimensions are comprised in the unreserved decision for the divine will. They are assured, advanced and realized in a life that has attained to perfection.

Perfection is a goal towards which the Christian has to strive, which however as a goal is not a possession from the beginning. Even St. Paul judges of himself, in the letter to the Philippians, that he has not yet obtained the goal of perfection, but is still pressing on to it (Phil 3:12-14). Hence one ought not to expect prematurely perfection from oneself or from others; and one ought not to be discouraged by the perception of one's shortcomings and imperfections. This in fact is the normal condition of human life. Reason to be frightened exists only when a person ceases to strive further and is no longer willing to take upon himself the efforts of continued progress and growth. But as long as a person proceeds on the way of holiness, he complies with the calling to be perfect, even though he actually still falls short of the ideal.

Hence the call to perfection must be understood as dynamic, not as static, in the sense that one is expected not to be perfect already here and now, but rather to keep striving towards the appointed goal. For this reason "the Christian, in virtue of his vocation to perfection, is not always obliged to do that which is more perfect in itself".[1] His obligation is to take that step which at the present moment corresponds to his growth and moral strength.

Perfection can also be called dynamic in the sense that even where a person has attained the goal of a mature character, he must still realize his virtue in always new tasks. He must try to be open for the new requirements of the times. From this point of view, human life can rightly be described with Holy Scripture as a "walking" in God's ways and wayfaring with the Lord.

Holiness, it must be noted, is not primarily a matter of a technique. The difficulty with the "language of growth and progress in the Christian life is that it can very easily be taken in a moralistic sense suggesting that by a rather mechanical stacking of one good act (work) on another we are somehow made better and better".[2] Growth in holiness consists in an always deeper union with the mind of Christ as the

---

[1] B. Häring, *Toward a Christian Moral Theology* (Notre Dame, Ind.: University of Notre Dame, 1966), 27.

[2] S. Hauerwas, *Character and the Christian Life* (San Antonio: Trinity University, 1985), 218f.

source and inspiration of one's conduct and way of life. "To be formed in Christ, to be sanctified, is to be committed to bringing every element of our character into relation with this dominant orientation. This is our integrity, when everything that we believe, do, or do not do, has been brought under the dominion of our primary loyalty to God."[1]

Holiness, furthermore, is not a merely individual affair. It is primarily a gift of grace, which is mediated through the Church as the community of the people of God. For it pleased God "to make men holy and save them, not as individuals without any bond or link between them, but rather to make them into a people who might acknowledge him and serve him in holiness" (LG 9). He therefore chose the race of Israel as his people and made it holy unto himself. This was done by way of preparation for the more perfect covenant in Christ, who founded the Church as the new people of God. Individual holiness is participation in the holiness of the Church, which she has received through Christ from God. Hence everybody belonging to the Church is sanctified in his innermost being. But it remains every person's personal task to live up to this existential holiness in concrete, daily life. The divine gift of sanctifying grace must find personal expression and development in a corresponding striving for perfection.

2. Universality of the call to perfection

The universal call to holiness and perfection is a particular concern of the Dogmatic Constitution on the Church of Vatican II. It states most clearly that "all the faithful, whatever their condition or state - though each in his own way - are called by the Lord to that perfection of sanctity by which the Father himself is perfect" (LG 11). All the members of God's people have the same filial grace and the same vocation to perfection, although not everybody is to proceed by the same path to this goal (LG 32). Not content with pronouncements of a brief nature, the Council Fathers dedicate an entire chapter to the subject, as already mentioned, entitled: "The call to holiness" (LG 39-42, chap. V). They leave no doubt that according to their conviction "the Lord Jesus, divine teacher and model of all perfection, preached holiness of life (of

---

[1] *Ib.* 222f.

which he is the author and maker) to each and every one of his disciples without distinction" (LG 40).

The reason for such emphasis must be sought in the above-mentioned doctrines and theological interpretations of the past, which used to distinguish between ordinary Christians, who live a modest life according to the commandments without higher aspirations, and the more generous souls, who do more than is their strict obligation and follow Christ's call to perfection. Particularly the religious life according to the three evangelical counsels and the priestly life of celibacy were considered as the embodiment of the more perfect fellowship with Christ; while the laity in the world were regarded as the ordinary Christians, who live life according to the commandments only. This led to an overemphasis on the religious and clerical state within the Church and to an undervaluation of the calling of the laity. The inadequacy of this theological and ascetic teaching was strongly felt by the Council and a correction set about.

Apart from the controverted passage on the rich young man, there is no doubt that the biblical call to perfection always addresses all the members of the chosen people and of the Christian community. Everybody is required to love God with his whole heart, to love his neighbour as himself and to be perfect in his love (Mt 5:48; 22:37-40 par; 1 Jn 2:5). All the Christians are summoned to live "as is fitting among saints" (Eph 5:3).

Theological reason leads to the same conclusion. God created man to make manifest in him and through him his glory. He wanted him to be a cooperator of his divine salvific plans. Since this task is the very reason for man's existence, he ought to live totally for it. He should perform it with all the abilities he possesses, as well as he can, and as a faithful servant of the Lord. This concerns not only Christians but all mankind. All men are called to bring the work of the creator and redeemer to completion.

The chief commandment of love of God and neighbour is most clearly revealed in Scripture, but also outside of Christian revelation men have been able to arrive at the knowledge of it. Sincere love does not set itself limits in charity, but wants to do as much good as is in its powers. The precept of love, writes St. Thomas, "is not confined by any limits, so that a certain degree of love would come under the commandment; a greater degree, which exceeds the limits of the commandment, would be only a counsel; on the contrary, everyone is commanded to love God as well as he can."[1] With growing intellectual, psychological and religious maturity, an ever more perfect love is not only regarded as desirable in a person but is expected from him.

The Dogmatic Constitution on the Church sees men's call to perfection grounded above all in their existential consecration by the grace of God. God wants all men to be sanctified by his Spirit and to be partakers of the divine nature. All "followers of Christ, called by God not in virtue of their works but by his design and grace, and justified in the Lord Jesus, have been made sons of God in the baptism of faith and partakers of the divine nature, and so are truly sanctified. They must therefore hold on to and perfect in their lives that sanctification which they have received from God" (LG 40).

The call to holiness is common for all, but the way to perfection is manifold and of greatest variety. Every person receives his individual measure of grace. God has given each one his own law of life according to the task assigned to him in the creator's divine plans and the work of salvation. In other words, each person has his own vocation. Vatican II states that each one "according to his own gifts and duties must steadfastly advance along the way of a living faith" (LG 41).

The individual realization of the common call to holiness depends on the personal gifts in the order of nature and grace, on the concrete circumstances and conditions of one's life, and on the personal guidance by the Holy Spirit. To find his true vocation, a person must be vigilant and open towards the call of grace in his heart. A life under "the perfect law, the law of liberty" (Jas 1:25; 2:12), requires confident docility to the Spirit of Christ and high-minded response to his inspirations.

IV. Pathways to holiness

Speaking of the ways to holiness, Vatican II writes that the first and most necessary gift is charity. Charity needs care

---

[1] *Contra retrahentes*, cap. VI; *Opuscula omnia* IV, ed. by P. Mandonnet (Paris, 1927), 276.

and unfolding. "If charity is to grow and fructify in the soul like a good seed, each of the faithful must willingly hear the word of God and carry out his will with deeds, with the help of his grace; he must frequently partake of the sacraments, chiefly the Eucharist, and take part in the liturgy; he must constantly apply himself to prayer, self-denial, active brotherly service and the practice of all virtues" (LG 42).

Holiness is not merely the absence of sin. Primarily it is creative love in the service of the kingdom of God. "It can be said that our holiness is proportioned to our capacity to serve as instruments of his love in establishing his kingdom and building up his Mystical Body."[1] Charity as the constitutive element of holiness is not possible without an interior poverty of spirit, which enables a person to practise solidarity with the unfortunate and dispossessed, and this in an efficient way. "A shortsighted and perverse notion of charity leads Christians simply to perform token acts of mercy, merely symbolic acts expressing good will. This kind of charity has no real effect in helping the poor."[2] The disciples must grasp the deep sense of charity which inspired Christ, in order to understand the full depths of Christian perfection.

Moreover, since holiness requires vigilant openness to the call of grace and the guidance of the Holy Spirit, it presupposes the spirit of prayer. The entire Christian life ought to be a permanent listening to God's invitation and call. The spirit of prayer includes the meditation on the word of God in Holy Scripture, participation in the liturgical life and the sacraments of the Church. The sacraments are mystical signs in which God works and which awaken our hearts and our minds to respond to God's action in our lives.

The liturgy links the believer to the community of God's people. Life in and with the Church is another requirement for growth in holiness and perfection. "just as God did not create men to live as individuals but to come together in the formation of social unity, so he willed to make men holy" in the common bond of "the family of God, in which love would be the fullness of the law" (GS 32). "We learn discipleship by being initiated

---

[1] Thomas Merton, *l. c.* 112.

[2] *Ib.* 116.

into it by others. Discipleship, life character, is a community achievement. To be like Jesus requires that we become part of a community pledged to be faithful to him."[1] With its heritage of ritual and religious images the Church is an indispensable point of reference for acquiring moral character and for the mould of Christian holiness.

Yet prayer and liturgy are not the only cornerstones of holiness. Faithful fulfilment of one's temporal duties is another. "In their pilgrimage to the heavenly city Christians are to seek and relish the things that are above: this involves not a lesser, but rather a greater commitment to working with all men towards the establishment of a world that is more human" (GS 57). The dichotomy of many between the faith which they profess and the practice of their daily lives is for the Council Vatican II one of the gravest errors of our time. It vigorously opposes the "pernicious opposition between professional and social activity on the one hand and religious life on the other" (GS 43). The one must be attended to without neglecting the other.

Christian perfection is the holiness of Christ in us. This is the ideal. But the full realization of the ideal stands at the end of a life and not at its beginning. We observe this in the lives of the apostles, who had to go a long way with Jesus, before they were entirely transformed by his spirit. The capacities of the different persons are different and so is their measure of freedom. Morals always again stands under the suspicion of being hard and overbearing, "without a feeling for the reality of life and without regard for the often very diverse and not always particularly great moral force of the individual. A standard of action is set which, if at all, only few can reach."[2] It is true that moral theology cannot dispense with setting down norms, because it is its task to give orientations for a well-integrated life, for a social life in justice and peace, and for the care of creation. There are basic demands which are inalienable, since the opposite would result in anguishing consequences for all concerned. But there are also gradations in moral life, where moral theology and the tolerance of fellow beings must grant a certain latitude.

---

[1] R.M. Gula. *l. c.* 197.
[2] H. Weber, *Allgemeine Moraltheologie* (Graz: Styria, 1991), 339.

Pastoral guidance must take the principle of gradualness into account. To be sure, it will not abandon the accepted moral standards of the community and not lose the ideal out of sight. Nevertheless it will have to respect the limited capacities of individual persons to embody the values upheld by the norms. Even though certain actions must be considered objectively (or materially) sinful, a person may not necessarily be subjectively guilty for doing them. The necessary freedom and insight may be lacking or just a sufficient evaluative knowledge may be missing. This is an accepted rule of moral theology past and present.[1]

Moral theology endeavours to give orientation for a meaningful, successful and therewith ultimately also felicitous life. In the train of the Gospel, Christian ethics wants to show "the way of salvation" (Acts 16:17). In the practical pursuit of this goal, however, we must know how to begin at the lowest rung of the ladder and climb step by step towards the summit, always with the help of the grace of God. This striving requires as a final virtue the virtue of perseverance. It is not hard to make a good start. But it is hard to continue, to carry on the work begun, and to persevere in it through many years until the end. The challenges of the monotony of daily routine and drudgery are the fire that tests the gold of a saintly life. "We are not 'converted' only once in our life but many times, and this endless series of large and small 'conversions', inner revolutions, leads finally to our transformation in Christ."[2]

---

[1] A helpful exposition on the question of pastoral moral guidance is found in R.M. Gula, *l. c.* 306-313.

[2] Thomas Merton, *l. c.* 158f.

BIBLIOGRAPHY

Manuals and dictionaries

Becker, L. C. and C. B., eds. *Encyclopedia of Ethics*, 3 vols. New York: Routledge Chapman & Hall, 2001, revised edition.

Gill, Robin. *A Textbook of Christian Ethics*. London/New York: T & T Clark, 2006, updated third edition (Anglican).

Grisez, Germain. *The Way of the Lord Jesus*, 3 vols. Chicago: Franciscan Herald Press, 1983, 1993, 1997.

Gustafson, James M. *Ethics from a Theocentric Perspective*, 2 vols. Chicago: University of Chicago Press, 1981 and 1984 (Protestant).

Häring, Bernard. *Free and Faithful in Christ. Moral Theology for Priests and Laity*, 3 vols. Middlegreen, England: St. Paul Publ., 1978-81.

Harrison, R. K., ed. *Encyclopedia of Biblical and Christian Ethics*. Appleton, Wis.: Nelson, 1987.

Kennedy, Terence. *Doers of the Word. Moral theology for hurnaniiy in the third millennium*, 2 vols. Middlegreen, Slough: St. Pauls, 1996 and 2002.

Macquarrie, John, and Childress, James. *A New Dictionary of Christian Ethics*. London: SCM, 1990, new edition (Anglican).

McClendon, James. *Systematic Theology. Ethics*. Nashville, Tenn.: Abington Press, 2002, 2nd edition (Protestant).

Pazhayampallil, Thomas. *Pastoral Guide: Moral-Canonical-Liturgical*, 2 vols. Bangalore: Kristu Jyothi College, 1996, revised edition.

Rendtorff, Trutz. *Ethics*, 2 vols. Philadelphia: Fortress Press, 1986 and 1989 (Protestant).

Sacramentum Mundi. An Encyclopedia of Theology, ed. by Karl Rahner et alii, 6 vols. London: Burns and Oates, 1968-70.

Vidal, Marciano. *Moral de Actitudes*, 4 vols. Madrid: PS, 1990-91, 6th printing.

Biblical ethics

Birch, Bruce C., and Rasmussen, Larry L. *Bible and ethics in the Christian life*. Minneapolis: Augsburg Publ. House, 1989, revised edition.

Birch, Bruce C. *Let Justice Roll Down. The Old Testament Ethics and Christian Life*. Louisville, Ken.: Westminster/John Knox Press, 1991.

Chilton, Bruce, and McDonald, J.I.H. *Jesus and the Ethics of the Kingdom*. London: SPCK, 1987.

Collins, Raymond F. *Christian Morality: Biblical Foundations*. Notre Dame, Ind.: University of Notre Dame Press, 1986.

Curran, Charles E., and McCormick, Richard A., eds. *Readings in Moral Theology 4: The Use of Scripture in Moral Theology*. New York: Paulist Press, 1984.

Dictionary of Biblical Theology, ed. by X. Léon-Dufour. London: G. Chapman, 1988, reprinted with revisions.
Encyclopedia of Biblical Theology, ed. by Johannes Bauer, 3 vols. London: Sheed and Ward, 1969.
Gallagher, John. *The Basis for Christian Ethics*. New York: Paulist Press, 1985.
Harvey, Nicholas Peter. *The Morals of Jesus*. London: Darton, Longman and Todd, 1991.
Lohse, Eduard. *Theological Ethics of the New Testament*. Minneapolis, Minn.: Fortress Press, 1991.
Schnackenburg, Rudolf. *The Moral Teaching of the New Testament*. London: Burns & Oates, 1967, 4th printing.
Schrage, Wolfgang. *The Ethics of the New Testament*. Philadelphia: Fortress Press, 1988.
Spohn, William C. *What Are They Saying About Scripture and Ethics*. New York: Paulist Press, 1984.

Fundamental moral theology, general works

Beach, Waldo. *Christian Ethics in the Protestant Tradition*. Atlanta, Ga.: Knox Press, 1988.
Böckle, Franz. *Fundamental Moral Theology*. New York: Pueblo Publ. Co., 1980.
Colling, Raymond F. *Christian Morality*. Notre Dame, Ind.: Notre Dame University Press, 1986.
Curran, Charles E. *Directions in Fundamental Moral Theology*. Dublin: Gill and Macmillan, 1986.
Frankena, William K. *Ethics*. Englewood Cliffs, N.J.: Prentice Hall, ^{2}1973. (Discusses in a concise way the various theories of ethics.)
Fuchs, Josef. *Personal Responsibility and Christian Morality*, 1983.
idem. *Christian Ethics in a Secular Arena*, 1984.
idem. *Christian Morality: The Word Becomes Flesh*, 1987.
idem. *Moral Demands and Personal Obligations*, 1993; all four books collected essays published by Georgetown Univ., Washington.
Gauthier, D. *Morals by Agreement*. Oxford: Clarendon Press, 1988.
Gula, Richard M. *Reason Informed by Faith. Foundations of Catholic Morality*. New York: Paulist Press, 1989.
Keeling, Michael. *The Foundations of Christian Ethics*. Edinburgh: T. & T. Clark, 1990.
Kennedy, Terence. *Doers of the Word. Moral theology for humanity in the third millenium*. Middlegreen, Slough: St. Pauls, 1996.
Lobo, George V. *Guide to Christian Living. A New Compendium of Moral Theology*, Theological Publications in India, Bangalore 1995. Westminster: Christian Classics, ^{5}1989; Anand, India: Gujarat Sahitya Prakash, 1985.
MacNamara, Vincent. *The Truth in Love. Reflections on Christian Morality*. Dublin: Gill and Macmillan, ^{2}1989.
May, William. *An Introduction to Moral Theology*. Huntington, Ind.: Our Sunday Visitor, 1991.

O'Connell, Timothy E. *Principles for a Catholic Morality*. San Francisco: Harper & Row, 1990, revised edition.
O'Donovan, Oliver. *Resurrection and Moral Order. An Outline for Evangelical Ethics*. Leicester, England: Apollos, ²1994 (Anglican).
O'Keefe, Martin. *Known from the Things that Are. Fundamental Theory of the Moral Life*. Houston: Center for Thomistic Studies, 1987.
Outka, Gene Harold, and Reeder, John P. Jr., eds., *Prospects of a Common Morality*. Princeton, N.J.; Princeton Univ. Press, 1993.
Spaemann, Robert. *Basic Moral Concepts*. London/New York: Routledge, 1989.
Williams, Bernard. *Morality. An Introduction to Ethics*. New York: Cambridge Univ. Press, ²1993.

Natural moral law, morality of law

Cronin, Kieran. *Rights and Christian Ethics*. Cambridge Univ. Press, 1993.
Crowe, Michael B. *The Changing Profile of Natural Law*. The Hague: Martinus Nihoff, 1977.
Curran, Charles E., and McCormick, Richard A., eds. *Readings in Moral Theology, No. 1: Moral Norms and Catholic Tradition*. New York: Paulist Press, 1979.
idem. *Readings in Moral Theology No. 2: The Distinctiveness of Christian Ethics*. New York: Paulist Press, 1980.
idem. *Readings in Moral Theology No. 7: Natural Law and Theology*. New York: Paulist Press, 1991.
Finnis, John. *Natural Law and Natural Rights*. Oxford: Clarendon Press, ²1989.
idem. *Moral Absolutes. Tradition, Revision and Truth*. Washington: Catholic University of America, 1991.
George, Robert P., ed., *Natural Law Theory. Contemporary Essays*. Oxford: Clarendon Press, 1992.
Greenawalt, Kent. *Conflicts of Law and Morality*. Oxford: Oxford University Press, 1989.
Lucien, Richard. *Is there a Christian ethics?* New York, N.J.: Paulist Press, 1988.
Messner. Johannes. *Social Ethics. Natural Law in the Western World*. St. Louis/London: B. Herder Book Co., ²1965.
Theron, Stephen. *Morals as Founded on Natural Law*. New York: Peter Lang, 1987.
Welch, D. Don, ed. *Law and Morality*. Philadelphia: Fortress Press, 1987.

Particular themes

Anglin, W. S. *Free will and the Christian Faith*. Oxford: Oxford University Press, 1990.
Bartner, Dorin. *Grace Abounding. Wrestling with Sin and Guilt*. London: Darton, Longman and Todd, 1993.
Black, Donald. *The Social Structure of Right and Wrong*. San Diego, Calif.: Academic Press, 1993.

Crossin, John W. *What Are They Saying About Virtue?* New York, N.J.: Paulist Press, 1985.
Das, Somen. *Christian Ethics and Indian Ethos.* Delhi: ISPCK 1989.
Donagan, Alan. *Choice. The Essential Element in Human Action.* London/New York: Routledge and Kegan Paul, 1987.
Fagan, Sean. *Has Sin Changed? A Book of Forgiveness.* London: Gill & Macmillan, ²1988.
Farley, Edward. *Good and Evil. Interpreting a Human Condition.* Minneapolis: Augsburg Publ. House, 1990.
Gualtieri, A. *Conscience and Coercion.* Montreal: Guernica, 1989.
Kekes, John. *Facing Evil.* Princeton, N.J.: Princeton University Press, 1990.
Keown, Damien. *The Nature of Buddhist Ethics.* London: Macmillan, 1992.
Kuic, Vukan, ed. *The Definition of Moral Virtue.* Bronx, N.Y.: Fordham University Press, 1986.
La Rondelle, H. K. *Perfection and Perfectionism. A Dogmatic-Ethical Study of Biblical Perfection and Phenomenal Perfectionism.* Berrien Springs, Mich.: Andrews University Press, 1984, 5th printing.
Lennon, Kathleen. *Explaining Human Action.* London: Gerald Duckworth, 1990.
Meilaender, Gilbert C. *The Theory and Practice of Virtue.* Notre Dame, Ind.: University of Notre Dame Press, 1984.
McCormick, Patrick. *Sin as Addiction.* New York, N.J.: Paulist Press, 1989.
Neuhaus, Richard John, ed. *The Structure of Freedom. Correlations, Causes and Cautions.* Grand Rapids, Mich.: Eerdmans, 1991.
O'Keefe, Mark. *What Are They Saying About Social Sin?* New York: Paulist Press, 1990.
Olen, Jeffrey. *Moral Freedom.* Philadelphia: Temple University Press, 1988.
Overberg, G. *Conscience in Conflict.* Cincinnati, Ohio: St. Anthony Messenger, 1991.
Smith, Barbara Darling. *Can Virtue Be Taught?* Notre Dame, Ind.: University of Notre Dame Press, 1992.
White, Morton. *The Question of Free Will. A Holistic View.* Princeton, N.J.: Princeton Univ. Press, 1993.
Whitney, Barry L. *What Are They Saying About Good and Evil?* New York, N.J.: Paulist Press, 1989.
Woodruff, Paul, and Wilmar, Harry A., eds. *Facing Evil. Light at the Core of Darkness.* La Salle, Ill.: Open Court, ²1989.
Zecha, Gerhard, and Weingartner, Paul, ed. *Conscience: An Interdisciplinary View.* Dordrecht: Reidel, 1987.

INDEX

A

Absolutes in moral theology 126f, 132f, 252-4, 270-2.
Action follows being, see *Agere sequitur esse*.
Acts, human, see Human acts.
Aequiprobabilism 191-3.
Agere sequitur esse,
meaning of the axiom 120f;
importance for the moral law 121-3, 128-30.
Alphonsus of Liguori, author of aequiprobabilism 193.
Analytical ethics, see Metaethics.
Anthropocentrism 30.
Anthropological sciences as source of moral law 9f.
Anthropology, theological, 4 footnote 1;
dialogical existence of man 13-21;
destiny of man 39-48;
ontological presuppositions 105-23.
Aristotle, moral theory 23-5.
Atheism,
possibility of sin in a. 296;
validity of the moral argument for atheists 7.
Attention, condition of imputability 229, 230, 242.
Attrition 332.
Authority, human, as source of moral obligation 58, 93f, 197;
see also Teaching office of the Church.
Autonomy, moral 92-95, 205;
impediment of the sense of sin 286;
in Kantian ethics 32-34, 92f.
Axiological ethics (Ethics of values) 36-39.

B

Basic and categorial freedom
Basic intention 223, 227.
Bentham, proponent utilitarianism 24, 27f.
Bias, sinful mind-set 307f.
Bible, see Holy Scripture.
Biblicism, ethical 102.
Bishops, see Teaching offic Church.
Body of Christ, relevance fo tian morality 215f, 294.

C

Canon law 67f;
see Human law.
Capital sins 309f.
Cardinal virtues 310, 347.
Categorial choice or optic 233.
Categorial character of th imperative 6, 53-57, 1
insufficient basis 26, 3
Categorical imperative 32, note 1.
Cessation of law 155-7.
Character formation 220-3
Bible as formative fact
Charismatic movement 57
Charity, see Love.
Christ,
faith in him, criterio cernment of spirits
norm and model of the life 19, 88, 90, 21
scandal of the world
style of his teaching
Christian ethics, definitio
see Moral theology.
Christological universalis
Church,

competence in moral questions 9, 109-11;
her authority and man's conscience 201-5;
mediator of holiness 362.
Circumstances as source of morality 254-6.
Civil disobedience 200f.
Civil law, see Human law.
Coercive power of human law, necessity 136f, 141.
Collective guilt 286, 320f.
Common good, object of the law 141f.
Communitarianism 61f, 217.
Community,
formative factor of character 221f;
matrix of moral identity 216-20;
mediator of moral values 9, 61f, 205-7, 331.
Community spirit, biblical motive 215f.
Compensatory conscience 184f.
Compromise, ethical 281-4.
Concupiscence, impairment of the human act 242-4.
Conflicts of conscience 197-200, 203f.
Conflicts of duties 185f.
Conscience,
biblical teaching 159-63;
concept 166-70, 172-4;
dependence on being 170-2;
division 174f;
existence 163-6;
formation of it, duty 201, 202, 205-7;
misapprehensions 158f, 170f;
obligatory force 179-88;
relation to authority 197-205;
stages in development 175-9;
"voice" of God 162, 169.
Conscientious objection 198-200, 203f.
Consent of free will,
condition of human acts 229f;
condition of sin 285, 301f.
Consensus fidelium 209.

Consequences of the human act as criterion of morality 9, 127, 129, 130-2.
Consequentialism 23, 127, 131f.
Contrition, perfect and imperfect 332f.
Conversion,
biblical teaching 327-30;
conditions 335-9;
nature 331-5;
necessity 330f;
sacramental enactment 339-41;
social dimension 328, 331, 334f, 339.
Cooperation in the sins of others 277-80.
Covenant theme, moral relevance 212;
see Old covenant and New covenant.
Creative responsibility 19-21.
Creativity of conscience 171f.
Criticism of Catholic ethics 101f, 109f.
Cultic, civil, and moral laws
in the NT 80f, 86;
in the OT 72f.
Cultural traits of moral law 109, 208f.

D

Damaging of others by material cooperation 279f.
Deontological foundation of moral norms 126-35.
Desire, efficacious and inefficacious 260, 306f.
Desire, evil 306f.
Determinism 232, 236.
Development of the world, purpose of human activity 45-47, 52f.
Dialogical character of morality 14-21.
Dichotomy between religion and temporal duties to be overcome 47.
Dictate of conscience 172-4.
Dignity of the human person as moral criterion 33 footnote 1.

Discernment
  of spirits 57-63;
  of values in Christian ethics 89-91.
Dispensation
  from human law 156f;
  from natural law 113-5.
Dissent of conscience 172, 198-200, 203f.
Distinctive character of Christian ethics 84-91.
Divine decrees 118-20.
Divine law 66f.
Docility,
  sign of prudence 349;
  to God's will 20;
  to the Holy Spirit 57-62, 364.
Dogma and moral teaching 4, 8.
Double effect, principle of 267-75.
Doubtful conscience and norms for action 174, 186-8.
Doubtful facts, duty to opt for the safer alternative 231, 233.
Doubtful laws, obligatory character 189-95.
Dynamic character
  of moral life 330f, 361, 365-7;
  of natural law 111-3.

E

Ecclesiastical law 67f;
  see Human law.
Education, moral 176f, 243, 248f, 348, 351.
Egotism 25.
Effects, see Indirectly willed effects.
Emotions, relevance for the discovery of the moral value 39.
Emotivism 39 footnote 1.
Empiricism, theory on conscience 164-6.
End intended by the agent, source of morality 256-9.
End, ultimate, see Ultimate end.
Epikeia
  in human law 148f, 152-55, 157;
  in natural law 114f.
Equality of the moral order for all 70.

Error
  of conscience and moral obligation 181-3, 198, 200;
  impairment of human acts 241.
Eschatological point of departure in ethics 9f, 123.
Eternal decrees as basis of natural law 118-20.
Eternal life as ultimate end 50.
Ethics of discourse 61f.
Ethics of values 36-39.
Eudaemonism,
  ethical system 23-29;
  in the OT 41.
Evolution of moral knowledge 111f.
Example,
  importance for moral education 350;
  misguided imitations 353-5;
  negative influence of bad e. 317, 322.
Excuses from human law 155f, 246.
Existential choice, see Fundamental option.
Existential ends 99f, 124f.
Existentialist ethics 29.
External act as source of morality 260f.

F

Faith,
  influence on conscience 161f;
  relevance for moral theology 4, 94f;
  source of moral identity 210-20.
Fear,
  impairment of human acts 244-7;
  reverential 245.
Finis operantis 256-9.
Finis operis 251-4.
Forgiveness of sins,
  grace of the sacrament of penance 340;
  held out by Christ 291.
Foundation of the moral norm, recent discussions 126-35.
Freedom and law, dialectic 64, 197, 205, 237.

Freedom of conscience 195-7, 199-201.
Freedom of action
   in cases of doubtful laws 190-5;
   value to be promoted 195, 232f, 237f.
Freedom of will,
   constituent principle of the human act 229f;
   presupposition of the human act 232-8, 251;
   presupposition of the moral law 5f;
   presupposition of sin 291f, 313;
   teaching of Holy Scripture 233-5.
Freud, Sigmund, on conscience 164-6.
Fundamental option 223-7;
   and holiness 360;
   fundament of virtue 343f, 341, 345;
   wrong, cause of mortal sin 300f, 226f.

G

Gifts of the Holy Spirit 57.
Glory of God as ultimate end 40-48, 52.
God, existence, presupposition of moral theology 5f.
Golden rule 36, 108.
Good intention 259, 261.
Grace,
   need of openness to the gift of 336f, 350;
   premise of man's sanctification 18f, 364.
Gradualness of moral growth 365-7.
Grave sin 296-9.
Group pressure, source of sin 322f.
Guilt 287f;
   depraved social structures as cause of 324f;
   see Sin.

H

Habit,
   formation in the service of virtue 350f;

impairment of human acts 248f.
Happiness as moral motive 26f, 28f, 32, 34, 37, 51.
Hartmann, Nicolai, exponent of ethics of values 37.
Hedonism 23.
Hermeneutics 8.
Heroic acts as object of the law 144.
Heteronomous ethics in dispute 32-34.
Historicity
   of human law 137f;
   of natural law 111-3, 122.
Holiness, see Perfection.
Holy Scripture,
   basis of Christian moral identity 4, 210-6, 219;
   source of moral theology 8f, 94.
Holy Spirit,
   docility to his guidance 57-63;
   inspiration of man's conscience 169;
   life according to the Spirit, vocation of Christians 338f, 364.
Human acts,
   concept 228-30;
   divisions 230f;
   impairments 238-50;
   sources of its morality 250-9.
Human law,
   biblical teaching 138-40;
   cessation 155-7;
   concept 67f, 135f;
   limits of obligation 68, 138, 140, 145f;
   moral obligation 68, 146-9;
   necessity 94, 140f;
   object of the law 141-6;
   properties 136-8.
Humanist personalism 29f.
Hume, critique of natural law 123-6.
Humility, condition of conversion 335f.

I

Identity, Christian 210-20.

Ignorance,
    impairment of human acts 239-41;
    reason for excusing from the law 155f, 240f.
Imitation of Christ 214.
Immutability of natural law 111-3, 122.
Impairments of human acts 238-50.
Impossibility,
    excusing from moral fault 282;
    excusing from observance of the law 156;
    impediment of just laws 144.
Imputability
    of human actions 285, 328-330;
    of indirectly willed effects 265-76;
    impairments of 238-50.
Inattention, impairment of the human acts 242.
Incapacitating laws 155f.
Indifferent acts 259f.
Indirectly willed effects,
    concept 230f, 265;
    imputability 265-75;
    moral relevance of the distinction 275.
Indispensability of natural law 113-5.
Individualistic ethics, insufficiency 29f, 216f.
Individuality of men, basis of moral obligations 116f, 122, 354.
Intention, source of morality 256-9.
Intention, basic 223, 227.
Internal acts as object of the law 145.
Internal sins 305-8.
Interpretation of the law 151f.
Intrinsically evil acts 252f, 270-2, 279f;
    see also Absolutes in moral theology
Intuition, relevance for the moral obligation 10, 39, 94f.
Involuntary sins, not warrantable 285.
Invalidating laws 155f, 247.

J

Joy in the good effect of an evil deed 306.
Jung, C. G., on conscience 164f.
Juridical guilt 288.
Justice,
    procedural 149-52;
    substantive (of human law) 141-6.

K

Kantian ethics 32-36.
Kingdom of God,
    as moral motive 213;
    as ultimate end 42-44, 47f, 52.
Knowledge, necessary
    for mortal sin 300-2;
    for a human act 228f, 230;
    requirement of virtue 347f.

L

Law in the OT 68-75.
Law (moral) in the NT 75-84.
Law, see
    Human law;
    Mosaic law;
    Moral law;
    Natural law;
    Positive law;
    Revealed law.
Law of Christ 77, 84, 97, 101f, 235.
Law (written), value and limits 64; 178f.
Lax conscience 183f.
Laxism 191f.
Legalism,
    antilegalism of Paul 234f;
    danger of it in the OT 73;
    insufficiency 20f, 77, 117.
Legislator,
    duty to keep within the bounds of jurisdiction 143;
    recourse to him in case of epikeia 154f.
Lesser evil,
    counselling the lesser sin 280f;

principle of the lesser evil, its moral relevance 130-2, 273f.
Lex talionis 72.
Liberation theology 52f, 324.
Liberty, see Freedom.
Liturgy,
  enactment of conversion by it 339-41;
  source of moral life 17f, 218.
Love (of God and neighbour),
  constitutive element of perfection 356, 358, 360, 363f, 365;
  criterion and measure of love 271, 345f;
  supreme but not only moral norm 345f.
Love of moral value, basic requirement for virtue 349f.
Lunatics, subject of natural law 106.

M

Magisterium of the Church, see Teaching office of the Church.
Man, nature of, see Anthropology, theological.
Marx, critique of religion 52.
Material cooperation in sin 277-80.
Material sin 285.
Maturity, moral 175-9;
  see also Perfection.
Meaning of human existence, see Ultimate end of men.
Mental sickness, impairment of the human act 250.
Mentally sick, subjects of natural law 106.
Merit, see Reward.
Metaethics 7 footnote 1.
Methods of moral theology 8-10.
Mill, John Stuart, advocate of utilitarianism 24, 27f.
Moral certainty, concept 180.
Moral identity,
  Bible as source of 210-16;
  faith community as matrix 216-20;
  relevance 208-10.

Moral law,
  concept 65-68;
  responsible care for it 20f.
Moral systems (on the use of probability) 190-95.
Moral theology,
  definition 3;
  division 10f;
  methods 8-10.
Mortal sin 225-7, 299-302.
Mosaic law,
  distinctive character 70f;
  limitations 71-73;
  nature 68-70;
  validity for Christians 75f, 81, 234f.
Motivation,
  source of morality 259;
  unconscious, impairment of freedom 248.
Motives of Christian ethics 212-6.
Mutability
  of human law 137f;
  of natural law 111-3, 122.
Mystical Body, see Body of Christ.

N

Narrative, moral relevance 78, 211.
Natural law,
  basis of human law 146f;
  concept 66, 97-106;
  existence 117-23;
  in the NT 81-84;
  in the OT 73-75;
  properties 106-17;
  relevance 95f.
Natural right 105f;
  see Natural law.
Nature as source of moral law 96, 97-101, 128-30, 134f.
Negatively voluntary effects 231.
Neurotic propensities, impairment of human acts 248 footnote 1.
New covenant, biblical motive 16, 212.
New law 76-82, 234f;
  see also Law of Christ.

O

Obedience to God,
  fundamental duty of men 20, 56, 77;
  disobedience against God, cause of sin 285, 289, 295.
Obedience to human authorities and laws 20, 138f, 197f.
Obedience to the guardians of the faith 61, 203f.
Object of the human act 251-4.
Obligation of human laws 146-9.
Obstacles of human acts 238-50.
Occasion of sin,
  duty to avoid it 312f;
  legitimate creation of an occasion 320.
Old covenant, foundation of OT morality 14f, 212.
Old law, see Mosaic law.
Omission, sins of 308f.
Ontological point of departure in ethics 9f, 123;
  see also *Agere sequitur esse*.

P

Passions,
  dominion over, requirement for virtue 350f;
  impairment of human acts 242-4.
Pathology, impairment of human acts 250.
Paul, apostle,
  attitude to the law 234f;
  on conscience 160-3;
  on natural moral law 83f;
  style of his teaching 79f.
Penal law theory 147-9.
Penance,
  fruit of conversion 338-40;
  means against temptation 312;
  sacramental 339-41;
  see also Conversion.
Perfection,
  biblical teaching 355-60;
  deficient ideals 353-5;
  nature 360-2;
  universality of the call 362-4.
Perplexed conscience 185f.
Perseverance, need in the striving for perfection 366f.
"Persona", unauthentic superstructure of conscience 165.
Personal calling, see Vocation of man by God.
Personalist character of moral law 115-7.
Pharisaic scandal 318.
Philosophical ethics, difference from moral theology 4f.
Philosophical sin 295f.
Pluralism, moral, 5 footnote 1, 202f.
Popes, see Teaching office of the Church.
Positive law,
  concept 67;
  excuse from it to avoid scandal 320;
  in the NT 80f;
  in the OT 72f;
  see also human law.
Practice, means for the knowledge of moral values 170, 349f.
Prayer,
  means in the pursuit of holiness 350, 365;
  mistaken practice 353;
  need of it for the discernment of spirits 58;
  provision against temptation 311f.
Predecision 224f.
Preference rules 262-5.
Pre-moral good and evil 254.
Prejudice 241, 307f.
Presumption,
  criterion for lawful action 188f;
  in favour of the Church's teaching office 203f.
Primary principles of natural law 107f.
Principle of double effect 267-75.
Principle of proportionate reason 268.
Privilege 157.
Probabiliorism 191f.
Probabilism 191, 193-5.
Probable laws, obligation 189-95.

Procedural justice 149-52.
Progress, temporal, as ultimate end 31f, 45-7.
Promulgation of the law, condition for its validity 149f.
Proportionalism 127.
Proprium of Christian ethics, see Distinctive character.
Protestant ethics,
    attitude towards natural law 85;
    objections against Catholic natural law 101-3, 109f.
Prudence, integral element of virtue 345, 348f.
Psychic disturbances, impairments of human acts 250.
Punishment as moral motive 54-6, 176.
Purpose of the human act, source of morality 256-9.

R

Rawls, contractual theory of justice 35f.
Reason,
    persons without its use as subjects of the law 106;
    source of moral law 9f, 98.
Reflex principles 188f.
Reliability of moral norms 109-11.
Religion, source of moral life 18-21.
Reparation for damages caused by scandal 319;
    by sin 338.
Repentance, see Conversion.
Responsibility
    before God 6, 14-21;
    for the sins of others 314-20;
    nature 14;
    see also Social responsibility.
Responsive character of morality 14-21.
Retribution as moral motive 54-56, 212.
Retroactivity of laws 150f.
Revealed law 66f;
    in the NT 75-81;
    in the OT 68-73.
Revelation, relevance for the moral law 5, 84-91, 94, 104;
    see also Holy Scripture and Magisterium of the Church.
Reward as moral motive 54-56, 212.
Rightness and wrongness, moral 175.
Rigorism 191f.

S

Sacraments,
    instruments of conversion and holiness 339-41, 365;
    source of moral life 17f.
Safer view, duty to follow it in doubtful facts 231, 233.
Salvation as moral motive 48-53.
Scandal 315-20.
Scandalum pusillorum 317f.
Scheler, Max, exponent of ethics of values 37.
Scintilla animae 167.
Scrupulous conscience 175, 185.
Seduction 314f.
Self-perfection (self-realization)
    as ultimate end 29-32, 344f;
    justified concern 31;
    obligation to it 45f, 360;
    see also Perfection.
Sensus fidei 209 footnote 2.
Side effect, see Indirectly willed effects.
Sin,
    biblical teaching 288-91;
    criteria for its gravity 149, 302-5;
    divisions 305-10;
    material and formal 286;
    mortal and venial 296-302;
    nature 285f, 291-6;
    social dimension 293-5;
    sources 310-25.
Sinful social structures 320-5;
    need of correction through communal conversion 328, 331, 334f.
Sins, internal 305-8.
Sins that cry to heaven 303.
Sinaitic covenant, see Old covenant.
Situation ethics 115f.

Situational character of natural law 115-7.
Slavery, teaching of Paul 80.
Social sin 322-5.
Social dimension
   of sin 293-5;
   of conversion 328, 331, 334f.
Social pressure,
   cause of sin 322f;
   impairment of human acts 244f.
Social responsibility,
   moral requirement 46, 339;
   sensibility for sins against 287.
Solidarity among men, purpose of human activity 46.
Solidarity in evil, source of sin 320-5.
Sonship, divine, as moral motive 214f.
Sources of morality 250-61.
State of perfection 351f, 357.
Subjects of natural law 106.
Substantive justice (of human law) 141-6.
Success and moral goodness 261.
Suffering,
   ethical significance 26, 47, 55, 313f, 338;
   liberation from it as Christian task 52f.
Superego 164, 176.
Supernatural virtues 344f.
Synderesis 169f.

T

Teaching office of the Church, authority in moral matters 61, 109-11, 201-5;
   factor of moral identity 219;
   source of moral theology 9.
Teleological constituent and foundation of the moral order 9f, 99, 122f, 126-35.
Temptation 310-4.
Theological virtues 310, 347.
Theology of liberation 52f, 324.
Theonomy of Christian ethics 39ff, 92-95.

Torah 68-73;
   see also Mosaic law.
Tradition, source of moral theology 8f, 61, 209, 218f.
Tutiorism 191f.

U

Ultimate end of men,
   deficient theories 23-39;
   disregard for it, essence of sin 295, 301, 304;
   importance for human law 142;
   importance for the moral law 21-23, 100f, 122f, 125f, 131-5, 258f;
   importance for the practice of virtue 343, and holiness 360;
   nature 21-3, 39-53, 90; unity of it for all mankind 5, 88f, 103f.
Universality of natural law 106-11.
Unjust laws, obligation 145f, 283.
Unjust social structures, see Sinful social structures.
Utilitarianism 23-29, 127.

V

Value, knowledge and love of it, prerequisite for rightful action 51, 229f;
   requirement for virtue 348, 349f.
Venial sin 226, 299-302.
Violence, impairment of human acts 247f.
Virtue,
   biblical teaching 342f;
   concept and nature 341, 343-5;
   division 346f;
   fundamental requirements 347-51;
   reservations today 341f.
Virtues,
   cardinal 310, 347;
   supernatural 344f;
   theological 310, 347.
Vocation of man by God,

of personal nature 13, 168f, 354f, 364;
  frustrated in sin 293;
  ultimate, one only for mankind 5, 21f, 103f.
Volition, inefficient desire 260.
Voluntarism, insufficiency 87.
Voluntary act and effect, divisions 230f.

W

Wisdom, cause of the primeval order of the world 73f, 119.
Women, status in the NT 80, 81.
Worship, source of moral life 218; see also Liturgy.

www.ingramcontent.com/pod-product-compliance
Lightning Source LLC
Chambersburg PA
CBHW071238300426
44116CB00008B/1094